Introduction to
PHYSIOLOGY

VOLUME 2

Introduction to
PHYSIOLOGY

VOLUME 2
BASIC MECHANISMS

PART 2

HUGH DAVSON

Physiology Department, University College
London, England

M. B. SEGAL

Sherrington School of Physiology, St. Thomas's Hospital
London, England

1975

ACADEMIC PRESS
and
GRUNE & STRATTON

U.K. edition published and distributed by
ACADEMIC PRESS INC. (LONDON) LTD.
24/28 Oval Road
London NW1

United States Edition published and distributed by
GRUNE & STRATTON INC.
111 Fifth Avenue
New York, New York 10003

Library of Congress Catalog Card Number: 75 5668
ISBN (Academic Press): 0 12 206802 5
ISBN (Grune & Stratton): 0 8089 0897 9

Printed in Great Britain by
The Whitefriars Press Ltd., London and Tonbridge

PREFACE

We can think of two ways of composing an Introduction to Physiology. First we may take a large standard text and sieve the material contained in it to free it of as much experimental material, argument and other "extraneous matter" to reduce its bulk to about one third of the original. Alternatively one may compose something entirely new, expounding as simply as feasible the basic scientific principles governing the functioning of the animal. The former method has, we think, been employed before, and the result has been a *synopsis* of, rather than an *introduction* to, physiology. By memorizing it almost word-for-word the medical student probably passes muster at an undiscriminating examination, and completes his medical education with a very poor understanding of the basic principles of medicine.

Pursuing the latter method we found that the first draft was embarrassingly large, and in reviewing what had been written with a view to shortening the book, it became clear that any serious surgery would destroy its character since it was, in effect, rather more than an Introduction containing—to use a musical term—a great deal of "development" too. Rather than abandon the project of producing an Introduction that was both short and adequate, we carried out a different kind of surgery, namely the division into several volumes. Volumes 1 and 2, which we now present, are an introduction to the basic mechanisms whereby the animal absorbs, distributes and transforms its energy-giving materials; and whereby the energy thus made available is utilized in such fundamental activities as muscular contraction, the transmission of messages by both nerves and hormones, the defence mechanisms and in reproduction.

The difficulties in understanding physiology arise in the fundamental principles governing the activities of the animal's parts, such as the flow of fluids, the conduction of the nervous impulse, the elimination of secretions from a cell or epithelium and so on. If the student has a firm grasp of these principles, the way is clear for the understanding of the rest of physiology, which consists in the analysis of control mechanisms. The remaining volumes are designed to enable the student to take up where the first two left off; thus Volume 3 is devoted to visceral control mechanisms and may be regarded as the "development" of the themes introduced mainly in Volume 1. Very arbitrarily the control of somatic motor activity and of reproduction have been put together to make Volume 4; this is only because their inclusion in Volume 3 would have made it too large for convenience. Volume 5 deals with sensory mechanisms and higher integrative processes, involving the cerebral cortex.

A few words on the way the volumes have been written. The present two volumes, being concerned largely with fundamentals, require little or no documentation, so that we have contented ourselves mostly with general references to reviews and texts at the end of each volume. This does not mean that the information has been culled only from these sources, and it is rare if we have quoted work that we have not read in the original. In the remaining volumes the subject matter has been treated in greater experimental depth, so that a more elaborate documentation, comparable with that found in Starling's *Principles of Human Physiology*, has been employed.

To conclude, we think that a study of the completed work will provide the student of physiology, taking this as part of a larger course, such as in medicine or dentistry, with knowledge of the subject sufficient for his requirements; for the student intending to make physiology his career the book will, we trust, be a proper "Introduction".

HUGH DAVSON
M. B. SEGAL

October 1974

CONTENTS

ACKNOWLEDGMENTS

We should like to record our indebtedness to those authors and publishers who gave us permission to reproduce illustrations, also to Jane Barnett for secretarial assistance, and to Moyra Harding for assistance with illustrations.

CHAPTER 1

The Nervous System

CONTROL MECHANISMS

In describing the basic principles of distribution of material in the body we have concentrated our attention on the mechanisms of the processes, showing how far the physiologist has been able to describe them in terms of concepts familiar to the physicist and chemist. We have, as far as possible, avoided touching on the mechanisms by which these physiological processes are brought into action and (of more importance) the mechanisms by which they are controlled to the point that the activities of the parts are smoothly integrated to ensure the adequate functioning of the whole organism.

Autoregulation

To a small extent many of the physiological processes that we have already described have a built-in control system, in the sense that they control themselves; this phenomenon is given the general name of *autoregulation*. For example, in the formation of the extracellular fluid, an increased filtration at the arterial end of a capillary creates the condition for an increased absorption at the venous end; the loss of fluid tends to raise the concentration of proteins in the remaining plasma, and this results in an increased colloid osmotic pressure. Again, Starling's Law of the Heart is an expression of an autoregulatory activity in the sense that, as the load presented to the heart is increased, the force of contraction augments and results in a greater output. In considering the functioning of the kidney, we found a remarkable degree of autoregulation which ensures that the rate of flow of blood through the organ remains constant in spite of large variations in arterial pressure, a process that occurs when the kidney is removed from all possible central control.

Feed-back

With all physiological activities, however, we find additional control mechanisms that permit a fine adjustment of a given physiological process to the needs of the organism as a whole. The basis of this control may be illustrated by the well known principle of the thermostat, illustrated in Fig. 1.1. The sensor (S) is able to respond in some manner to a change in the feature that we wish to regulate, in this case the temperature; it does this by expanding, and the result of the expansion is to close an electrical switch, which operates a relay that

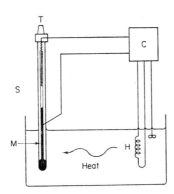

Fig. 1.1. The thermostat. The sensor (S) detects changes in temperature of the bath by changes in length of the column of mercury (M). If the bath temperature exceeds that set on the thermostat (T), the column of mercury rises and completes the circuit that switches off the current to the heating coil (H) by means of a relay in controller (C). Conversely, a fall in temperature opens the circuit and the heating coil now warms the bath to the preset temperature.

finally cuts off, or reduces, the supply of heat from an electrically heated source (H). We call the heater the *effector* in so far as it carries out the function that we are concerned with, namely keeping the bath warm. Between the sensor and the effector we have a communicating or *feed-back* system that carries the information regarding the temperature of the tank to the control centre and from the control centre to the effector; in the mechanical example considered this is contributed by the wires and relay. In living animals the sensor is called the *receptor*; the major communicating system is the *nervous system*, and the effectors are muscle fibres or other cells specialized to carry out specific functions, such as secreting enzymes in digestion.

Hormone Control

Working alongside this nervous system of control we have a *hormonal* or *endocrine system*, in which the communication is carried out by transport of a chemical ejected into the blood-stream, through which it reaches its "target cells"—effector cells that respond to this blood-carried humoral agent. As we shall see, the distinction between the nervous and humoral mechanisms is often not as striking as at first thought; the transmission processes are indeed fundamentally different, in so far as, in the one case, the information is carried along nerve fibres and in the other, is carried in the blood-stream. However, in both cases the effectors are brought into action by a chemical agent, either a hormone such as secretin or adrenaline or a neurotransmitter like acetylcholine or noradrenaline.

THE NERVOUS SYSTEM

The Neurone

The basic unit in nervous control is the neurone, a cell that has become specialized to respond to a change in its environment—the *stimulus*—and to carry this response as a message to be transmitted either to another neurone or, more rarely, directly to an effector cell. According to their functions, the neurones have a wide variety of forms, as illustrated in Fig. 1.2 which shows several types. They have a common structure, in the sense that there is the cell body or *perikaryon* (also called the *soma*) containing the nucleus and most of the metabolic apparatus of the cell; there are also the *axon* and one or more processes called *dendrites*. The variability in form of neurones is largely caused by the wide variety of dendritic ramifications. It is along the axon that the neurone transmits its message, whilst it is along the dendrites that influences from other neurones are transmitted. Thus the message passes from the dendrites to the perikaryon, and away from the perikaryon along the axon. Where interconnections between neurones are concerned, the axon of the "transmitting" neurone may make its connections with the dendrite of the "receiving" neurone, or with its perikaryon (an "axo-somatic contact") or even with the initial part of its axon (an "axo-axonic contact").

Grouping of Neurones

The processes from neurones are grouped together to form *nerves*, or *tracts*, many of these being visible to the naked eye. The perikarya,

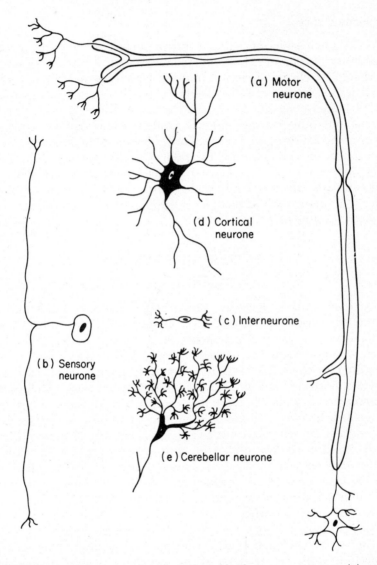

Fig. 1.2. Some of the types of neurone found in the nervous system. (a) motor; (b) bipolar sensory; (c) spinal interneurone; (d) cortical; (e) cerebellar.

or cell bodies, are likewise grouped together to form *nuclei* or *ganglia* which may be situated within or outside the *central nervous system*, the latter being defined as the brain and spinal cord.

The Axon

The basic organization of the nervous system can only be adequately appreciated with a knowledge of the nature of the messages a given neurone can transmit and the manner in which a stimulus, applied.

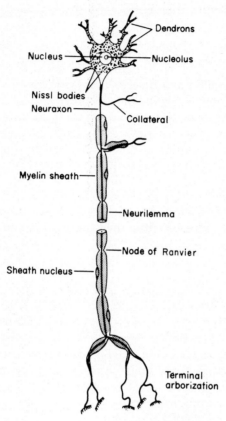

Fig. 1.3. A motor neurone and investing membranes. The neurone consists of a cell body with nucleus and cytoplasm. The cell body gives off projections, the dendrites, and the long axon in the case of the motor nerve. The axon is covered by a neurilemma or Schwann sheath, which encloses a layer of lipid or myelin, the electrical insulator of the axon. (Greep, "Histology", 1966, McGraw Hill.)

say, to the surface of the skin, can initiate the message that the nerve, with its endings in the skin, transmits to the brain. The neurone (Fig. 1.3) is a cell, and like all cells is separated from its environment by a plasma membrane which extends over its whole surface. The axon consists, from without inwards, of an outermost cellular covering (the *neurilemma* or *Schwann sheath*); a myelin sheath of mainly lipoid material which acts as an electrical insulator—this may be thick in the typical *medullated* or *myelinated* axon, or very thin or non-existent in the *non-myelinated* axon; beneath the myelin sheath is the plasma membrane enclosing the *axoplasm*, the fluid or semi-fluid cytoplasm of the axon.

Ultrastructure

The endosplasmic reticulum of the neurone is concentrated in the perikaryon, where it was recognized by the light microscopists by virtue of its basophilia and described as *Nissl substance*; in the electron microscope its homology with that of other cells is easily recognized. Both perikaryon and the processes contain mitochondria. More recently two other structures have been identified, namely microtubules and microfilaments similar to those described in other cells (Vol. 1). The organization of these fine structures varies with the neurone and the particular process; thus in the dendrites of most neurones the filaments are rare, the major component being the microtubule, an inverse relation being found in the axon. Separation and analysis of the microtubules showed that they were built up of the protein, *tubulin*.

Schwann Sheath

The Schwann sheath is made up of characteristically flattened cells which remain *in situ* as apparently permanently fixed elements. However, they have by no means lost the powers of movement or reproduction so that when the underlying axon and myelin degenerate, as when the nerve fibre is severed, the Schwann cells tend to become more spherical, exhibiting continuous changes in shape until they finally take up new positions on regenerating material. In order to be able to re-sheathe a growing axon-stump they must, of course, migrate, and they move at some 49–90 μ per 24 hr.

Axon–Schwann Cell Relations. The relations of the axon to the myelin sheath and Schwann cell have been indicated earlier (Vol. 1, Ch. 2) when discussing the origin of the myelin as a lamellar arrangement of plasma membrane derived from the enclosing Schwann cell. To recapitulate, the axon with its limiting plasma membrane is enveloped by the Schwann cell, whilst the myelin sheath is derived from the Schwann cell's own plasma membrane and is to be regarded as part of the Schwann cell (Fig. 2.13, Vol. 1). The non-myelinated axon is likewise enclosed in a Schwann sheath, being enveloped within the Schwann cell, as illustrated in Fig. 1.4, where it is called a *Remak*

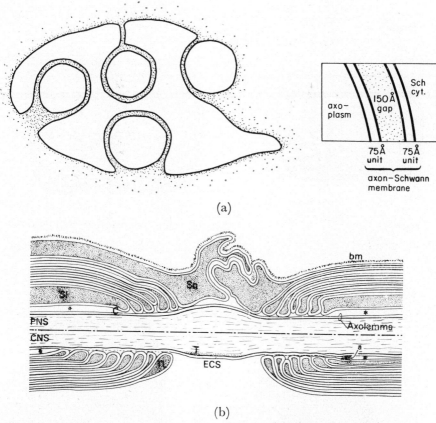

(a)

(b)

Fig. 1.4. (a) Illustrating Remak axons embedded to different extents in a single Schwann cell. (Courtesy J. D. Robertson.) (b) The node of Ranvier. The upper half of the diagram illustrates the structure found in peripheral myelinated nerve (PNS), and the lower half illustrates that found in the central nervous system (CNS). In the PNS the Schwann cell provides both an inner collar (Si) and an outer collar (So) of cytoplasm in addition to the compact myelin. Outer collar (So) is extended into the nodal region as a series of loosely interdigitating processes. Terminating loops of the compact myelin come into close apposition to the axolemma in region near the node apparently providing some barrier (arrow at a) for movement of materials into or out of the periaxonal space (marked by *). The Schwann cell is covered externally by a basement membrane. In the CNS the myelin ends similarly in terminal loops (Tl) near the node and there are periodic thickenings of the axolemma where the glial membrane is applied in the paranodal region. These may serve as diffusion barriers and thus confine the material in the periaxonal space (marked *) so that movement in the direction of the arrow at (a) would be restrained. At many CNS nodes there is considerable extracellular space (ECS). (Bunge, *Physiol. Rev.* 1968, **48,** 197.)

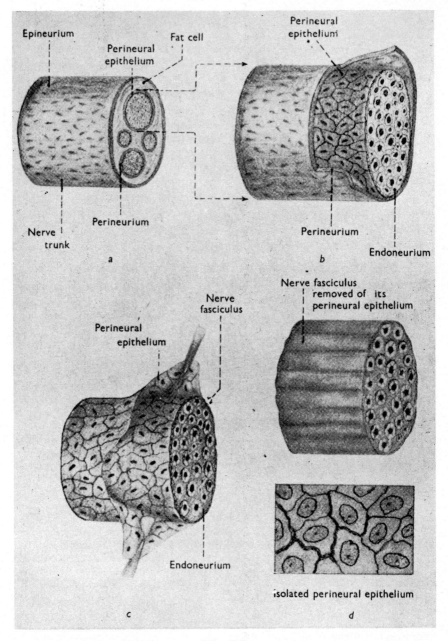

Fig. 1.5.

fibre, the stalk or *mesaxon* being the channel constituted by the plasma membranes of the enveloping Schwann cell. It must be appreciated that the extracellular environment of the axon is very limited in volume by virtue of this enclosure within the Schwann sheath, so that losses of ions from the axon, e.g. of K^+ during the conduction of an impulse, can build up quite high concentrations immediately outside.

Node of Ranvier. When an axon has a thick myelin sheath, this is interrupted, at intervals of about 1 mm, to give the *nodes of Ranvier*, where myelin is absent. As we shall see, the myelin sheath, with its high electrical resistance, is a modification that permits a high velocity of transmission of the impulse; however, this high resistance must be interrupted at nodes, i.e. regions of lower resistance, through which electrical current can flow. Fig. 1.4 illustrates the relations between a typical axon to its myelin sheath and Schwann cells at the region of the node; the myelin laminae end in terminal loops whilst the investment of Schwann cytoplasm continues over the node in the form of loosely interdigitating processes; access to the axon thus requires diffusion between the processes of Schwann cytoplasm. This is relatively unrestricted compared with diffusion through the myelin layers, and enables the nodal region to function as a "low resistance pathway".

Central Neurones. In the vertebrate central nervous system—brain and spinal cord—the myelinated fibres are also ensheathed in a cellular covering analogous with Schwann cells—the *oligodendroglia*—which provide the myelin sheath in precisely the same way as the Schwann cells do. In the lower half of Fig. 1.4 the analogous structures

---

Fig. 1.5. The outer membranes of peripheral nerve; the figures demonstrate the various stages of isolation of this "perineural epithelium" under a binocular dissection microscope. (a) The nerve trunk as a whole, with many fasciculi along with their connective tissue components, the epi-, peri-, and endoneurium. The perineural epithelium is shown in the diagram surrounding each nerve fasciculus, lying under the perineurium. (b) One nerve fasciculus is removed along with the perineurium, perineural epithelium and endoneurium. Part of the perineurium is removed to show the multiple layered perineural epithelium, lying immediately under the perineurium and on the entire surface of the nerve fasciculus. (c) The nerve fasciculus removed from its entire perineural connective tissue layer, leaving the perineural epithelium covering the nerve fasciculus. The multiple layered nature of the perineural epithelium is indicated. (d) Nerve fasciculus removed of its perineurium and perineural epithelium, leaving the nerve fibres of the fasciculus and the endoneurium intact. The isolated perineural epithelium can be seen lying flat on the glass slide. A capillary network in this perineural epithelium is also shown. (Shanthaveerappa and Bourne, *J. Anat.* 1962, **96**, 527.)

at the node are shown, and it is seen that a larger area of the axon at the node is left bare of glial covering.

Outer Sheath

As indicated above, the axons are grouped together in bundles, and the individual bundles are enclosed by a membrane, the *perineurium*, which acts as a protective layer, in so far as it restricts the access of materials from the extracellular space of the tissue in which the nerve runs. In general, these perineurium-enclosed bundles are grouped together within a thicker connective-tissue sheath called the *epineurium*, and it is this epineurium-enclosed bundle that is called a nerve (Fig. 1.5).

AXONAL PROPAGATION OF THE MESSAGE

The Action Potential

When two recording electrodes are placed on the axon—and for this purpose the giant axon of the squid is a useful preparation—there is usually no difference of potential between the two. When the nerve discharges into the muscle, however, there is a rapid series of potential changes described as an action potential, as illustrated by Fig. 1.6. The electrode nearest to the brain, from which the discharge emanates, becomes negative in relation to the more distal one, and a little later the situation is reversed, the nearer, or proximal, electrode becoming positive in relation to the distal one. Finally, the situation returns to

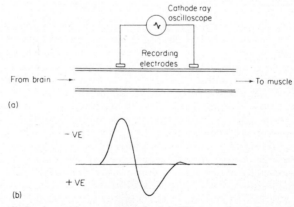

Fig. 1.6. A diphasic action potential. (a) The method for recording electrical activity as impulse passes along the nerve. (b) The changes in potential between the two electrodes as the impulse passes. Upstroke means negativity of left-hand (proximal) electrode in relation to right-hand (distal) electrode.

the original state of no potential difference between the electrodes. This *diphasic action potential* may be over in a millisecond or so, and usually the message transmitted from the brain along the nerve consists of a succession of these diphasic "spikes" at a frequency which may be just one or two per second or as high as a thousand per second in some sensory axons.

Velocity of Transmission

The action potential is transmitted along the axon towards its terminals. This can be demonstrated by placing several pairs of recording electrodes at different distances from the central origin of the neurone; spike potentials will be recorded in succession, and the latency between any pair, divided by the distance, will give a measure of the conduction velocity of the impulse. This varies with the type of neurone, being some 100 metres/sec in the largest myelinated mammalian axons and as low as 0·5 metres/sec in the fine non-myelinated fibres of the frog.

Electrical Stimulus

The same type of "message" can be caused to flow along an axon by applying an electric shock; in this case it is found that the action potential moves in both directions along the axon. A general feature of conducting cells is that wherever the action potential originates it spreads in all directions; since, in the normal course of events, the action potential of many neurones originates on the cell body, or very close to it on the *axon-hillock*, the normal direction of transmission, the *orthodromic direction*, is from perikaryon to axon terminals; the *antidromic impulse* passes in the reverse direction.

The Mechanism of the Action Potential

Monophasic Spike

The study of the action potential is best carried out by confining attention to the events taking place at a single electrode, since the diphasic record described above is essentially the successive effects of changes taking place at the points of contact of the two electrodes on the axon. We may achieve this *monophasic* recording by simply placing a microelectrode inside the axon and recording the changes of potential taking place between this and a distant, neutral, electrode that completes the electrical circuit but is otherwise unaffected by the changes taking place along the axon. Thus, if the axon is surrounded in a saline bath, the neutral, or indifferent, electrode can be placed in this.

Reversal of Resting Potential. We have seen that an electrode within the axon records its resting, or membrane, potential; and this is of the order of 60–70 mV, the inside being negative. When the axon is stimulated at a distance from the recording electrode, the potential changes take place after the required conduction time, and these now consist in the reversal of the resting potential, as indicated in Fig. 1.7 where the resting value of the potential is given by the lower horizontal line. Movement upwards of the record indicates a decrease in negativity of the electrode inside the axon, and at the point where it crosses the upper horizontal line the resting potential is zero, i.e. there is no

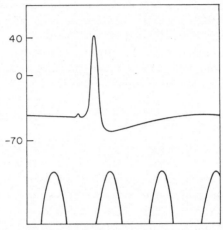

Fig. 1.7. Membrane action potential of the squid giant axon, recorded between the inside and outside. The vertical scale indicates the potential of the internal electrode in millivolts, the sea-water outside being taken as zero potential. Time-marker, 500 c.p.s. Note the "overshoot" of some 40 mV, the inside electrode becoming positive in respect to the outside. (Hodgkin and Huxley, *J. Physiol.* **104,** 176.)

difference of potential between the inside and outside of the axon. The process continues, and the active electrode inside the axon becomes still less negative, i.e. it becomes *positive* in relation to the surrounding saline, and finally reaches a peak of positivity of about 40 millivolts; it then falls rapidly to give a small "after-potential", in the sense that the inside of the axon becomes more negative than before; finally this *negative after-potential* subsides.

Diphasic Spike

If a second internal electrode is placed a little distance along the axon, and the potential changes from each electrode are recorded separately, then obviously the second electrode goes through the same

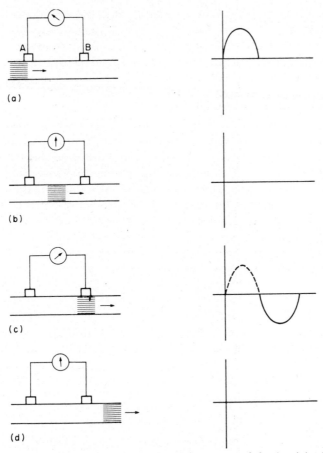

Fig. 1.8. The nature of the diphasic action potential. At (a) the active region has arrived at the first electrode A so that A is negative with respect to B. At (b) the active region has moved away from A and not yet reached B so that both electrodes are at the same potential. At (c) the active region has reached B so that B now becomes negative with respect to A and at (d) the active region has passed both electrodes so they are again at zero potential difference.

reversal of membrane potential; if it is downstream of the stimulus this action potential occurs a short time after the first. Thus the *propagation* of the electrical change enables us to understand the diphasic character of the action potential recorded between two electrodes on the surface. This is illustrated by Fig. 1.8; at (*a*) the change in the membrane potential has begun at the first electrode; the potential between inside and outside has reversed, making electrode A positive in relation to B; at *b* the action potential at A has subsided so that the potential at A is now zero, the same as at B; at *c* the action potential has begun at B, so that the electrode here is positive in relation to A and at *d* the action potential has subsided and A and B are at equal (zero) potential.

Increase in Sodium Permeability

We may now ask why it is that the resting potential has changed its polarity, the inside becoming positive in relation to the outside. The answer was provided by Hodgkin and Katz, who showed that the height of the action potential, i.e. the extent to which this reversal took place, depended on the concentration of sodium in the medium. Thus we have seen that the magnitude of the resting potential depends on the effective impermeability of the axon membrane to Na^+, it being a potential dependent on the high internal concentration of K^+. We also saw that, if the membrane had some degree of permeability to Na^+, the correct measure of the potential was given by the equation:

$$E = \frac{RT}{nF} \ln \frac{[K]_i + a[Na]_i}{[K]o + a[Na]o}$$

with a equal to the ratio of Na^+ to K^+ permeabilities. In the resting state this ratio is small, so that Na^+ contributes little to the resting potential. If, however, a became very large indeed, i.e. if the membrane became highly permeable to Na^+, then the potential would be effectively determined by the equation:

$$E = RT/F \ln [Na]_i/[Na]_o$$

i.e. it would become a *sodium-potential* instead of a potassium- or chloride-potential. The theoretical sodium-potential is about 40 mV, so that the maximum degree of positivity, i.e. of "overshoot", indicated by the height of the potential above the zero baseline of Fig. 1.7, will be given by this; in fact overshoots close to this can be recorded. We can understand, now, why the size of the action potential is affected by the concentration of Na^+ in the medium (Fig. 1.9).

Increase in K^+-permeability

The increase in sodium-permeability lasts a very short time, and is succeeded by a subsidence towards its original value accompanied by a large increase in K^+-permeability; and it is these two effects that restore the resting potential rapidly to its original value.

Negative After-potential. The negative after-potential may be explained on the basis of this increased permeability to K^+. Thus the resting potential of the squid's giant axon is normally less than the theoretical Nernst potential that would be expected on the basis of the relative concentrations of K^+ inside and outside; this is because of a significant permeability to Na^+ even in the resting state, and the Goldman equation tells us that, because of this, the resting potential will be lower than the full K^+-potential. A large increase in permeability to K^+ would tend to make the potential closer to the theoretical, i.e. the inside would become more negative and thus give rise to the after-potential. It is only after this phase of high K^+-permeability has subsided that the negative after-potential disappears.*

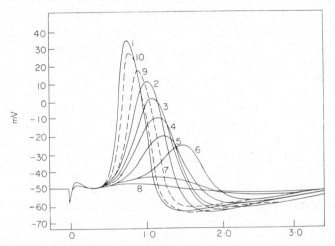

Fig. 1.9. Effect of external concentration of sodium on the size of the action potential of squid nerve, measured as the change in the potential of an internal electrode relative to the external fluid when an impulse is conducted past. Curve 1, normal nerve; 2–8, outside fluid replaced by isotonic dextrose, records taken every 15 sec; 9, 10, after restoration to seawater. (Hodgkin and Katz, *J. Physiol.* 1949, **108**, 37.)

Refractoriness

Immediately after the occurrence of an action potential the membrane across which the potential occurred is refractory, in the sense that it is impossible to initiate another spike. This is because the membrane's capacity to increase its Na^+-permeability has been lost, and it requires time for it to be re-established. As the axon recovers, the size of action potential that can be evoked gets larger until, when

---

* This high K^+-permeability gives to the axon the power of rectification, so that it is often called *delayed rectification,* delayed because it comes on after the increase in Na^+-permeability.

this *relatively refractory period* is over, the spike-height is back to its original value.

Initiation of the Response

Let us study, first, the classical mode of stimulation employed before the development of microelectrodes which could be inserted into the axon. We place two electrodes, fairly close to each other, on the surface of the axon, as in Fig. 1.10a, and make the circuit with a switch. We may apply a rectangular pulse, in the sense that the switch is put on for a short time and then switched off. Now it has been known for a long time that, to initiate a spike, the axon under the stimulating electrode must be made negative when the circuit is completed. Thus the spike begins at the negative pole in the set-up illustrated by Fig. 1.10a. Essentially what we have done, then, is to partially depolarize the membrane. Initially it had a membrane potential with the outside positive; by applying the negative electrode we have, in effect, reduced the resting potential, and to apply the electrical analogy of the membrane described in Vol. 1, we have partially discharged the condenser reducing the potential E_M to E' (Fig. 1.10b). Because the membrane has a finite resistance, current flows through the electrodes in the manner illustrated in Fig. 1.10b, and we may regard the stimulus as either the reduction of the membrane potential or as the flow of current such that positive current flows out of the axon.

Threshold. When the amount of depolarization is small, there is no spike, and as the applied potential is increased a *threshold* is reached at which the spike is fired off. It is customary to speak of the spike, then, as an *all-or-none response* that occurs when a certain threshold depolarization is reached; up to a point this is true but modern work has shown that the transition from no response to the full spike is not so abrupt as was at first thought (p. 27).

Trans-membrane Stimulation. That it is the depolarization of the membrane that is important is easily demonstrated by trans-membrane stimulation, one stimulating electrode being inserted into the axoplasm and another placed on its surface. The internal electrode must be made positive, and the passage of current from inside to outside induces the spike, whilst reversal of the polarity fails to excite. If the applied potential is only, say, 5 mV, the membrane is depolarized to that amount but nothing further happens, the response being said to be passive and to represent the partial discharge of the condenser. As the applied potential is increased, we reach a critical depolarization that leads on to the spike; in other words the depolarization becomes *self regenerative*. Once this critical value has been reached the inside

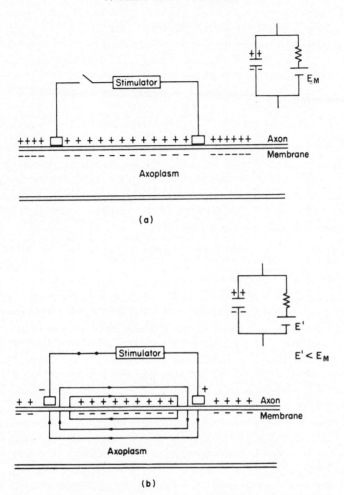

Fig. 1.10. The initiation of the action potential. Two electrodes from a square-wave stimulator are placed close together on a neurone as shown in (a). The electrical analogy of the resting membrane potential E_M is shown in the inset. If now the switch is closed a new potential (E') is established across the membrane, the area of the membrane under the negative electrode becomes partially depolarized (that is the membrane potential is reduced) and an action potential is initiated.

becomes less and less negative and reverses its polarity, becoming positive in relation to the outside.

Partial Depolarization. Thus the event for the onset of the increased Na^+-permeability, required to cause the regenerative spike, is the partial depolarization of the cell membrane. This depolarization is most simply achieved by an electrical impulse, but it may also be brought about by applying a high concentration of K^+ to a localized region on the outside of the axon; we have seen that the membrane potential decreases as the outside concentration of K^+ is increased, in accordance with the Nernst Equation:

$$E = -\frac{RT}{nF} \ln [K]_i/[K]_o$$

Na^+-permeability and Potential. Why the permeability of a membrane to Na^+ should be increased by a small degree of depolarization is still only a matter for speculation; the Na^+-permeability is doubtless of the facilitated transfer or carrier-mediated type, and we may postulate that the availability of the carriers is somehow governed by the potential across the membrane.

The Flow of Current

Recharging of Condenser

The studies with electrodes inside and outside the axon permitted the description of the changes in potential across the membrane which take place during the action potential, or spike. They consisted in a rapid depolarization, or reduction, of the resting potential to zero, which continued into a reversal of the membrane potential, the inside now becoming positive. These changes were followed by a reversal leading to a repolarization of the membrane, the inside finishing up negative. If we represent the equivalent electrical circuit as in Fig. 1.11, i.e. treating the membrane as a leaky condenser with an electromotive force, E_K, applied across it and thus giving an internal negativity, we may treat the spike as a discharging of the condenser and a recharging of it with opposite polarity through the establishment of a new electromotive force, E_{Na}, governed this time by the concentrations of Na^+ on each side of the membrane instead of by K^+ (Fig. 1.11).

Capacitative Current. Such a change must be accompanied by the flow of current, flowing across the membrane through the resistance, R, and across the condenser to charge it with the opposite polarity, this latter being described as a "capacitative current". It becomes of great interest to be able to measure the actual flows of current taking place during the establishment of the new potential across the membrane, and subsequently when the *status quo* is re-established.

Voltage Clamp

Hodgkin and Huxley were able to do this by exploiting the technique of *voltage clamping*, which permitted the establishment of any required

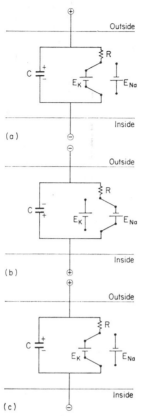

Fig. 1.11. The flow of current during an action potential. (a) In the resting state an excitable membrane can be represented as a leaky condenser (C) with an electromotive force E_K applied across it. The size of E_K is governed by the concentration gradient of potassium ions across the membrane. (b) When an action potential passes down the membrane, the condenser is discharged and a new EMF, E_{Na}, is switched into the circuit. The current now flows in the opposite direction and the size of the EMF is dependent on the concentration of sodium ions on either side of the membrane. (c) The action potential has passed and the membrane is restored to its original state with the EMF again dependent on the distribution of K^+ ions.

potential across the membrane and maintained this potential constant in spite of the flows of current that would otherwise have resulted in change. Thus if we establish a depolarizing potential across the axon normally, and if this depolarization is greater than threshold, we have seen that the depolarization continues; the task of the voltage clamp is to prevent this further depolarization. This is achieved by a feed-back circuit which pumps current into the circuit to oppose the change in potential that would have occurred. The amount of current that must be pumped in is clearly a measure of the current that was flowing through the axon, i.e. the voltage clamp provides a direct measure of the current flowing and of any changes that take place while the clamping potential is maintained (Fig. 1.12).

Inward Na$^+$-current. Hodgkin and Huxley found that the first effect of a depolarizing clamp, sufficient to have caused a spike, was a flow of positive current inwards. This current could be shown to be carried by Na$^+$-ions, since it was reduced by reducing the concentration of Na$^+$ in the medium and was abolished in a Na$^+$-free

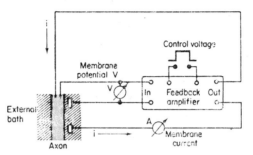

Fig. 1.12. The voltage clamp. This device detects the natural flow of current across the excitable membrane and by means of the feedback amplifier applies an equal but opposite current which holds the membrane potential constant. The size of this external current is thus a direct measure of that flowing across the membrane, and by varying the potential in a step-wise fashion, the magnitude and direction of current-flow during the action potential can be determined. The feedback circuit opposes the sudden potential swing that normally occurs when the membrane potential is raised above the threshold value. (Katz, "Nerve Muscle and Synapse", McGraw-Hill, 1969.)

medium. The magnitude of this initial inward current increased with increasing degree of depolarization, so that the *current–voltage curve* may be represented by Fig. 1.13, where the ordinate is the value of the peak current measured immediately on establishing a membrane potential given by the abscissa. It will be noted that the current signs reverse at a membrane potential of about 40 mV, inside positive. This is what would be expected were the current due to the switching on of an E.M.F. governed by the Na$^+$-potential which, according to the Nernst equation, should be about 40 mV with the inside positive.

Outward K$^+$-current. The flow of current, after depolarizing the membrane, is a Na$^+$-current and is due to the very high permeability of the membrane to Na$^+$ by comparison with the permeability to K$^+$

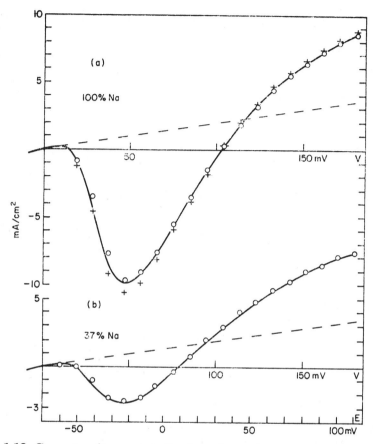

Fig. 1.13. Current–voltage curves for the voltage clamped myelinated axon. The ordinate is the value of the peak current measured immediately on establishing the values of membrane potential shown on the abscissa. (a) Normal Ringer solution; (b) Normal Ringer solution containing 37% of the normal Na^+-concentration. (Dodge and Frankenhaeuser, *J. Physiol.* 1959, **148,** 188.)

and Cl^-, the Na^+-ion entering the axon more rapidly than Cl^- can accompany it or than K^+ can move out in exchange. This current is transient, however, and is followed by a persisting current in the opposite direction which could be shown to be due to an onset of high K^+-permeability accompanied by the return of Na^+-permeability to its original low value. This steep change in K^+-permeability, revealed in the voltage-clamped condition as an outward-flowing current, would, in the normal state, lead to a rapid re-establishment of the normal resting potential, i.e. a repolarization. Thus the spike is seen as the consequence of an initial rapid increase in Na^+-permeability, followed by a return to its original value in company with a large increase in K^+-permeability. This may be described as a switching on of the K^+-E.M.F. as the Na^+-E.M.F. is switched off (Fig. 1.11).

Inactivation of Na^+-permeability

We may ask whether the fall in Na^+-permeability, which is necessary if the resting potential is to be re-established, occurs passively, or whether there is an active switching-off mechanism. Hodgkin and

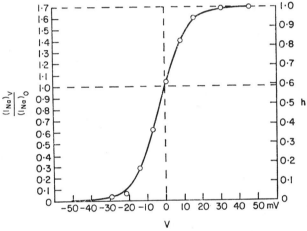

Fig. 1.14. The influence of membrane potential on the "inactivation" of the sodium permeability. Abscissa: displacement of membrane potential from its resting value during conditioning step. Ordinate: sodium current during test step relative to maximum sodium current. The smooth curve has been calculated. The inactivation of the sodium permeability increases as the membrane is depolarized. (Hodgkin and Huxley, *J. Physiol.* 1952, **116**, 497.)

Huxley showed that there was what they called an "inactivation" process, favoured by depolarization of the membrane. As the spike developed, the Na^+-permeability mechanism was inactivated, thus making it possible for the increased K^+-permeability to repolarize the membrane. This inactivation process is revealed by maintaining a definite depolarization across the membrane for a long period of time. Under these conditions it is found that the ability to develop a Na^+-current with further depolarization is impaired—the greater the degree of membrane depolarization applied, the greater this "inactivation". The inactivation took time to develop, following a simple logarithmic curve with a rate-constant of 0·14 msec^{-1}, and was thus much slower than the establishment of the initial Na$^+$-current which had a rate-constant of 15 msec^{-1} representing a "half-life" of about 0·05 msec.

Dependence of Inactivation on Membrane Potential. The degree of inactivation achieved by a sustained depolarization may be represented by the ratio of the peak Na$^+$-current obtained by a fixed depolarizing step, e.g. 50 mV, over the maximum peak Na$^+$-current obtainable; this is indicated by h and varies from 1, when the axon has been maintained in a hyperpolarized state, to zero when it has been maintained at a depolarization of some 50 mV below the normal resting potential (Fig. 1.14). It will be clear that this inactivation process, which if complete makes the membrane incapable of increasing its Na$^+$-permeability, contributes to the repolarization process after the initial inward Na$^+$-current, since it increases with the degree of depolarization.

Predicted Action Potential

Quantitative studies of the changes in Na$^+$- and K$^+$-permeability, as measured by the currents flowing through the nerve membrane when potentials were applied across it and using the voltage-clamp technique, allowed Hodgkin and Huxley (1952) to develop a series of equations whose solution enabled them to predict the course of the action potential (Fig. 1.15), as well as to predict the effects of a changed

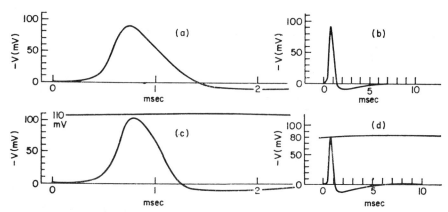

Fig. 1.15. A comparison of the potential changes calculated theoretically from current measurement during voltage clamp conditions with those recorded during the normal action potential. The upper traces (a) and (b) are the *calculated* potential changes on two different time-scales while (c) and (d) are the *recorded* action potentials on similar time-scales. (Hodgkin and Huxley, *J. Physiol.* 1952, **116,** 473.)

environment of the nerve on its action potential, e.g. the effects of altered concentration of Ca^{2+}.

Accommodation

It has been known for a long time that, when stimulating a nerve electrically, in order to specify the threshold it is not sufficient to give the magnitude of the applied depolarization since the rate at which this depolarization is established is of great importance. Furthermore, the length of time during which a given depolarization is applied is also important.

Strength–Duration Curve

Thus, to consider the latter point first we may plot the duration of an applied potential against the intensity required to elicit a response.

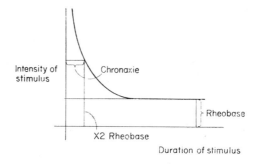

Fig. 1.16. The strength–duration curve. The curve represents the threshold values of stimulus intensity plotted against duration of stimulus necessary to elicit an action potential. The rheobase is the value of stimulus intensity below which the current may be applied indefinitely without exciting the nerve. Conversely there is a limit to the duration of stimulus below which the strength of stimulus can be increased indefinitely without eliciting a response, and was said to be a measure of the excitability of the tissue. (Katz, "Electric Excitation in Nerve", OUP, 1939.)

This gives the well known *Strength–Duration Curve* of Fig. 1.16; and it is seen that there is a critical value of the depolarization, the *rheobase*, below which it can be maintained indefinitely without evoking a response. In general, the shorter the stimulus the greater the current required to stimulate. The *chronaxie* is defined as the duration of a stimulus, of twice the rheobase, required to excite.

Minimum Current Gradient

The importance of the rate of establishing the depolarization is manifest in the *minimal current gradient*, and is illustrated in Fig. 1.17 which shows the threshold for stimulation in terms of the current-intensity as a function of the time required to reach this current-intensity. When the rate of rise is below the minimal current gradient, excitation fails.

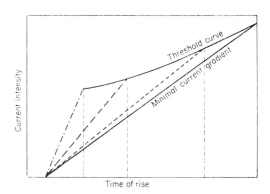

Fig. 1.17. Diagram illustrating the relation between rate of rise, and threshold strength of a linearly increasing "triangular" current pulse. The steeper the rate of rise of current intensity the lower is the threshold. (Katz, "Electric Excitation in Nerve", OUP, 1939.)

Ionic Basis of Accommodation

The classical investigators of the quantitative aspects of the stimulus concluded that, when a potential was applied to the excitable tissue, two processes came into play—an *excitatory* one tending to fire off the all-or-none response, and an *accommodative* response, tending to raise the threshold, i.e. acting against the excitatory process. This term "accommodation" is still retained, and indicates the adaptation of the tissue to the applied stimulus. Analysis of the flow of currents across the membrane during the application of the stimulus, using the voltage-clamp technique referred to above, has revealed that the fundamental process in accommodation is a reduction in the power of the excitable tissue to increase its Na^+-permeability for a given degree of depolarization. Associated with this "inactivation" of the Na^+-permeability system there is the increased permeability to K^+ associated with the applied depolarization. As we have argued above, the increased K^+-permeability, by forcing the membrane potential to the theoretical K^+-potential, will antagonize the depolarizing effect of the applied potential. Thus accommodation, manifesting itself as a progressively increasing threshold for firing the spike, reflects the development of the Na^+-inactivation process and the onset of the "delayed rectification" or increased permeability to K^+ that follows the transient increase in Na^+-permeability. Both processes increase with the degree of depolarization of the membrane and, in contrast to the initial increase in Na^+-permeability, they are sustained and not transient. Thus, if the Na^+-current is not turned on rapidly, the opposing processes succeed in aborting the action potential. The phenomenon of minimal current gradient is explicable in terms of the accommodation process: too slow a rate of depolarization allows the Na^+-inactivation and delayed rectification to inhibit the development of Na^+-permeability required for the spike.

Propagation of the Impulse

Electrotonic Potentials

When the nerve membrane is artificially depolarized by a small amount, say 5 mV, the response is passive, in the sense that the resting potential remains at this reduced level; it is as though we had partially discharged the condenser, as in Fig. 1.10, by an inward flow of current. The change in membrane potential is described as an *electrotonic potential* to differentiate it from the regenerative type of depolarization

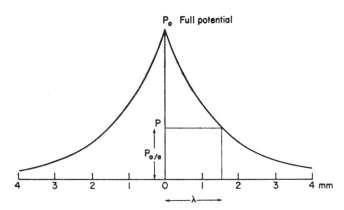

Fig. 1.18. The electrotonic potential. The diagram represents the fall in value of an applied potential (P_0) as it spreads out along the nerve membrane. P_0 is a subthreshold stimulus. λ, the length constant, is the distance from the point of application to the point at which the potential has fallen to $1/e$ of its value. Myelinated fibre has a high transverse resistance, and λ is some five times the value for non-myelinated fibres; hence the potential spreads further in the myelinated fibre.

that leads to the spike. When we examine the effects of this depolarization at increasing distances from the applied electrode we find that they fall off rapidly, in the sense that the depolarization at, say, 5 mm is only a small fraction of that immediately under the applied electrode (Fig. 1.18).

Length-constant. The spread is predictable from the theory of cables, and follows the exponential equation:

$$P = P_0\, e^{-x/\lambda}$$

where λ is called the *length-constant* or *characteristic length* and is given by

$$\lambda = \sqrt{\frac{r_m}{r_1 + r_2}} \qquad (1)$$

where r_m is the transverse resistance across the membrane, and r_1 and r_2 are the resistances of the outside and inside media of the nerve, i.e. the intracellular fluid, r_1, and the bathing medium, r_2. Inspection of Equation (1) shows that λ is the distance from the point of application of P_0 to the point at which the potential, P, becomes $1/e$ of the applied potential P_0. In myelinated fibres, with high transverse resistance, the length-constant is some 2–3 mm whilst in a non-medullated fibre it is of the order of 0·5 mm.

Time-constant. We may note, also, that the electrotonic potential takes time to develop and to decay after the applied potential has been switched off. The time-course is defined by the time-constant, τ_m, which is approximately the time required for the potential to reach 85 per cent of the steady value.

Local Subthreshold Responses

When the applied depolarization is made greater and greater, a point is reached when the action potential is generated, and this propagates away from the applied electrode so that now the spread is no longer predictable in terms of passive cable theory. We may ask how it is that the reversal of the membrane potential that takes place under the stimulating electrode is propagated to neighbouring parts of the membrane. The answer was given by Hodgkin's application of local-circuit theory many years before the true nature of the response was understood.

Hodgkin started from the observation that, if he established larger and larger depolarizations at a given point, the change-over from the passive, non-propagated, to the active, propagated, response was gradual, so that at intermediate depolarizations there was some, but limited, active depolarization which subsided before the self-regenerative spike developed (Fig. 1.19). These "local subthreshold responses", as they were called, propagated a little way but died out—they were said to "decrement to extinction". Thus failure of propagation, i.e. of the locally developed action potential to move away from its seat of origin, was due to its failure to stimulate adequately the adjoining regions.

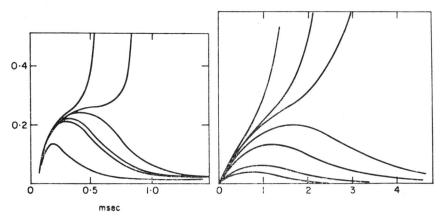

Fig. 1.19. Showing the transition from the local responses of subthreshold stimuli to the fully propagated action potential when the stimulus is above threshold in a crustacean nerve fibre. (Hodgkin, *Proc. Roy. Soc. B*, 1938, **126**, 87.)

Local Circuits. We may ask how can a local depolarization affect the adjacent membrane? This follows simply from cable theory, and the analogy between the effects of an applied potential, as in electrical stimulation, and a local depolarization is shown in Fig. 1.20. Thus, when a cathode is applied to the axon membrane, positive current flows as in Fig. 1.20a, positive ions being "pulled" through the membrane under the cathode to establish circuits of current of larger and larger radius. The adequate stimulus is reached when the local current under the electrode reaches a definite value. In Fig. 1.20b we have an active region of the axon, i.e. a region that has developed its action potential so that positive current from the surface tends to flow into the "negative sink" created by this active region. For the current to flow a circuit must be made, and this is given by the flow of positive current out of the axon in the region just adjacent to the active region, i.e. it is a local circuit induced by the change in potential across the active region. As soon as this local current acquires the necessary magnitude, the membrane develops its high Na^+-permeability, passes through its spike, and is in a position to induce an adequate local circuit to cause further propagation.

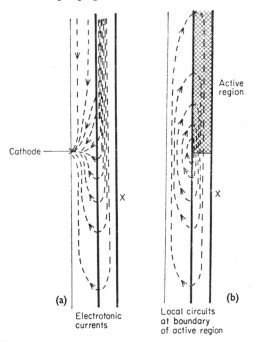

Fig. 1.20. Illustrating the analogy between electronic currents (a) due to an applied stimulus and (b) the local circuits at the boundary of an active region. (Hodgkin, *J. Physiol.* 1937, **90**, 183.)

Extrinsic Currents

The local currents due to an active region of membrane are called *extrinsic*, and they may be demonstrated in a number of ways. For example the spread of the spike may be prevented locally by, say, cooling the nerve; the spike reaching the cooled portion is extinguished, but if the cooled region is small, it is possible to demonstrate an in-, creased excitability of the nerve beyond the block at the moment when the spike is extinguished. This is illustrated by Fig. 1.21: stimulating at S_1 caused an action potential which was extinguished by the block so that no response was recorded at (c); however, application of a subliminal stimulus at S_2, which by itself would not excite, when applied at the time the spike from S_1 reached the block was effective in evoking a spike, which was recorded at (c).

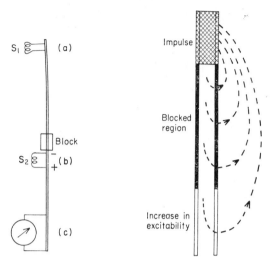

Fig. 1.21. The electrotonic spread of potential. In the left hand diagram a nerve is blocked by cooling and action potentials generated at S_1 are extinguished by the block. If, however, a subthreshold stimulus is applied at S_2 at the time the spike reaches the block, an action potential is recorded at (c). The right hand diagram shows the spread of local current around the block lowering the threshold so that a subthreshold stimulus is now sufficient to depolarize the nerve. (Hodgkin, *J. Physiol.* **90,** 183.)

Foot of Action Potential. If the action potential is spreading ahead of itself through its effect on the passive cable properties of the axon, then the initial upstroke of the action potential, the so-called *foot* of the spike, represents the flow of extrinsic current rather than development of activity under the recording electrode; only when the regenerative increase of permeability to Na^+ has started does the curve of potential rise steeply. Cole and Curtis were the first to demonstrate

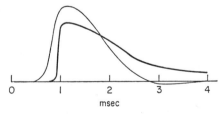

Fig. 1.22. The relation between the increase in sodium permeability, as represented by change in membrane conductance (thick line) and the action potential (thin line). The change in conductance is seen to occur during the rising phase of the action potential. (Cole and Curtis, *J. Gen. Physiol.* 1938, **22,** 37.)

this sudden change in the membrane characteristics during the action potential; this is shown in Fig. 1.22, where they recorded both the action potential and the transverse resistance across the squid giant axon. It is seen that the change in membrane resistance, which reflects Na^+-permeability, comes on well after the onset of the foot of the action potential.

Velocity of Propagation

A factor favouring speed of conduction will be the distance to which the extrinsic currents stretch in advance of the spike. This depends on the cable properties of the axon and in particular on the transverse resistance. The development of a thick lipid sheath—the myelin sheath—represents an adaptation favouring increased conduction-

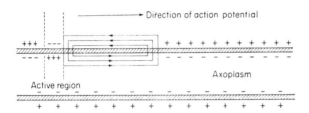

(a) Non myelinated nerve fibre

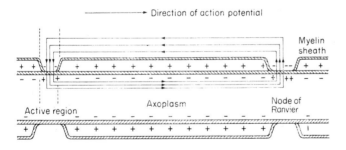

(b) Myelinated nerve fibre

Fig. 1.23. Velocity of propagation. The distance ahead that local currents spread depends on the transverse resistance of the membrane, and the greater the spread the faster the action potential can travel. (a) Non-myelinated nerve, the local currents depolarize the region immediately adjacent to the active part of the membrane. (b) The myelinated nerve has a high transverse resistance as myelin forms an effective insulator. The electrotonic spread of local currents is between nodes of Ranvier.

velocity; however, this militates against the flow of current through the membrane, and Nature has reached a compromise by the development of the nodes of Ranvier, regions where the myelin is absent. It is at these regions that current is allowed to flow across the axon, i.e. the conduction along a myelinated nerve fibre is *saltatory*, the extrinsic current ahead of the spike passing through the next node instead of, as in non-myelinated nerve, through the immediately adjacent region (Fig. 1.23). Thus measurements of the electrical resistance across the node showed it to be about one ten-thousandth of that across the internode.

Fibre Diameter and Velocity

It follows from the application of cable theory to the analysis of the spread of electrotonic currents, that the rate of conduction should increase with fibre-diameter; in fact, with unmyelinated fibres, velocity should be proportional to the square root of the diameter. With myelinated fibres, too, conduction velocity should increase with diameter, and if the distance between nodes is proportional to the diameter, a linear relation may be predicted. The dependence of conduction velocity on fibre diameter forms the basis for the classification of the individual fibres in a mixed nerve, as shown in Table I, where the conduction-velocities of the different fibres are grouped according to diameter.

TABLE I

Frog fibres; conduction velocity as function of fibre diameter

	Type	Diameter (μ)	Velocity (m/sec)
A $\{$	α	18·5	42
	β	14·0	25
	γ	11·0	17
B		—	4·2
C	(Unmyelinated)	2·5	0·4–0·5

Myelin Thickness. When considering the effects of diameter of myelinated fibres, it must be appreciated that changes in total diameter are compounded of changes in both myelin thickness and diameter of the axis-cylinder—the name given to the unmyelinated part of the axon. Thus we may expect velocity to be a complex function of total axon diameter. According to Smith and Koles, the optimal ratio of axis cylinder to total diameter, d/D, should be 0·6, and this is approximately what is found experimentally. As Fig. 1.24 shows, the increase in conduction velocity with axon diameter, D, is largely governed by the increasing thickness of the myelin sheath.

Mixed Nerve. Any given nerve contains a mixture of fibres of widely varying diameter, and to a large extent we can correlate function with this parameter. Thus very rapid conduction is required for conducting impulses *to* fast skeletal muscle; and also *from* their spindles, to provide the motor centres with information regarding their length

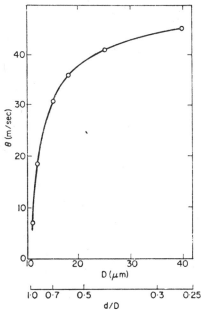

Fig. 1.24. Conduction velocity (θ) computed for various external axon diameters (D). The axis cylinder diameter (d), the unmyelinated portion of the axon, was held constant at 10·5 μm. Temperature 20°C. The ratio: axis cylinder diameter/total fibre diameter, d/D, is shown on the lower abscissa. (Smith and Koles, *Am. J. Physiol.* 1970, **219**, 1256.)

at any moment. A great deal of sensory information is not so urgent, so that it is more economical to employ finer, and less rapidly conducting fibres, to carry this, e.g. information on the temperature of the skin, the tension in the urinary bladder, and so on. Usually it is possible to resolve the sense of pain into a fast and slow component according to the time taken to reach consciousness, and these components are carried by different types of fibre, "fast pain" being carried by relatively rapidly conducting myelinated fibres and "slow pain" by very slowly conducting unmyelinated (C) fibres.

Temperature

In warm-blooded animals the velocity of conduction, for a given axon diameter, is considerably greater; thus the velocity in the most rapidly conducting A-fibres in the cat is 100 m/sec, comparing with some 40 m/sec for the frog axon of comparable diameter.

Invertebrate Fibres. Invertebrate nerve fibres have only very thin myelin sheaths, if any, so that when high conduction-velocity is required, as in the mantle-nerves of the squid, this is achieved by the fusion of many neurones to form a single giant neurone with a diameter of over half a millimetre, compared with only 10 μ for a frog myelinated sciatic fibre conducting at about the same rate of 25 metres per second.

Repetitive Discharges

When a constant sustained depolarization is applied to the axon, usually only a single spike is evoked, and this is presumably because the constant current is maintaining the Na^+-permeability mechanism in an inactivated state while the increased K^+-permeability is maintained. Thus the axon may be said to accommodate rapidly to the applied stimulus. When a sensory neurone is stimulated naturally, e.g. by a touch to the skin in which its axon-endings occur, the response is repetitive, a series of spikes passing along the axon in rapid succession; the reasons for this difference will be discussed later. For the moment it is sufficient to appreciate that the usual message is a series of spikes rather than a single one, and we may assume that the axon, when stimulated electrically, is exhibiting a far greater degree of accommodation than when stimulated naturally through its nerve endings.

Altered Accommodation

This accommodation can be disturbed, however, by quite small changes in the environment of the axon; thus, merely lowering the concentration of Ca^{2+} in the medium will cause a repetitive discharge in the squid giant axon in response to an applied constant current. The analysis of the causes of this change in response shows that the single spike response is, indeed, rather the exception than a usual state of affairs, depending on the rapid inactivation of the Na^+-mechanism and the onset of the increased K^+-permeability. An upset in the time-relations of these processes could easily lead to repetitive discharge; in fact, with appropriate changes in the electrical parameters it is possible to envisage spontaneous rhythmic discharges independent of any external stimulus, and this, of course, is the basis for the pacemaker activity of the heart muscle fibres (Chapter 2).

NEURO-EFFECTOR TRANSMISSION

The neurone transmits its message, consisting of a series of action potentials, either to another neurone—as for example, when the message from a sensory neurone is transmitted to a motor neurone in the spinal cord—or else it may transmit its message to an *effector cell*. The best studied of the effector cells is the voluntary muscle fibre. Whether transmission is from neurone to neurone, or neurone to effector cell, the process takes place at a specialized junctional region; in the neurone-to-neurone transmission this region is called a *synapse*; at the skeletal muscle fibre it may also be called a synapse, but usually it is called a *neuromuscular junction*. The essential features of the junction, or synapse, are the very close approximation of the cell membranes of the axon and the recipient cell, and usually the liberation, from the terminals of the axon, of a *transmitter substance* that initiates an electrical change in the post-junctional cell, be it muscle fibre or neurone.

SKELETAL NEUROMUSCULAR TRANSMISSION

The End-plate

The voluntary muscle fibre is a long cell containing many nuclei; it is surrounded by a connective-tissue type of membrane, the *sarcolemma*, beneath which lies the plasma membrane that is responsible for its permeability characteristics. The junction between the motor nerve fibre and the muscle fibre is frequently in the form of the *end-plate*; at the nerve terminal, the nerve fibre loses its myelin sheath whilst its perineurial sheath fuses with the sarcolemma thereby giving the axon access to the underlying plasma membrane of the muscle fibre. In the electron microscope it can be seen that the plasma membranes of both cells remain separated by a measurable gap. Thus, according to Robertson's description, the terminal axon becomes enveloped in a gutter formed by a depression in the surface of the muscle fibre, the membrane in this gutter being thrown into a series of *post-junctional folds* some $0 \cdot 5 \ \mu$ to $1 \cdot 0 \ \mu$ long and 500–1000 Å wide. The arrangement is illustrated schematically in Fig. 1.25. The nerve terminals are only partially invested by Schwann cells, so that the naked axon comes into close relation with the plasma membrane of the muscle fibre.

Synaptic Vesicles

The cytoplasm of the terminal axon contains numerous *synaptic vesicles*, some 300–400 Å in diameter; and there is little doubt that these

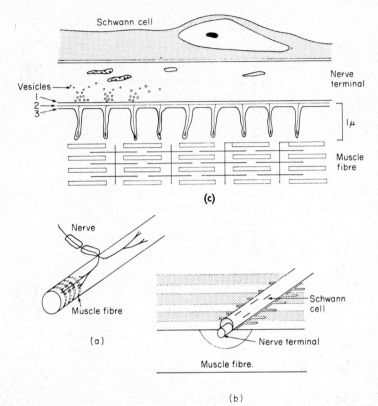

Fig. 1.25. Neuromuscular junction. (a) The ending of motor axons on the
muscle fibres. (b) A three-dimensional representation of the relation between
nerve terminal and muscle fibres. The Schwann cell covers only the top
half of the nerve fibre and the base is embedded in a gutter on the muscle
surface. The depressions alongside the nerve fibre are the folding of the post-
synaptic membrane of the muscle fibre. (c) A transverse section of the motor
end plate: (1) is the terminal axon membrane; (2) the basement membrane;
(3) the folded post-synaptic membrane of the muscle fibre (post-junctional
    folds). (Katz, "Nerve, Muscle and Synapse", McGraw-Hill, 1969.)

are the containers of the transmitter substance released from the
terminal into the junctional spaces, namely *acetylcholine.*

The Effector Response

All-or-None

Stimulation of the motor neurone to a single muscle fibre causes it
to contract. The mechanical features of this contraction will be discussed in a later Chapter; here we may note that the response is usually

all-or-none, like the action potential of nerve, and this "all-or-none-ness" is due essentially to a feature common to the two types of cell, namely that both transmit over their whole surface a wave of action potential. It is the wave of action potential, rapidly passing over the surface of the muscle fibre, that induces the underlying myofibrils to contract. Thus, if we place recording electrodes on the nerve and muscle of the classical nerve-muscle preparation of Fig. 1.26, and stimulate the nerve, we obtain action potentials from both nerve and muscle, that of the muscle being followed by mechanical contraction.

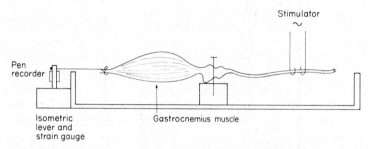

Fig. 1.26. The nerve-muscle preparation. A frog gastrocnemius muscle is dissected free with its sciatic nerve supply from the cord. Stimulation of the nerve produces contractions of the muscle which can be recorded on a pen recorder.

Synaptic Delay

By applying electrodes very close to the entry of the nerve to the muscle it can be estimated that there is a delay in transmission from neurone to muscle fibre longer than would be anticipated by the mere electrical transmission of the action potential from the neurone to the muscle fibre, i.e. the idea, originally propounded by Eccles, that the nerve spike transmitted its effects by virtue of its extrinsic current is unsound. The delay is short, however, being of the order of 1 msec.

Acetylcholine as Transmitter

The chemical nature of the transmission is best revealed, perhaps, by the study of the effects of drugs; thus acetylcholine, applied to the end-plate region of an isolated nerve-muscle preparation, causes a contraction of the muscle. By applying this through a micro-pipette electrophoretically, Krnjevic and Miledi found that extremely small amounts were effective, namely 10^{-17} to 10^{-16} moles. Stimulation of the nerve causes release of acetylcholine into the medium, and if its hydrolysis is prevented by an appropriate inhibitor of cholinesterase, the amounts collected per impulse can give an approximate idea of how much was required for transmission. Krnjevic and Mitchell estimated, on this basis, that only some 1.10^{-17} moles, i.e. some 6 million molecules, were liberated per impulse at an individual junction. This is smaller than the amount required to excite when applied locally, but it is likely that the natural mode of liberation, directly into the clefts between nerve terminal and muscle membrane, is the more efficient and therefore requires less.

Nicotine and Muscarine Actions. The effects of acetylcholine may be mimicked by several drugs, notably nicotine, so that the action of acetylcholine on the neuromuscular junction is often described as its *nicotine action*, by contrast with its *muscarine action* on effectors that are controlled by the autonomic nervous system, such as the heart. Thus, although, as we shall see, acetylcholine is the transmitter of impulses from the vagus-nerve to the heart, its action on the heart cannot be mimicked by nicotine. It would seem that the "receptive substance" on the heart's S.A.-node is slightly different from that on voluntary muscle; both "accept" acetylcholine and respond, but nicotine will only meet the voluntary muscle's requirements—and also those of certain synapses—whilst muscarine meets the requirements of autonomic junctions such as those in the heart and intestine.

Cholinesterase. Liberation of a transmitter might be expected to cause repetitive discharges unless it was in some way inactivated, or alternatively it might be expected to cause indefinite refractoriness. In fact, the response to a single action potential in the neurone is a single response in the muscle; this is because the liberated acetylcholine is rapidly hydrolysed to acetic acid and choline by the enzyme *acetylcholinesterase*, which is concentrated in the junction. This is revealed

$$CH_3\overset{O}{\overset{\|}{C}}OCH_2CH_2\overset{+}{N}(CH_3)_3 + H_2O \longrightarrow CH_3\overset{O}{\overset{\|}{C}}OH + HOCH_2CH_2\overset{+}{N}(CH_3)_3$$

| Acetylcholine | Cholinesterase | Acetic acid | Choline |

histochemically by incubating the muscle with a sulphur derivative of acetylcholine, acetylthiocholine, in the presence of a copper salt; the primary reaction product is precipitated as copper sulphide and this appears as dense accumulations in the end-plate regions. For electron microscopical studies, the heavier lead sulphide was precipitated, and this was found on the plasma membrane of the muscle fibre in the space between the axon and muscle and in the space formed by the junctional folds (Fig. 1.27).

Potentiation. An inhibitor of cholinesterase, such as *eserine*, may be expected to prolong the effects of a nerve stimulus, and this does indeed occur giving rise to the phenomenon of *eserine-twitching*, although the cause of this repetitive response is rather more complex than originally thought. We may say, at any rate, that eserine and other cholinesterase inhibitors *potentiate* the action of acetylcholine, so that

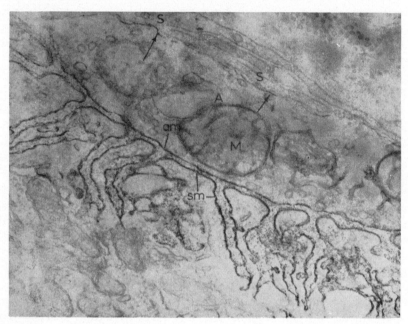

Fig. 1.27. Localization of acetylcholinesterase at the neuromuscular junctions. The pre-junctional (am) and post-junctional (sm) membranes are distinctly stained. Moderate staining is also present in the axonal plasma membrane (arrows) facing the teloglial Schwann cell (S) covering mitochondrion (M). A: axon. × 63,500 approx. (Davis and Koelle, *J. Cell Biol.* 1967, **34,** 157.)

smaller doses are more effective and longer lasting. Thus eserine applied to the surface of the eye causes the pupil to constrict; this is because the constrictor fibres to the pupil are activated by acetylcholine, liberated from the oculomotor nerve. There is normally a continuous discharge of nerve impulses to the pupil, maintaining its diameter at a value corresponding to the degree of illumination. The applied eserine allows the acetylcholine, liberated by this "tonic discharge", to remain unhydrolysed, and thus the muscle contracts more vigorously.

Curarine

This drug, which is the active principle of the South American arrow poison, blocks neuromuscular transmission; and there is no doubt that its action is on the post-synaptic membrane, i.e. its influence is on the muscle rather than on the neurone. More specifically, it does not affect the liberation of acetylcholine but prevents this from activating the muscle fibre, probably by a process of competitive inhibition, as the curarine molecule has such a strong affinity for the receptive groupings on the muscle membrane that it occupies them to the exclusion of acetylcholine.

End-plate Potential

The study of the curarized end-plate has permitted the analysis of the electrical events taking place at the junction; thus in the normal nerve-muscle preparation, the arrival of the nerve impulse, and the initiation of the muscle spike, tend to obscure the electrical events taking place in the muscle fibre preliminary to the initiation of its spike. Eccles and O'Connor had found suggestive evidence that, before the muscle spike was fired, there was a slower development of depolarization of the muscle in the end-plate region, which they called the *end-plate potential (e.p.p.)*, but this was obscured by the large all-or-nothing spike that was immediately fired off in the muscle. They made use of the refractory state of the muscle, following a single stimulus, to show that this end-plate potential occurred.

Relation to Muscle Spike. By recording with an electrode immediately in the end-plate region, Fatt and Katz were able to show that the action potential here was characteristically different from that recorded from a point far away from the end-plate; in the latter event the spike rose steeply from its base-line, but in the former there was an initial slow rise, followed by the steep rise, characteristic of the spike taken from the muscle fibre distant from the end-plate. It appeared that the spike was "taking off" from the slower depolarization of the end-plate potential. By applying curarine, which depresses the end-plate potential, the relation between e.p.p. and the spike could be studied, as in Fig. 1.28; here the record *a* is from the end-plate region of the normal fibre; the spike takes off from the slower e.p.p. The records from *b–e* indicate successive degrees of curarization; the e.p.p. is depressed, and the delay between the beginning of the e.p.p. and the spike increases, until finally in *e* only the e.p.p. is left.

The evidence suggests that the e.p.p. is a necessary preliminary step to the evolution of an all-or-none spike in the muscle membrane;

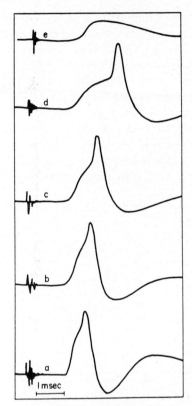

Fig. 1.28. The effects of curarine on the potentials recorded at the end-plate region of a single-fibre nerve-muscle preparation in response to a nerve stimulus. (a) Before curarine; (b)–(d) progressive curarization showing the diminution of the initial end-plate potential and progressive lengthening of the spike latent period; (e) pure end-plate potential, no spike being set up. (Kuffler, *J. Neurophysiol.* 1942, **5**, 18.)

if it fails to build up to the required height it subsides without setting off the muscle spike.

Relation to Transmitter Release. Further analysis of the e.p.p. indicated that it represented a period of depolarization of the end-plate membrane caused by the liberation of transmitter over a brief period. The localized depolarization spread electrotonically, in the same way as the spread of an applied potential discussed above, i.e. in accordance with the cable-characteristics of the muscle membrane, and it decayed electrotonically; Fig. 1.29 illustrates the likely course of events at the hypothetical transmitter site.

Summation. A remarkable feature of the end-plate potential is its power to summate the effects of successive stimuli. In the normal preparation a single nerve impulse always fires off a muscle response, so that if the end-plate potential is to be regarded as the initial step leading to transmission, this potential always reaches the required value for firing off a spike. As we have seen, in the curarized preparation the end-plate potential may be reduced to the point where no muscle spike takes off; however, if two or more nerve impulses reach this curarized end-plate in succession, then, provided the delay between impulses is not too large, the end-plate potential evoked by the first stimulus may add with that evoked by the second, and the

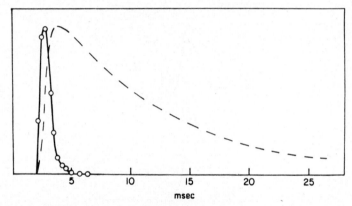

Fig. 1.29. End-plate potential and transmitter action. Broken line represents the end-plate potential of frog's sartorius muscle at 17·5°C with a time constant for decay of 9·8 msec. Solid line represents the probable course of "transmitter" action. Ordinates in arbitrary units. Abscissa: time after stimulation. (Eccles, Katz and Kuffler, *J. Neurophysiol.* 1941, **4,** 211.)

result may be a sufficiently large e.p.p. to set off a spike. Thus we may say that the first nerve impulse has *potentiated* the second, permitting it to overcome the curare-block.

Non-regenerative Response. This finding, and many others, indicate that the muscle membrane in the end-plate is electrically different from that elsewhere on the fibre. Thus acetylcholine, applied to the non-endplate regions of muscle, usually has no effect; curarine, applied elsewhere than at the end-plate, has no effect, and, as we have seen, a spike recorded from non-end-plate regions shows no slow rise; only when the record is taken from very close to the end-plate do we get the slow rise which we call the e.p.p. The evidence, developed mainly by Katz and his collaborators, indicates that the end-plate membrane is capable of being depolarized either by the application of a de-polarizing current, or chemically by acetylcholine or nicotine, but that it is incapable of the regenerative type of response, i.e. it is not capable of reversing its polarity of resting potential.

Generalized Increase in Ionic Permeability. The depolariza-tion could be due to a generalized increase in membrane permeability, permitting the breakdown of the resting potential; without the highly specific increased Na^+-permeability, which takes place in nerve and non-end-plate regions of muscle, the membrane potential cannot reverse. An indiscriminate increase in ionic permeability would cer-tainly reduce the membrane potential, which depends on a low permeability to Na^+. The actual point to which the potential would fall would depend on the relative magnitudes of the ionic permeabili-ties, in accordance with the Goldman equation (Vol. 1); it has been estimated that this would be about 15 mV, inside negative, i.e. that the resting potential would fall from an initial value of about 100 mV to 15 mV; the maximum end-plate potential that could be developed would therefore be 85 mV. As indicated, it is not easy to estimate the maximum e.p.p. because the spike intervenes, but indirect estimates indicate that this might be reached.

Initiation of Muscle Spike

It is now possible to envisage the events leading to the initiation of the muscle spike. The nerve spike travels as far as the terminals and, as a result of its arrival, acetylcholine is liberated into the junctional clefts; this depolarizes the muscle membrane by virtue of a brief transmitter action; the electrical effects spread and decay slowly by virtue of the cable properties of the muscle fibre; and, as a conse-quence of the local currents generated through the non-end-plate muscle membrane, a spike is fired off. Usually the e.p.p. is more than adequate to generate a muscle spike, since a spike is fired off when the e.p.p. has reached only about 35 mV, considerably less than its theoretical 85 mV. In its refractory state following several impulses, or after treatment with curarine, the e.p.p. is reduced to the point that the spike can no longer be initiated. However, the special feature of the e.p.p. is that it is not an all-or-none phenomenon, so that in its dimin-ished form it may add with a new one, and in fact nerve impulses in rapid succession will cause the e.p.p. to build up to the point where muscle excitation occurs. Thus, under certain special conditions, we have the phenomenon of a single nerve impulse failing to evoke a muscular response, whereas a tetanus, i.e. a rapidly repeated series of impulses, does.

Facilitation. In this case the first stimulus has *facilitated* the response to a succeeding one, and we have envisaged the facilitation as the release of a quantum of transmitter some of which remains at the end-plate and adds to the second quantum produced by the second stimulus. As we shall see, facilitation is a complex phenomenon, depending mainly on the circumstance that the quantum of transmitter released by a nerve impulse is not constant, but is affected by the previous history of the terminal. In a similar way, fatigue is mainly a reflection of a reduced quantum of transmitter released.

Spontaneous End-plate Potentials

An important discovery relating to the development of the end-plate potential in response to nervous stimulation was that, in the absence of any stimulus, the end-plate gave rise to a series of spontaneous e.p.p.'s that were much smaller than that recorded after a nerve stimulus, namely 0·5 mV on average compared with the estimated 50 mV for the spike-producing potential.

These could be shown to occur randomly, and their amplitude was diminished by curarine and increased by eserine which also increased the duration of individual potentials. It could, in fact, result in summation of successive miniature potentials that eventually led to a spike. It was considered that the miniature potentials resulted from the release of "packets" or quanta of transmitter, so that the large e.p.p. in response to a nerve stimulus represented the synchronized release of many packets. When transmission was steadily blocked by increasing the concentration of Mg^{2+} and decreasing that of Ca^{2+}, the e.p.p. in response to a nerve stimulus decreased, until finally it became the size of a single miniature e.p.p. By statistical analysis of the effects of varying the sensitivity of the junction it was concluded that, in the mammalian end-plate, for example, some 310 quanta were released in response to a nerve impulse. The miniature potentials are definitely not due to spontaneous electrical discharges in the nerve terminals since they are unaffected by blocking nervous conduction with tetrodotoxin; however, there is no doubt that depolarization of the nerve terminal increases the *frequency* of miniature e.p.p.'s, and this is the cause of the large e.p.p. that results from the arrival of the propagated impulse.

In general, then, it would seem that the size of the end-plate potential, and therefore the likelihood of transmission, is determined by the frequency with which miniature potentials occur (and this is a *pre*-junctional matter), together with the size of the quantal response, this being determined by the characteristics of the *post*-junctional membrane.

Fatigue

Pre- and Post-synaptic Events

When a nerve is stimulated repetitively, the force of the muscular contraction decreases and eventually there may be a complete block—*Wedensky inhibition*. The fatigue is not due to failure of the nerve to conduct impulses, nor yet to the ability of the muscle to contract, since direct stimulation of the muscle evokes a normal contraction. It is the end-plate that has become "fatigued", and the cause is the failure of the nervous impulse to liberate sufficient acetylcholine from the terminals. It must be appreciated, however, that in any situation where transmission has been altered there is the possibility that the cause is either *pre-synaptic*, involving liberation of transmitter, or *post-synaptic*, involving the sensitivity of the end-plate to transmitter, or else both factors may be involved. Thus the action of curare is post-synaptic or post-junctional. On the other hand, raising the concentration of Mg^{2+} causes block at the junction, but this is due to the failure of the nerve impulse to liberate adequate transmitter, an effect that is antagonized by Ca^{2+} which causes an increase in liberation per impulse. The effects of Mg^{2+} and Ca^{2+} are thus pre-synaptic. To separate pre- and post-synaptic effects we must measure the size of the e.p.p. in response to a single nerve impulse. A diminution in this could be due to either factor, but if the response to a known amount of transmitter, injected by the microelectrophoresis technique in the immediate neighbourhood of the junction, is unchanged, then we may assume that the reduced size of e.p.p. is due to reduced output of transmitter.

Output of Transmitter

The fatigue of repetitive stimulation is almost certainly due to reduced output of transmitter per nerve impulse. This is most simply demonstrated by measuring the output of transmitter in the perfused tissue, when hydrolysis is prevented by an anticholinesterase. When this, and other techniques, are employed, it is found that, shortly after beginning repetitive stimulation, the output per impulse begins to fall, until a steady level of output is reached which is maintained for long periods. Under these conditions the rate of synthesis of new transmitter apparently keeps pace exactly with the loss due to release.

Exponential Decline. If synthesis is prevented, by use of the drug hemicholinium, which inhibits acetylcholine synthesis by blocking the uptake of choline by the nerve terminal, so depleting the terminal of substrate, then repetitive stimulation leads to an exponential decline in output per impulse, as illustrated in Fig. 1.30, until finally there is no output, revealed, for example, by the absence of measurable e.p.p. At this point the stores of transmitter are completely depleted. This exponential decline in output, when synthesis is inhibited, means that the output depends on how much transmitter is present in the store, being probably a constant fraction of this.

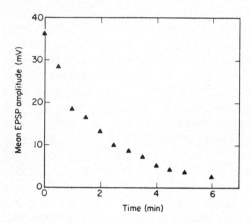

Fig. 1.30. The changes in amplitude of the excitatory post-synaptic potential (EPSP) in a cell in the superior cervical ganglion during continuous stimulation of the cervical sympathetic trunk when acetylcholine synthesis is blocked. The EPSP amplitude declined until no response was detectable $6\frac{1}{2}$ min after the beginning of the stimulation. (Bennett and McLachlan, *J. Physiol.* 1972, **221**, 651.)

Release from Stores

Thus, when repetitive stimulation takes place with uninhibited synthesis, the course of events is probably release of the constant fraction of the existing stores, which are high. This release provokes the synthesis of new transmitter, which, however, is not adequate in rate to maintain the stores at the original high level; and the output per impulse falls because the stores have fallen. Ultimately rates of synthesis and release balance. Since the output per impulse during steady stimulation is independent of rate of stimulation between 5 and 20 Hz, it is clear that the rate of synthesis is accurately adjusted to rate of release, otherwise we would expect the output per impulse to fall at the higher rates, with their consequent larger outputs of transmitter in unit time.

Synthesis and Release

Thus the situation may be presented by Fig. 1.31; acetylcholine (ACL) is synthesized in the cytoplasm of the terminal and stored in vesicles; released ACh is hydrolysed by acetylcholinesterase outside the terminal, and the choline liberated is taken up and used in resynthesis of ACh. The rate of synthesis is accelerated by the decrease in concentration of transmitter in the terminal, which is a consequence of its

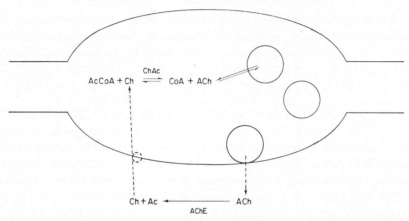

Fig. 1.31. Diagram of the varicosity of a preganglionic nerve terminal showing the principal features of the storage and synthesis of acetylcholine (ACh). Ac: acetyl group; CoA: coenzyme A; Ch: choline; ChAc: choline acetyl transferase; AChE: acetylcholin esterase. Acetylcholine is synthesized in cytoplasm and stored in vesicles. The population of vesicles represents the single store from which transmitter is released by nerve impulses. Released ACh is hydrolysed by acetylcholinesterase and the choline from this reaction is taken up into the terminals and used in the resynthesis of ACh. The rate of synthesis is accelerated by the decrease in concentration of transmitter in the terminal, which is a consequence of its release by nerve impulses. (Bennett and McLachlan, *J. Physiol.* 1972, **221,** 651.)

release by nerve impulses. This system provides a homeostatic mechanism that enables a constant level to be maintained over long periods of stimulation, at a value of about 40 per cent of the resting stores.

Significance of Fatigue

The block of neuromuscular transmission following excessive stimulation must be regarded as a protective mechanism that prevents the nervous system from overworking a muscle or, more generally, from overworking the animal as a whole.

Thus large amounts of work, as in marathon running for example, might well lead to the production of more lactic acid than could be dealt with, and the consequent acidosis could lead to collapse and death, so that the intervention of neuromuscular fatigue, which prevents the animal, however willing, from contracting a muscle, acts as a safety mechanism.

Mechanism of Release of Transmitter

Transmitter is normally released spontaneously and gives rise to the miniature end-plate potentials. Blocking of nervous activity completely, with, say, tetrodotoxin, blocks the output due to nervous stimulation but leaves the spontaneous output at the skeletal neuromuscular junction unchanged. Thus any explanation of the mechanism of transmitter output must explain both the spontaneous release and the action-potential induced release. So far as the latter is concerned, it is clearly the wave of depolarization that causes the additional release, and we must ask: What are the events between this depolarization and the release of transmitter? The strong analogy between facilitation of the neuromuscular junction and the effects of Ca^{2+} on the junction suggested that, as in the activation of the contractile machinery (Vol. 2, Ch. 2), the fundamental step is an increase of ionized Ca^{2+} in the cytoplasm of the nerve terminal, where it in some way favours the release of transmitter.

Effects of Calcium and Magnesium

It was early discovered that removal of Ca^{2+} from the medium bathing a nerve-muscle junction abolished transmission. This was shown to be a pre-synaptic event, being due to a failure to liberate acetylcholine at the junction. Raising the concentration of Mg^{2+} above normal had a similar effect, and there was a definite antagonism between the two ions, Ca^{2+} favouring release of transmitter and Mg^{2+} blocking this, so that a given size of end-plate potential in response to nerve stimulation could be obtained with various proportions of Ca^{2+} and Mg^{2+} in the bathing medium. Sr^{2+} and Ba^{2+} tended to behave like Ca^{2+}, whilst Na^+ was similar to Mg^{2+}, in the sense that, when the Ca^{2+}-concentration was low, reducing the Na^+ content favoured transmission, and increasing it diminished it. It seems that Na^+ and Mg^{2+} compete with Ca^{2+} for specific sites on the nerve terminal. The studies of Katz and Miledi leave little doubt that the wave of depolarization, when it reaches the nerve terminals. causes an influx of Ca^{2+}, and it is the increased concentration of this ion within the nerve terminal that is the link between depolarization and transmitter release.

Ca^{2+} and Exocytosis. If the release of transmitter consists in the fusion of the vesicle membrane with that of the nerve terminal accompanied by emptying, or partial emptying of its contents into the synaptic cleft, then we may assume that the extra Ca^{2+} favours this exocytotic membrane fusion process. It could favour this possibly by attaching to negatively charged groups on the vesicle surface, thereby reducing their surface charge and favouring close approximation of the membranes. Another suggestion is that an ATPase in the membrane is concerned in release of transmitter, and that Ca^{2+} inactivates this; and certainly the finding that ouabain, an inhibitor of ATPase, reduces the output of acetylcholine at the junction with intestinal muscle lends some support to this hypothesis.

Facilitation

Repeated stimulation of a nerve fibre leads, as we have seen, to reduced output of transmitter per impulse, which is the physical basis of fatigue. During the first few impulses in a high-frequency train, however, each impulse releases successively greater amounts of transmitter. The course of events, therefore, during repetitive stimulation is a growth in the amount of transmitter released per impulse, which passes through a maximum so that eventually a steady state is reached with a lower output per impulse than initially, as illustrated schematically in Fig. 1.32. The period of rising output is a manifestation of facilitation, in so far as the first, or "conditioning", stimulus

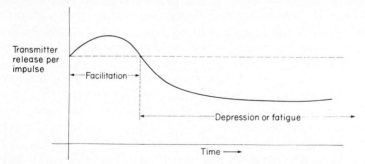

Fig. 1.32. A schematic curve showing the release of transmitter per impulse during repetitive stimulation of a nerve-muscle preparation. The first few impulses release more transmitter with each impulse, but after this facilitation the transmitter pool is depleted and fatigue occurs as the level of transmitter release falls.

increases the response of the second stimulus. Thus normally the first few impulses of a train attempt to release greater and greater fractions of transmitter from a "pool", but after the first few impulses this "pool" is depleted leading to a depression of transmitter release—fatigue. Treatment of the nerve-muscle junction with Mg^{2+}, which depresses release of transmitter, lengthens the period of facilitation, whilst the onset of depression or fatigue is correspondingly delayed.

According to Katz and Miledi, facilitation at the end-plate can be regarded as the manifestation of an increased probability that an impulse will release quanta of acetylcholine, so that the frequency of spontaneously occurring miniature end-plate potentials is increased. They emphasized the analogy with the effects of Ca^{2+} since application of this ion locally to the end-plate, with a micropipette, caused large end-plate potentials. Thus if, as seems likely, the release of transmitter involves a primary entrance of Ca^{2+} into the nerve terminal in response to the nerve action potential, then facilitation can be regarded as the effects of a "carry-over" of Ca^{2+} within the terminal. Thus facilitation represents a build-up of the concentration of Ca^{2+}, or some specific Ca^{2+}-complex, within the terminal, favouring exocytosis of synaptic vesicles, whilst fatigue is due to the depletion of the stores of transmitter within these vesicles.

Excitation–Secretion Coupling

It must be appreciated that release of transmitter by the emptying, or partial emptying, of a vesicle from the cell is only one example of release of segregated material. Thus we have seen that the exocrine secretions of the salivary and pancreatic glands involve emptying of enzyme-containing granules into an acinus (Vol. 1), and we shall see that endocrine secretion, e.g. that of adrenaline from chromaffin cells, involves emptying of granules into the extracellular space of the gland, whence they are carried away in the blood. All these processes are subject to nervous or hormonal control, and it seems that the *"excitation–secretion coupling"* process, like that involved in muscular contraction, represents the primary entry of Ca^{2+} into the effector cell in response to the stimulating agent. The analogy is indicated in Fig. 1.33; in (*a*) we have the depolarization of the nerve terminal at the end-plate causing entry of Ca^{2+} and release of transmitter; in (*b*) we have the arrival at an exocrine cell of a stimulus, which may be a neurotransmitter such as acetylcholine or a hormone such as secretin; here the chemical agent has depolarized the effector cell—exocrine gland

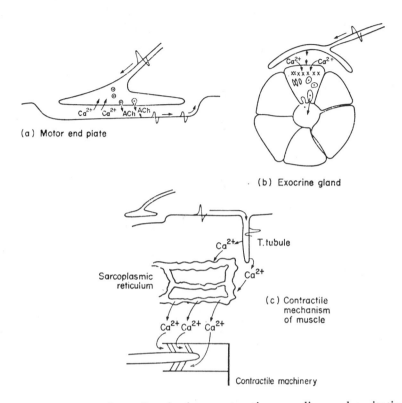

(a) Motor end plate

(b) Exocrine gland

(c) Contractile mechanism of muscle

Fig. 1.33. A comparison of excitation–contraction coupling and excitation–secretion coupling. (a) The motor end-plate. The nerve terminal is depolarized and Ca^{2+} ions enter, which in turn cause release of transmitter. (b) Exocrine secretion. The exocrine cells are depolarized by either transmitter released from nerve endings or by hormones, such as secretin; this causes the entry of Ca^{2+} which triggers off vesicle fusion and eventual release of the secretion. (c) Excitation–contraction coupling in the muscle. The arrival of the muscle action potential at the base of the tubule (T) system causes the release of Ca^{2+} ions from the sarcoplasmic reticulum leading to contraction of the myofilaments.

cell—and the depolarization has caused entry of Ca^{2+} which has triggered off the fusion of vesicles containing, this time, enzymes. In (c) the arrival of the stimulus at the muscle cell has likewise caused depolarization, and this has mobilized Ca^{2+} in the cytoplasm, causing contraction of the myofilaments. In this last case the depolarization has caused Ca^{2+}, *already in the effector cell*, to become effective by dissociating an un-ionized complex, rather than causing penetration from outside. However, in so far as the link between the excitatory process and the effector's response is through the appearance of ionized Ca^{2+} in the cytoplasm of the effector cell, the analogy remains. Moreover, it may well be that the stimulus to emptying a vesicle from a cell likewise involves mobilization of intracellular Ca^{2+}; recent work of Matthews on the pancreatic acinus, secreting amylase, certainly suggests this.

Twitch and Slow Fibres

Before passing to the study of the nerve–nerve synapse, we must mention the distinction between two types of vertebrate muscle, especially prominent in submammalian orders such as the frog. Thus the responses of the muscle fibre so far described are those of the *fast* or *twitch* type; they give rise to an all-or-none propagated spike and muscular contraction in response to a single impulse in the nerve fibre; their nerve fibres end in typical end-plates, with only one or two on a single fibre. The slow fibre of the frog has a multiple innervation, in the sense that the endings are distributed over the whole surface—*terminaisons en grappe* (Fig. 1.34)—and it is through this distributed innervation that the whole of the fibre contracts synchronously, by contrast with the twitch-fibre that relies on the spread of the action potential.

Small-junction Potential

The slow fibres give rise to slow contractions, which increase in strength as the frequency of nerve stimulation increases. The response to the nerve action potential is the development of what has been called *the small-junction potential*, which may be recorded from an intracellular electrode; these summate with repetitive stimulation until a plateau of depolarization, of some 30–35 mV, is reached but no propagated spike arises from this. When a single fibre was studied by Burke and Ginsborg, they found that, with an internal microelectrode, they could depolarize the fibre completely without evoking a propagated spike. The whole fibre was behaving like an end-plate and, like this, it seemed that the response to an electrical or nerve stimulus was a general increase in ionic permeability.

Function. The significance of this difference in muscle types is probably to be found in their differing functions—the slow being concerned with sustained postural contractions and the twitch with rapid phasic movements. In mammals no such differentiation with respect

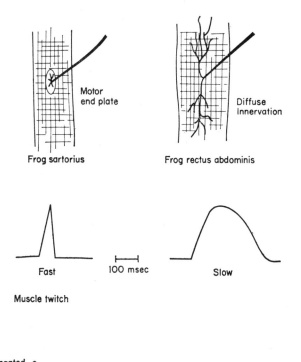

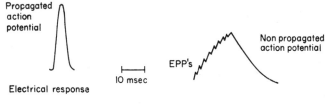

Fig. 1.34. The fast and slow fibres of the frog. On the left is shown the fast or twitch sartorius muscle with its discrete muscle end-plate. Stimulation of the motor nerve leads to propagated action potentials which spread out rapidly across the muscle fibres leading to a rapid twitch. On the right is the slow rectus abdominis muscle with a diffuse innervation. The contractile response is slow and the muscle membrane does not support a propagated action potential.

to this type of nerve ending has been found, except in the eye muscles. In general, as we have seen, fibres do belong to either a twitch-type, with rapid contraction and relaxation, or a slow type in which the response to a stimulus is slower and more sustained. The slow muscles are relatively red because of their high concentration of myoglobin and, like the slow frog fibres, they are concerned with sustained contractions.

Effects of Denervation

Loss of Direct Excitability

Cutting off the nerve supply to a muscle has two effects, a loss of indirect excitability and a state of hyperexcitability. The loss of indirect excitability takes some days to develop, but finally the muscle remains excitable to direct stimulation, and the end-plate may be excited by applied acetylcholine, but transmission from the nerve is blocked. This is due to exhaustion of the stores of transmitter, which cannot be renewed through loss of the appropriate enzyme, *choline acetyltransferase*, which presumably has to be synthesized by the perikaryon. As we should expect, spontaneous e.p.p.'s cease in parallel with the loss of indirect excitability. In the electron microscope degenerative changes in the junction occurred at the time of transmission block; these consisted in the appearance of masses of what appeared to be agglutinated synaptic vesicles, which eventually became surrounded by Schwann cytoplasm and then appeared to make a synaptic type of contact with the muscle fibre. Later, the axon disappeared completely leaving the Schwann cell making a synaptic contact that was difficult to distinguish from the normal axon–muscle contact except that the arrangement of vesicles in the Schwann cell was so much more irregular than in the axon. Associated with this development of a synaptic type of contact the end-plate showed miniature e.p.p.'s with a lower frequency than normal. It was not responsive to nerve stimulation, however.

Hypersensitivity

After these effects have manifest themselves the muscle becomes hypersensitive to acetylcholine, the so-called "denervation hypersensitivity" that is shared by many other tissues. The striking feature of this hypersensitivity is that the whole length of the muscle fibre becomes sensitive to acetylcholine, as opposed to the normal situation where sensitivity is confined to the end-plate region; moreover, the end-plate region itself does not become hypersensitive, so that the hypersensitivity of the whole fibre is due to this spatial extension of sensitivity. Electrically, moreover, the whole fibre tends to behave like an end-plate, although it is possible to record propagated action potentials from it. It would seem, then, that the nerve fibre normally prevents the development of "extrajunctional receptors" as Miledi calls them, and this represents one example of the way in which a nerve fibre can influence the normal physiology of a muscle fibre.

Regeneration of Axon

When a motor nerve fibre to a muscle is cut, the peripheral axon regenerates, and it is interesting to follow the changes in the muscle fibre as it resumes its normal innervation. The first stage is the increase in amplitude and frequency of the miniature e.p.p.'s, until they return to the values they had before nerve-section; at this point transmission becomes possible, but not before. Associated with this resumption of transmission, there is a narrowing of the acetylcholine-sensitive zones on the muscle fibre.

Movement of Material within the Axon

The main synthetic machinery of the neurone, i.e. the nucleus, endoplasmic reticulum and Golgi apparatus, is concentrated within the cell-body or perikaryon. The most peripheral regions of a neurone, namely the axonal endings, may lie several feet away from the cell body, so that the replacements of protein, lipids, etc. and the supply of mitochondria may well have to rely on a special transport mechanism rather than the slow process of diffusion and Brownian movement. Furthermore, where the axon is concerned, transmission of the message from one neurone to another, or to the effector cell such as a muscle fibre, taking place at the axon terminals, involves the liberation of a chemical transmitter. This is released from the axon into the junctional space outside and, so far as acetylcholine is concerned, it is rapidly broken down by hydrolysis after performing its function.

Replacement of Vesicles

There is no doubt that most of the lost transmitter is replaced by local synthesis in the nerve terminals, but these transmitters are contained within vesicles, which are complex structures containing specific proteins, and the release of transmitter from these, involving as it does an exocytosis mechanism, undoubtedly involves considerable wear and tear. New vesicles must be synthesized in the cell body of the neurone and must be carried down to the axon terminals. The vesicles containing the transmitter noradrenaline also contain the enzyme dopamine β-hydroxylase that catalyses the conversion of dopamine to noradrenaline, and so they must be regarded as synthetic as well as storage sites.

Effect of Axon Ligatures

The migration of the storage granules can be studied by ligating a nerve and measuring the accumulation of transmitter immediately above the ligature, making use, for example, of the green fluorescence of noradrenaline for studying an adrenergic nerve. Figure 1.35 illustrates schematically the effects of two ligatures; accumulation takes place at both, suggesting that the process governing the movement is generated within the axon rather than farther back at the cell body. However, the accumulation at the proximal ligature, i.e. that close

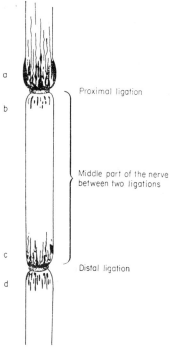

Fig. 1.35. Schematic illustration of the fluorescence-histochemical appearance of a double-ligated sciatic nerve 12 hours after the ligation. The accumulation at (a) is considerably larger than at (c) while the distal, retrograde accumulations are larger at (d) than (b). (Dahlström, *Symp. Soc. Int. Cell Biol.* 1969, **8**, 153.)

to the cell body, continues indefinitely whilst that at the lower one ceases after a few hours. Calculations derived from this sort of experiment indicate a rate of movement of 3–10 mm/hr. If this is a normally occurring event, then it is easy to show that the life-span of the granule is of the order of 4–5 weeks in the rat, indicating that there is a continuous breakdown and replacement from the perikaryon. Since the release of transmitter from these noradrenaline-containing granules apparently does not involve breakdown of the whole granule but rather a loss of its core, this turnover of the granules is probably independent of neural activity. Measurements of the turnover of the noradrenaline in the terminals indicate that the content may be renewed several times during the life-span of a granule.*

Slow Movement

The rate of movement of transmitter granules seems to be of a different order of magnitude from the much slower migration of the axonal substance described by Weiss; according to this author, the axon may be considered to be growing continuously but retaining a static length by casting off material at its termination. This type of axonal flow occurs at about a few millimetres a day and thus is very much slower than that discussed above. The process is best studied by placing a partial constriction on a nerve and examining the changes in the axon above and below, which consist in a bulging and thinning respectively; and when the constriction is removed there is a tidal flow from the dilated region, rather like the flow of lava, so that the thinned distal region fills out. In the dilated region the mitochondria accumulate, so that, whereas in a 500 Å section only some three profiles of mitochondria would normally be seen, there are now a hundred or more. This suggests that the renewal process includes the supply of mitochondria, presumably formed by reproduction in the perikaryon. In fact, Weiss calculates that the perikaryon produces some 1000 mitochondria per day in a typical motor neurone. These organelles are self-replicating, in the sense that they contain DNA and can synthesize some of their proteins; nevertheless they require the cooperation of the cell's ribosomes for synthesis of specific proteins such as cytochrome-c, so that it is certain that any "new" mitochondrion appearing in the axon has come from the cell body.

Labelled Protein Movement

With the use of isotopically-labelled amino acids, the proteins in the perikaryon may be labelled, and their movement along the axon may be measured. For example Ochs has injected the dorsal root ganglion or the ventral horn of many mammals with ^{3}H-leucine and, after 24 hours, he has dissected out the nerve and its central connections.

---

* The idea that all transmitter, e.g. noradrenaline, is synthesized in the perikaryon and carried in vesicles to the terminals cannot be sustained, since experiments in which the turnover of noradrenaline in the terminals is measured indicate that the existing stores are replaced with a half-life of a few hours, whereas the contribution from the cell body, as measured by the rate at which vesicles accumulate at a ligature, would be only some 3 per cent of the stores in a day.

Analysis of segments shows in all cases a progressive wave of radioactivity passing along the neurone away from the cell body (Fig. 1.36).
The rate of movement was on average some 410 mm/day, varying
between 389 and 423, and taking place just as rapidly in sensory as in
motor nerves, in large and small, myelinated or non-myelinated. This
remarkable uniformity in behaviour suggests a common mechanism,
and similar to that causing the movement of transmitter granules.

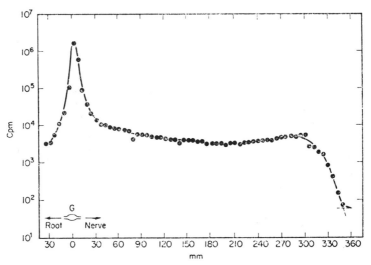

Fig. 1.36. The movement of protein labelled with ³H-leucine along the
goat's sciatic nerve. The ganglion was injected with ³H-leucine and its
nerve was removed 24 hours later and divided into segments which were
analysed for radioactivity. Radioactivity (Cpm) has been plotted against
distance from the ganglion; and from the position of the abrupt fall in
activity an axoplasmic rate of transport of 382 mm/day was computed.
(Ochs, *J. Physiol.* 1972, **227**, 639.)

Block by Colchicine. Thus this "fast" movement may be blocked
by colchicine which has also been shown to block the movement of
transmitter granules; the slow movement, on the other hand, is unaffected by colchicine. The finding that colchicine, which disorganizes
the microtubular system (Vol. 1), when injected under the perineurium
blocks the movement of noradrenaline-containing granules suggests
that these structures are implicated in the movement, possibly, as
suggested by Schmitt, by making and breaking links with the surface
of the granule to give a cog-wheel-like progression. As we have indicated
earlier, the cytoplasm of the neurone, be it the perikaryon or axon or

dendrites, contains both microfilaments and microtubules, so that either or both structures may be implicated in the fast movement. Since slow movement is unaffected by colchicine, we may suspect the involvement of the microfilaments. These might well be responsible for the minute peristaltic-wave-like motions passing over the surface of the neurone described by Weiss; they had a periodicity of some 16 minutes. Similar results were found by Lubinska and Nimierko with cholinesterase, the remarkable feature being the speed with which movement occurred (being some 260 and 134 mm/24 hr distally and proximally and thus corresponding to the "fast rate"); however, only a small proportion of the total enzyme content was migratory.

Two-way Flow

The accumulation of mitochondria and other organelles has been interpreted on the basis of a continuous supply from the perikaryon. The possibility that movement might also occur from the distal to the proximal portions of the axon has been suggested frequently. Thus, according to Zelena, when an axon is cut through, mitochondria accumulate to form pellets at both stumps, suggesting a two-way motion; again, if an axon was cut across in two places, separating it from the perikaryon on one side and its terminals on the other, then mitochondria tended to disappear from the central region, passing to the two cut ends.

Degeneration and Regeneration

Section of a peripheral nerve leads to degeneration of the axons peripheral to the cut, the so-called Wallerian degeneration. This degeneration indicates the reliance of the axon on the perikaryon for its normal maintenance, a dependence that we have already seen when discussing the formation of transmitter vesicles on the endoplasmic reticulum (Nissl substance) of the perikaryon and the subsequent migration of the vesicles to the axon terminals. The signs of Wallerian degeneration appear within a day or two of section, so that it has been concluded that the peripheral regions rely on the fast movement of matter, as typically manifest in the movement of vesicles, rather than the slower axonal flow described by Weiss.

Chromatolysis. The perikaryon and dendrites remain intact after axotomy, but usually there are pronounced changes in the perikaryon, described as *chromatolysis*, suggesting that some signal has reached the perikaryon provoking the metabolic reactions required for the synthesis of new material involved in regeneration of the cut axon from the central stump. The characteristic reaction of the cell body is a swelling whilst the nucleus moves away from the axon hillock, and the large Nissl bodies (which are stacked membranes of the endoplasmic reticulum with their attached ribosomes) become dispersed. This chromatolysis is a sign of enhanced RNA synthesis since, if this is blocked with actinomycin D at the time of axotomy, the process of chromatolysis is also blocked.

Signal for Chromatolysis. The nature of the signal provoking chromatolysis is a matter of conjecture. It could be that the neurone produced a substance that depressed RNA production, and that some of this depressor was lost by diffusion away from the cut axon. It seems likely, however, that some signal moves from the cut end to the peri-karyon, since the closer the section to the perikaryon the sooner is the reaction.* The rate of movement of the signal has been computed at 4–5 mm/day.

Regeneration. Regeneration of the axon takes place by a sprouting from the proximal stump, whilst the Schwann cells in the cut region tend to round up and multiply finally reassuming fixed positions bridging over the sectioned region. Degeneration of the peripheral nerve is confined to the axons, so that the sprouting new axons utilize the original neurilemmal tube which acts as a guide. So far as skeletal muscle is concerned, the regenerated nerve terminals enter the original end-plates provided access has not been prevented by degenerative changes in the muscle; in this latter event, new end-plates are established.

Trophic Action of Nerve

Denervation of a tissue usually leads to significant changes in its metabolism, and it is customary to describe the maintenance of the normal condition as being the result of the *trophic action* of the nerve. The studies on the migration of material along the axon, especially the slow movement of axoplasm, might provide the physiological basis for this trophic action, but it could be argued that the effects of denervation were due to the absence of nerve stimuli.

Denervation Atrophy. Thus a muscle fibre tends to degenerate— *denervation atrophy*—if it is maintained quiescent for long periods, and this may be simply a disuse phenomenon. Apart from this, the failure of nerve stimuli entails a failure of transmitter release, e.g. acetylcholine at the neuromuscular junction. Is the trophic substance acetylcholine? In general it is fairly certain that denervation atrophy of muscle

---

* It must be appreciated that the results of axotomy vary; some neurones show no chromatolysis with regeneration; others show chromatolysis with or without regeneration and others die without regeneration.

involves something more than disuse, since muscle may be "inactivated" by separation from its central connections in the cord but leaving its motor innervation intact, and it is found that, although disuse atrophic changes take place, they are by no means identical with those taking place following denervation.

Cross Innervation. An example of trophic action that lends itself to quantitative study is the effect of experimentally altering the innervation of a muscle by surgical means. Thus a slow muscle, such as the soleus, can be transformed into a fast one by cutting its motor nerve and causing it to be re-innervated by the nerve from a fast muscle; associated with the change in mechanical response there were characteristic biochemical changes, e.g. the high α-glycerophosphate dehydrogenase activity appropriate to the predominantly anaerobic utilization of glycogen of fast muscle. Although it would be wrong to say that the cross-innervated fibre acquires completely the characteristics of the muscle from which it derives its new nerve, the changes are sufficiently striking to warrant the conclusion that the nerve fibre influences the biochemistry of the muscle fibre that it supplies.

Multiple Neurotization. Another example of trophic action is the circumstance that multiple neurotization of a single skeletal muscle fibre is rare, so that when a nerve regenerates, the growth of a nerve terminal into an end-plate apparently inhibits the growth of further terminals to form multiple end-plates. Experimentally the presence of some inhibitory process is revealed by the fact that it is only possible, surgically, to cause a nerve fibre to innervate a muscle fibre provided the muscle fibre has no innervation, and the phenomenon is reminiscent of the block to polyspermy where the penetration of an ovum by one sperm prevents the access of others. The release of acetylcholine by the nerve undoubtedly plays a role in preventing multiple neurotization, since, if the nerve is previously treated with botulinum toxin, which prevents release of acetylcholine, it is possible to cause multiple neurotization by implanting a new nerve in an end-plate-free region, new end-plates developing to give multiple innervation of individual fibres.

Acetylcholine Release. Finally we may mention the nervous control over acetylcholine sensitivity of the muscle fibre; we have seen that denervation of a muscle fibre causes a "denervation hypersensitivity" consisting of a spread of sensitivity from the end-plate region so that the whole fibre eventually becomes as sensitive to locally applied acetylcholine as the end-plate. According to Thesleff's studies, involving the use of botulinum toxin, it is primarily a lack of acetylcholine release that gives rise to the spread of sensitivity (i.e., acetylcholine, released at the junction, prevents the rest of the fibre from becoming sensitive to it) but it is unwise to be dogmatic on this point and it may well be that several factors, including acetylcholine release, combine together to restrain spread of sensitivity.

Transneuronal Degeneration. Evidence of trophic action within the central nervous system is also found; thus when an axon is cut, the neurone with which it makes synaptic connections may show signs of degeneration—*transneuronal degeneration*—indicating that it depended on connections with other neurones for its normal condition.

Nerve Growth Factor

Of particular interest with respect to regeneration is the nerve growth factor (NGF) isolated originally from certain mouse tumours, but later found in much higher concentration in the submaxillary gland of the mouse and in snake venoms. This factor (or factors, since they differ according to their source) is a protein of molecular weight 5000 to 40,000. When injected into, say, the yolk-sac of embryonic chicks it causes massive increases in the size of the sympathetic ganglia, due to an increase in the size and number of the sympathetic neurones. Injection into newborn mice has the same effects, leading to hyper-innervation of such structures as the intestine, blood vessels and iris. The factor seems essential for the continued maintenance and growth of sympathetic neurones since injections of an antiserum to the factor into young mice virtually destroy the sympathetic system.

Site of Synthesis. Where the factor is actually synthesized and whether it is required for normal maintenance of sympathetic neurones in adult animals are points that have not yet been clarified; certainly the submaxillary glands synthesize the factor, but this may be a capacity common to many tissues of the body although on a smaller scale. Removal of the glands from newborn animals has no deleterious effects so that it would be wrong to ascribe to them an endocrine function in addition to their exocrine one. As Levi-Montalcini emphasizes, a similar situation exists with regard to erythropoiesis-stimulating factor (p. 308); the function of the factor is unquestionable, but its source and mode of secretion into the blood-stream are by no means clear.

Invertebrate Muscle Fibre

The nerve–muscle junction that we have so far described in detail behaves in an essentially all-or-none manner, in the sense that, if transmission occurs, the muscle fibre contracts in an all-or-none fashion because transmission has involved the development of an all-

or-none action potential on the muscle fibre. In a later chapter we shall discuss the manner in which this action potential fires off the contractile process. There are many junctions, especially in invertebrates, where a single action potential, reaching the junction, does not evoke an all-or-none muscular action potential and all-or-none muscular response.

Junction Potential

Thus, in order to obtain a propagated spike over the crab muscle fibre it is usually necessary to stimulate the nerve repetitively, and this is accompanied by the development of "*excitatory junctional potentials*" whose magnitudes summate to a critical value when the spike takes off. The crustacean muscle is thus similar to the curarized vertebrate fibre. The endings of the nerve fibres on the muscle fibre are characteristically different, being distributed over the whole surface instead of being confined to one or two end-plates as in the vertebrate system. In general, the response of a given fibre is the summated response of junctional potentials distributed over the surface; these effects spread, owing to the large space-constant of the invertebrate fibre, and so give the impression of a uniform depolarization. Each junctional potential is graded, in the sense that it increases in size with increasing frequency of nerve stimulation, until finally a spike is fired off.

Ca^{2+} and Ba^{2+}

It is interesting that replacement of some of the external Na^+ by Ca^{2+} or Ba^{2+} will convert a graded non-propagated response to an all-or-none propagated one, probably because these ions can carry the inward current normally carried by Na^+ in the vertebrate system.

Miniature Potentials

As with the vertebrate system, the crustacean fibre exhibits miniature spontaneous junctional potentials; facilitation, manifest as the increased muscular response with repetitive stimulation of the nerve, is due to the liberation of more quanta of transmitter in response to the nerve impulse, i.e. it is a presynaptic phenomenon.

Inhibition

We shall see that control over vertebrate muscular activity may be exerted through both excitatory and inhibitory influences. However, the inhibition cannot be exerted directly on the muscle fibre, the only response to nerve stimulation being excitatory, so that inhibition in the vertebrate must be exerted on the motor neurone—its discharge must be reduced or abolished. The situation in the invertebrate muscle is different, a given muscle fibre being innervated by one type of fibre that excites and by another fibre that will cause relaxation if stimulated at the same time as the excitatory fibre, i.e. it inhibits the excitatory effect of the latter fibre. When the excitatory fibre is stimulated, we have seen that an excitatory junctional potential may be recorded from a localized region of the muscle fibre; when the inhibitory fibre is stimulated at the same time this excitatory junctional potential subsides more rapidly. Since, therefore, contraction depends on the summation of many junctional potentials, we can understand the inhibitory effect of this action.

Inhibitory Junctional Potential. However, when the membrane potential is recorded under the influence of the inhibitory nerve alone, the inhibitory junctional potentials are very small or non-existent, and may be depolarizing or hyperpolarizing, according to circumstances. We may ask: How would it theoretically be possible to inhibit the effects of an excitatory impulse? At the junction, the excitatory effect is due probably to an increase in Na^+-permeability, or perhaps in both Na^+- and Cl^--permeabilities. The increase in Na^+-permeability must depolarize the membrane, since it permits K^+–Na^+ exchanges across the membrane, exchanges that remove the restraint on K^+-movements which is the basis of the potential. If the inhibitory impulse increases the permeability to K^+ it will tend to stabilize the membrane potential, and oppose the depolarizing effect of the excitatory impulse. As to its own effect on the membrane potential, this will depend on the value of the potential and how it is determined. Thus, if it is equal to the theoretical K^+-potential, as given by the Nernst equation, this means, most probably, that the permeability to K^+ is very high in relation to that of other ions, and it is this ion that is determining the membrane potential. Increased permeability should have little or no effect on the membrane potential, but it could still prevent the depolarizing effect of an excitatory impulse. If the membrane potential is low, because of a significant permeability to Na^+ in the resting condition, then an increase in K^+-permeability will tend to raise the membrane potential, i.e. it will be hyperpolarizing. If the resting potential is initially greater than the K^+-potential, due, say, to the fact that Cl^- is determining the potential and this has a distribution across the membrane such as to give a higher potential (i.e. $[Cl^-]_{Out}/[Cl^-]_{In}$ is greater than $[K^+]_{In}/[K^+]_{Out,}$) then increasing K^+-permeability will drive the membrane potential towards the lower K^+-potential, and the inhibitory nerve will actually depolarize. Thus an inhibitory discharge can hyperpolarize, depolarize, or have no effect.

Equilibrium Potential. This effect of an inhibitory discharge was elegantly displayed by Dudel and Kuffler, who varied the degree of polarization across the invertebrate junction by passing current through an internal electrode; at different artificial values of the membrane potential, achieved in this way, they measured the effects of an inhibitory stimulus. When the membrane potential was 80 mV, i.e. when they had hyperpolarized it, the inhibitory junctional potentials were depolarizing; at 72 mV the junctional potentials were negligibly small, and they became hyperpolarizing when the membrane potential had been set at lower values (Fig. 1.37). The potential at which reversal

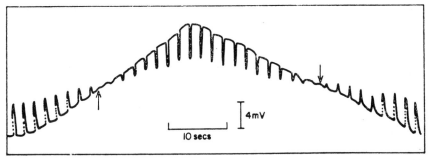

Fig. 1.37. Inhibitory potentials at an invertebrate junction obtained with varying resting potentials, beginning with 80 mV and falling to 61 mV by passing a current through a second intracellular microelectrode. Arrows indicate the reversal point at 72 mV. (Dudel and Kuffler, *J. Physiol.* 1961, **155**, 543.)

occurred was called the *inhibitory equilibrium potential,* and it is the potential to which the membrane potential is driven as a result of the inhibitory discharge.

TRANSMISSION IN THE NERVOUS SYSTEM

The Nerve–Nerve Synapse

The endings of axons on nerve cells are so varied in type that it is no more possible to speak of a typical synapse than to speak of a typical neurone. The axon generally ramifies at its termination, and a common way of making contact with the dendrites or soma of the post-synaptic neurone is in the form of *terminal boutons,* small swellings of the terminal fibres that are apposed to the surface. Thus the motor neurone of the anterior horn of the spinal cord, studied so extensively by Eccles, has large numbers of these boutons occupying perhaps 80 per cent of its

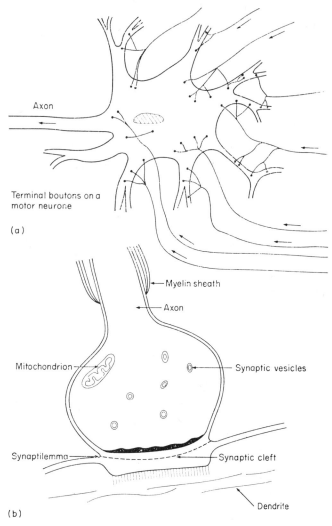

Fig. 1.38. The nerve synapse. (a) A few of the terminal boutons on the cell body of a motor neurone. These boutons occupy 80% of the cell surface. (b) A simplified diagram, from an electron micrograph, of a single synaptic bouton.

total surface (Fig. 1.38); these are derived from many individual axons, so that the motor neurone may be subjected to influences from many other neurones; in other cases, a single axonic termination may occupy a large proportion of the neurone's surface, in which case we may expect the neurone from which this axon is derived to have a more or less exclusive effect on the post-synaptic neurone.

Synaptilemma

In the electron microscope the junction between axon and post-synaptic neurone can be seen to represent a close apposition of the plasma membranes, with a 200 Å separation. If the pre-synaptic axon is myelinated, it loses its sheath a short distance from the surface of contact, whilst the Schwann cell surrounds the terminal axon right down to the depression on the post-synaptic cell, but it does not extend to the very end of the fibre, so that the *synaptilemma*, as the region of junction is called, consists in the apposition of plasma membranes.

Synaptic Vesicles

The pre-synaptic terminals are easy to distinguish from post-synaptic parts of the neurone by the presence of numerous *synaptic vesicles* in the former, together with the high concentration of mitochondria.

The vesicles, which, like those in the neuromuscular junction, contain the transmitter, are of different size and appearance according to the nature of the transmitter. Thus, cholinergic synapses, liberating acetylcholine, contain vesicles of 300–500 Å in diameter, of uniform density in the electron microscope, whilst those liberating catechol-amines, such as noradrenaline, are predominantly in the region of 300–600 Å in diameter and contain a dense core of 150–250 Å; larger vesicles, of 600–1500 Å in diameter, also with a granular core, probably also contain catecholamines and may represent different states of the same basic vesicle.

Synaptosomes. Experimentally the vesicles within the nerve terminals of the brain may be separated by homogenizing the brain and, by differential centrifugation, a suspension of *synaptosomes* is obtained; these are membrane-bound bodies—probably broken-off nerve terminals—containing the vesicles. By placing them in a hypo-osmolal medium the synaptosomes could be caused to swell and burst, leaving the synaptic vesicles free. Analysis showed that they contained transmitter—acetylcholine—and also the synthesizing enzyme, choline acetyl transferase.

Organization of the Nervous System

Before analysing further the electrical events in the neurones during transmission, we must study the elementary organization of the vertebrate nervous system.

Sensory Neurone

The neurone directly involved in the sensory process is called a sensory neurone; let us follow its long receiving process, which we may call a dendrite, from the point where this process terminates in the skin or a muscle, to the point where it disappears from view in the spinal cord, and thence onwards. As illustrated in Fig. 1.39, the process is derived from a fine nerve which has been derived by dichotomy

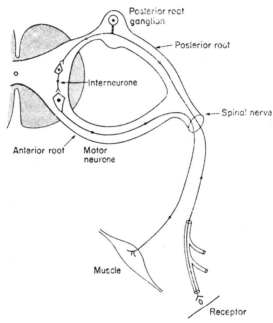

Fig. 1.39. The cell body of a sensory neurone lies in the dorsal root ganglion with a long receiving process extending to the peripheral sensory receptor and a transmitting process to the spinal cord.

from larger nerves. These larger nerves finally approach the spinal cord as a thick white bundle, which splits into two main *roots,* and it is into the posterior root that the sensory process finally penetrates. Just outside the cord, near the point of bifurcation into posterior and anterior roots, the fibre enters a swelling, the *posterior root ganglion.* It is here that the cell body or soma of this sensory neurone is located, together with the cell bodies of the many hundreds of sensory neurones subserving similar functions.

The sensory neurones of the posterior root ganglion are described as unipolar, because they have no axon-dendritic polarity; instead, a single process, which may be described morphologically as an axon, bifurcates to give two processes, the one carrying the sensory message towards the perikaryon, and often called on that account the dendrite, and the other carrying the message away into the spinal cord.

Connection in the Cord. As Fig. 1.39 illustrates, this sensory neurone terminates within the spinal cord, in the sense that it passes its message on to another neurone, which has its cell body in the part called the *posterior gray column*. The *interneurone*, receiving the message, passes it on to another neurone in the anterior region of the cord on the same side or on both, and a process from this motor neurone emerges in the *anterior* or *motor root* of the spinal nerve, where its axon merges with the bundle of entering axons of the sensory neurones.

Basic Organization

Thus Fig. 1.39 illustrates the basic principle on which the central nervous system is organized: information is brought into it through the sensory neurones with their cell bodies grouped into ganglia outside the cord; the information is "processed" within the central nervous system, and the messages to the effectors, be they muscle fibres or glandular cells, are transmitted through the motor cells located in the central gray matter. The essentially sensory basis of the posterior root is easy to demonstrate by section of this, when messages fail to enter the cord however hard the spinal nerve is stimulated.

Figure 1.39 illustrates a section through one arbitrarily chosen level of the spinal cord; moreover, it illustrates only one pathway (and this a very simple one) by which a stimulus, applied to the surface of the body, can influence the motor neurones of the ventral horn. This involves a single interneurone, which may pass its message on to a motor neurone on the same side of the cord or it may cross to the opposite side before making its synapse, thereby giving rise to a "crossed response".

Ramification of Sensory Axon

In fact, of course, the possibilities of transmission from the sensory neurone to other neurones at the same or different levels of the cord are far greater; thus there are some thirty-one pairs of nerves, corresponding to the appropriate segments of the cord. A sensory axon, entering the cord at its given level, does not by any means confine itself to this level, as suggested by the section in Fig. 1.39; instead, the axon passes up and down, communicating with interneurones at each level (Fig. 1.40). The ordered arrangement of these ascending

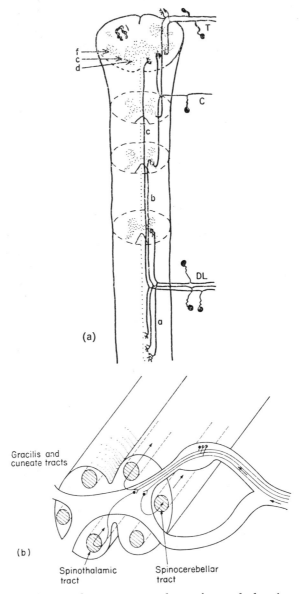

Fig. 1.40. (a) Scheme of a sensory pathway in cord showing fibres both ascending and descending. DL: lower lumbar root; C: cervical root; T: trigeminal root; d: nucleus of Goll's column; c: nucleus of Burdach's column; f: sensory root of trigeminal (Cahal, "Histologie du Système nerveux de l'Homme et des Vertébrés"). (b) A diagram of the principal ascending tracts.

and descending fibres gives rise to specific *tracts* of *white matter*, white because many of the axons are myelinated (p. 5).

Descending Tracts

In a similar way, descending axons from neurones at high levels of the cord, or from the brain, communicating with neurones situated at lower levels, are gathered into *descending tracts*.

Propriospinal Neurones

In general, the cord contains, in addition to the cell bodies of the motor neurones sending messages out of the cord (i.e. the typical motor neurones), groups of cell bodies of neurones that transmit only within the central nervous system, either to other parts of the cord, at the same or different levels, or from the cord to the brain. The tracts formed by such special neurones are called *propriospinal* (belonging to the spinal cord).

Reflex Behaviour

Spinal Motor Neurones

It is possible to study the activities of neurones in the spinal cord, or other regions of the central nervous system, by inserting electrodes into localized regions, and measuring the responses to afferent stimuli, which may be evoked naturally, for example by stretching the tendon of a muscle or pinching the skin, or less naturally by applying an electric shock to the afferent nerve or the posterior root. The recording of the response can be made with an intracellular electrode; although when dealing with groups of small interneurones, a "focal" external electrode can often provide useful, but not such accurate, information. Before such refined techniques of recording were developed, the characteristics of the motor neurones were deduced from the responses of the muscles of the limbs to sensory stimuli, as in Sherrington's studies of the spinal reflexes, or alternatively their activities could be measured by the strength of the discharges in the anterior root.

The Reflex Arc

The basic functional unit in animal behaviour is the reflex, which may be defined as the motor response to a specific form of stimulus; and the *reflex arc* is defined as the series of neurones required for the elicitation of the reflex.

Thus we may stimulate the skin of the foot by pinching it; this noxious stimulus causes a withdrawal of the foot—the *flexor reflex*.

Associated with this there is an extension of the opposite foot, which ensures that the body will be adequately supported while the stimulated foot is lifted—this is the *crossed extensor reflex*.

Spinal Transection. Removal of all influences from the brain can be achieved by cutting the spinal cord above the point of emergence of the roots concerned with the limbs in question. At first, the animal becomes completely unresponsive to cutaneous stimuli—it is in a condition of *spinal shock*, so that even powerful electrical stimuli applied to the sensory roots, stimuli that would, in the intact animal, have evoked powerful pain responses, have no influence at all. After a time, responsiveness returns and now the same type of reflex may be elicited in this "spinal animal". The condition of shock indicates that the neurones of the cord are held in some sort of "readiness" by influences from the brain; technically, we should say that they were being *facilitated* by descending impulses from the brain, so that cutting of these messages leaves them in a strongly refractory condition.

Sherrington's Technique. Sherrington studied reflexes of this type, usually by attaching the tendons of leg-muscles, involved in either extension or flexion of the leg, to a device for measuring the force exerted by the muscle in response to a stimulus which was applied either to the skin or to the sensory nerve.

Fractionation. With this technique he deduced many important features of the behaviour of the motor neurones concerned in muscular contraction. Thus, when a given sensory nerve was stimulated with a maximal shock, so that all fibres were stimulated, the reflex contraction of a given muscle was only a fraction of the total force it could develop when the motor root, or its motor nerve, was stimulated directly. It appeared that a given muscle was supplied with a large "pool" of motor neurones in the cord, so that it had a wide range of possible activity—when more neurones were brought into play, more fibres were caused to contract and the more powerful was the response. However, a given sensory neurone does not have access to all the motor neurones but only to a fraction, and the phenomenon is described as *fractionation* of the available motor neurone pool. This fractionation ensures that the force of contraction of a given muscle in a reflex will be determined by afferent impulses from several sensory nerves, thus promoting a well coordinated response; opposed to this is the condition where a single sensory nerve could monopolize the whole motor neurone pool and leave the muscle reflexly insensitive to messages arriving over closely related sensory nerves.

Occlusion. The phenomenon of *occlusion* is a direct consequence of fractionation. Thus if two sensory nerves can exert their effects through common motor neurones, then one nerve, by activating some of the neurones "belonging" to the pool of the other, occludes the other, in the sense that, while it is being stimulated, it prevents the second nerve from increasing the strength of the muscular response by as much as the force it would develop by itself.

Irradiation. Another phenomenon is that of *irradiation*, manifest as a contraction of the extensor muscles of the opposite leg when the sensory stimulus is increased in strength. This irradiation is presumably based on the widely distributed collaterals of the afferent fibres illustrated in Fig. 1.40, and also of the interneurones.

Reciprocal Innervation

It has already been mentioned that, in vertebrates, the response of a muscle to stimulation of its motor nerve is only excitatory, so that inhibition of muscular activity must be carried out by inhibition of the motor neurones in the cord. Sherrington showed that a scratch-reflex, brought about by stimulating touch—or hair—receptors behind the ears of a dog, could be inhibited by application of a noxious stimulus to the pad, i.e. the withdrawal reflex replaced the scratch reflex, which was inhibited. The importance of inhibition in the execution of ordinary movements was emphasized by the phenomenon of *reciprocal innervation*, namely the simultaneous inhibition of the extensor muscles at a joint when the flexors were activated, or *vice versa*. The process is illustrated by Sherrington's classical diagram of Fig. 1.41; here the nerve fibre a represents the sensory fibre from the skin; this synapses with two groups of neurones in the cord, namely those that excite neurones within the cord and those that inhibit motor neurones to the antagonistic muscles. In Fig. 1.41 the central terminal branches of a are excitor for the flexor and inhibitor for the extensor muscles of the same side, and the reverse happens for the muscles of the opposite side.

This reciprocal innervation is by no means confined to the activation of skeletal muscles, and is widely spread throughout the body's control systems. Thus the size of the pupil is governed by a sphincter muscle and a dilator muscle supplied by separate nerves; if the pupil becomes smaller, this is a result of simultaneous contraction of the sphincter muscle and relaxation of the dilator; similarly dilatation is due to contraction of the dilator muscle with inhibition of the sphincter.

Stretch Reflex

When a stretch is applied to a muscle, especially an extensor to a limb, the muscle actively opposes the stretch by contracting. This is a

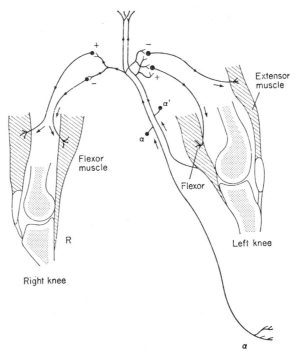

Fig. 1.41. Reciprocal innervation. The sensory nerve fibre *a* from the skin synapses with neurones that excite the flexor muscle of the same side and the extensor muscle of the opposite side, while inhibiting the antagonistic muscles. Thus on one side the terminal branches are excitatory for the flexor muscles and inhibitory for the extensors, while on the other side the innervation is reversed. (The diagram is from Sherrington and does not show the inhibitory interneurone which must be present at each inhibitory site, since no single neurone can release different transmitter substances at its nerve endings).

reflex response, in the sense that it operates through the sensory nerve from the muscle, since cutting the dorsal root abolishes the reflex. The stretch reflex is highly localized, in the sense that, if the quadriceps tendon is divided up and only a part is stretched, only that part of the muscle will contract. As with the flexor reflex, however, the phenomenon is associated with inhibition of the antagonistic muscles.

Spindle and Golgi Tendon-organ. The afferent pathway for this reflex is the sensory nerve supplying the particular muscle involved. This nerve terminates in special receptors in the muscle called *muscle spindles* which, when the muscle is stretched, cause a discharge in the sensory nerve (Fig. 1.42a). Thus the spindle is an organ that provides information to the spinal cord regarding the state of stretch of the muscle fibres, and its activity is typically seen in the stretch reflex. Another organ, also connected with indicating the tension in a muscle, is the tendon-organ of Golgi; it is formed around a bundle of small tendon fascicles close to the junction between the tendon and the muscle fibres. The sensory nerve terminals ramify amongst the fascicles in such a way that, when the tendon is stretched, these terminals probably become stretched too and thus are stimulated to discharge

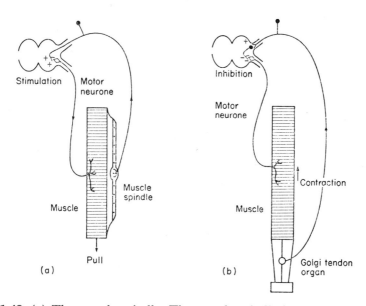

Fig. 1.42. (a) The muscle spindle. The muscle spindle is arranged parallel to the muscle fibre as shown. When the muscle is stretched the muscle spindle discharges and stimulates the motor neurone which in turn causes the muscle to contract. (b) The tendon organ. The tendon organ is arranged in series with the muscle fibre and discharges when the muscle contracts. This discharge activates an inhibitory interneurone which inhibits the motor neurone.

(Fig. 1.42b). It would seem that the reflex response due to the tendon-organ is inhibitory to its own muscle, whilst it tends to excite the antagonists. It thus works in opposition to the muscle spindle, which tends to excite its own muscle when stretched, and we may look upon the tendon-organ as a protective device for preventing a muscle from pulling too strongly on its tendon, and this is typically seen in the *lengthening reaction*, i.e. the sudden reversal of the stretch-reflex and the resistance of the muscle to stretch giving way suddenly to a passive relaxation, which may be shown to be the result of inhibition of the motor neurones controlling the stretched muscle.

Monosynaptic Nature of Reflex. The stretch-, or *myotatic*, reflex is of fundamental interest to the experimenter on the central nervous system since it is the one reflex whose arc is definitely established as involving only two neurones, namely the sensory and motor neurones

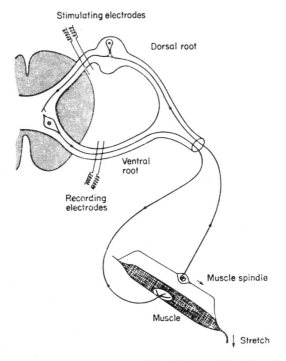

Stimulating electrodes

Dorsal root

Ventral root

Recording electrodes

Muscle spindle

Muscle

Stretch

Fig. 1.43. The monosynaptic reflex. Stimulation of a dorsal sensory root causes a motor response in the fibres of the ventral root, and since this occurs with an extremely short latency of 0·5 msec it is considered not to involve more than one synaptic delay.

(Fig. 1.43). Lloyd recorded electrically from the roots of a spinal animal; when he stimulated the posterior (or dorsal) root, he found that the motor response differed according to the strength of the applied stimulus, the differences being due primarily to the different thresholds of the sensory fibres in the dorsal root. Thus, when the stimulus was just strong enough to evoke a reflex response, as recorded by a discharge in the anterior root, the response was a sharp spike with an extremely short latency, namely some 0·5 msec, so short that the reflex could not have involved more than one synaptic delay, i.e. he was recording a monosynaptic reflex. With stronger stimuli the same monosynaptic response was followed by more delayed responses indicating the evocation of polysynaptic reflex responses. Subsequent analysis showed that the monosynaptic response had resulted from stimulating the fibres from a muscle-nerve rather than one ending in the skin, and it could be shown, further, that it was the large rapidly conducting "Group Ia" fibres that were the responsible sensory fibres that supplied the muscle spindles. Thus the stretch-reflex, initiated by activation of the muscle spindle, was the monosynaptic response.

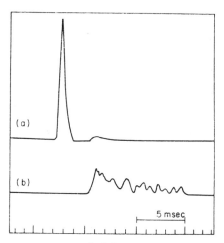

Fig. 1.44. Reflex responses recorded from a ventral root. (a) Response to afferent stimulation of a muscle nerve; (b) response to stimulation of a cutaneous nerve. The upper trace is a monosynaptic reflex discharge whilst the lower trace is a polysynaptic discharge without the spike seen in (a). (Lloyd, *J. Neurophysiol.* 1943, **6**, 111.)

Figure 1.44 illustrates the differing effects of stimulating sensory nerves from a muscle and from the skin, the former giving the rapid large monosynaptic response with its short latency, and the latter the more prolonged discharge with longer latency involving one or more interneurones.

Quantitative Analysis. With the type of recording used by Lloyd, where the responses to many individual fibres were led into the appropriate recording device, the increasing height of the recorded potential was essentially a measure of the number of neurones responding, and of the frequency of their discharge. In this way, then, it was possible to measure the responsiveness of the spinal motor neurones, and to confirm that they could be reflexly inhibited. In addition it was shown that they could be *facilitated,* in the sense that an afferent volley of impulses arriving up one sensory nerve, whilst not necessarily evoking any overt response in the motor neurones, could increase their sensitivity to a volley in another sensory nerve (Fig. 1.45).

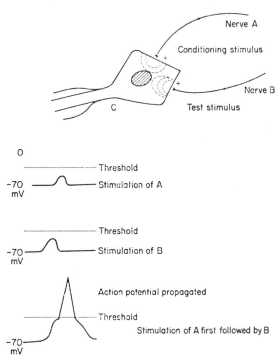

Fig. 1.45. Facilitation. The afferent volley of impulses arriving down nerve A, although not large enough to generate a spike in the motor neurone C, can nevertheless increase the sensitivity of C to the stimulus from another nerve B, so that although the stimulus of B is subthreshold by itself the pre-conditioning by A enables the threshold to be exceeded and causes the motor neurone to discharge.

Facilitation and Inhibition. Thus we may apply a "conditioning" shock to one muscle-nerve and examine its effect on the response to the "test" shock applied to another afferent nerve. If the conditioning shock is facilitatory, then the response to the test shock is increased; but the magnitude of the increase depends on the delay between conditioning and test stimuli, being greatest when the interval is zero and decaying rapidly, so that after about 10 msec there is no facilitation. Thus the excitability of the motor neurones involved in this monosynaptic response has been increased for a short period of time. In a similar way, by choosing an appropriate nerve, we may examine the inhibitory action of an afferent impulse on the motor neurones; this also decays, so that if the delay is greater than about 10 msec there is little or no evidence of inhibition.

Electrical Studies of Spinal Motor Neurones

Post-synaptic Potentials

The study of reflex activity, by both Sherrington's and Lloyd's techniques, provided a great deal of knowledge as to the basic responses of the motor neurones. However, this knowledge was derived by inference rather than by direct study of the neurones; and it was not till Eccles made recordings from individual motor neurones, by inserting microelectrodes into them, that the true nature of the excitatory and inhibitory processes was revealed. Eccles found that the motor neurones had resting potentials of 50–80 mV. When an excitatory volley of impulses from the posterior root reached the neurone

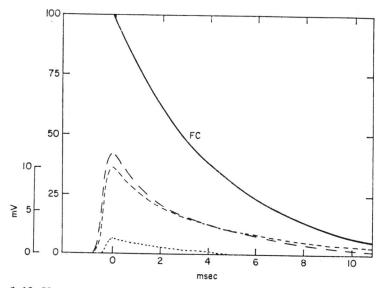

Fig. 1.46. Showing the correlation between EPSP and the facilitation of the monosynaptic reflex. Dotted and broken lines indicate time course of EPSP recorded from a motor neurone after stimulation of a sensory root muscle nerve at three different strengths. Curve marked FC shows facilitation of monosynaptic reflex, expressed as percentage of the maximum, which is at zero time interval between the conditioning and testing volleys. (Eccles, *Cold Spr. Harb. Symp. Quant. Biol.* 1952, **17**, 175.)

there was a brief depolarization, called by Eccles the *excitatory post-synaptic potential* (*EPSP*), analogous with the end-plate potential of the neuromuscular junction but differing from this in that it did not necessarily lead to a spike response. The spike response only occurred when the potential had built up to a critical value of about 15 mV.

Relation to Facilitation. The EPSP decayed over a period of 10 msec, during which time it would add with the response to a new stimulus, and it is this finite decay course of the EPSP that doubtless represents the facilitation described by Sherrington and Lloyd. This is illustrated by Fig. 1.47, which shows the time-courses of the EPSP when the sensory nerve is stimulated at three different strengths. The line marked FC shows the facilitation of the monosynaptic reflex, expressed as a percentage of the maximum, which occurs at zero time-interval between conditioning and test stimuli.

Inhibition

In general, then, the motor neurone is unlikely to respond with a discharge if it only receives a single afferent stimulus; it requires the mutual facilitation of perhaps hundreds of impulses, reaching the many synaptic knobs on the motor neurone's surface within 10 msec of each other, to raise the EPSP to the critical magnitude. The importance of this *integrating* action of the motor neurone is emphasized even more when we examine the effects of an inhibitory afferent discharge; thus Eccles measured the membrane potential when a muscle nerve, known to inhibit, was stimulated. The result was the *inhibitory post-synaptic potential* (*IPSP*), a small wave of hyperpolarization that increased the resting potential by a few millivolts. An interesting feature of the IPSP is the longer latency, indicating the intervention of at least one extra synapse, so that inhibition of a motor neurone always, apparently, involves an interneurone, which is localized in the intermediate nucleus of the spinal cord. By inserting a microelectrode into a single inter-mediate neurone, graded EPSP's were set up in response to afferent stimulation; and these summated to give a discharge which could have a latency as small as 8 msec. Thus Fig. 1.47 illustrates the probable nervous pathways for the simultaneously evoked excitatory and inhibitory actions on the motor neurones of a pair of antagonistic muscles; the excitatory response is monosynaptic, whilst the inhibition of the antagonist takes place through an intermediate neurone (IN).

Mechanism of IPSP. As with the end-plate potential, it would seem that the IPSP is due to an indiscriminate increase in ionic permeability. With the EPSP the evidence suggested that the mem-

brane became more highly permeable to anions, such as Cl⁻, so that
the resting potential was dominated by the permeability to this ion.
As we have argued earlier (p. 64) an increased permeability to either
this ion or to K^+ would have the effect of stabilizing the membrane
potential, in the sense of driving it towards a potential governed by the
distributions of these ions, i.e. keeping the inside strongly negative in
relation to the outside.

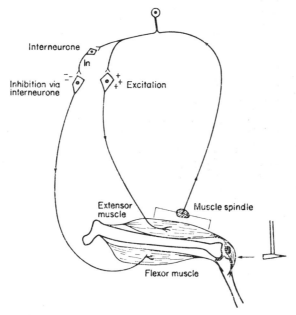

Fig. 1.47. A diagram of the pathways for the simultaneously evoked
excitatory and inhibitory actions on the motor neurones of a pair of antagonistic muscles. The patella tap stretches the muscle and causes a spindle
discharge which excites its own muscle via a monosynaptic reflex, but
inhibits the antagonistic muscle via an interneurone.

Interaction of EPSP and IPSP. As with facilitation, inhibition
decays, and the time-course corresponds with the decay of the IPSP.
The IPSP, by hyperpolarizing the motor neurone's membrane or,
what is more important, by stabilizing its membrane potential, tends
to antagonize the EPSP, which is depolarizing. Thus at any given
moment the motor neurone is receiving perhaps many hundreds of
impulses, some of these tending to depolarize and others tending to
prevent depolarization through stabilization of the membrane potential.
According to the interaction of these opposing influences, the neurone

may be entirely inactive or it may show varying degrees of discharge, degrees that are measured by the frequency of its action potential.

Higher Influences. Many of these interactions can be demonstrated in the spinal animal, and even when the segment of cord has been separated from adjacent segments, but the phenomenon of spinal shock shows how the condition of the motor neurones is influenced by descending discharges from higher centres, and these may be either facilitatory or inhibitory. Thus the phenomenon of *decerebrate rigidity* (Vol. 4), whereby, on cutting off the influences of only part of the brain, the stretch reflexes become exaggerated, reveals the normal incidence of inhibitory impulses to the motor neurones as well as of excitatory ones. Removal of the connections with the inhibitory region of the brain, leads to enhanced excitability.

Final Common Pathway

In fact, as we shall see when we consider some of the more complex aspects of control of the bodily movements, the motor neurones of the spinal cord and brain are the objects of very many influences indeed, some of these exerted directly from centres in the brain, such as the vestibular nuclei, through the descending tracts in the cord, and others by the preliminary interaction of many brain centres, before finally the result of this interaction is reflected in a descending discharge to the motor neurones. Truly, then, the motor neurones are described as the *final common pathway* (Fig. 1.48).

Initiation of the Response

As we have seen, the response of a motor neurone to afferent stimuli is graded, building up to an all-or-none type of propagated discharge when the EPSP has exceeded a critical amount. The value of such a system is obvious, enabling, as it does, the integration of afferent influences from many sources before the final decision to discharge is made. We may ask whether the membrane of the body of the neurone and its dendrites is different from that of the axon which gives rise, essentially, to the all-or-none propagated type of response only. The answer is probably "yes", in so far as the dendrites and perikaryon are probably similar to the end-plate in being depolarized or hyperpolarized in response to chemical mediators. Unlike the end-plate, they are capable of all-or-none spike activity involving high Na^+-permeability.

IS- and SD-spikes. Thus the depolarization of the perikaryon causes this region of the neurone to act as a "potential sink", causing local circuits to flow that finally activate the axon in the region of the axon

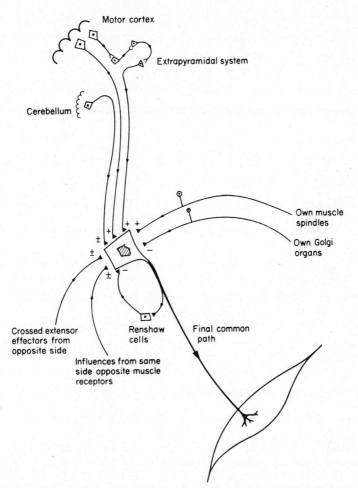

Fig. 1.48. The motor neurone as the final common pathway. The variety of excitatory and inhibitory inputs to a motor neurone that contribute to its state of excitability at any moment.

hillock, i.e. the region of emergence of the axon from the perikaryon (Fig. 1.49). This series of events was made clear by Eccles' analysis of the events in the impaled motor neurone; the spike (Fig. 1.50) has an inflexion on its ascending limb, and the evidence suggests that this initial rise, the *IS-spike*, is due to activity in the initial segment of the axon, i.e. the unmyelinated proximal part of the axon and the axon hillock. The second elevation is considered to be the result of the spread of the activation to the soma or perikaryon, and is called the

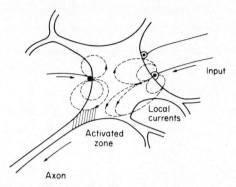

Fig. 1.49. The spread of currents from locally depolarized regions of the perikaryon. These regions act as "potential sinks" and may finally depolarize the axon hillock and generate an action potential.

SD-spike (soma and dendrites). The threshold for evoking the IS-spike is only about one-third of that for the SD-spike, so that the initial segment is clearly the place where the spike originates, and it then spreads over the soma and dendrites.

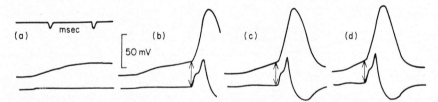

Fig. 1.50. Intracellularly recorded potentials in a motor neurone in response to monosynaptic activation of increasing strength from (a) to (d). The onset of the IS-spike is indicated by the arrow; this merges into the SD-spike. The differentiated records below, i.e. records of *rate of change of potential* against time, show clearly the point of inflexion corresponding to the SD-spike. In (a) only an EPSP has been set up. (Coombs, Curtis and Eccles, *J. Physiol.* 1957, **139**, 198.)

Acetylcholine in Central Transmission

Synaptic Vesicles

There is little reason to doubt that transmission in the spinal cord, as in the rest of the central nervous system of higher vertebrates, is through the liberation of transmitter. The synapses of the cord reveal the presence of vesicles in the terminals of the axons; these may be separated as *synaptosomes*, membrane-bound bodies containing the

vesicles; on osmotic bursting in hypotonic solutions, the contents are
liberated, and in this way the presence of acetylcholine as one of the
central transmitters may be established.

Collateral Inhibition

So far as the cord is concerned, acetylcholine is unequivocally the
transmitter in the process of collateral inhibition. Thus the axon
running from a motor neurone in the cord gives off a collateral branch

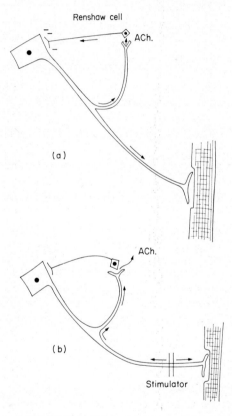

Fig. 1.51. Collateral inhibition. The axons running from lower motor
neurones give off collateral branches as shown in (a). These collaterals
synapse with Renshaw cells which inhibit the motor neurone. (b) Antidromic
stimulation. Impulses are propagated backwards up the motor nerve; they
cause the Renshaw cells to be stimulated by the release of acetylcholine
from the collateral endings. This acetylcholine can be collected by perfusing
the spinal cord and measuring the activity of the perfusate with a bioassay
technique.

on its way out of the cord, synapsing with what has been called a
Renshaw cell, a neurone in the intermediate nucleus (Fig. 1.51). Thus
an action potential, initiated at the axon hillock of the motor neurone,
passes down to the muscle fibre causing it to contract, but at the same
time the action potential passes back along this collateral to activate
the Renshaw cell, and this latter sends inhibitory impulses to the motor
neurone. In other words, the motor neurone tends to inhibit its own
activity through this collateral pathway, a common form of feedback
control in the central nervous system.

Renshaw Cell Discharge. The inhibitory activity in the Renshaw
cells can be picked up by an electrode in the intermediate nucleus,
being recognized by its characteristically high-frequency spike-
discharge. Local application of a cholinergic inhibitor, such as dihydro-
β-erythridine, blocks the Renshaw discharge indicating that the motor
neurone, besides liberating acetylcholine at its peripheral termination
on the motor neurone, also liberates acetylcholine at its synapse with
the Renshaw neurone. It will be clear from Fig. 1.51 that, if the motor
neurone's axon is stimulated electrically, the Renshaw cell will be
stimulated synaptically through the collateral; this is because action
potentials spread in both directions. This *antidromic stimulation* (Fig. 1.51)
causes the release of acetylcholine, which may be collected experimentally in the fluid, passing over the perfused spinal cord.

Non-cholinergic Transmission

Other transmitter substances that have been either proved, or are
suspected, to behave in this way are noradrenaline, 3-hydroxytyramine
(dopamine), 5-hydroxytryptamine (5-HT or serotonin) and possibly
amino acids such as glycine, glutamic acid and gamma-aminobutyric
acid (GABA).

Catecholamines

Thus the catecholamines, such as noradrenaline and dopamine,
can be recognized in formaldehyde-treated sections of brain tissue by
virtue of their fluorescence, using the technique of Falck and Hillarp,
and in this way definite tracts may be identified within the brain.
The technique consists essentially in exposing a microtome section of
the tissue to formaldehyde vapour, which reacts with the amine, leading eventually to a fluorescent compound which thus causes the tissue
to fluoresce with a characteristic colour. Noradrenaline and dopamine
can be differentiated by treatment with HCl, which reduces the fluores-

cence of noradrenaline specifically. Secondary catecholamines, such as adrenaline, produce their fluorescent compounds much more slowly and can be differentiated on this basis. Indolamines, such as 5-HT, also produce fluorescent compounds, but the spectral characteristics of the fluorescent light are different, permitting differentiation on the basis of the yellow colour emitted by 5-HT.

Glycine. Again, there is a high concentration of the amino acid glycine in the ventral gray matter of the spinal cord in the region where inhibitory neurones are concentrated, and the microinjection experiments carried out by Curtis certainly indicate that glycine depresses the activity of spinal motor neurones causing the appearance of inhibitory post-synaptic potentials (IPSP's).

Convulsants

Just as transmission at the neuromuscular junction may be blocked by substances like curare, so central transmission can be blocked. Of especial interest is the block of inhibitory neurones, since this leads to hyperactivity of the central neurones that are now released from their tonic inhibition. In this way we can account for the convulsive effects of *strychnine*, which blocks the reflexly evoked IPSP of the motor neurone, probably by competing with the inhibitory transmitter for active sites on the post-synaptic membrane. *Tetanus toxin* is another convulsant; it probably acts by reducing the amount of inhibitory transmitter released from nerve terminals.

Glycine–Strychnine Interaction

Of the transmitters that are considered to act as inhibitors of spinal motor neurone activity, glycine, dopamine, GABA and noradrenaline have been implicated, and it is interesting that strychnine has a specific effect in antagonizing the action of one of these, namely glycine. Thus we may depress the activity of spinal motor neurones by local injections of the various putative inhibitory transmitters, but the effectiveness of strychnine in overcoming this depression is far greater when it has been induced by glycine than with the others. An example of this specific antagonism of glycine by strychnine is shown in Fig. 1.52. Here the top line shows the spontaneous discharge of a neurone of the reticular formation of the medulla; the lowest line shows the discharge of the same neurone depressed by either glycine or GABA; treatment with strychnine removes the depression caused by glycine but not that by GABA.

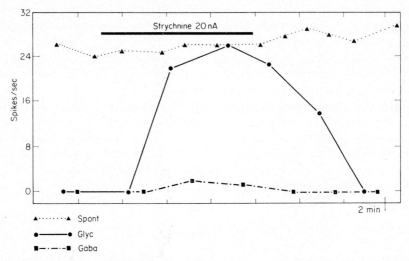

Fig. 1.52. The strychnine antagonism of glycine inhibition. The top line is the spontaneous discharge of a neurone of the reticular formation of the brain, the lowest line shows the same neurone depressed with GABA (squares) or glycine (circles). As can be seen, the injection of strychnine antagonizes the glycine-induced inhibition but does not affect that induced by GABA. (Hosli and Tebecis, *Exp. Br. Res.* 1970, **11,** 111.)

The Brain

The spinal cord continues upwards (Fig. 1.53) from the cervical region as the *medulla,* a region where many of the ascending branches of the sensory neurone, illustrated by Fig. 1.40, terminate to relay with new neurones that transmit the sensory message higher in the brain. The medulla continues through the *pons* into the *midbrain.*

Cranial Nerves

These regions are built on the same plan as the cord, in the sense that they contain groups of the cell bodies of motor neurones, which emerge from the brain to pass to their effector sites. Some of these *cranial nerves* (Fig. 1.54) are exactly analogous with the spinal nerves, containing both motor and sensory fibres. As with the spinal nerves, the sensory contribution is from groups of sensory neurones situated outside the brain proper, in ganglia, e.g. the *Gasserian ganglion* of Nerve V. The axons of the sensory neurones pass into the brain and relay in regions of gray matter called the *sensory roots,* e.g. we may speak of the *sensory root* of the trigeminal in the midbrain. Some of the cranial nerves seem to be purely motor [e.g. the oculomotor nerve

(N. III)] whilst others are purely sensory, such as the optic nerve (N. II). In general, the cranial nerves are concerned with controlling activities in the head, but in addition some, such as the *vagus*, are entirely concerned with the control of visceral processes.

Oculomotor Nerve. As examples of the analogy and difference between cranial and spinal nerves, we may examine the oculomotor nerve (N. III) and the trigeminal (N. V). The neurones, whose axons

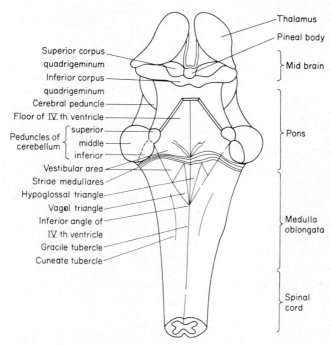

Fig. 1.53. The structures of the brain-stem.

constitute the oculomotor nerve, occupy a part of the gray matter of the midbrain, so that a section of the midbrain at the level of the superior colliculus reveals these neurones—*the nucleus of N. III*—as a bilaterally organized mass of gray matter, giving rise to axons that emerge from the anterior aspect of the brain-stem as the two oculomotor nerves. By examining sections of the midbrain at successive levels, the three dimensional shape of the nucleus can be established, and by studying the effects of electrical stimulation of different parts, or the effects of lesions on the degeneration of the different fibres in the nerve, it can be established that the motor neurones are grouped together in accordance with the different muscles of the eye that they activate. Furthermore, there is an autonomic group (p. 105) concerned with the involuntary muscles of the eyes controlling the size of the pupil and the act of accommodation; this group is called the *Edinger–Westphal nucleus.*

Trigeminal Nerve. The oculomotor nerve is purely motor; by contrast, the trigeminal is both sensory and motor, and is thus more

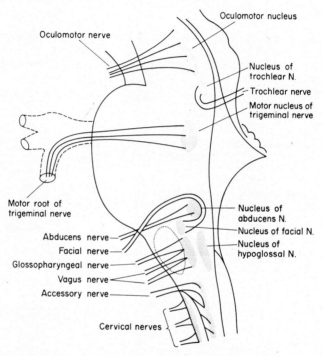

Fig. 1.54. A diagrammatic representation of the motor nuclei of the cranial nerves, lateral aspect. (Kuntz, "Textbook of Neuroanatomy", 5th edition, Baillière, Tindall and Cox.)

similar to a spinal nerve. The motor neurones have their cell bodies grouped in the pons as the *motor nucleus* (Fig. 1.54), and their axons pass forward through the Gasserian ganglion, which contains the cell bodies of the sensory neurones (Fig. 1.55) and is thus analogous with the posterior root ganglion of a spinal nerve. The sensory neurone sends one axonal branch to the periphery along one of the three branches (hence the name trigeminal), where it ends in a sensory organ, such as touch-spots of the skin, whilst the central axonal branch passes into the brain-stem to relay with a central neurone. The regions of synapse are called the *sensory nuclei* (Fig. 1.55), and are groups of neurones that may be relay-neurones, carrying the sensory message to the thalamus and cerebral cortex, or they may be concerned with motor reflexes, in the same way that the interneurones of the cord are concerned with spinal reflexes. Thus its close connection with the

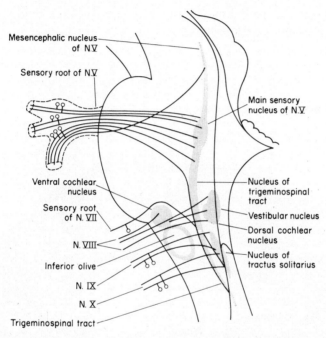

Fig. 1.55. A diagram of the nuclei of termination of the afferent cranial nerves; lateral aspect. (Kuntz, "Textbook of Neuroanatomy", 5th edition, Baillière, Tindall and Cox.)

motor nucleus of the facial nerve (N. VII) permits reflex motor responses in the facial muscles, whilst other motor reflexes are brought about through the motor nucleus of N. V. An exception to the rule that sensory neurones have their cell bodies outside the central nervous system in ganglia is given by some of the sensory neurones of N. V. Thus the *mesencephalic root*, illustrated in Fig. 1.55, is made up of the cell bodies of sensory neurones whose axons pass out into the trigeminal nerve (N. V); they probably carry mainly information from the muscle spindles concerned in mastication.

Brain-stem

The medulla and pons are described as the *rhombencephalon*, and it will be seen from Fig. 1.56 that they lie in relation to the IVth ventricle. The pons, in addition to brain-stem nuclei, contains the large tracts connecting the two sides of the cerebellum. The midbrain is called the *mesencephalon*, and is related topographically to the aqueduct of Sylvius, which is the fluid channel connecting the IIIrd and IVth ventricles.

In addition to containing the motor neurones and acting as relay stations for sensory neurones, these structures which, because they are

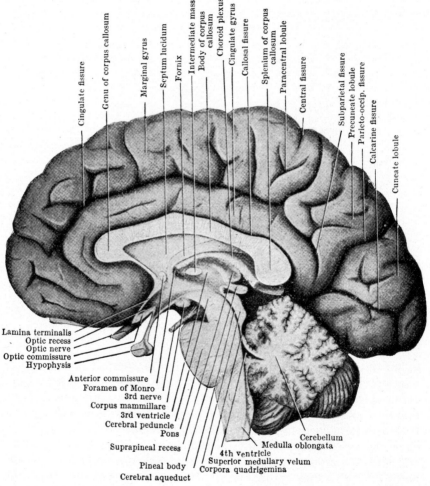

Fig. 1.56. Medial section of the adult human brain. (J. Symington.)

on the main ascending and descending pathway of the central nervous system, are described collectively as the *brain-stem*, contain groups of neurones that act as integrating centres for several important functions. These are notably the *respiratory centres* in the medulla, the *vasomotor centres*, *swallowing*, and *vomiting* centres, and so on.

Higher Sensory Pathway

To continue with the basic topography of the brain, we may note that the ascending pathway for sensory impulses from the environment continues through the medulla and midbrain to reach the *thalamus*, a large body of gray matter that acts as a relay station for sensory information. From here the information is transmitted by new neurones

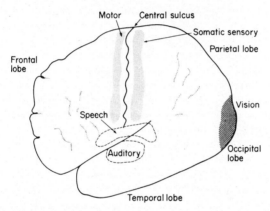

Fig. 1.57. The features of the cerebral cortex with known functional areas.

to the cerebral mantle or *hemispheres*. The important functional neurones of the hemispheres are contained in the outer layer, or *cerebral cortex*, the underlying white matter representing the various tracts that bring information to the cortex, carry efferent discharges to the lower regions, and generally provide connections between different parts of the cortex. Thus the cerebral cortex is the highest region to which information can be transmitted.

Cerebral Cortex. Connections between the cerebral cortex and the lower regions of the brain are made through the cerebral peduncles, which are thus made up of large tracts, both ascending and descending. There is, in the cortex, an obvious separation of functions, in the sense that certain regions are concerned with sensations and others with initiating motor activities, and still others with coordination of the parts.

Somatotopic Organization. Furthermore, the sensory regions may themselves be divided according to the type of sensation, e.g. vision is represented by the posterior or occipital region (Fig. 1.57) whilst cutaneous sensation is represented by a region on the parietal cortex called the post-central gyrus. Again, as Fig. 1.58 illustrates, the different regions of the body are represented in an orderly fashion. This "somatotopic organization" is revealed experimentally by stimulating the anaesthetized animal on various parts of its body and determining where the "evoked response" can be recorded from the surface of the

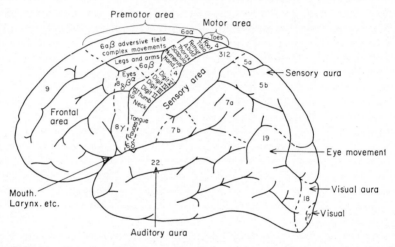

Fig. 1.58. A diagram of the extent of the sensory cortex associated with various regions of the body. As far as the cortex is concerned, man is mostly a fingers, lips and tongue animal. (Penfield and Rasmussen, "The Cerebral Cortex of Man", 1950, Macmillan.)

cerebral cortex. Alternatively, in the conscious human subject, we may stimulate different regions of the cortex and ask the patient his sensations. The organization of the bodily movements shows likewise a somatotopic arrangement. Thus the various parts of the body may be represented on a part of the frontal cortex called the precentral gyrus; stimulation of different regions gives rise to movements localized to different parts of the body as indicated in Fig. 1.59.

Pyramidal Tracts

As indicated in Fig. 1.59 the motor pathway from this part of the cerebral cortex is by way of the *pyramidal tracts*, also called *corticospinal tracts*. These descend through the brain-stem and cord where, in primates, the axons terminate directly on the motor neurones whose characteristics we have already described. It is considered that voluntary activity is initiated in the motor cortex and is effected through the pyramidal tracts; stimulation of the tracts certainly causes bodily movements. Examination of the motor neurones at a given level of the cord when pyramidal tract impulses reach them shows that they may

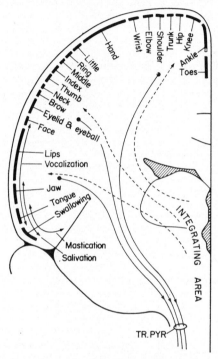

Fig. 1.59. Cross-section through right hemisphere along plane of the precentral gyrus indicating somatotopic localization of motor function. The broken lines suggest that there is subcortical control over the initiation of voluntary activity. (Penfield and Jasper, "Epilepsy and the Functional Anatomy of the Human Brain".)

be facilitated, i.e. a reflex response operating through the cord (e.g. the stretch reflex) is made more powerful, or its threshold is reduced, if simultaneously the pyramidal neurones are caused to discharge. Again, under appropriate conditions of discharge the cortical tract can be made to inhibit the spinal motor neurones.

Sensory-motor Co-ordination. This very direct communication of the motor cortex with the spinal motor neurones shows that reflex movements involving the cortex may well be carried out through a

5-neurone arc, three sensory neurones being employed, the third-order one from the thalamus activating the pyramidal tract neurone which finally activates the motor neurone in the cord. In this way we can understand how the motor activity, for example of the fingers during writing, may be accurately controlled by the sensory information arising from the skin of the fingers. Thus the close proximity of the somatic sensory and motor regions on the post- and pre-central gyri reveals its significance.

Basal Ganglia

Immediately beneath the hemispheres are the *basal ganglia*, the most prominent of which is the *corpus striatum*, concerned with the control of bodily movements. They are, in general, centres concerned in the

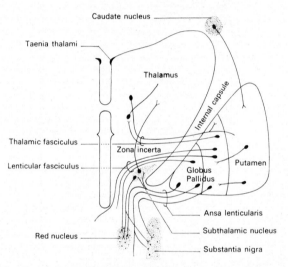

Fig. 1.60. Diagram illustrating some of the relationships of the fasciculi that traverse the ventral thalamus. (Kuntz, "A Text of Neuroanatomy", 5th edition, Baillière, Tindall and Cox.)

integration of activities involving higher and lower stations; so complex are the interrelationships, however, that it is not easy to specify a given function for any part. As Fig. 1.60 shows, the anterior thalamus is closely related to the basal ganglia, so that the thalamus must be regarded as much more than a sensory relay station.

Parkinsonism. A number of characteristic defects in motor activity are associated with lesions in these ganglia, or their related brain structures, and thus emphasize their importance in coordination of muscular activity. Thus the characteristic syndrome of Parkinsonism is associated with lesions in the substantia nigra, a brain-stem region with close neural relations with the caudate nucleus and putamen (Fig. 1.60). Analysis of the concentrations of dopamine—a central transmitter—in the caudate nucleus and putamen showed that it was unusually low in Parkinsonian patients, suggesting that it is an interruption in the circuit involving these basal ganglia and the substantia nigra that is the root cause of the defect. Again, the involuntary movements in Wilson's disease, or *hepatolenticular degeneration*, result from pathological accumulation of copper in the lenticular nucleus, the name given to the globus pallidus plus putamen.

The Cerebellum

The *cerebellum* lies off the main track and receives impulses from the cord and medulla below, and from the cerebral hemispheres above. Its functions have become better defined as a result of recent work, and the principal one is undoubtedly that of assisting in the performance of skilled tasks. Thus it is continuously fed information relating to the state of the muscles through tracts of white matter in the cord, e.g. the spino-cerebellar tracts, whilst the neurones responsible for controlling motor activities, e.g. the pyramidal tract neurones of the frontal cerebral cortex, send collateral branches to the cerebellum, so that it is kept informed, not only of the state of the muscles but also of the motor impulses being sent to them. The most prominent feature of cerebellar damage is thus disturbance in the coordination of the bodily movements.

The Colliculi

At the midbrain level there are four protuberances called the *superior* and *inferior colliculi*; these are relay-stations and integrating centres for visual (superior) and auditory (inferior) stimuli. It must be appreciated that the main relay stations for visual impulses from the optic nerves and tracts are the *lateral geniculate bodies*, situated higher up in the diencephalon and analogous with the thalamus.

The Hypothalamus

The *hypothalamus* is a region of the brain concerned with the integration of many forms of visceral activity; it is a part of the diencephalon and is thus close to the thalamus and to the IIIrd ventricle, and lies between the midbrain (below) and the forebrain (above). Its importance as a coordinating centre is revealed anatomically by its receiving afferent impulses from all parts of the brain; its main efferent output is probably to the neurones of the autonomic nervous system, i.e. to that part of the system that controls such visceral activities as movements of the intestine, contraction of the heart, and so on.

Visceral Control Centres

Studies based on localized damage to the hypothalamus, or on stimulation by implanted electrodes, indicate the presence of several coordinating centres, such as *feeding* and *drinking centres*. Thus Andersson implanted electrodes in the hypothalamus of the goat and, when electric shocks were passed through these, the goat would almost immediately begin to drink water. The presence of a *temperature-regulating centre*, with neurones highly sensitive to the temperature of the blood passing through the brain, is well established. The main *vasomotor centre*, controlling the blood circulation, is in the medulla. However, the control of the dilator mechanism, through which the blood supply to the muscles during exercise may be increased, operates apparently through a localized region of the hypothalamus. Finally, we may note that the hypothalamus is closely related to the endocrine control of bodily activity; thus we have seen that the osmolality of the blood is carefully controlled through the kidney. Within the hypothalamus there are cells especially sensitive to changes in osmolality of the blood—the *osmoreceptors* of Verney—and these transmit their responses to the pituitary body, causing it to secrete an *antidiuretic hormone* into the blood that reduces the excretion of water by the kidney. This hypothalamic-endocrine control is by no means confined to the excretion of the antidiuretic hormone; we shall see that release of very many hormones, influencing all aspects of bodily behaviour, is controlled through *releasing factors* liberated from specific cells in the hypothalamus. Thus the hypothalamus may be regarded as the main site for integration of the neural and hormonal control mechanisms of the body.

Cortical Relations. The hypothalamus is under cortical control, having close connections with what has been called the *limbic system*, and containing, among other structures, the hippocampus, regions of the frontal lobe, fornix and so on. Stimulation of the pyramidal tracts, which represent the axons from neurones in a large part of the cerebral cortex, causes a number of visceral responses in cats, such as sweating, relaxation of the bladder, altered gastric motility and so on. This indicates that, although the complex reflex activities involved in visceral control are largely determined by the hypothalamus, the cortex may exert an influence as well. In humans, the various psychologically induced stress phenomena that lead to excess secretion of hormones and hyperactivity of the gastrointestinal tract are obviously brought about by cortical activity.

The Tracts of the Spinal Cord

At this point, it is worth examining the spinal cord in more detail, since its tracts of white matter and its columns of gray matter constitute, essentially, a synopsis of function of most of the nervous system. Figure 1.61 illustrates the main descending (left) and main ascending (right)

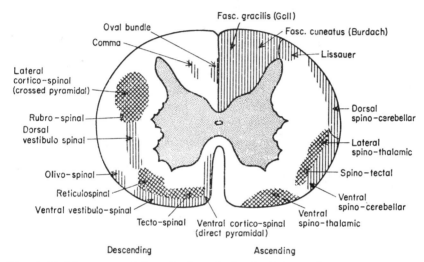

Fig. 1.61. The tracts of the spinal cord. On the left are the main descending pathways and on the right the main ascending pathways. (Davson and Eggleton (Eds.), "Principles of Human Physiology", Churchill, 14th edition, 1968.)

tracts. The pyramidal tracts are seen to occupy two regions, according to whether the descending fibres have remained on the same side of the cord as the cortex from which they are derived, or from the opposite side. The maintenance of posture is achieved largely through the vestibular apparatus in close relation to the ear. The sensory neurones in N. VIII, carrying the information from the vestibular apparatus, relay in the medulla, in the *vestibular nuclei*. Neurones in these nuclei send down axons to the spinal motor neurones and interneurones in the two *vestibulospinal tracts*. Another part of the brain, the *reticular formation*, is also closely connected with control of bodily movements, and this gives rise to the *reticulospinal tract* that, once again, influences the final common path—the spinal motor neurones. Sensory information takes several routes up the cord according to the organs from which the information is derived. Thus fine tactile impulses from the skin and proprioceptive impulses from the muscles travel in the large dorsal tracts, the *fasciculi gracilis* and *cuneatus*, whilst other cutaneous information regarding temperature and pain, as well as of touch, is carried in the ventral and lateral *spinothalamic tracts*; the cerebellum receives information from the muscle and joint receptors which passes up the dorsal and ventral *spinocerebellar tracts*. The tectum is the name for the roof of the midbrain, which is constituted by the colliculi, hence the *tectospinal* and *spinotectal* tracts are descending and ascending fibres from and to this region. The superior colliculi are closely connected with vision, in the sense that coordination of bodily movements with visual information is probably mediated here. Hence the tectospinal tract influences the motor neurones of the cord in the light of visual information, whilst information from the muscles and skin is carried to the colliculi by the spinotectal tract.

THE AUTONOMIC SYSTEM

The experimental study of the central nervous system has been so intimately concerned with the control of bodily motor activity and sensation that there is a tendency to describe the organization of the central nervous system in terms of these *somatic* activities, relegating the control mechanisms in *visceral*, or non-somatic, activities to a supplementary description. In fact, of course, the nervous control of the viscera and blood vessels is just as vital, if not more so, than any control of the somatic system; thus a very small lesion in the medulla can bring respiration, and thus life, to a halt; a correspondingly small lesion in the motor cortex, or in one of the basal ganglia, can impair motor activity, but this would not be fatal.

Pre- and Postganglionic Fibres

In general, the visceral outflow from the brain and cord is separate in origin from that of the somatic outflow, although the axons travel together for at least part of their respective journeys. A special feature of the visceral or autonomic outflow is the relaying of impulses from the motor neurones of the cord or brain in certain *ganglia*, which are collections of neurones outside the brain and cord usually enclosed in a connective-tissue sheath. Thus the effector neurone to the viscus, or to a blood vessel, is not derived from the brain or cord, but from the ganglion. We may speak of the *preganglionic neurone* as belonging to the central nervous system, and the *postganglionic neurone* as belonging to the peripheral nervous system. The analogy between the somatic and visceral motor systems is illustrated by Fig. 1.62 which compares the two types of reflex. The motor neurone of the cord concerned with the viscus belongs to a group in the *intermediolateral column* of gray matter, and its axon emerges in the ventral root along with axons from the ventral horn governing the voluntary motor system.

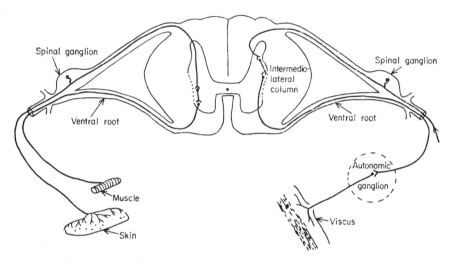

Fig. 1.62. A diagram of the somatic and visceral reflex arcs.

Sympathetic and Parasympathetic Division

The visceral system may be divided, on both functional and anatomical grounds, into a *sympathetic* and *parasympathetic* system. Functionally, they differ in that, when both branches innervate an organ, almost invariably the one is excitatory and the other inhibitory. Furthermore, the sympathetic motor axon usually (but not always) liberates noradrenaline as its transmitter, whilst the parasympathetic motor axon liberates acetylcholine. Anatomically the systems are distinguished by the origins of their motor neurones.

Sympathetic Division

In the sympathetic division, the preganglionic fibres are derived exclusively from the spinal cord, so that the reflex illustrated in Fig. 1.62 involves the sympathetic system. The spinal neurones relay, in the *sympathetic trunk,* a chain of ganglia running alongside the spinal cord as illustrated in Fig. 1.63. Alternatively they may pass through one of

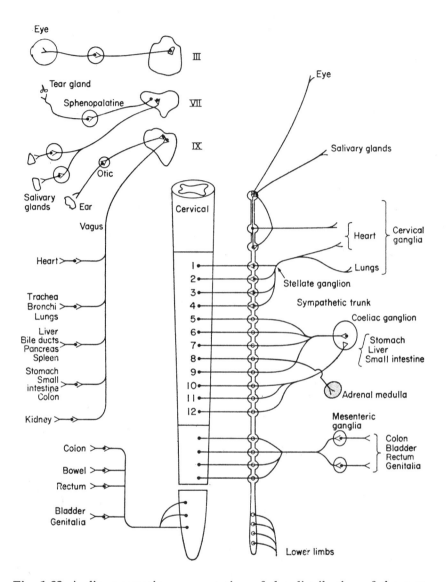

Fig. 1.63. A diagrammatic representation of the distribution of the sympathetic and parasympathetic parts of the autonomic system. On the left is the parasympathetic distribution with long preganglionic fibres and short postganglionic fibres, the parasympathetic ganglion being very close to the innervated organ. On the right is the sympathetic distribution with the chain of sympathetic ganglia alongside the cord. Note that there is a bilateral distribution of both systems and one from each side has been shown in the diagram.

these ganglia and relay in a more peripherally located ganglion close to the site of action, e.g. the coeliac ganglion lying on the abdominal aorta close to the stomach (Fig. 1.63). From the ganglion, postganglionic neurones send their axons to the effector site, e.g. the smooth muscle of the stomach wall, the smooth muscle of an arteriole, etc.

Ganglia. Not all segments of the cord give rise to a sympathetic outflow, which is confined to the segments T2 to L3. As Fig. 1.63 shows, however, there are ganglia on the sympathetic trunk corresponding to all segments except in the cervical region, where there are only the *superior, middle* (often absent), *intermediate* and *inferior cervical ganglia.* The inferior cervical ganglion is usually fused with the first thoracic, when it is called the *stellate ganglion.*

Postganglionic Pathways. The postganglionic axons pass to their effectors by one of two routes: either in the ventral root and its continuation as the spinal nerve, in which case its axon is mixed with those of the somatic motor system; alternatively the axon may pass along the large blood vessels, and reach its destination with these. It is this latter mode of innervation that makes it difficult, experimentally, to denervate a viscus, such as the stomach, completely. As indicated above, some of the spinal sympathetic neurones pass through the ganglia of the sympathetic trunk without relaying. They travel to the *collateral ganglia* in the abdomen which lie in special relation to the viscera; these collateral ganglia are the *coeliac,* and *superior* and *inferior mesenteric ganglia.* The fibres emerging from the sympathetic chain on their way to these ganglia make up the *splanchnic nerves.*

Parasympathetic Outflow

The parasympathetic outflow from the central nervous system is derived from certain cranial nerves, i.e. the oculomotor (N. III), the facial (N. VII), the glossopharyngeal (N. IX) and the vagus (N. X), and also from the second and third sacral roots of the spinal cord. The axons from the brain and cord do not relay in the ganglia of the sympathetic chain, but in peripherally located ganglia in close relation to the organ that they innervate.

Ciliary Nerves. Thus the autonomic fibres from the oculomotor nucleus in the brain-stem pass with the motor fibres innervating the voluntary striped muscles controlling the eye movements (Fig. 1.64), the extraocular muscles. Their function, however, is to control the smooth involuntary muscle within the eye, namely the ciliary muscle (controlling the accommodation process), and the sphincter muscle of the iris (controlling the size of the pupil). The fibres run to the *ciliary* *ganglion,* a small ganglion behind the globe of the eye in the orbit. From this ganglion, postganglionic fibres penetrate the globe as *short ciliary nerves,* and run to the appropriate muscles.

Vagus. The *vagus* has its motor neurones in the gray matter of the medulla (Fig. 1.54); the axons run to most of the abdominal viscera by way of various autonomic nerve plexuses in which, as well as in the organs themselves, are scattered the ganglia from which the postganglionic fibres are derived.

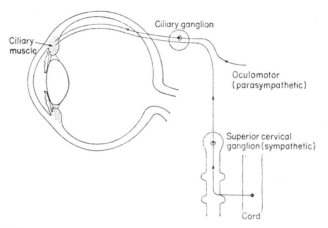

Fig. 1.64. The autonomic distribution to the ciliary muscle of the eye.

Sacral Outflow. The *sacral outflow* leaves the cord as the *pelvic visceral nerves,* or *nervi erigentes*; these supply the pelvic viscera. Thus erection of the penis results from the dilatation of the blood vessels caused by discharge in the nervi erigentes.

Sensory Inflow

The visceral sensory inflow to the brain and cord follows the sensory somatic pathway. Thus sensory fibres from the blood vessels of the skin are derived from neurones in the dorsal root nucleus. Sensory fibres from the cornea of the eye are derived from the Gasserian ganglion, the cranial equivalent of a dorsal root ganglion; they pass out of the eye in ciliary nerves. The axons from the Gasserian ganglion enter the brain-stem to relay in the gray matter called the sensory root of the trigeminal (N. V). Figure 1.65 illustrates schematically the general relations of the sympathetic and parasympathetic systems in the head region.

Although the viscera are, in general, remarkably insensitive to environmental change, at any rate in so far as conscious sensation is concerned, the actual sensory innervation is remarkably extensive. The vagus, for example, often considered as a predominantly motor nerve, controlling the heart, lungs and abdominal viscera, contains a majority of sensory fibres.

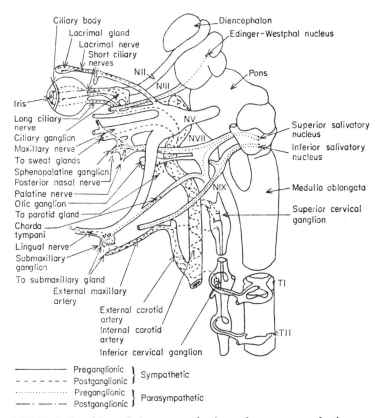

Fig. 1.65. Relationships of the sympathetic and parasympathetic nerves in the cephalic region. (Kuntz, "The Autonomic Nervous System", Lea and Febiger.)

Transmission in the Autonomic System

Transmission of messages from the central nervous system, i.e. the brain or spinal cord, to the effectors governed by the autonomic system, be they cardiac muscle fibres, smooth muscle fibres of the gastro-intestinal tract, or secretory cells of a variety of glands, involves two steps. These are transmission from a pre-synaptic to a post-synaptic neurone within a ganglion, and transmission from the terminal ramifications of the post-synaptic neurone on the effector cell.

Cholinergic Ganglionic Transmission

In general, the preganglionic fibres, be they of the parasympathetic or sympathetic division, are cholinergic and liberate acetylcholine at their terminals. These terminals contain characteristic vesicles similar to those at the neuromuscular junction. Thus we may experimentally perfuse the superior cervical ganglion of the sympathetic chain with an artificial blood, collecting the venous effluent, and by stimulating the ganglion in the presence of an inhibitor of cholinesterase, which prevents hydrolysis, we may collect the liberated acetylcholine. It was, in fact, the pioneering studies of Birks and McIntosh on this ganglion that provided a great deal of information about cholinergic transmission, information that assisted in planning comparable experiments on the neuromuscular junction.

Nicotine. The conditions of liberation are very similar in ganglion and neuromuscular junction, depending on a suitable concentration of Ca^{2+}, whilst transmission is blocked by high concentrations of Mg^{2+}. The action of the transmitter may be mimicked by nicotine, just as at the neuromuscular junction, so that autonomic transmission is another of the "nicotinic" actions of acetylcholine. High doses of nicotine, however, block transmission. This was the drug employed by Langley in determining whether a given preganglionic nerve actually relayed in a ganglion; if transmission was blocked by painting the ganglion with nicotine, a relay occurred; if not, since conduction along the axon was unaffected by nicotine, it could be stated that the nerve passed through without relaying.

Blocking Agents. As with the neuromuscular junction, curare blocks autonomic ganglionic transmission, whilst a number of synthetic compounds, such as *hexamethonium*, tend to block autonomic junctions specifically. If the number of methylene groups in the molecule is increased to ten, as in *decamethonium*, the drug has a preference for the neuromuscular junction, being a powerful muscle relaxant

$$CH_3-\overset{\overset{\displaystyle CH_3}{|}}{N^+}-(CH_2)_{10}-\overset{\overset{\displaystyle CH_3}{|}}{\underset{\underset{\displaystyle CH_3}{|}}{N^+}}-CH_3$$

Decamethonium

Post-synaptic Cholinergic Neurones

The post-synaptic neurones of the parasympathetic system are like-wise cholinergic, liberating acetylcholine at their terminals, so that parasympathetic action can be mimicked either by acetylcholine itself or by other compounds which, because of their chemical similarity, are parasympathomimetic. However, there is a subtle difference between the reactive groupings on the parasympathetically innervated effector cells, such as those of the heart, and those on the somatically innervated skeletal neuromuscular junctions. This difference is that nicotine does not mimic acetylcholine on these parasympathetically innervated organs, whereas *muscarine* does, and *vice versa*. Dale spoke of the *muscarinic action* of acetylcholine when he was referring to its action at parasympathetic postganglionic terminals, by contrast with the *nicotinic action* at the preganglionic terminal or at the neuromuscular junction. Whereas curare blocks the nicotinic action of acetylcholine, the specific blocker for the muscarinic action is atropine. Thus atropine causes a dry mouth because it blocks secretion of saliva, normally promoted by parasympathetic action; it causes a dilated pupil by blocking the tonic parasympathetic discharge to the pupilloconstrictor muscle of the iris, and so on.

Nicotinic and Muscarinic Receptors. In considering this difference in the way in which the action of acetylcholine may be brought about, we may imagine that there is a certain reactive grouping on the effector cell, e.g. on the muscle end-plate or on the secretory cell of the salivary gland. This reactive grouping is such that the acetylcholine molecule in some way fits on and thereby causes a depolarization of the membrane. At both the muscle end-plate and the secretory cell the receptive grouping accepts acetylcholine, but the groupings are different in a subtle way so that, although they both accept acetylcholine, the one cannot accept muscarine and the other cannot accept nicotine.

Pharmacological "Receptor"

In this connection we may note a terminology introduced by the pharmacologist, namely the use of the term *receptor* to characterize the special chemical grouping at a drug-sensitive site. Thus the pharmacologist would state that the parasympathetic receptor on the cardiac muscle was similar to that on intestinal muscle but different from that on skeletal muscle. To the physiologist this may be confusing, since to him the receptor is, or was, the cell responsive to environmental

7*

change, e.g. the rod or cone of the eye, sensitive to light, the hair-cell of the ear, and so on.

Post-synaptic Adrenergic Transmission

Most postganglionic neurones of the sympathetic system liberate the catecholamine, noradrenaline (Fig. 1.66), at their terminals, but there are exceptions (e.g. sympathetic fibres to the sweat glands

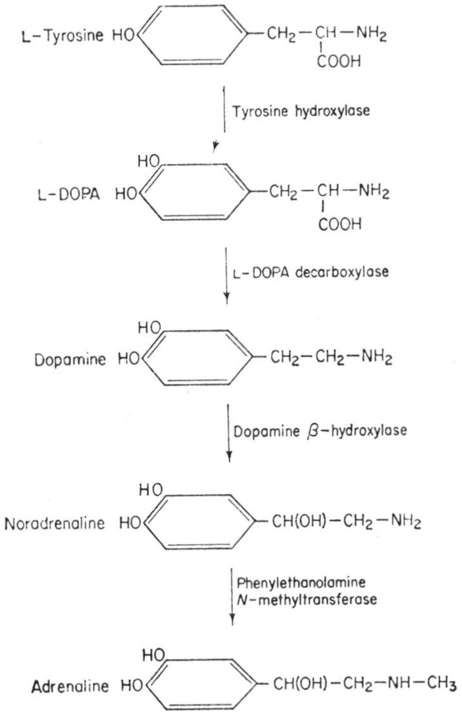

Fig. 1.66. The intermediate stages in the formation of adrenaline. (Blaschko, *Brit. Med. Bull.* 1972, **29,** 110.)

liberate acetylcholine), and hence it is advisable to use the terms *cholinergic* and *adrenergic* to describe the mode of action of a given autonomic effector system.

Noradrenaline Vesicles. The transmitter of the adrenergic neurone is localized in vesicles, where it can be recognized by its characteristic fluorescence after treatment with formaldehyde, as indicated earlier. In the electron microscope, moreover, the vesicles are distinguishable from cholinergic vesicles by the dense granular central core; they fall into two main size-groups—small, of 300–600 Å diameter with a central core of 150–250 Å, and large, of 600–1500 Å diameter with a core of 400–700 Å diameter. As we shall see, when discussing the section on smooth muscle, there are no well defined neuromuscular junctions or end-plates, as in fast skeletal muscle. However, in many instances the fine unmyelinated neurone forms varicosities or swellings in its course between muscle cells, and these varicosities are filled with the granular vesicles containing noradrenaline, which are presumably emptied, or partially emptied, of their contents in response to depolarization. The fluorescence technique enables quantitative estimates of the amount of noradrenaline in different parts of the neurone, and this varies from some 10–100 μg/g in the cell body and main axon to perhaps 10,000 μg/g in the terminal varicosities.

We have seen that there is a migration of vesicles from the perikaryon to the terminals, so that it might be suggested that transmitter was synthesized in the perikaryon and carried by this movement to the site of action at the terminals. However, the rate of turnover of the transmitter is so much greater than that which could be provided by such a movement that we must postulate local synthesis in the axon and terminals. Nevertheless, the perikaryon, containing as it does the protein- and lipid-synthetic machinery of the neurone, is necessary for providing the materials of the vesicles, i.e. its lipid membrane, and also for the enzymes and other proteins belonging to it.

Noradrenaline Synthesis. The steps in the synthesis of noradrenaline are indicated in Fig. 1.66, where it is seen that several enzymes are required for the total reaction, beginning with the hydroxylation of the amino acid tyrosine, to the final conversion of dopamine to noradrenaline. The enzyme for this last step, *dopamine β-hydroxylase*, is apparently confined to the vesicles, or at any rate it is the only one of the enzymes present in them, so that the final stage in synthesis must take place in the vesicles. The vesicles, moreover, have an active "pump" that enables them to remove dopamine rapidly from the cytoplasm. The remaining enzymes are present in the cytoplasm, and we may assume that tyrosine is taken up from the blood into the neurone where the synthetic process continues to the point of dopamine. The vesicles, manufactured in the perikaryon, migrate downwards, and since they contain the β-hydroxylase, the final step in synthesis occurs within them. Because of the slow turnover of vesicles, but rapid turnover of noradrenaline, we must assume that the emptying of the vesicle during transmission is not "all-or-none" but that, after losing some noradrenaline, the vesicle accumulates dopamine and makes further supplies of noradrenaline. However, because β-hydroxylase, and other proteins, are lost during exocytosis, eventually the vesicle be-comes "used up" and is replaced by a new one from the perikaryon.

Life-cycle of Vesicle. The hypothetical life-cycle of a vesicle is illustrated in Fig. 1.67. According to this, the presence of large and small vesicles is due to the circumstance that small vesicles result from partial emptying of the large ones, as indicated by Stage 3. These subsequently recycle during transmission until they become exhausted of transmitter.

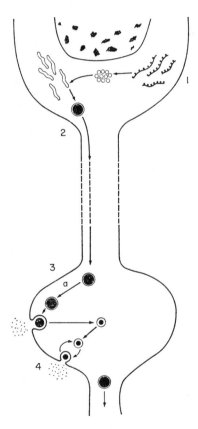

Fig. 1.67. Hypothetical life-cycle of synaptic vesicles in sympathetic neurone. Broken lines indicate shortening of axon for convenience of diagrammatic representation. Successive stages are: (1) synthesis of vesicle components in soma; (2) axoplasmic transport of vesicles to varicosities; (3) transformation of large vesicles into small ones occurs in axon terminals by exocytosis; (4) vesicles recycle during transmission until they become exhausted. (After Geffen and Livett, *Physiol. Rev.* 1971, **51,** 98.)

Catabolism of Noradrenaline

The metabolism of noradrenaline is complex, as illustrated by Fig. 1.68, which shows its catabolic pathways. It will be recalled that cholinesterase serves to hydrolyse transmitter after it has fulfilled its function at its effector cell, but that the liberated choline is not all wasted, a large fraction being recaptured and converted back to

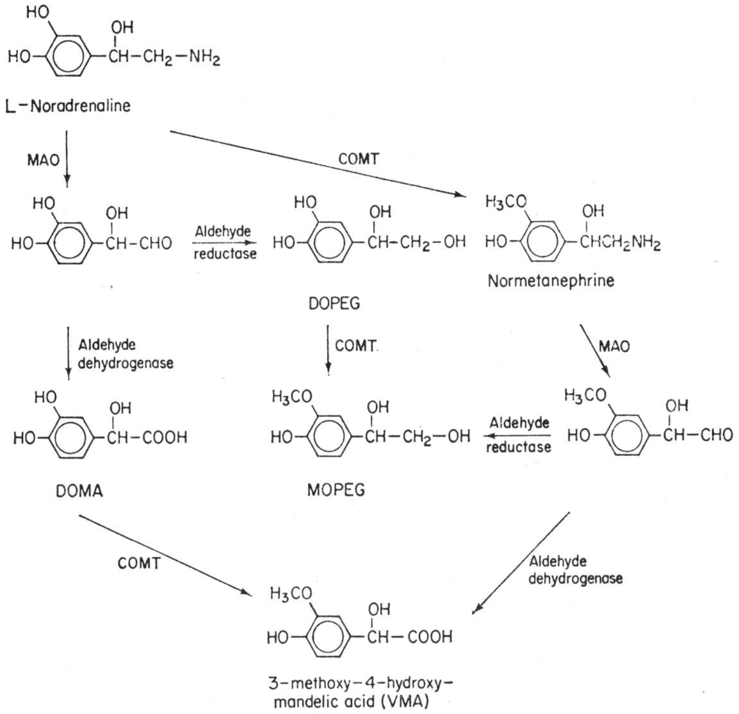

Fig. 1.68. The major pathways of noradrenaline catabolism. (Geffen and Livett, *Physiol. Rev.* 1971, **51**, 98.)

acetylcholine by the enzyme choline acetyl transferase. At the neuromuscular junction this hydrolysis is an important feature, since it prevents repetitive firing of the post-synaptic neurone. In the adrenergic system it seems that chemical inactivation of the transmitter does not play an important role in this respect, the main factor being uptake of the liberated noradrenaline by the neurone or effector tissue.

Uptake of Liberated Transmitter

Thus the neurone can actively take up noradrenaline, either liberated from its cytoplasm or injected experimentally into the extracellular space. This "amine pump" is similar to other active transport processes directed towards amino acids, sugars, etc. in that it apparently depends on a downhill movement of Na^+ (Vol. 1), maintained by a primary uphill active transport of this ion, a transport that is inhibited by ouabain. The process is also inhibited by cocaine, and this accounts for the potentiating action of cocaine on adrenergic transmission, since it causes the liberated transmitter to remain in contact with its effector cell for longer than normal.

Function of MAO

Nevertheless, there are enzymes that convert noradrenaline into inactive compounds, namely catechol-O-methyl transferase (COMT) and monoamine oxidase (MAO). MAO is located in the mitochondria but is by no means confined to the neurone—as much as a half of that in a tissue, such as the vas deferens, being extraneuronal. The enzyme MAO occurs in many tissues and thus is not exclusively concerned with adrenergic transmission. We shall see that many of the effects of noradrenaline may be mimicked by the hormone adrenaline, which has a widespread action, and since the enzyme will attack many amines, including adrenaline, it is presumably concerned with in-activation of the hormone. Within the nerve terminal the enzyme will clearly play a role in metabolizing any free transmitter outside the vesicles, presumably preventing the level from rising too high.

Importance for Noradrenaline Uptake. Moreover, the re-uptake of noradrenaline by the terminals, which represents the main "in-activation" process, seems to depend on the presence of MAO in the terminals, since this depends on the concentration of free intraneuronal amines in the cytoplasm. MAO keeps this concentration down and thus favours re-uptake, so that a MAO inhibitor actually causes an increase in catecholamines in the neurones. Its function within non-neuronal tissue, such as smooth muscle cells, may well be that of oxidation of transmitter, which, as we have seen, is taken up not only by the neurones that liberated it but also by adjacent effector cells.*

Function of COMT

The other metabolic pathway for catabolism of noradrenaline is through methylation, to give normetanephrine (Fig. 1.68), catalysed by the enzyme catecholamine O-methyl transferase, and thence a variety of products that have been identified in blood and tissues.

---

* MAO will oxidize a variety of primary, secondary and tertiary monoamines, so that 5-HT (serotonin), a probable central transmitter, and dopamine, besides adrenaline and noradrenaline, are affected by inhibitors of the enzyme.

The enzyme is probably responsible for catabolism of extracellular transmitter.

Effects of Enzyme Inhibitors. In the adrenergic system the removal of transmitter, necessary to curtail the duration of its action, is brought about largely by a re-uptake mechanism, as opposed to the destruction that takes place in the cholinergic system. In consequence, we need not expect an inhibitor of catecholamine destruction, such as Marsalid (which inhibits MAO) to potentiate the action of noradrenaline. This is generally true; inhibitors of MAO certainly have actions, but this is quite often due to a mimicking of the action of noradrenaline because of their similar chemical composition, or else the general effects on amine metabolism lead to pronounced pharmacological effects.

Release and Resynthesis of Noradrenaline

The synthesis of noradrenaline must occur continuously, to make up for material lost through the catabolic pathways. The strong dependence of functional activity on replacement is revealed by the effects of the drug reserpine, which leads to a virtual adrenergic denervation of the animal through depletion of its stores of transmitter. The effect is not a simple blockage of the synthetic pathway, but in the functional activities of the vesicles, preventing them from accumulating and storing amine, so that recovery from reserpine involves synthesis of a new set of vesicles; thus the longer the nerve, the longer the time for recovery from reserpine action.

Model. A variety of experimental studies have led to the picture of noradrenaline storage, release, synthesis and breakdown, illustrated by Fig. 1.69. Within the vesicle the bulk is stored as a complex with protein—chromogranin—ATP and Ca^{2+}; in this form it has little osmotic activity, and thus presents no problems of osmotic lysis due to the hyperosmolality were the noradrenaline free in solution. This store is in equilibrium with a mobilized form, NA_2, within the vesicle, and which is in dynamic equilibrium with the cytoplasmic store, NA_3. Synaptic liberation involves partial exocytosis in which, besides noradrenaline, chromogranins, including β-hydroxylase, are liberated.

β-Hydroxylase. The key factor in controlling the synthesis of noradrenaline from tyrosine, within the neurone, is the circumstance that the first step in this synthesis, catalysed by tyrosine hydroxylase, is rate-limiting, and is inhibited by noradrenaline—*product inhibition.* Thus, as noradrenaline is used up through transmitter action and catabolism by MAO and COMT, the cytoplasmic concentration falls; this causes disinhibition of the tyrosine hydroxylase, thereby accelerating synthesis of dopamine, which enters the vesicle and is converted to noradrenaline.

Specificity. The catecholamine transmitter released by the postganglionic neurone at its effector site is noradrenaline. As indicated earlier there are other monoamines that act as transmitters [i.e.,

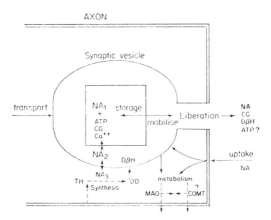

Fig. 1.69. Topochemical model of sympathetic transmission. (The NA represents noradrenaline.) The transmitter is contained principally within the synaptic vesicles in a bound form (NA_1) together with ATP, chromogranins (CG), and Ca^{2+}. NA_1 exchanges with unbound but intravesicular norepinephrine (NA_2), which is derived from uptake and synthesis across the vesicle membrane. NA_2 in turn exchanges with a small extravesicular pool (NA_3) which is derived from uptake across the axon membrane and outward diffusion from the vesicles. NA_3 is susceptible to the action of monoamine oxidase (MAO) in mitochondria and possibly catechol-O-methyltransferase (COMT). Nerve impulses liberate transmitter and other soluble constituents of the vesicle by a process of partial exocytosis. Vesicle stores of norepinephrine are replenished by drawing on NA_3, thus removing inhibition of tyrosine hydroxylase (TH) and accelerating synthesis of norepinephrine through dopa decarboxylase (DD) and dopamine β-hydroxylase (DβH). The important contribution to the functional compartmentation of transmitter stores of the distribution of the vesicle population within a nerve terminal and of impulse activity between different nerves is not shown. (Geffen and Livett, *Physiol. Rev.* 1971, **51**, 98.)

dopamine and 5-hydroxytryptamine (5-HT)] and their general behaviour, in so far as re-uptake by neuronal membranes and storage in granules are concerned, is similar to that of noradrenaline. It is interesting that storage within the granule is highly specific so that a noradrenaline-containing neurone will not *store* dopamine or 5-HT, and, in fact, the requirements for storage are remarkably rigorous;

this is in marked contrast to the active pump mechanisms that transport the transmitter across the neuronal or granule membrane, where selectivity is not marked. Thus, it seems that the *storage* function, as opposed to the *transport* function of the granule, or neuronal membrane, is the determining factor where accumulation of a transmitter in a given neurone is concerned.

Adrenaline

The strong analogy between the action of adrenaline, the hormone secreted by the medulla of the adrenal gland, and the effects of sympathetic stimulation, led to the belief that adrenaline was the transmitter at the sympathetic nerve terminals. Thanks to the work of Von Euler, however, the non-methylated primary amine, *noradrenaline,* has been identified as the transmitter (p. 108).

TABLE II

Actions mediated by α and β receptors (After Jenkinson, *Br. Med. Bull.*)

System or Tissue	Action	Receptor
Heart	Increased rate and force	β
Blood Vessels	Constriction	α
	Dilatation	β
Bronchial Smooth Muscle	Relaxation	β
Longitudinal Muscle of Gut	Relaxation	β
Gut Sphincters	Constriction	α
	Relaxation	β
Uterus	Contraction	α
	Relaxation	β
Bladder	Contraction (mainly trigone)	α
	Relaxation (mainly detrusor)	β
Adipose tissue	Increased lipolysis	β

Alpha and Beta Actions. Adrenaline, usually liberated at times when the sympathetic system is being activated (as in fear), will usually mimic the action of noradrenaline at sympathetic terminals—for example, it will accelerate the heart—but it has been shown to have two types of activity on an organ. These have been described by Ahlquist as *alpha* and *beta* actions, due to the presence of *alpha* or *beta* types of receptive groupings (receptors) on the effector membrane. Thus, as indicated by Table II, the alpha receptor, when activated by adrenaline, usually excites, causing vasoconstriction, cardiac acceleration, dilatation of the iris, and so on; beta receptors usually mediate inhibition, e.g. relaxation of blood vessels. Noradrenaline, and thus adrenergic excitation, is thought to act mainly on the alpha receptors whilst adrenaline acts on both, so that its effects on a tissue are usually complex. The beta activity is imitated by the synthetic compound *isoproterenol* (*isoprenaline* or *isopropylnoradrenaline*). The alpha action is blocked by ergotoxin, phentolamine and dibenamine, whilst the beta action is blocked by dichloroisoprenaline, propanolol, and practolol.*

Long and Short Sympathetic Neurones

As conventionally indicated, the sympathetic outflow consists of a preganglionic neurone, with its cell body in the spinal cord, which relays either in the chain of ganglia close to the spinal cord (Fig. 1.70a) or in a collateral ganglion, such as the inferior mesenteric ganglion which acts as relay station for the sympathetic supply to the genitalia, etc. (Fig. 1.70b). Thus postganglionic sympathetic fibres running from, say, the inferior mesenteric ganglion in the hypogastric nerve would be treated as post-synaptic, the axons being derived from neurones with their cell bodies in the ganglion (Fig. 1.70b). On this basis, then, a ganglion-blocking agent should have no effect on the sympathetic response to stimulating the hypogastric nerve, e.g. the contraction of the vas deferens, since the nerve would run direct to the effector without further relay. In fact, however, the blocking agent does obliterate the response, suggesting that the sympathetic fibres in the hypogastric nerve, running to the pelvic organs of the urogenital tract, are preganglionic, relaying with postganglionic neurones in small ganglia in close relation to the vas deferens and other pelvic organs, in a similar fashion to the parasympathetic system (Fig. 1.70c). Thus the postganglionic neurone is long in Fig. 1.70a and short in Fig. 1.70c, and modern methods of identification of sympathetic neurones, by virtue of their noradrenaline content, have confirmed this arrangement.

"Receptors"

The depolarization of the post-synaptic membrane by the transmitter is so highly specific that we must postulate the binding of the transmitter with a specific chemical grouping in the cell membrane, a grouping presumably located to a specific macromolecule, be it protein, lipid, or lipoprotein. As indicated earlier, this grouping is described as a "receptor". Modern research on the mechanism of transmission is directed to isolation of the receptors concerned in

* More recent work has suggested sub-classification of the β-receptors (see Vol. 3 Ch. 2).

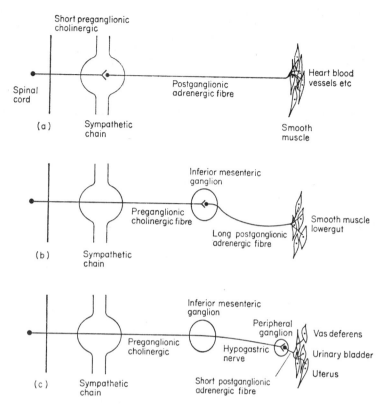

Fig. 1.70. The organization of the sympathetic innervation showing the various types of adrenergic neurones. (a) The short preganglionic type with the long postganglionic fibre, which originates from the sympathetic chain, supplying, for example, heart and blood vessels. (b) Intermediate type with the sympathetic ganglion not in the sympathetic chain, found in the gut. (c) The long preganglionic type with the short postganglionic fibre; the sympathetic ganglion in this case lies within the tissue, e.g. vas deferens, uterus and urinary bladder. (Modified from Livett, *Brit. Med. Bull.* 1973, **28**, 93.)

cholinergic and adrenergic transmissions; the first step is to label the receptor *in situ* and subsequently to release the labelled material from the membrane.

Isolation

A useful starting point is the electric organ of certain fishes; this may be regarded as a massive end-plate, or series of end-plates, weighing many grammes, and activated by a cholinergic mechanism. The best label is clearly a substance with very similar specificity in its affinity for the receptor, but which binds much more strongly so as to remain bound during the subsequent preparative steps. Many inhibitors of transmission exert their effects precisely because their affinity for the binding site on the post-synaptic membrane is very high, so that the inhibitor, e.g. curare, prevents access by the true transmitter, acetylcholine. Thus ^{14}C-curare was one of the first labels used in an attempt to isolate a protein from the electric organ that corresponded with the "receptor substance". The label employed by Miledi was the snake venom, bungarotoxin.

Binding of Drugs

When a suitable label has been found for the receptor, the preparative techniques may be developed, and subsequently the binding of a range of drugs, e.g. carbachol, muscarone, nicotine, etc. may be

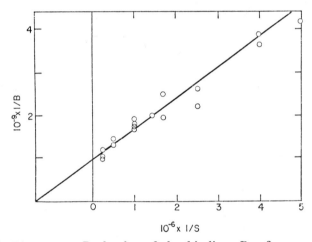

Fig. 1.71. Lineweaver–Burk plot of the binding, B, of muscarone to a preparation of electroplax. The reciprocal of the binding, 1/B, is placed against the reciprocal of the concentration of muscarone, 1/S. (O'Brien *et al.*, *Proc. Nat. Acad. Sci., Wash.* 1970, **65,** 441.)

measured quantitatively. The binding may be measured, as with comparable studies on hormone binding to their carrier proteins (p. 145), the receptor preparation being placed in a dialysis-sac and surrounded by a saline medium. A known amount of, say, acetylcholine is added and the concentration in the outer medium determined at equilibrium. From this, and the amount added, the fraction bound to the receptor material can be computed. The binding at different concentrations may be plotted as a Lineweaver–Burk plot (Vol. 1) and from this an affinity constant may be determined as in Fig. 1.71.

Pitfalls

If the "pharmacology" of the preparation agrees reasonably well with the natural pharmacology, i.e. if the relative affinities for a series of cholinergic drugs are in the same order, then we may be fairly certain that we are dealing with material containing the receptive substance, but of course there are many pitfalls. Thus acetylcholinesterase is a protein closely associated with the receptors for acetylcholine, and its affinity for cholinergic drugs is very similar to that of the receptor itself, as we should expect. It is important, therefore, to be certain that the preparation of, say, the cholinergic receptor is not acetylcholinesterase. The preparation described by Edelfrawi from the electroplax of the electric eel could be differentiated from cholinesterase, since by centrifuging at 100,000 g, all the binding power for acetylcholine could be removed, yet the supernatant fluid still contained some cholinesterase activity. The material was inactivated by chymotrypsin and trypsin, and also by phospholipase C, so that a lipo-protein structure may be postulated.

CHAPTER 2

Hormonal Control

The nervous control of physiological processes studied in the previous chapter is brought about by the propagation of an electrical change in the neurone. This change in the state of the neurone is initiated by some sort of chemical influence on its surface, such as, for example, when the neurone has been directly excited by another. This excited neurone likewise exerts its effect, almost invariably, on the effector cell by means of a chemical liberated from its endings, the *neurotransmitter*, such as acetylcholine, noradrenaline, dopamine, and so on. In this way organs, spatially remote from the central controlling system, can be kept under control. An additional mode of control, also capable of operating over large distances, is provided by the *hormones* which are carried in the blood-stream from their point of secretion by the controlling gland or tissue to their "target" tissue or organ.

HORMONES

Hormone is the name given by Bayliss and Starling to the active principle in an extract of duodenum which, when injected into the blood, caused secretion of juice by the pancreas. The experiment was carried out because it had been found that in an isolated piece of small intestine, i.e. without nervous connections with the rest of the animal, there was a copious secretion of juice by the pancreas when acid was placed into the lumen. Thus the loop of intestine, with its intact blood supply but unable to communicate with the nervous system, was able to provoke secretion by ejecting into the blood a chemical agent, called *secretin*, that activated the secretory cells.

Endocrine Glands

In this case the chemical, which has since been identified as a polypeptide, is synthesized by certain specific cells belonging to the intestinal tissue. The hormones subserving other control mechanisms (such as *prolactin*, controlling milk secretion, *thyroxine*, controlling metabolic rate, and many others) are synthesized and stored in special organs called *glands*, and because the secretions, by their very nature, are ejected into the blood-stream in order for them to exert their control functions, they are called glands of internal secretion or *endocrine glands*. This differentiates them from the glands of external secretion, or *exocrine* glands, such as the salivary, sebaceous and sweat glands, whose secretions are ejected on to the surface of the body.

Pancreas

The interior of the gastro-intestinal tract may be regarded as an extension of the surface of the body, so that the pancreatic, gastric, duodenal, etc. secretions are legitimately called exocrine. However, the pancreas, which, as we have seen, secretes the enzymes for intestinal digestion, is also an endocrine gland, synthesizing two hormones, *insulin* and *glucagon*, controlling carbohydrate metabolism. In general, then, an endocrine secretion is a hormone operating in a control mechanism, whilst an exocrine secretion is not a hormone in the accepted sense of the word.* The exocrine secretion usually contains enzymes, but not necessarily, as with the sweat glands, whose function is that of moistening and not digestive. In the mixed gland, such as the pancreas, the cells of origin of the different secretions are easily distinguishable. Thus the exocrine cells, producing the enzymatic mixture that must be ejected into the gut, are organized into acini (Vol. 1) and their secretions are identified as well defined granules that are ejected into the acinus-lumen by a process of exocytosis (Vol. 1).

α- and β-Cells. The endocrine cells are easily differentiated. Those synthesizing insulin occupy the so-called *islets of Langerhans*, the cells constituting them being called *beta cells*. Their synthesized hormone may be recognized by the fluorescent antibody technique (Vol. 1) in granules within the cells. The other enzyme, glucagon, is contained within the alpha cells of the islets. Again, a gland such as the pituitary, which secretes a number of different hormones, is composed of different types of secretory cell (each type probably responsible for a single secretion) stored in granules within the cytoplasm.

Peptides and Proteins

The chemical nature of the hormones varies widely. Some are made up of amino acids which are described as polypeptides when the

* The word "hormone" is derived from the Greek word meaning to arouse.

number of such amino acids is fewer than a hundred and proteins when it is greater; thus oxytocin and vasopressin (Fig. 2.1), from the posterior pituitary, contain only eight amino acids. The hypothalamic "releasing factor" that causes secretion of the thyrotropic hormone,

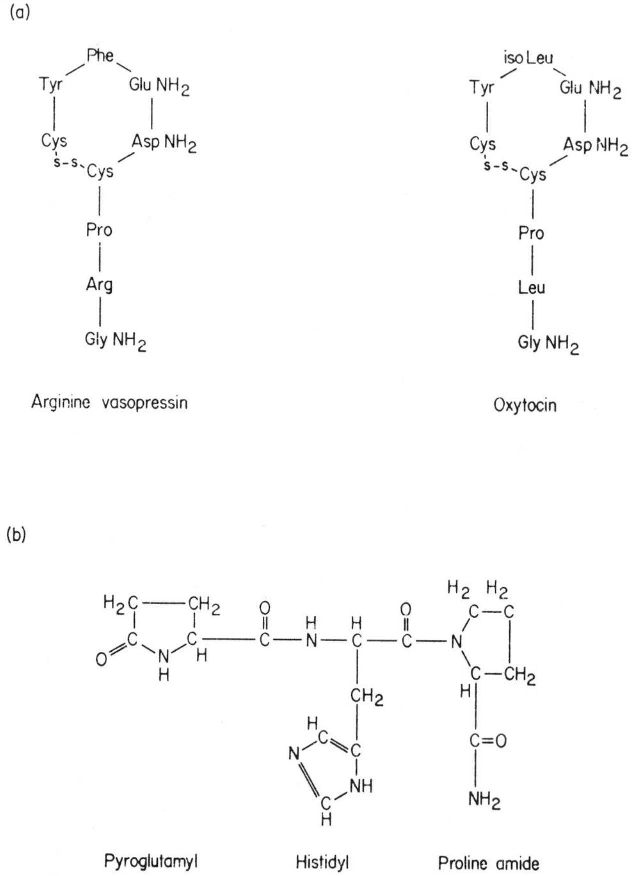

(a)

Arginine vasopressin

Oxytocin

(b)

Pyroglutamyl   Histidyl   Proline amide

Fig. 2.1. The formulae of vasopressin and oxytocin, released from the posterior pituitary gland and the thyroid stimulating hormone releasing factor TSHRF which controls the release of TSH from the anterior pituitary (b).

TSH, is a tripeptide; insulin contains 150 in two interlinked chains, as illustrated in Fig. 2.2. The secretions of the anterior pituitary are glycoproteins of molecular weights varying between 25,000 and 50,000. The polypeptide hormones are interesting in that, with some at any rate, their activity can be mimicked by quite a small sequence of amino acids. For example the hormone gastrin consists of a polypeptide chain of seventeen amino acids, yet the activity of the hormone can be evoked by the C-terminal tetrapeptide; on the other hand the hormone secretin, with 27 amino acids, requires to be intact if it is to show significant activity.

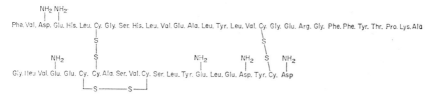

Fig. 2.2. The structure of insulin. (Sanger, *Brit. Med. Bull.* 1960, **16,** 183.)

Steroids

Another class of substances is given by the steroids, the chemical basis for the secretions of the adrenal cortex and sex hormones. The basic skeleton of these molecules is a saturated phenanthrene ring to which is attached a five-membered ring (Fig. 2.3); thus cholesterol, the constituent of cell membranes and of the myelin sheath of nerve, occurs in the blood and forms the basis for the synthesis of many steroid hormones; some examples are shown in Fig. 2.4.

Nomenclature of Steroid Compounds.* Many biologically active steroid compounds are now known and more are being described almost daily. No student can be expected to remember the formulae of all these compounds, but it is of importance that he should be able to identify the formula from the name if necessary. The method of naming these compounds is based on conventions which form a language and the object of this section is to explain the rules of this briefly, so that the student may be able to construe it. To have a key to this language is no less important for the student of physiology than for the student of chemistry. More detailed accounts will be found in Klyne (1957), Fieser and Fieser (1959) and Shoppee (1964).

The basic carbon skeleton of steroids is a tetracyclic compound with one five-membered ring and three six-membered rings, *cyclopentanophenanthrene*. The rings are called A, B, C, and D, and the carbon atoms are numbered as in Fig. 2.3(a). All lines have a single carbon atom at each end.

All the free carbon valencies are filled by hydrogen atoms which are not drawn in. There are three places in the basic tetracyclic nucleus at which carbon containing side chains are found—R_1, R_2 and R_3. R_2 and R_1 are usually methyl groups containing, thus, only 1 carbon atom each. These are called "angular" methyl groups and their carbons are numbered 18 and 19 respectively. The R_3 chain can contain up to 10 carbon atoms which are numbered from 20 upwards. The actual chain above is that of *cholestane*. The tetracyclic nucleus may be regarded for the sake of simplicity as approximately flat, though it need not always be so. In it there are seven asymmetrical carbon atoms, i.e. atoms in which all four valency bonds are attached to different neighbouring atoms. These centres of asymmetry are atoms 5, 8, 9,

* Reproduced from "Principles of Human Physiology" (Eds. Davson and Eggleton) 14th edition, 1968, by kind permission of Dr. R. D. Harkness and J. and A. Churchill.

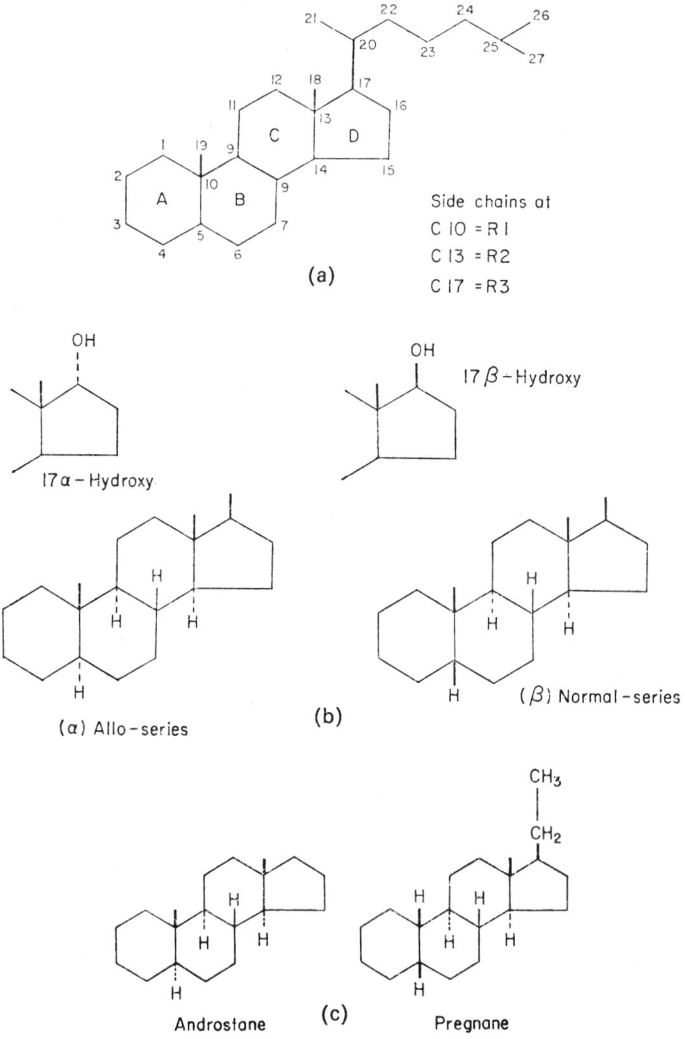

Fig. 2.3. The cyclopentophenanthrene ring. An explanation of the nomenclature of steroids is given in the text.

10, 13, 14 and 17. At these points the free valency of the carbon, i.e. the one which
does not form part of the ring system, may either project at an angle towards the
reader, forwards from the plane of the ring which is supposed to be in the plane of
the page, or it may project backwards out of the other side of the paper away from
the reader. The former direction can be indicated by the convention of a thick line,
the latter by a dotted line. In naming the compounds the direction is conventionally
given relative to the direction of the angular methyl groups (R_2 and R_1, carbons 18

and 19) which project forwards. Substituents or H atoms which project forwards in the same direction as the angular methyl groups are labelled β, those that project backwards in the opposite direction α as shown in Fig. 2.3(b). If the configuration is not known it may be specified by the Greek letter ζ (*xi*).

A special nomenclature is used to describe the configuration of C 5. If this configuration is β the relation of rings A and B is said to be *cis* and the compounds are called *normal*-compounds. If the configuration is α the relation of rings A and B is said to be *trans* and the compounds are called *allo*-compounds.

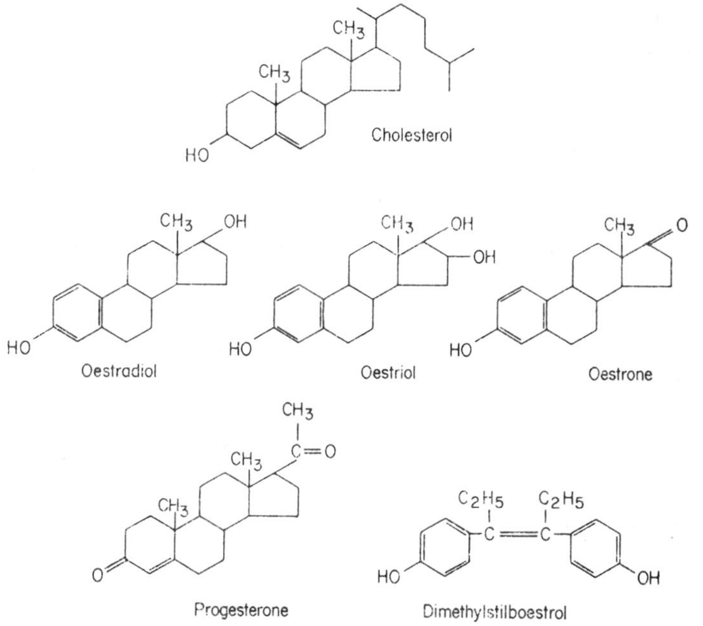

Fig. 2.4. The chemical structure of cholesterol, some oestrogens and progesterone. Diethylstilboestriol is a synthetic molecule with hormone-like activity.

The relation of rings A and B is trans in most natural steroids and so is the relation of C and D. Any compound which differs from the typical steroid in configuration of a C–C or C–H link at a site of nuclear asymmetry other than C 5 is known as an *iso*-compound; for example if in the above two compounds the H at C 14 had the β configuration instead of the α, as now, these would be called the 14-*iso* compounds. If the asymmetry involves an OH group rather than a C–C or a C–H link the compound is described as an *epi*-compound. In all names the number of the C atom is put before other descriptions referring to it, for example the compound above is described as 14-*iso*. If the same description refers to two carbon atoms they are written together as for example 3β: 17α-dihydroxy meaning that there is a hydroxyl group on both the 3 and 17 carbon atoms, and in this case that on the 3 has the β configuration, on the 17 the α configuration. Double bonds in the rings are specified by the Greek capital Δ (delta) or the suffix -ene or -en after the first of the carbons between which the bond goes, for example Δ^4 or 4-ene means a double bond between C 4 and C 5. If the double bond is not to the next carbon numerically, the carbon to which it goes is put in brackets, for example 5(10)-ene.

In steroids with a side chain at C 17 this may also have asymmetrical carbon atoms, e.g. C 20 of which the two isomers are distinguished by the suffixes α and β.

Because full names may be unwieldy, shorter ones are often used to describe a basic structure which several compounds have in common, for example the whole compound shown at the beginning of this section is called *cholestane* if at C 5 the hydrogen is in the α (trans) configuration to C 10; and *coprostane* if it is in the β (cis) configuration. Coprostane could be called 5β-cholestane. Basic structures which will occur later in nomenclature are given in Fig. 2.3(c). In such basic structure the name is terminated by the syllable -*ane*.

Two other points require mention; firstly the use of the prefix *aetio-*. This means that the C 17 side chain has been lost and replaced by hydrogen; for example, androstane above might be called aetio-coprostane. Secondly the use of the prefix *nor-* which means that a methyl group has been replaced by H. This prefix is said originally to have stood in German for "N ohne Radicale" or "N without radical" (cf. *nor*-adrenaline).

Nervous and Endocrine Mechanisms

In general, the essential difference between the nervous and hormonal control systems is the fact that the nervous system is concerned with short-term measures of adaptation to a given situation (an adaptation that must, of its nature, be rapid) whilst the endocrine system controls longer-term adaptations.

Thus the acceleration of the heart and constriction of the peripheral arterioles at the onset of vigorous physical exercise are brought about by direct nervous control over the target organs operating through the sympathetic nervous system. These immediate adaptations to a situation demanding physical exertion are reinforced and sustained by endocrine secretions, notably those of the adrenal medulla, which liberates adrenaline and noradrenaline into the blood-stream. These ensure that the vascular adaptations are maintained, and also accelerate the production of metabolic energy through increased transport of sugar and amino acids into the liver, and so on.

Growth and Development. Again, the control of growth, involving the control over a variety of syntheses, is essentially a hormonal phenomenon, whether it be the growth of the whole animal (as with *growth hormone* of the pituitary) or of special tissues to meet the demands of pregnancy (as with the ovarian hormone, *oestradiol*, which is responsible for uterine growth or *prolactin* that controls the development of the mammary glands). Here the actions of the hormone are difficult to differentiate from those of an essential metabolite or vitamin. Thus maintained growth of the uterus during pregnancy requires the continuous secretion of oestrogens which pass into the uterine cells to their nuclei and are subsequently released and finally excreted. The amounts of hormone synthesized by the ovary or placenta and ultimately excreted may amount to one or more grammes per day in a pregnant woman, representing an apparently extravagant use of this humoral control factor.

Transmitters and Hormones

Nervous and hormonal controls have a great deal in common in so far as they both utilize chemical agents in their mechanism of activation of the effector, or target organs. In the one case the agents are called *transmitters*, or neurohumours, and in the other they are called *hormones*, and the essential difference in the two modes of control is the circumstance that the hormones are carried bodily in the blood-stream from the control point to the point of action whilst the nervous transmitters are released by "remote control" from stores in the nerve endings, which make very close contact with the effectors. The latter method has the obvious advantage of rapid and direct communication with the effector organ, as opposed to the slower and more diffuse communication provided by a substance liberated into the main blood-stream and therefore carried to all tissues of the body.

Hypothalamus. In general, as we shall see, the two methods of control are very closely interlinked; thus the liberation of the hormones adrenaline and noradrenaline by the adrenal medulla is itself brought about by excitation of the sympathetic innervation of the gland. Such excitation is mediated through the hypothalamus which, we have seen, is very closely related to the control over visceral functions. Thus, centres in the hypothalamus are capable of activating the visceral organs separately, through their direct neural connections, and more generally through this activation of the adrenal medulla.

Storage and Release of Hormones

The analogy between the neurotransmitter and humoral processes extends to the mode of storage and release of the respective factors. Thus we have seen that the neurotransmitter is stored in vesicles which empty by a process of exocytosis in response to depolarization of the nerve terminal and penetration of Ca^{2+}. Many of the endocrine cells secreting hormones were early recognized by the classical cytologists by their contents of "granules", which, in the electron microscope, could be shown to be membrane-covered vesicles; separation of these vesicles by ultra-centrifugal methods showed that they contained the specific hormone. Where a gland secreted several hormones, the different hormones were shown to be confined to specific types of cell and the release of a given hormone could be recognized often by the depletion of the granules confined to a specific cell type.

Synthesis

It must be emphasized, however, that storage of hormones in vesicles represents only a supply for immediate use. This is similar to the transmitter stored in the nerve terminals which will only suffice for a limited number of post-synaptic potentials; when synthesis of transmitter is blocked, repetitive stimulation of the nerve soon leads to failure of transmission. Thus nerve stimulation is accompanied normally by a signal for accelerated synthesis of transmitter. In the same way stimulation of hormonal secretion, e.g. by a trophic hormone, is followed not only by release but by synthesis. In fact the amount of hormone in a gland is employed very frequently as a measure of its secretory activity, i.e. of its *output*, the provoked synthesis far out-weighing the immediate loss. When the output of steroid hormones by the adrenal cortex was measured under the influence of ACTH, it was found that, during the first ten minutes, there was no increased output, but only increased synthesis. By 40 minutes there was some output, but the gland still contained as much as it had after the ten-minute interval, suggesting that the gland only secretes its hormone when it has built up a critical level in the tissue by synthesis.

Steroid Storage

With the steroid hormones, storage in well-defined granules seems not to occur, and this may well reflect the lipid character of the hormones, their probable sites of accumulation being lipid droplets or the membranes of the Golgi apparatus, just as with the synthesis and accumulation of fat in mammary cells (Ch. 5). Since the hormones are secreted in a more water-soluble conjugated form, e.g. as sulphate or glucuronide, it is likely that this conjugation takes place in the Golgi apparatus, the site of sulphation of mucopolysaccharides.

Ca^{2+} and Release

It seems very likely that the release of hormone, stored in granules, from the endocrine cell is similar in mechanism to the release of neuro-transmitter (such as noradrenaline and acetylcholine) which is itself similar to the release of secretions by the exocrine glands. In all cases the material is contained in a granule or vesicle which fuses with the cell membrane, allowing release of the contents to the exterior (p. 135). The evidence implicating entry of Ca^{2+} into the secretory cell is very strong in the case of the neuromuscular synapse, and Douglas has extended this concept to both exocrine and endocrine secretion, the common event in this "excitation–secretion coupling" being the increased concentration of ionized calcium in the cytoplasm. We have seen that colchicine, which inhibits microtubular activity, blocks migration of transmitter vesicles along the nerve axon, and it is interesting that it also blocks release of hormones from some, but not all, glandular cells, e.g. glucagon from a-cells of the pancreas, or ACTH from the pituitary.

Action Potential

In certain instances it may well be that the primary event is a depolarization of the secretory cell; thus Dean and Matthews showed that the resting potential of the pancreatic islet cells was dependent on the glucose concentration of the medium; moreover, action potentials could also be recorded and the number of cells discharged increased

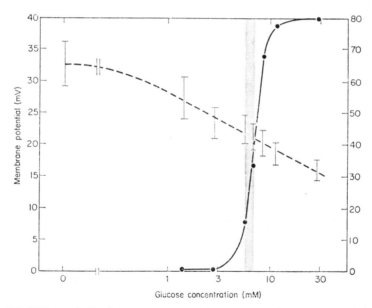

Fig. 2.5. Effect of D-glucose concentration on membrane potential and electrical activity in cells of the pancreatic islets. Membrane potential (dashed line) SE of mean indicated by vertical bar. Electrical activity: expressed as the percentage of impaled cells which show action potential discharge (continuous line). The stippled column shows the normal range of blood glucose concentration in the mouse. (Dean and Matthews, *J. Physiol.* 1970, **210,** 255.)

from a threshold at 4 mM glucose to a maximum at 28 mM corresponding precisely to the dependence of insulin secretion on glucose concentration (Fig. 2.5). The electrical response to glucose concentration depended on the external concentration of Ca^{2+} just as the rate of insulin secretion depended on this variable.

Non-Granular Secretions. With the steroid hormones, e.g. those of the adrenal cortex, the absence of a storage mechanism in the form of granules might well require a different form of activation. Thus the

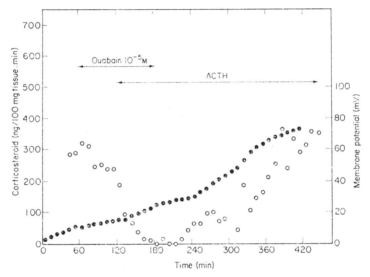

Fig. 2.6. The independence of corticosteroid secretion on the cellular membrane potential in the isolated adrenal cortex. Corticosteroid production (filled circles); membrane potential (open circles). Effect of ouabain 10^{-5} M on the response to ACTH (10 mu/ml). Open circles are means of membrane potentials in successive 10 min periods. (Matthews and Saffram, *J. Physiol.* 1973, **234,** 43.)

stimulus in this case is probably simply the stimulus to synthesize the hormone, its release requiring no special mechanism. By contrast with a hormone stored in the form of granules, such as insulin, the stimulus is first to bring about exocytosis and second to induce synthesis to replenish stores. In fact, studies on the influence of external ions and membrane potential on steroid synthesis by isolated adrenal cortex have shown a marked independence of secretion and membrane potential (Fig. 2.6). External Ca^{2+} is important so that synthesis may be blocked by complete sequestration of this by EDTA, but it seems likely that Ca^{2+} is also important for a step in hormone synthesis (perhaps the induction of enzyme synthesis), rather than for any mechanical events such as seems the case with granule-containing endocrine cells.

THE PITUITARY GLAND

Another, and interesting mode of control over the secretion by an endocrine gland is shown in the relations between hypothalamus and the pituitary gland. This is a gland of internal secretion, situated in close relation to the brain, that plays a central role in the endocrine control of bodily activities and represents the primary mechanism through which the neural and endocrine control mechanisms are integrated. It is enabled to play this role, first through its close neural connections with the central nervous system, having a direct connection with the hypothalamus through the *hypothalamohypophyseal tract*, and secondly by being able, not only to liberate specific hormones of its own—e.g. growth hormone controlling growth processes—but also to liberate several hormones whose function is to stimulate other endocrine glands, such as the thyroid, to liberate their hormones.

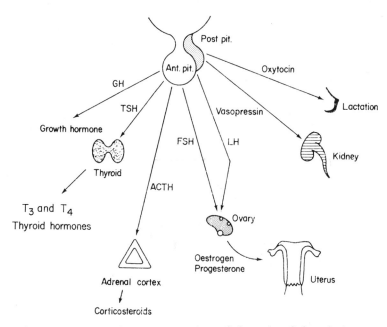

Fig. 2.7. A diagrammatic representation of the role of the pituitary gland in endocrine secretion. The pituitary hormones are indicated on each arrow and the principal target organ. No feed-back routes are shown or hypothalamic releasing mechanisms.

Thyroid Stimulating Hormone

Thus the thyroid gland is not under direct nervous control since it continues to function normally in controlling metabolic rate, whether it is in its correct position or whether it has been transplanted to another part of the body and separated from its nerve supply. So long as its vascular supply is adequate, it will function; and this means that it not only sends its outward control messages chemically through the blood but it also receives its control messages by the same medium, and it is the *thyroid stimulating hormone*—TSH—liberated from the pituitary and carried to the thyroid gland in the general blood stream, that provokes the liberation of thyroxine. This, in turn, accelerates the metabolic activities of the tissues (Fig. 2.7). TSH is a mucoprotein of molecular weight 25,000–28,000.

Structure of Pituitary Gland

Neurohypophysis and Adenohypophysis

The pituitary is illustrated in Fig. 2.8; it consists of two parts of different embryological origin, the *posterior lobe*, or *neurohypophysis*, and the *anterior lobe* or *adenohypophysis*. As Fig. 2.8 illustrates, the neurohypophysis is divided into three parts, namely the *median eminence of the tuber cinereum*, the *infundibular stem* and the *infundibular process*. The first two parts are collectively described as the *neural stalk* and constitute the pathway of the hypothalamic neurones on their way to the in-

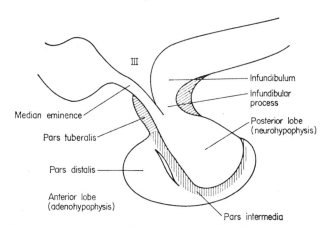

Fig. 2.8. The gross structure of the pituitary gland. The gland is divided into two principal regions of different embryological origins—the anterior lobe (adenohypophysis) and the posterior lobe (neurohypophysis).

fundibular process. The adenohypophysis is likewise divided into three parts, namely the *pars tuberalis*, sheathing the neural stalk, the *pars intermedia* and the *pars distalis*.

Functions of Anterior Lobe

The distinction between the posterior and anterior lobes is fundamental in terms of both embryology and function. The anterior lobe secretes a variety of hormones controlling many functions; and, as indicated above, this may be a direct control of the tissue, such as that exerted by growth hormone, or less directly through trophic hormones, such as TSH, acting on the thyroid, ACTH, stimulating the secretion of the adrenal cortical hormones, and FSH, stimulating the follicles of the ovary to secrete, and so on. Each of the hormones secreted by the anterior lobe is formed by a characteristically different type of cell. This may be demonstrated by suppressing the release of a given anterior lobe hormone by a feed-back mechanism (p. 142), and when this has been achieved it can often be shown that certain histologically recognizable cells have a reduced number of granules in them.

Functions of Posterior Lobe

The *posterior* lobe or *neurohypophysis* is not a true gland, or part of a gland, in so far as the cells producing its secretions—*oxytocin*, acting on the mammary glands and causing uterine contractions during pregnancy, and *antidiuretic hormone* or *vasopressin*, acting on the kidney—are actually neurones, with their cell bodies located in the *hypothalamus* and their axons running in the hypophyseal stalk to the median eminence and posterior pituitary.* In response to an appropriate stimulus these neurones of the hypothalamus are activated, a wave of action potential passing to their endings; as a result, the hormones, called now *neurohormones*, are released from the nerve endings into the adjacent extracellular spaces and carried away in the general blood stream to their target organs. The hormones, which are octapeptides, are contained in granules in the axoplasm of the neurones; they are presumably synthesized in the cell bodies and carried by axonal flow, like the granules of neurotransmitters, towards the axon terminals.

---

* An additional hormone secreted by the neurohypophysis has been called *coherin*. It causes an immediate inhibition of the jejunum which is followed by a prolonged rhythmic contraction beginning at the cephalad end of a loop and propagated in uninterrupted sequence to the end. It is a polypeptide of molecular weight about 4000.

Supraoptic and Paraventricular Nuclei

The neurones responsible for the release of these neurohormones—oxytocin and vasopressin—are large-celled and phylogenetically and ontogenetically distinct from other groups; it is customary to ascribe vasopressin synthesis to the large-celled neurones of the *supraoptic nucleus,* and oxytocin synthesis to similar large-celled neurones in the *paraventricular nucleus,* but modern work suggests that such an anatomical separation is not always correct, and it may well be that the neurosecretory cells responsible for oxytocin and vasopressin activity are scattered throughout the supraoptic and paraventricular nuclei.

Osmoreceptors

In his classical study of the release of the hormone, vasopressin, in response to blood hypertonicity, Verney postulated the existence of "osmoreceptors" in the hypothalamus that would be activated when the blood became hypertonic; in turn, some cells would release antidiuretic hormone, or vasopressin, and this would bring about water conservation by inhibiting the excretion of water by the kidney.

Osmosensitive Neurones. Subsequent studies, employing microelectrodes for recording from single neurones in the hypothalamus, have revealed the existence of neurones that are specifically responsive to changed osmolality of the blood, it may be argued that these osmosensitive neurones themselves are the osmoreceptors of Verney; alternatively, they could be neurones that are synaptically related to osmoreceptors, situated elsewhere. Other neurones of the hypothalamus have been identified as those that discharge in response to a suckling stimulus, releasing oxytocin into the blood by a comparable mechanism; these are classically stated to be concentrated in the paraventricular nucleus but, as indicated above, it is more likely that the neurosecretory cells are scattered throughout both supraoptic and paraventricular regions irrespective of the hormone synthesized and liberated.

Neurosecretory Cells

These large-celled neurones of the hypothalamus are of obvious interest from an ultrastructural point of view, since their hormone must be synthesized and carried to the nerve endings; the prominent feature is the large amount of Nissl substance at the cell periphery together with a large Golgi apparatus close to the nucleus. It will be recalled that the Nissl substance is in reality the ergastoplasm of the cell, the site at which protein synthesis takes place, its basophilia being due to the large amounts of ribonucleoprotein in the form of ribosomes attached to the membranes of the ergastoplasm or endoplasmic reticulum.

Synthesis of Hormone

It would seem that the neurohumour is synthesized on the endoplasmic reticulum and converted to the mature secretory granules in the Golgi system. These granules, generally some 1000 to 2000 Å in diameter, are surrounded by a single membrane. When these neurones were brought into activity, by keeping the animal short of water, Zambrano and De Robertis found that the granules increased in size; when dehydration was maintained the most obvious effect on the cells was an increase in the number of ribosomes. Takabatake and Sachs showed that extracts of the median eminence of the hypothalamus were capable of synthesis of vasopressin, a process that was inhibited by puromycin, indicating synthesis of the polypeptide on the ribosomes.

Exocytosis

The liberation of the hormone from the granule could take place by elimination of the complete membrane-bound granule or, as with secretion of pancreatic and parotid enzymes, by the emptying of the granule through the axon terminal membrane after fusion with this membrane, i.e. by exocytosis. The latter hypothesis is favoured by the general absence of granules in the extracellular space adjoining the axon terminals.

Neurophysin

The hormones vasopressin and oxytocin are linked by a non-covalent linkage to carrier-proteins of molecular weight about 20,000, known as *neurophysins*. Liberation of the hormone runs parallel with release of neurophysin, so that the neurosecretory granules probably consist of "packets" of the hormone linked to neurophysin.

Transport

Transport of the neurohypophyseal hormones from the hypothalamus to the hypophysis may be measured by labelling them with ^{3}H-tyrosine injected into the cerebrospinal fluid. This is incorporated into newly synthesized hormone, and the time required for it to appear in the gland gives some measure of the rate of transport. This suggests a minimum rate of some 2 mm/hr, being closer to the "fast rate" observed in transport of biogenic amines along axons (p. 56) than to the slow migration described by Weiss for axoplasmic renewal.

Hypothalamic Control of Adenohypophysis

We have seen that with most glands transplantation to another part of the body, separating it from its normal neural connections, does not prevent it from exerting its endocrine control over the body approximately normally. This is not true of the anterior pituitary, even though it survives and preserves its structure apparently intact; but this does not mean that the normal functioning of the adenohypophysis relies on nervous discharges, and in fact the nervous supply to its different parts is very small or non-existent.

Releasing Factors (or Releasing Hormones)

The loss of function is due to the interruption of certain vascular connections between the gland and the hypothalamus, so that the *releasing factors* (or *releasing hormones* as they are now called), liberated by the hypothalamus and normally carried from here to the endocrine secreting cells of the adenohypophysis along these connections, fail to reach their destination (Fig. 2.9). The cells that secrete these releasing factors into the portal system are hypothalamic neurones distinguished from those secreting into the posterior pituitary by their smaller size and their distribution in the basal part of the hypothalamus. Their axons run to the median eminence and presumably, after passage of an action potential, their secretions, called releasing factors, are liberated into the extracellular space in immediate relation to a capillary which carries it into the portal system connecting the median eminence with the anterior lobe of the pituitary, or adenohypophysis.

Portal System

By a portal system is meant, in general, a system of vessels that begins as a capillary plexus, or network and ends in another capillary plexus. The most obvious instance of this is the portal system of the liver, the capillaries of the intestine joining to become the portal vein which breaks into a new set of capillaries in the liver whence the blood is ultimately carried away in the hepatic vein (Vol. 1). Popa and Fielding showed that the prominent blood vessels of the pituitary stalk were, in fact, portal, ending in capillaries in the median eminence of the tuber cinereum, at the one pole, and in the hypophysis at the other pole. Essentially, arterial twigs supply a rich vascular plexus in the pars tuberalis, and it is from this plexus that capillary loops and tufts penetrate into the substance of the median eminence; these constitute the *primary plexus* of the portal vessels, and they impart a pink colour to the tissue of the median eminence distinguishing it from the hypothalamus proper. Blood from the primary plexus runs along large portal trunks in the stalk and these break up into sinusoids in the pars distalis of the adenohypophysis (Fig. 2.9).

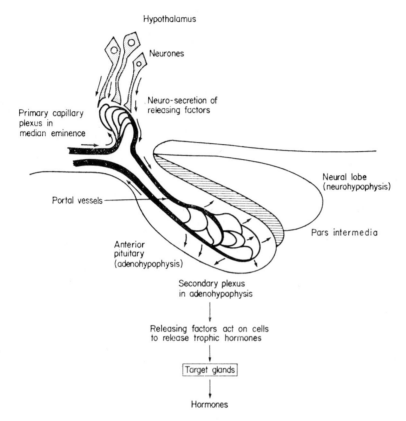

Fig. 2.9. The hypothalamic control of the anterior pituitary gland. Neurones from the hypothalamus secrete releasing factors from their endings, which are in close proximity to the capillaries of the portal vessels, as shown. The releasing factors diffuse into the blood-stream and are carried by the portal system into the anterior pituitary where they cause the release of their specific trophic hormone. The trophic hormones act on their target gland and cause release of the hormone into the blood.

Carriage of Releasing Factors. The capillaries of the primary plexus in the median eminence come into close relation with nerve fibres from the hypothalamus. With the unequivocal demonstration that the direction of blood-flow is from the median eminence to the pituitary gland, the suggestion that the nerve fibres from the hypothalamus liberated certain "releasing factors" into the blood, which were carried down to the endocrine cells, became of real significance. The demonstration by Harris that section of the stalk, such as to interrupt the portal blood supply, abolished the hypothalamic control over the secretion of gonadotrophic hormones from the anterior pituitary provided further proof of the hypothesis. If, in experimental animals, there was regeneration of the portal system of blood vessels, then it was found that normal gonadotrophic secretion returned.

Identification of Releasing Factors. Further proof of chemical control by the hypothalamus of the activity of the anterior pituitary was given by the preparation of extracts of the hypothalamus that, when injected into the local portal system, caused the liberation of hormones. Subsequent work on the purification of these extracts has enabled the chemical identification of more than one releasing factor. We have already seen that the thyroid releasing factor, TRF (or thyroid releasing hormone, TRH, as it is now called), is a simple tripeptide—pyroglutamyl-histidyl-prolineamide (pGlu-His-ProNH$_2$); the factor causing release of luteinizing hormone (LHRH) and follicle stimulating hormone (FSHRH) is a decapeptide (PyroGlu-His-Trp-Ser-Gly-leu-Arg-Pro-GlyNH$_2$). The factor that causes release of melanocyte stimulating hormone, MSHRH, is a pentapeptide: H-Cys-Tyr-Ile-Gln-AsN-OH, which is a fragment of the 20-membered ring component of the larger neurohypophyseal hormone, oxytocin, concerned with uterine movements and lactation. A further example of the economy practised by Nature is that the factor that inhibits the release of MSH—*MSH Release Inhibiting Factor (MSHRIF)*—is a tripeptide, split off from oxytocin by an exopeptidase (Pro-leu-gly-amide) present in median stalk microsomes.

Finally, blood may be collected directly from the portal system by insertion of a fine cannula, and this blood, when injected into rats, will stimulate the release of anterior hypophyseal hormones, such as TSH or ACTH.

Hypophysiotropic Areas

By placing lesions in specific regions of the hypothalamus and observing the consequent changes in the releasing factor content of the hypothalamus it has been possible to allocate specific areas to the probable synthesis of the RF's. Thus FSHRF is in the paraventricular region, LHRF in the suprachiasmatic and arcuate region of the ventromedian nucleus; TSHRF is much more widely distributed. This, and other experimental approaches, have led to the delineation of the so-called *hypophysiotropic area* of the hypothalamus, an area which, when cut off from higher cerebral influences, is able to maintain nearly normal anterior pituitary function. The area is delineated in Fig. 2.10.

In Vitro Effects

In the electron microscope quite striking and rapid changes were observed in the anterior pituitary cell after treatment with releasing

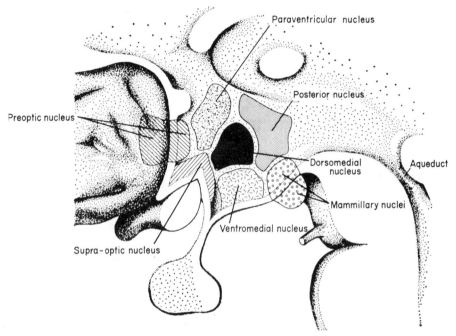

Fig. 2.10. The hypophysiotrophic area of the hypothalamus. (Netter. "Ciba Collection of Medical Illustrations." Vol. 1.)

factor, or rather of a hypothalamic extract presumed to contain these. There was an increase in the number of secretory granules within five minutes of the injection, and frequently granules were seen fused with the plasma membrane apparently undergoing exocytosis into the pericapillary space. It seemed that both release and synthesis of hormone, in this case growth hormone, had been stimulated by the releasing factor.

8*

Mechanism of Release

As to the mechanism of action of the releasing factor, it has been suggested that it causes a primary depolarization of the secreting cell. This could cause, or be accompanied by, penetration of Ca^{2+} which might then activate release of the hormone. That depolarization is a likely first step is shown by the influence of increasing the external concentration of K^+ on the release of hormones from incubated

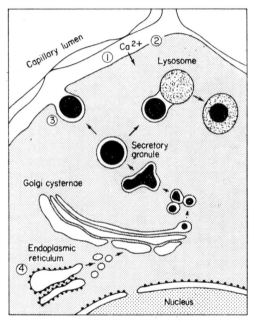

Fig. 2.11. The possible time sequence in the activation of a hypophyseal cell by a releasing factor. (McCann and Porter, *Physiol. Rev.* 1969, **49,** 269.)

pituitaries *in vitro*, an effect that is additive with the releasing factors. The importance of Ca^{2+} is shown by the blocking of the effects of depolarization or releasing factors by employing a Ca^{2+}-free medium. The complete mechanism of release is indicated schematically in Fig. 2.11. Since the hormones of the pituitary that are released by the releasing factors are held in granules, the basic mechanism of release is doubtless similar to that involved in the release of enzymes, e.g. amylase from the parotid or pancreas, and may be classed as a manifestation of excitation–secretion coupling. The matter will be discussed more generally later (p. 282).

Neurohumours and Neurohormones

There are obvious analogies between the neural and hormonal control mechanisms since the fundamental basis in transmission of an influence of one cell on another is through a chemical mediator. The difference between the neurotransmitter or neurohumour (involved characteristically in the synaptic type of transmission) and the neurohormone (involved in the blood-carried mode of transmission) rests mainly on the different types of chemical employed, the degree of localization of the application process to the effector cell, and the rapidity of onset and termination of the neurotransmitter's effect. Thus the neurohumours are usually biogenic amines, such as noradrenaline, dopamine, acetylcholine, and so on, whilst the neurohormones are usually polypeptides, the liberating cells often being called *peptidergic*. In both cases it seems that the chemical is liberated from the terminal by the wave of action potential; with the neurohumour the liberation very frequently occurs at a specialized junction between neurone and effector cell, an arrangement that serves to confine the liberated messenger to a highly localized region; by contrast the neurohormone is liberated into the blood-stream. With those liberated into the posterior lobe, the pathway is long and involves the whole of the systemic circulation, so that all parts of the body are exposed to the messenger. With the releasing factors the messenger's spread is more restricted, being confined to the portal circulation.

It must be emphasized that, when non-mammalian and invertebrate animals are considered, the distinction between the "ordinary neurone", acting by a neurotransmitter, and the neurosecretory cell, acting through a neurohormone, tends to fade. In some species some neurones may be found that make no special type of contact with their effector cells and may even liberate their transmitter into the cerebral ventricles, whilst some neurosecretory cells show the presence of synaptic vesicles and specialized contacts with their effector cells. Even the chemical distinction is not rigid, so that endocrine function may be mediated by a biogenic amine instead of a polypeptide as, for example, with adrenaline.

Neuroendocrine Integration

The elucidation of the relations between the hypothalamus and the endocrine system enables us to understand, in general terms, how the brain may influence all aspects of bodily activity, either through direct neural control, or less directly by liberation of neurohormones. These latter may be releasing factors or such hormones as ADH. Thus the hypothalamus receives messages from most parts of the brain, so that it is easy to see how a great variety of sensory input can influence visceral activity. As an example we have the well known circumstance that a pigeon will only lay eggs if there is another pigeon in sight, and this occurs even if it sees only an image in a mirror. Here the visual input reacts on the hypothalamus, and this causes the release of luteinizing and follicle-stimulating hormones (LH and FSH) through the appropriate releasing factors. This, of course, is not the only means by which the hypothalamus can control bodily function; its close relations with centres controlling respiration, gastrointestinal motility and so on, permit it to have a direct nervous action.

Feedback

The relations between the endocrine and nervous systems are reciprocal, so that the release of a given hormone is usually closely related to the concentration of this in the blood. Thus it is possible to inhibit the release of thyroid stimulating hormone—TSH—by the simple expedient of raising the blood level of thyroxine, the hormone secreted by the thyroid gland. In this case the hormone is acting directly on the anterior pituitary, since injection of thyroxine directly into the anterior pituitary (but not the hypothalamus) inhibits TSH secretions; with other glands this negative feedback operates on the hypothalamus. Such a feedback can be mimicked by implanting small crystals of hormone into the median eminence. Thus implantation of oestradiol caused failure of ovulation in rabbits; in this species ovulation occurs only after mating, the act of coitus causing the release of gonadotrophic hormone. It is clear that this simple feedback system is able to maintain a steady basic level of hormone in the blood, but of course, in order that the hormonal system be effective, this homeostasis must be overriden in accordance with the needs of the organism.

Neuronal Inhibition of Oestrus Behaviour

This feedback operating through the central nervous system is an example of the influence of a steroid hormone on the neurones of the hypothalamus. Thus the hormone can not only operate on its effector target cells, e.g. the uterus, but it can also operate on neurones, presumably by affecting their excitability or perhaps by a direct synaptic action. The case just cited is one in which a high concentration of a steroid hormone inhibited release of the same hormone by a reflex mechanism, namely through coitus; it represented negative feedback. A more positive action of steroid hormones in stimulating central nervous activity is shown by a variety of experiments involving not only the hypothalamus but higher cerebral centres. Thus many of the aspects of oestrus behaviour in animals involve central nervous-controlled activity and are collectively referred to as "heat manifestations"; these are abolished in the female by ovariectomy, to return when the animal is injected with oestrogen and progesterone.

When Mayerson examined the interrelations of nervous and hormonal activity, he found that the effects of the hormones were opposed by nervous activity, operating through a monoaminergic pathway, so that the effects of the hormone, whether injected or secreted naturally, could be enhanced by treating the animal with reserpine, which depletes the neurones of their transmitter. By treating them with a monoamine oxidase inhibitor the oestrus phenomena could be enhanced and, in the ovariectomized animal, could be brought about by a lower dose of hormone. When the activities of a variety of steroid hormones and synthetic analogues were studied, it was found that there was a strong parallelism between the response of target organs, such as the uterus, and the induced central nervous activity, such as lordosis, so that it seems that the same receptor may well be present in both the effector tissue—such as uterine muscle—and in the central neurones.

Electrical Stimulation of Hypothalamus

The hypothalamus contains various centres which, when stimulated electrically, have well defined effects. Thus when an electrode is implanted in a given region in a goat and is stimulated, the goat will automatically drink water and the region is described as a *drinking centre*. Other centres, when stimulated, evoke satiety, so that an animal stops eating; and so on. These responses are immediate, and operate presumably through purely neural pathways. Implantation of electrodes in certain regions, in particular the tuber cinereum, brings about changes that are clearly hormone-induced. Thus Harris was able to induce ovulation in the rabbit by stimulating the tuber cinereum, an effect that could not be obtained by repeated stimulation of the anterior pituitary, pars intermedia, or infundibular stem.

BINDING OF HORMONES TO CARRIER PROTEINS

The hormones are able to exert their actions on target cells when they are in extremely low concentration in the blood plasma or extracellular fluid, concentrations of the order of perhaps 10^{-11} Molar. We must therefore expect their molecules to have a special affinity for the surface of the target cell in preference to the surfaces of other cells and connective tissue elements.

Attachment to Target Cell

In this way we can envisage the target cells "capturing" the hormone molecules as they come into their vicinity, the other cells of the body letting them go by. Such a mechanism must be regarded as an ideal one, however, since it is extremely difficult to design a molecule that will attach, or adsorb, to one surface and not attach to another. The best that can be achieved is to have a molecule with a *preferential* affinity for one cell surface and a smaller affinity for other surfaces. This means, then, that the hormone "designed" to attach, say, to the thyroid cell, will also attach to every other cell of the body to some extent, so that unless a further step is taken to ensure specific attachment to the thyroid cell there will be very little hormone for this cell, practically all of it being trapped by the other cells of the body by virtue of their greater number. If we appreciate, furthermore, that not only the cell surfaces, but the proteins circulating in the blood also have an affinity for hormones, the amount left free for the target cell will be very small.

Relative Affinities

However, it is through this latter form of attachment that target specificity is achieved, namely the development of special *carrier proteins* with very strong and specific affinity for a given hormone. In this way they are protected from being taken up by non-target tissue, whilst the target cells are able to attach the hormone to their own surface entirely by virtue of their greater affinity for the hormone. Thus, in the immediate neighbourhood of the cell surface we may picture the local concentration of the hormone as being very low, because of the powerful uptake by the cell. Since the binding, or adsorption, to the carrier protein, is reversible, the amount bound will be governed by the concentration in the medium in accordance with simple equilibrium dynamics:

$$[S] \times [C] \rightleftharpoons [CS]$$
Hormone Carrier Complex

Thus the uptake by the target cell causes the carrier to give up some of its hormone, and in this way the very small amounts of hormone ejected into the blood-stream are able to exert specific effects on the target tissue.

Specific Carriers

The carriers that have been so far identified are proteins. One such, with a strong affinity for thyroxine, the thyroid hormone, is called *thyroxine binding globulin* (TBG); another, which binds certain steroid hormones, is called *corticosteroid hormone binding globulin* (CBG) or *transcortin*; and it also binds progesterone. The carriers responsible for transport of the two neurohypophyseal hormones, vasopressin and oxytocin, are called *neurophysins*.

Since binding is reversible, we may expect some competition for the CBG, and in fact it is found that aldosterone will compete for the carrier, e.g., will displace cortisol and progesterone.

Binding Affinity

The affinity of any carrier for a hormone may be characterized by the reciprocal of the dissociation constant in the equation:

$$\frac{[S] \times [C]}{[SC]} = K_d$$

$$\text{Thus Affinity} = 1/K_d = \frac{[SC]}{[S] \times [C]} = Ka.$$

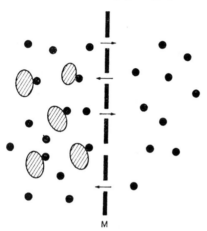

M

Fig. 2.12. The dialysis of a hormone (filled circles) with its carrier (cross-hatched) against an aqueous solution. The carrier molecules cannot cross the dialysis membrane (M) whereas the hormone can, so that at equilibrium the concentration of hormone in the solution outside the dialysis sac represents the concentration of unbound hormone.

Experimentally we may measure the affinity* by dialysing a mixture of the hormone with its carrier against an aqueous solution, as illustrated by Fig. 2.12. The carrier is unable to pass through the dialysing membrane, M, whereas the hormone can, so that at equilibrium, the

---

* The binding capacity of a carrier is often indicated by J, the average number of molecules bound per molecule of carrier. It is given by:

$$J = \frac{n \, K_a[S]}{1 + K_a[S]}$$

where n is the number of binding sites, K_a is the association constant for binding at each site and [S] is the molar concentration of unbound hormone. If J/[S] is plotted against J, a straight line is obtained, with intercepts on abscissa and ordinate equal to n and nK_a respectively.

concentration of hormone in the solution outside the dialysis-sac represents the concentration of unbound hormone. The total amount of hormone added to the system is known, so by subtraction the concentration of hormone-complex is known, and also the remaining amount of free carrier. If the concentration of hormone is steadily increased, by adding more to the system, a point is reached when the carrier is saturated. If the molecular weight of the carrier is known, e.g. 50,000 for CBG, then we may estimate the maximum number of molecules of hormone carried by a molecule of carrier, i.e. the number of "carrier sites" on the protein molecule. This is frequently found to be unity.

Storage

The importance of the carrier has already been stressed in so far as it allows the hormone to reach its target effectively. Now it may be shown that when the hormone is attached to its carrier it is ineffective, hence the presence of carriers in the blood-stream means that there is a reserve of hormone in the blood, and this may be quite significant in amount. Thus the concentration of thyroxine in the blood of a normal animal is actually of the order of 1.10^{-7}M, but because of the binding to carrier, the concentration of free thyroxine is only about one ten-thousandth of this, $3–6.10^{-11}$ M. A further useful function of the carrier is to stabilize the hormone; thus cortisol will oxidize spontaneously in the absence of CBG, whereas it remains stable in its presence.

Types of Carrier

We may distinguish three main types of carrier in the blood: there are the highly specific ones, with a low concentration in the plasma but very high affinity; those so far identified are TBG, CBG and one binding oestradiol and testosterone called *steroid-binding β-globulin*. A second group also show specificity for types of hormone, but their affinities are much smaller so that they contribute much less to the carrying function; one of these is *thyroxine binding prealbumin* (TBPA) for thyroid hormone and a glycoprotein (AAG) that binds steroids. Thirdly, it must be appreciated that the albumin of plasma has some affinity for a great variety of compounds, be they hormones or exogenous drugs, such as sulphonamides, aspirin, etc. The affinity for a given hormone is relatively weak, but the vastly higher concentration of albumin in the plasma means that a significant proportion of the total amount of circulating hormone will, in fact, be carried in this less specific manner. Thus so far as thyroxine is concerned, some 75 per cent is carried by TBG, 15 per cent by the lower-affinity TBPA and 10 per cent by serum albumin.

Variations in Binding Capacity

For any given level of endocrine activity the binding capacity of the blood is of obvious importance in determining at any moment how much hormone is available at the target site. Hence the study of alterations in binding capacity, whether occurring naturally or through drugs, is of some interest. Figure 2.13 shows the increase in binding of progesterone during pregnancy. Interestingly this is accompanied by

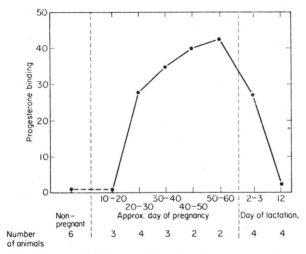

Fig. 2.13. Progesterone binding activity in the serum of pregnant and lactating guinea pigs. (Westphal, "Biochemical Actions of Hormones". G. Litwack, ed., Academic Press.)

an increase in the total amount of hormone in the blood, suggesting that the increased binding reduces the free hormone level and that this acts by the negative feedback mechanism (p. 142) causing more hormone to be secreted.

ASSAY OF HORMONES

The degree of activity of a hormone varies with its concentration in the blood, so that a fair idea of the activity of a given endocrine gland at a given moment is provided by the concentration in the circulating blood. Frequently, too, the concentration within the secreting gland of an experimental animal will also provide a clue, since secretion of the hormone into the blood is often accompanied by synthesis, which more than replaces the secreted hormone, and in this case an elevated concentration in the gland betokens increased activity. Because of the low concentrations at which the hormones are active, usually the amounts in the volume of blood that it is practicable to withdraw are too small for straightforward chemical analysis.

Use of Target Organ

In this event less direct methods of assay are employed, the most usual being to measure the effects of a known volume of blood, or an extract of this, on an experimental target preparation. Thus we may measure the increase in metabolic rate of rats injected with a preparation considered to contain thyroxine, and compare this with the effects of known amounts of the pure hormone. If the hormone provokes the contraction of smooth muscle, as with some prostaglandins, adrenaline, oxytocin, etc., then the effects of varying amounts of the unknown preparation in causing contraction of an appropriate smooth muscle preparation may be determined, and the dose–response curve compared with one obtained using a pure preparation of the hormone.

Isotopic Labelling

A great improvement in the sensitivity and accuracy of the assay has been provided by the use of radioactive isotopes; thus the thyroid hormones of an animal may be easily "labelled" by injecting it with a dose of radioactive iodide, $^{131}I^-$, so that after a short time practically all the radioactive iodine in the animal is in the form of these hormones. Any physiological change provoking an increased thyroid excretion, e.g. lowering of body temperature, will result in an increased radioactivity in the blood, and this can be measured with considerable accuracy. In this case the experimenter is fortunate in that the radioactive precursor is taken up almost exclusively into the gland with which he is concerned, any residue being fairly rapidly excreted. If the precursor to a steroid hormone, e.g. cholesterol, is presented to the animal body, in the radioactive form, e.g. by labelling with ^{14}C, then of course many different steroid hormones will become radioactive. It will not be easy therefore to relate changes in blood radioactivity with secretion of a particular hormone unless preliminary preparative procedures are undertaken to separate the hormone in which one is interested from the remainder. If this is practicable, then the fact that one may measure radioactivity quantitatively with high accuracy, even when dealing with very low concentrations, means that the steroid hormone can indeed be measured with some accuracy.

Radioimmunoassay

The technique of radioimmunoassay, developed by Berson, is based on the general principle of the specificity of the reaction between antigen and antibody. Thus we may prepare an antibody to the protein or peptide hormone we are interested in, e.g. prolactin or growth hormone, by injecting the purified hormone of one species into that of another. This *antigen* provokes the synthesis of *antibodies*, which appear in the serum of the animal so injected (Chapter 4). The reason why this hormone provokes an immune reaction is because the amino acid sequence of, say, a human prolactin is different in certain regions, from that of, say, a rabbit, and it is this difference that is detected by the reactive cells of the recipient animal. These antibodies will only react with prolactin molecules with amino acid sequences that are closely similar to that which evoked their production. Thus the requirements for the assay are a purified preparation of the hormone of the species we are studying, e.g. human prolactin, and an immune antiserum. The hormone is labelled, and this is done most conveniently with ^{131}I, which reacts with the tyrosine groups of the hormone.

Competition with Antibody. The basis of the technique is to cause the hormone in the blood sample to compete with a fixed quantity of labelled hormone for binding with a fixed quantity of antibody. Thus if the supply of antibody is insufficient to react with all the hormone present in the mixture, then the labelled and unlabelled hormones will compete, and the relative amounts actually bound will be proportional to their concentrations. If we take a series of mixtures all containing the same amounts of antibody and the same amounts of labelled hormone, we can add to them successively larger amounts of the blood-extract containing the hormone. After the reaction has taken place we separate, by an appropriate technique, the hormone–antibody complex from the hormone remaining in solution as unbound material, and we measure the radioactivities in the bound and unbound material. Clearly the more unlabelled hormone that was added to the mixture the smaller will be the proportion of the radioactivity in the bound fraction, so that the ratio:

Radioactivity in Bound Fraction/*Radioactivity in Unbound Fraction*

will vary inversely with the concentration in the blood-extract. The technique is illustrated schematically in Fig. 2.14.

Technical Problems. The main problems are thus the preparation of the pure hormone with which to obtain the antibody, and then the separation of the bound hormone from the free hormone, and this is usually based on their different molecular weights, electrophoretic mobilities, and so on. Perhaps the most ingenious method of separation involves the preliminary attachment of the antibody to the wall of the incubation tube. This happens if the immune serum is used as a coating for a polypropylene or polystyrene tube, so that any hormone attached to the antibody remains firmly attached to the tube through

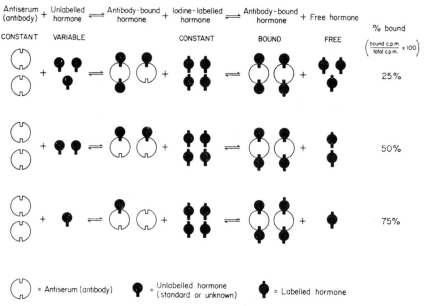

Fig. 2.14. Diagrammatic representation of the radioimmunoassay technique for the assay of hormones. An antibody is prepared specific for the hormone to be assayed. By adding a constant proportion of this antibody and a constant proportion of radioactively labelled hormone at a known concentration, and by then adding the unlabelled hormone at unknown concentration to a series of samples the bound and free radioactivity can be measured and an estimate made of the unknown concentration, (Cowie and Tindal, "The Physiology of Lactation", Arnold).

its link with the antibody. Thus, after the reaction, the contents of the tube are removed and counted and the tube itself is counted for radioactivity, the gamma radiations from the ^{131}I-label passing easily through the material of the tube.

THE "SECOND MESSENGER": CYCLIC AMP

Adenosine triphosphate (ATP) can split off two of its phosphate groups in the form of pyrophosphate to give a cyclic compound, adenosine-3′, 5′-phosphate, or cyclic AMP (cAMP)

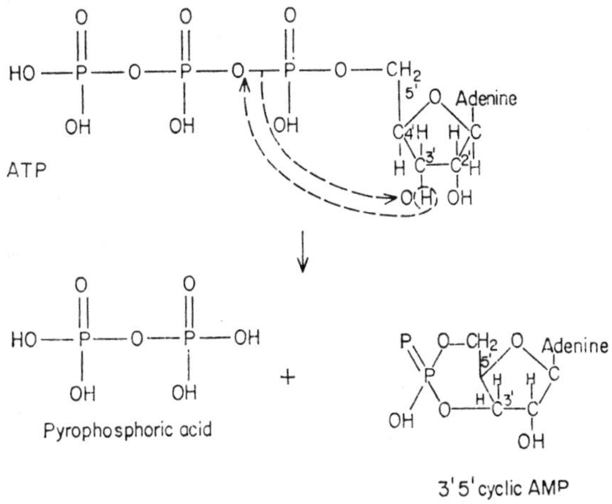

$$
\begin{array}{ccc}
O & O & O \\
\parallel & \parallel & \parallel
\end{array}
$$

HO—P—O—P—O—P—O—CH₂

ATP

OH   OH   OH

Adenine

ATP

↓

HO—P—O—P—OH +

OH   OH

Pyrophosphoric acid

Adenine

3'5' cyclic AMP

a reaction catalysed by the enzyme *adenyl cyclase* present in practically all cells and most probably either strongly attached to, or forming an integral part of, the cell membrane. The compound is broken down in cells to 5'-AMP by an enzyme *phosphodiesterase*.

Glycogenolysis

In 1961 Rall and Sutherland emphasized the possible role of cAMP in hormone action; they based their argument primarily on the studies of the increased breakdown of glycogen—*glycogenolysis*—brought about by the adrenal hormone adrenaline, a breakdown that is necessary to support the increased metabolism induced by the hormone. This increase in glycogenolysis was brought about by the activation of an enzyme—*phosphorylase kinase*—that was necessary for the conversion of the inactive phosphorylase of muscle to its active form, thereby permitting it to catalyse the first step in glycogen breakdown, namely the reaction:

Glycogen + nATP ———→ nGlucose-1-phosphate + nADP.

It seemed that this activation of phosphorylase kinase involved a direct participation of cAMP, which was found to accumulate in muscle in parallel with the increase in active phosphorylase. In a similar way, the effect of the pancreatic hormone, glucagon, in promoting glycogenolysis, was associated with an increase in liver cAMP. Finally, the action of the adrenocorticotrophic hormone (ACTH) on the adrenal cortex, which stimulates steroid synthesis, was likewise associated with an increase in cAMP in the adrenal tissue.

Cellular Formation of cAMP

Rall and Sutherland made the broad suggestion that, not only were the actions of adrenaline and ACTH mediated through the formation of cAMP in the cell, but that many other hormonal effects were also mediated in the same way, namely the action of TSH on the thyroid, the action of LH on the growth of ovarian tissue, and so on. Furthermore, they suggested that hormonal actions not directly concerned in glycogenolysis (such as the synthesis of fatty acids, proteins and ketone bodies by the liver which are induced by adrenaline) might also be mediated through cAMP, which thus acted as a "second messenger" in the chain of events beginning with the liberation of the hormone into the blood stream and ending with the final intracellular event whether it was breakdown of glycogen, synthesis of protein, iodination of protein, and so on.

Mimicking Hormone Action

The evidence supporting the Rall–Sutherland hypothesis is now overwhelming, not only in respect to the glycogenolytic system, to which they specifically applied it, but to many other known hormone-target interactions. Perhaps the hormonal system most extensively studied is the interaction between thyroid stimulating hormone— TSH—and the thyroid gland, since the manifestations of TSH action are easy to observe, e.g. the increased vesicle formation in thyroid cells, the increased uptake of I^-, its increased organification, and so on. Experiments carried out largely on isolated tissue, e.g. isolated thyroid cells separated from each other by treatment of the tissue with trypsin, have shown a remarkable parallelism between the action of TSH on the tissue and the action of cAMP. Where failure to obtain an effect is reported, this is usually due to the failure of the cAMP to penetrate the target cell, so that a synthetic compound, dibutyryl cAMP (DBAMP) which is more lipid-soluble, is often found to be effective when cAMP is not.* In a similar way the actions of many other hormones on their target tissues may be mimicked by cAMP or DBAMP, e.g. the increased synthesis of steroid hormones by the adrenal gland provoked by ACTH.

---

* With respect to the mimicry of hormone actions of cAMP and DBAMP, Tata has emphasized that this is sometimes illusory, especially in regard to the longer-term actions. Thus the increase in RNA and phospholipid of thyroid cells in response to TSH is a slow process, yet it apparently occurs rapidly in response to DBAMP. However, this response is illusory and represents only a rapid uptake of the isotopically labelled precursors used to identify the RNA and phospholipid, and not an actual synthesis of new material.

Binding of Hormone to Cell

The question arises as to how the experimentally observed increase in cAMP in the target tissue is brought about by the hormone. There are strong experimental and *a priori* reasons to believe that the primary attack of the hormone is on the cell surface. On *a priori* grounds it may be argued that the hormones usually have a strong tendency to attach themselves to other molecules, and are usually transported by carrier molecules to which they are firmly attached; to act, they must detach themselves from the carrier, and this is made possible by the very special affinity that the hormone molecule has for certain "receptor sites" on the target cell. This is the essential basis for hormone specificity, the ability of the hormone to choose the cell on which it is going to act. Thus this "recognition" and interaction depend on specific chemical groupings on the cell's surface, probably constituting part of its plasma membrane.

Experimental Demonstration of Binding. Experimentally this preliminary binding of the hormone to the cell may be demonstrated by exposing the target tissue to the hormone at a low temperature, then washing the tissue with a saline medium so as to remove as much of the hormone as possible, and then to allow the tissue to warm to its normal temperature of 37°C. If the hormone is firmly attached to the target cells we may expect it to remain there in spite of the washing, and thus to show its activity after this as soon as the tissue is warmed. With TSH acting on thyroid tissue this is exactly what happens. It could be argued that the hormone has entered the cell and remained there during the washing procedure, but it is found that if the cell is treated with an antibody to TSH, before the warming up, then it no longer shows the TSH response. The antibody to TSH is a globulin and too large to be expected to enter a cell, so that the evidence that the hormone is bound to the surface is strong. Another way of demonstrating the surface attack of the hormone is to attach it to a very large molecule, thereby preventing it from entering a cell; thus Schimmer linked ACTH to cellulose fibres and, even though these were visible microscopically, the ACTH bound in this way was effective in increasing the production of steroids by the adrenal gland.

Adenyl Cyclase

The first step, then, is the binding of the hormone to a specific receptor, or "recognition" site on the cell membrane. How does this bring about the accumulation of cAMP? A clue to the mechanism is provided by the finding that the enzyme, adenyl cyclase, which catalyses the formation of cAMP from ATP, is intimately connected with the cell membrane, so that when the cell is fragmented and subjected to differential centrifugation the enzyme activity is found in the microsomes, i.e. attached to fragmented membrane. There is evidence that it is the plasma membrane, rather than the endoplasmic reticulum, to which the enzyme is attached. Thus the hormone could act by stimulating the adenyl cyclase in the cell membrane, presumably by inducing some change in its shape that caused it to expose its active groupings. Alternatively the link between hormone and cell membrane might induce the liberation of a soluble compound that activated the cyclase.

Mechanism of cAMP Action

We come now to the mode of action of the cAMP. All the evidence indicates that when cAMP acts on an enzyme to increase its activity it binds strongly to it, and it is in this way that the site of action of the cAMP can often be determined if the tissue, or cell, is treated with cAMP labelled with radioactive carbon. By appropriate fractionation procedures the radioactivity can be found in association with a certain protein which may be the enzyme that cAMP is activating.

Activation by Splitting

There are doubtless many mechanisms by which cAMP can activate a given enzyme; one mode is described by Lipmann who studied the activation of a protein phosphokinase concerned in protein synthesis. He found that the enzyme would bind strongly to cAMP, although on fractionation of the product of binding, using ^{3}H-labelled cAMP to identify this, he obtained a preparation that showed very high enzyme activity but without any cAMP bound to it. Thus it seemed that cAMP had caused the production of a highly active form of the enzyme without remaining attached to the original enzyme molecule. The activity of this fraction was independent of adding further amounts of cAMP, yet in the intact system the original enzyme was promoted by cAMP. Measurement of the molecular weights of the several components of the system treated with cAMP revealed three compounds, with molecular weights of 140,000, 80,000 and 60,000 respectively; and it seemed that the two smaller molecules had been obtained by splitting of the large one by the action of cAMP, as illustrated in Fig. 2.15. Thus the large 140,000 molecule was inactive; it reacted with cAMP to form a complex with cAMP, of molecular weight 80,000, and an active enzyme of molecular weight 60,000 that did not require cAMP for its activity. We may say, in this case, that the inactive enzyme was made up of an active portion and an inhibiting portion, and that cAMP acts by "dis-inhibiting" or "de-repressing" the enzyme.

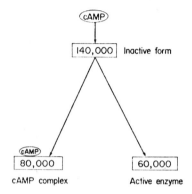

Fig. 2.15. Activation of a protein kinase by cAMP, which by attaching itself to the large molecule causes it to split into two; the active portion contains no bound cAMP.

Messenger RNA and Hormonal Action

This de-repression of enzyme activity is one method of control of metabolism. In the general discussion of metabolic control in Vol. 1, other methods were mentioned, especially the synthesis *de novo* of enzyme by the protein-synthesizing system of the cell. As we have seen, this involves the "translation" of a messenger-RNA, which acts as the template for the linking together of the amino acids in their correct sequence. A step before this is the synthesis of new messenger-RNA using the gene's DNA as a template, a process that is called "transcription". In bacterial systems the production of enzyme usually requires the transcription from the gene material, and it is therefore inhibited by actinomycin D; this is because the messenger RNA's are not stable and have to be resynthesized.

Inhibition of Translation

In mammalian tissues the messenger-RNA's required for enzyme synthesis seem to be more stable, so that we may expect the stimulatory effect of cAMP on enzyme synthesis, if it occurs, to act on the translational process, i.e. the linking together of amino acids on the messenger-RNA attached to the ribosomes (Vol. 1). This process is unaffected by actinomycin D but is inhibited by puromycin or cycloheximide, and it is interesting that the stimulation of synthesis of the steroid hormones of the adrenal cortex, induced by ACTH, may be inhibited by puromycin and cycloheximide, but not by actinomycin D. Thus cAMP, in this case, acts by promoting translation of a stable messenger-RNA, presumably by activating a key enzyme in this process, possibly the enzyme concerned with activating the amino acid that permits it to attach to the soluble RNA.

RNA Synthesis

That the transcriptional process is important, too, is shown by the action of follicle-stimulating hormone (FSH) which stimulates protein synthesis in the testes of immature rats whose pituitaries have been removed; this is independent of an increase in transport of amino acids, or of their activation in the protein synthetic mechanism. An increased synthesis of RNA, as revealed by increased incorporation of tritium-labelled uridine into the nuclear RNA stores, precedes the increase in protein synthesis, and this is inhibited by actinomycin D. The evidence thus indicates that it is the messenger-RNA of the nucleus that is involved. Since FSH stimulates cAMP production by the testis, it may well be that the increased amounts of cAMP are the primary step that provokes the increased RNA synthesis.

Prolactin

A very thorough analysis of the molecular biology of hormone action is that of Turkington who investigated the changes in nucleic acid turnover in the mammary gland in response to treatment with pro-lactin, the pituitary hormone that induces development of the gland during pregnancy and initiates and maintains the production of milk. Thus the production of the milk involves the synthesis of a new protein, caseinogen, and this may be recognized by labelling with $^{32}PO_4$ since it is a phosphoprotein. The development of new RNA is followed by labelling with tritium or ^{14}C as indicated earlier.

RNA Synthesis. Figure 2.16 shows the rapid rise in nuclear RNA and the larger and more protracted rise in ribosomal RNA together with the appearance of ^{32}P-casein. In this instance, then, the synthesis of RNA within the nucleus and its subsequent migration into the cytoplasm, where it appears in the ribosomes, are probably the primary events in response to the hormone prolactin. All these increases are inhibited by actinomycin D as well as cycloheximide, showing that RNA synthesis on a DNA template is required as well as protein synthesis. Further analysis of the changes in RNA composition showed that t-RNA, as well as ribsomal RNA, were produced in response to prolactin, whilst the increased rate of synthesis of casein was accompanied by an increase in polysome formation, i.e. in the formation of groups of ribosomes linked together with a messenger RNA, a formation that is the necessary prerequisite for polypeptide synthesis (Vol. 1). Thus prolactin stimulates the formation of all three types of RNA.

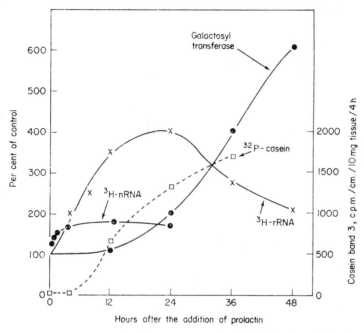

Fig. 2.16. The sequence of molecular events in the induction of milk protein by prolactin. Mouse mammary explants were incubated with insulin and hydrocortisone for 96 hr prior to the addition of prolactin to the medium. The first rise in radioactivity is seen in the nuclear RNA (^{3}H nRNA) followed by a rise in the ribosomal RNA (^{3}H rRNA) and then an increase in ^{32}P caseinogen and galactosyl transferase. (Turkington, "Lactogenic Hormones", CIBA Symposium.)

Involvement of cAMP. As to the mechanism whereby the appropriate genes are activated by prolactin, which almost certainly remains attached to the surface of the cell, once again the suggestion has been made that adenyl cyclase in the membrane is activated. The connection with cAMP is not so simple, however, since prolactin does not cause increased cAMP accumulation in the mammary cell, nor does cAMP mimic the action of prolactin. Nevertheless the secreting cell contains a phosphokinase that is activated by cAMP and also a protein that binds specifically to cAMP, and these are increased in amounts in cells stimulated to secrete in response to prolactin.

Activation of Protein Kinases

The concept of the second messenger role of cAMP was derived from a study of the protein kinases of muscle and liver, i.e. enzymes that promote the phosphorylation of protein. Where the protein is an enzyme, this phosphorylation may result in converting it into its active form. Thus the phosphorylase of muscle must be acted on by a *phosphorylase kinase* to make it active. Furthermore, the tissue contains two phosphorylase kinases, the one active and the other inactive, and the conversion of the inactive to the active form once again involves the action of a phosphokinase, and it is this *"phosphorylase kinase kinase"* that is activated by cAMP. Thus the chain of events in epinephrine-stimulated glycogenolysis is:

Epinephrine ⟶ Adenyl cyclase ⟶ cAMP ⟶ Protein kinase ⟶
Phosphorylkinase ⟶ Phosphorylase ⟶ Glycogen

Diversity of cAMP-stimulated Actions

The protein kinase, acted on by cAMP, may well be one of a large number contained in the cell, and in this way we may explain the diversity of actions of cAMP in a given cell, as for example the multiple actions of TSH on the thyroid cell all mediated by cAMP. These protein kinases would act on a variety of inactive enzymes, converting them to active forms (or they might conceivably activate some and inactivate others), but ultimately exerting the control of the metabolic activities of the cell required by the hormone. It is certainly true that cAMP-sensitive protein kinases may be isolated from a large variety of tissues.

Breakdown of cAMP

The phosphodiesterase within the cell catalyses the conversion of cAMP to the non-cyclic 5′-AMP, so that the level of cAMP at any moment is governed by the relative activities of the adenyl cyclase and phosphodiesterase. The stimulating action of theophylline and caffeine on a variety of metabolic and transport processes has been well recognized and the explanation lies in their inhibitory action on phosphodiesterase, thereby allowing the accumulation of cAMP in the cell. Thus, in general, the methyl xanthines have effects similar to those of hormones, and this may well explain the more powerful contraction of the heart induced by caffeine.

Control of Lipolysis

Under conditions of metabolic stress the supply of energy from fat becomes important, as in severe exercise or in the arousal from hibernation when, as we have seen, fatty tissue is specifically involved. As with glycogenolysis, the adrenergic neurohormone—noradrenaline—stimulates lipolysis in adipose tissue and this, once again, is secondary to the activation of the adenyl cyclase system to give increased levels of cAMP.

cAMP in Adipose Tissue Cells

Thus the individual cells of adipose tissue may be separated and the accumulation of cAMP in response to hormones may be measured directly; all those that increased lipolysis *in vivo*, namely ACTH, catecholamines, glucagon, LH and prolactin caused an increase in cAMP in the cells. By causing the cells to lyse and studying their "ghosts", consisting mainly of their cell membranes, Birnbaumer and Rodbell were able to show that the hormones increased the adenyl

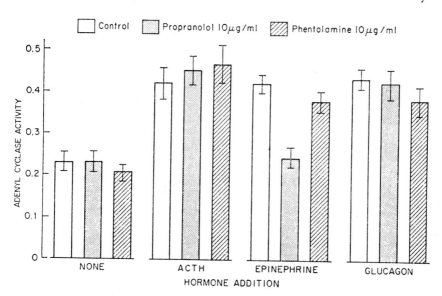

Fig. 2.17. Control of lipolysis. Effect of α- and β-adrenergic blockers on adenyl cyclase activity, measured in the absence and presence of 0·2 g/ml ACTH, adrenaline or glucagon. Fat cell ghosts were incubated for 10 min at 37°C. As can be seen, the α- and β-blockers did not affect the stimulation by ACTH or glucagon, which would indicate that they act on different receptor sites for the same system. (Birnbaumer and Rodbell, *J. biol. Chem.* 1969, **244**, 3477.)

cyclase activity, which survived this lysis because the enzyme was a part of the cell membrane. The actions of the various hormones did not add, so that it seemed that they all acted on the same enzyme, their differing activities being due to the presence of differing receptor sites for the hormones. Thus the inhibitor of β-adrenergic activity, propanolol, completely inhibited the action of adrenaline, but left that of the peptide hormones glucagon and ACTH unaffected (Fig. 2.17). The cAMP presumably activates a lipase that hydrolyses the neutral fat in the tissue to fatty acids and glycerol.

Insulin Inhibition. Insulin, the pancreatic hormone, is a powerful antilipolytic substance, and its action is accompanied by a reduced accumulation of cAMP in the tissue. It is not at all certain, however, whether it acts by an inhibition of adenylcyclase, or by stimulating phosphodiesterase. Thus the mechanism of insulin action in this respect remains obscure (Vol. 3).

Synaptic Transmission

The essential similarities between hormonal and nervous transmission have been emphasized earlier, but nowhere is the analogy better demonstrated than in the synaptic transmission process. There is evidence accumulating that the event succeeding the liberation of the synaptic transmitter is the activation of adenyl cyclase which, by allowing an accumulation of cAMP, might then initiate the post-synaptic events, be they electric discharge as in nerve or muscle, or the secretion of a hormone by a cell, and so on.

Brain Enzyme Concentrations

The evidence on which this involvement of cAMP in synaptic action is based is largely the very high concentrations of adenyl cyclase and cAMP phosphodiesterase in the brain; it is higher, in fact, than in any other tissue. Moreover, when the brain is homogenized and subjected to differential centrifugation, it is the fractions rich in nerve endings and synapses (synaptosomes) that have a high activity, an activity that is greatly increased when the particulate material is solubilized with a detergent, which suggests that the enzymes are located inside membrane vesicles. The activation of enzymes following the transmitter action on a neurone provides an obvious basis for memory, in the sense that the consequent chemical changes might leave a permanent mark on the character of the excitable cell membrane and thus modify its response to succeeding stimuli.

Corticosteroids

Receptor Proteins

It must be emphasized that not all hormones utilize cAMP as a second messenger. Thus the steroid hormones of the adrenal cortex probably do not do so; instead they penetrate their target cells, e.g. those of the liver or thymus, where they become immediately bound to "receptor proteins". The subsequent steps leading to increased synthesis of critical enzymes, e.g. tyrosine aminotransferase, are only a matter of conjecture. Since the histones bound to nuclear DNA probably act to inhibit its powers of RNA transcription, it has been suggested by Karlson that the hormones interact with histones, thereby activating transcription sites on the gene material of the cell.

HORMONAL CONTROL OF TRANSPORT

The hormonal control over metabolism becomes intelligible in terms of the activation or inhibition of key enzymes in the chain of chemical reactions. This activation may consist in a chemical conversion, the removal of an inhibitor group, or in some simple change in shape, the so-called *allosteric modification* of Monod.

Enzyme Synthesis

As indicated earlier in discussing the control of metabolism, the *synthesis* of enzymes plays an important role. This could consist in the production *de novo* of enzymes that are normally not present in the cell; in this case the gene material must be activated, or "de-repressed", to permit its transcription to give a new messenger-RNA that begins the synthetic process. Such a process has been shown to take place in the stimulation of bodily growth, by growth hormone, or in the enlargement of the uterus by ovarian hormone. The process would be inhibited by actinomycin D, the inhibitor of transcription from a DNA template. Alternatively, the synthesis of existing enzymes could be accelerated, and this might well be achieved by accelerated translation of existing messenger-RNA. As such it would be inhibited by puromycin or cycloheximide, but not by actinomycin D.

Substrate Availability

One important mode of control of metabolism is through substrate availability, so that if the rate of chemical reaction were critically determined by, say, the availability of glucose, then an acceleration of the transport of glucose to the site of its chemical change would accelerate the metabolic process. An important mode of increasing availability is through altering the permeability of the cell membrane to the substrate. This seems to be the manner in which insulin favours carbohydrate metabolism, the pronounced fall in blood-glucose level following an injection of insulin being, at least in part, due to an accelerated transport into most of the cells of the body (not those of the brain, however).

Facilitated Transfer

It will be recalled that the transport of many metabolizable substances into cells requires the presence within the membrane of postulated carriers; these are essentially specific arrangements of atoms on the cell membrane that permit selected substances to pass through much more rapidly than they otherwise would, as judged by their molecular size and lipid-solubility. The process has been described as *facilitated transfer*, or *catalysed permeability*.

Synthesis of New Carrier

The transport of many sugars and amino acids exhibits this type oᵢ facilitated transport, and it has been suggested that the mode of hormone acceleration of permeability, as revealed by insulin action, is through the synthesis of new carriers. On this basis there have been a variety of attempts to show that hormone-induced changes in transport are inhibited by inhibitors of protein synthesis. So far as the effects of insulin on sugar transport are concerned, this theory does not apply, and it seems that insulin modifies the affinity of sugars for the hypothetical carriers.

Amino Acid Transport

However, the stimulation of amino acid uptake by insulin does seem to be inhibited by puromycin. It will be recalled that the transport by facilitated transfer can be described in terms of two main parameters—the affinity of the substance for the carrier (proportional to $1/K_m$, K_m being the dissociation constant for the carrier–substrate complex) and V_{max}, the maximum rate of transport, this latter being governed by the number of theoretical carriers on the membrane. Analysis of the effects of puromycin indicated that V_{max} was reduced, suggesting a loss of carriers.

Glucocorticoid Action. Again the so-called glucocorticoids, i.e. the steroid hormones of the adrenal cortex that influence metabolism (cortisol and corticosterone), promote the process of gluconeogenesis, i.e. the synthesis of glucose from non-glycogen sources. They do this partly by promoting the catabolism of proteins and amino acids, and this is accompanied by accelerated transport into the liver where the amino acids are de-aminated so that their carbon-skeletons may be employed in the synthesis of carbohydrate. Associated with this accelerated transport into the liver there is diminished transport into skeletal muscle. Hydrocortisone certainly increases the uptake of amino acids by the isolated perfused liver, but this was maintained after treatment with actinomycin D. The increased uptake induced by insulin, on the other hand, was 50 per cent blocked by actinomycin D, suggesting once again the synthesis of new carrier material.

Salt and Water Transport

The transport of salt and water is strongly influenced by the posterior pituitary hormone, vasopressin, or antidiuretic hormone, and by the adrenal cortical hormone, aldosterone; this influence is exhibited in the kidney but also in a variety of other transport systems, such as the frog's skin or toad bladder. Whilst there is little doubt that these hormonal actions are mediated by cAMP, the actual mechanism whereby transport of water and salt is increased by, say, vasopressin in frog's skin, is by no means clear; the involvement of protein synthesis, for instance, has not been established.

Aldosterone. By contrast, the action of aldosterone, which favours transport of sodium out of the renal tubule (Vol. 1), is closely related to protein synthesis. Thus the time taken for the renal effects to manifest themselves is long, and they are blocked by actinomycin D.

Non-transport Hormonal Effects

It must be emphasized that any action on transport is only one of a variety of actions of a hormone. Thus insulin will definitely accelerate the incorporation of amino acids into proteins independently of accelerating their transport into the cell, as may be shown by introducing the amino acids into the cell before allowing the insulin to act. Again, artificial protein synthetic systems may be employed, using ribosomes from hormone-treated tissues, and it is found that, where the hormone increases protein synthesis, there is enhanced ribosomal activity, and *vice versa*. This is well illustrated by the action of cortisol, which has an anti-anabolic action on non-liver tissues, such as the thymus, and promotes protein synthesis by liver; the ribosomes of thymus are inhibited and those of liver are activated by treatment of the animal with cortisol. Moreover, as Spaziani has emphasized, the effects of inhibitors of protein synthesis on hormone action may not be due to a primary action on protein synthesis since often the effects, e.g. those of oestradiol on the glucose transport into uterus, are rapid in onset and may be due to a non-specific action of the inhibitor in increasing blood-flow. Often, too, the effects of the hormone, such as that of oestradiol on uptake of sugars by the uterus, occur so soon after administration of the hormone that it is difficult to envisage the preliminary synthesis of carriers.

Permease

The basic concept of the synthesis of a factor favouring cell membrane transport was developed by Monod, who coined the term "permease" to describe what is now called a carrier. Thus he found that the bacterium *Escherichia coli* could utilize galactose, provided that the enzyme galactosidase had been induced in the bacterium by growing it in a galactose-containing medium. The ability to synthesize this resides in the presence of a gene operon (Vol. 1), and some mutants can be found which lack this gene and are therefore incapable of synthesizing the enzyme. Monod found another "cryptic" mutant that also could not utilize galactose, but this was not because it could not synthesize galactosidase—it could—but because it lacked a means of transporting galactose into its cell. Monod found that the presence of this transport mechanism, or permease, was genetically controlled, so that the permease, or carrier, could be synthesized provided the genic material was present and activated.

PROSTAGLANDINS

In recent years the physiological actions of certain complex fatty acids have acquired great interest since they share many of the characteristics of hormones and neurotransmitters and may, indeed, be regarded as local tissue hormones. These lipids have been given the generic name of *prostaglandins*, the name originally given by Von Euler in 1935 to a lipid material of unknown structure extracted from human seminal plasma. On intravenous injection the material lowered arterial pressure through a relaxation of the vascular muscle tone; it stimulated contraction, however, of isolated intestinal and uterine muscle. Subsequent work has shown that the origin of this material was the seminal vesicles rather than the prostate gland. Since then active lipid material has been found in a variety of tissues and fluids, and chemical studies have revealed that their activities are due to mixtures of several fatty acids based on prostanoic acid:

Prostanoic acid

These prostaglandins are synthesized in nature from arachidonic acid and dihomo-λ-linoleic acid, both being derived from linoleic acid in the diet; this is presumably why linoleic acid is an "essential fatty acid". They have been isolated from such diverse tissues and fluids as seminal plasma, menstrual fluid, lung, brain, thymus, the renal medulla* and the iris of the eye.

Irin

Thus, to choose the eye as an example, it had been recognized for many years that injury to the eye was usually associated with a constriction of the pupil, i.e. a constriction of the smooth circular muscle of the iris. A similar constriction could be induced by antidromic stimulation of the sensory nerve—the trigeminal. Ambache found in the iris a lipid material, which he called *irin* and which caused contraction of smooth muscle, and he was able to exclude such substances as histamine, acetylcholine, etc. as being responsible. Irin was subsequently shown to be a mixture of several prostaglandins among which are $F_{2\beta}$ and E_2. It is possible, then, that irritative stimuli cause the release of these prostaglandins either from the iris tissue or from the terminals of the sensory neurone. In other tissues the prostaglandins may be released spontaneously (as with an *in vitro* preparation of the frog's intestine), in response to a nervous stimulus (as with the frog's gastric mucosa), or in response to a hormone (as with the release of PGA, PGE and PGF from liver by glucagon).

Structural Basis

Prostanoic acid is the basic skeleton of the prostaglandins, and numerous changes on this theme can be rung by alterations in its cyclopentane ring to give series described as PGE, PGF, PGA and PGB (Fig. 2.18). Modifications within any of these series are achieved by the presence of double bonds in the side-chains; thus PGE has one at the C_{13} position, E_2 has a second double bond at C_5 as well as

* The substance extracted from the renal medulla, medullin, which causes a sustained depression of blood pressure, is a prostaglandin-E, and it seems likely that its renal effects, (promoting excretion of sodium) are due to altered blood-flow, dissipating the medullary gradients necessary to operate the countercurrent mechanism (Vol. 1).

one at C_{13}; E_3 has three double bonds, and so on. If it is appreciated, furthermore, that PGE has four asymmetric centres at C_8, C_{11}, C_{12} and C_{15}, giving eight possible stereoisomers, the number of possible prostaglandins is enormous. Thus, so far the seminal vesicles have been shown to secrete some thirteen different compounds and doubtless many more remain to be identified.

Individual prostaglandins may be either excitatory or inhibitory on smooth muscle, so that the action of any fluid containing several must be the outcome of mutually inhibitory and synergistic tendencies; thus the PGE of human seminal plasma has a strong inhibitory action on the muscular wall of the uterus (myometrium) whereas PGF excites.

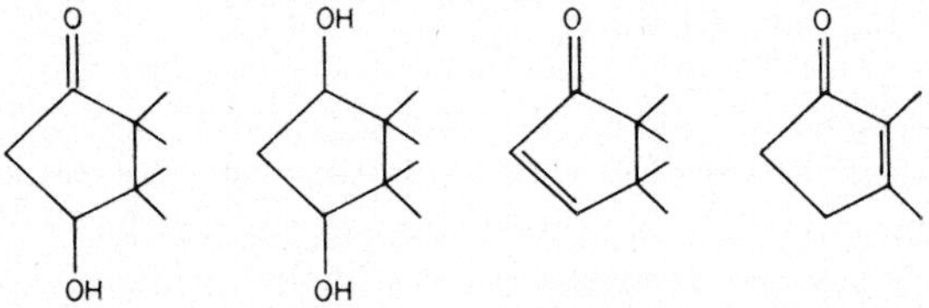

Fig. 2.18. The structural differences between prostaglandins of the E, F, A and B series. (Horton, *Physiol. Rev.* 1969, **49**, 124.)

Possible Transmitter Action

Prostaglandins have been isolated from most tissues, including the brain where their concentration is high although, when different regions of the brain are compared, only slight differences are found; this is in marked contrast to the situation with accepted transmitters such as dopamine. They are present in the cerebrospinal fluid, and there is an increased output into the fluid superfusing the cortex as a result of sensory stimulation, so that a transmitter function for prostaglandins has been postulated. Evidence on this point is by no means conclusive, however; thus the prostaglandins liberated into splenic smooth muscle on sympathetic stimulation do not act as transmitters, in that the smooth muscle response cannot be mimicked by them. Nevertheless microinjections of prostaglandins into the brain produce well-marked excitatory or inhibitory actions on neurones, whilst injection of small amounts into a cerebral ventricle in the unanaesthetized cat has a strong sedative effect, so that the animal retires to a corner and remains inactive and somnolent for long periods. In the cerebellum, moreover, it will antagonize the inhibitory effects of noradrenaline on spontaneously firing Purkinje cells.

Action on Adenyl Cyclase

The suggestion has been made that prostaglandins are able to antagonize the action of noradrenaline by acting on the adenyl cyclase system. Thus if noradrenaline exerts its action by activating the enzyme and causing accumulation of cAMP on the Purkinje neurone, then PGE_1 and PGE_2, by inhibiting adenyl cyclase, antagonize the action of noradrenaline.

Inhibition of Transmitter Release

Another possible mode of action is by reducing the amount of transmitter released at a nerve terminal. Hedqvist showed that PGE_2 reduces the output of noradrenaline from the spleen in response to sympathetic stimulation. PGE_2 is certainly released during splenic stimulation, so that it might well act in this manner rather than as a transmitter of nervous activity.

Cyclic AMP and Prostaglandin Action

Many of the effects of prostaglandins are manifest in those systems where cyclic AMP is thought to mediate the hormonal response; thus PG inhibits the antidiuretic action of vasopressin—a hormonal action closely connected with cAMP as a "second messenger". Again, the lipolytic and antilipolytic responses in fat tissue, induced by noradrenaline or insulin respectively, are almost certainly mediated through the adenyl cyclase–cAMP system, and it has been found that PGE_1 inhibits noradrenaline-stimulated lipolysis, an inhibition that is accompanied by inhibition of accumulation of cAMP. Finally, nervous stimulation of the fat pads caused release of sufficient prostaglandins to affect lipolysis, a quantity as small as one nanogramme being adequate to inhibit nerve-stimulated lipolysis.

Insulin-like Action

Thus PGE_1 is like insulin in inhibiting hormone-induced lipolysis; as with insulin this only happens when the cell membrane is intact, i.e. when adenyl cyclase, which is apparently strongly attached to the membrane, is in a position to influence cell cAMP. Thus, as illustrated in Fig. 2.19, it is possible that prostaglandins may participate in a negative feedback system, the cAMP produced as a result of the hormonal activation of cyclase causing release of prostaglandin, which inhibits adenylcyclase. In many other systems, however, prostaglandins may mimic the action of the stimulating hormone, in which case it may be postulated that they activate adenyl cyclase.

Inactivation

In vivo the main inactivation pathway is through conversion of the OH-group at C_{15} to a ketone by a dehydrogenase. Prostaglandins are also susceptible to β- and γ-oxidation, and hydrogenation of the double bonds leads to the formation of more saturated products that are excreted in the urine. The lungs and the liver are mainly responsible for this inactivation and so efficient is this that a single circuit of blood through the lungs causes inactivation of at least 90 per cent of the prostaglandins. Hence the actions of prostaglandins must be essentially local, i.e. at the site of their release.

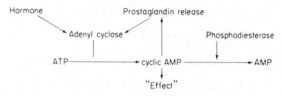

Fig. 2.19. The postulated negative feed-back role of prostaglandins. The cAMP produced, as a result of hormonal activation of adenylcyclase, may cause the release of prostaglandins as well as having an effect in the cell, and this prostaglandin release could cause inhibition of adenylcyclase. (Horton, *Physiol. Rev.* 1969, **49**, 124.)

Functions of the Prostaglandins

Since prostaglandins have been isolated from all tissues examined, we may reasonably implicate their release with some aspect of the tissue's function, e.g. the constriction of the pupil of the eye in response to eye-trauma, the modification of synaptic activity in the central nervous system, the excitation of uterine contractions during labour, and so on. It is reasonable to look upon them as local hormones interacting with the better understood and more definitive mechanisms.

Vascular Effects

Of special interest is the effect on vascular smooth muscle. PGE_1 and PGE_2 lower systemic arterial pressure by lowering peripheral resistance so that there is increased blood-flow in muscle and skin. Consequently the intervention of prostaglandins in the increased peripheral blood-flow during exercise (Vol. 3) has been suspected, but by no means proved. As with other systems, it must be emphasized that it is quite incorrect to state that prostaglandins as a class have a given effect; for example, E_1 and E_2 do indeed cause lowered arterial pressure through relaxation of vascular muscle but $PGF_{2\beta}$ causes a powerful constriction of veins and, by increasing venous return, tends to *raise* arterial pressure.

Opposing Influences

In general, whenever a prostaglandin is found to exert one effect another may be found to exert the opposite; furthermore there are many species variations in response, e.g. PGE_1 inhibits gastric secretion in rats but not in man.

THE FATE OF HORMONES

We have seen that a neurotransmitter is removed from its site of action by chemical or other means, a process that serves to limit the period of its activity and thus to leave the target organ responsive to further quantities. Clearly, if there were no removal mechanism, control over the target organ through changes in amount of transmitter released would be impossible. In the same way the blood-borne hormones must be removed from the blood so that control over the target organ can be exerted through variations in the blood concentration. Because removal from the blood must of necessity take some time, by virtue of the large volume of blood that must be treated, the time-scale of turnover of the hormone will be much greater than that of removal of neurotransmitter. Physiologically this may be revealed by the time-lag between the stimulus for hormonal activity and the actual response of the target organ. Thus the control over water excretion is exerted through the posterior pituitary hormone, *vasopressin* or the *antidiuretic hormone*, and there is normally a basic level of this hormone in the blood. When water is ingested, thereby reducing the osmolality of the blood, the osmoreceptors are inhibited and the secretion of vasopressin into the blood ceases. However, the stimulus to urine formation takes time to manifest itself, since this consists in the reduction in the level of circulating hormone (i.e., it depends on the metabolic removal of the hormone), so that the slower the turnover of the hormone in the blood the longer the time-lag between water ingestion and urinary excretion.

Half-life

Experimentally the turnover of a hormone is measured by injection of labelled hormone into the circulation and measuring the decay of the label in the blood; from this a "half-life" is calculated, i.e. the time required for the concentration to fall to half its initial value. The hormones fall into three categories, namely those with a rapid turnover with half-lives of a few minutes, such as ACTH and the releasing factors; those with half-lives of 15–20 minutes such as vasopressin and insulin, and those with a long half-life of many hours, such as oestrogens and cortisol.

Kidney and Liver. The mechanism for removal varies with the hormone and is not unique for a given hormone. The target organ presumably inactivates the hormone after it has exerted its effect, but the turnover is often so rapid that other mechanisms must be invoked, such as metabolism by the liver with subsequent excretion of the products. A pathway for this excretion is the bile, but the liver also conjugates many hormones with glucuronic acid or sulphate, making them sufficiently water-soluble to allow the kidney to excrete them easily, so that the main route for excretion becomes the urine.

Involution of Secretory Apparatus

We may note that the cessation of secretion of a hormone after a period of vigorous activity would leave the secretory cells with large quantities of secretory granules in their cytoplasm, so we may envisage a mechanism coming into play that would not only prevent continued synthesis but cause destruction of the synthesized hormone. In fact, electron microscopical studies of the anterior pituitary have shown that, when lactation is inhibited by removal of the suckling animals from the mother, there is a progressive involution of the protein-secreting machinery, brought about by sequestering of the endoplasmic reticulum in lysosomes or autophagic vacuoles. Not only is the synthesizing apparatus engulfed but also the secretory granules, presumably containing prolactin; the high concentration of acid phosphatase present in the lysosomes indicates a breakdown function. It may be that this sequestering and lysis of secretion represents one of the mechanisms of braking the secretory activity of a gland; at any rate an increased secretory activity by anterior pituitary cells is accompanied by increased acid phosphatase activity in them.

THE ADRENAL GLAND

We may complete this general account of endocrine action with a description of the structure and main functions of the adrenal gland, which provides an instructive example of the cooperation of the endocrine and nervous control systems in a variety of functions.

Medulla and Cortex

In the mammal the two adrenal glands, or *suprarenal bodies*, lie on or near the upper lobe of each kidney. The gland is a dual structure in mammals, the central core, or *medulla*, having a quite different embryological origin from the outer shell, or *cortex*. The medulla is derived from neural ectoderm and is to be regarded as an extension of the nervous system, secreting adrenaline and noradrenaline—the latter being, as we have seen, the transmitter in peripheral adrenergic mechanisms. Adrenaline is closely related to noradrenaline, being the methyl derivative:

Noradrenaline   PNMT   Adrenaline

the process of methylation taking place in the adrenal medulla and being catalysed by the enzyme *phenylethanolamine-N-methyl transferase* (PNMT). The adrenal cortex secretes steroid hormones, e.g. cortisol, aldosterone, etc. In general, the medullary hormones cooperate with the adrenergic nervous system in immediate responses to emergencies, so that adrenaline causes increased rate and force of heart beat, dilatation of blood vessels to muscles, and so on. The cortical hormones come into play in adaptations to long-term stresses, such as starvation, water and salt lack, and so on. As we shall see, there is a very intimate relation between cortex and medulla so that adequate function of the medulla relies on a continuous supply of steroid hormones from the cortex; and the close association of the two types of tissue in a single organ is to be regarded as a phylogenetic development permitting this cooperation.

Vascular Supply

This association is revealed by the special features of the blood circulation which ensure that blood leaving the cortex passes deeper into the medulla in sinusoidal-type vessels before finally being collected into a few veins that leave the gland. Figure 2.20 illustrates the basic features of the blood supply. The arterial supply is of two types; the majority of the arteries ramify in the subcapsular tissue and give rise to an anastomosing sinusoidal network of cortical arteries that surrounds the cords of cortical cells; the sinusoids get progressively wider and coalesce on approaching the centre of the medulla. As indicated by Fig.2.20, another type of artery—the arteriae medullae—passes directly through the cortex to ramify in the medullary tissue, so that the medulla receives blood mainly through the multitude of cortical

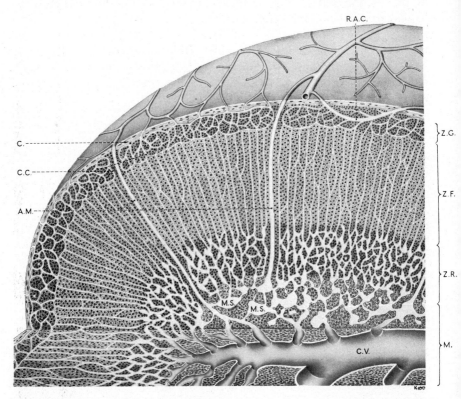

Fig. 2.20. Stereogram of mammalian adrenal gland showing the medulla (M) with its central vein (CV) and the cortex with its three zones, the zona glomerulosa (ZG), zona fasciculata (ZF) and zona reticularis (ZR) enclosed by the capsule (C). Two arteriae medullae (AM) and an arteria corticis (RAC) are shown. The columns of cortical cells are mostly separated by capillary sinusoids (CC). MS: Medullary sinus (Harrison and Hoey, "The Adrenal Circulation", Blackwell, 1960.)

capillaries but also through these medullary arteries. Both sets ultimately drain into the suprarenal vein. According to Bennett and Kilham the medullary cells are bathed at one pole by blood from the cortex and at the other by blood from the medullary artery; we may presume that it is at this latter pole that the cell's nutrition takes place since the blood is true arterial blood. At the other pole the cell receives its hormonal stimulus from the cortex, and it may be at this pole that it empties its granules. As we shall see, the hormonal stimulus from the cortex is a stimulus to methylate noradrenaline, thereby converting it into an adrenaline-storing cell. The actual stimulus for ejection of the hormone from the cell is nervous, however.

Adrenal Medulla

The medulla is made up of cords of cells surrounded by blood vessels, and its tissue is easily differentiated from the surrounding cortex by the darkening after treatment with bichromate due to the oxidation of the catecholamines synthesized within the medullary cells. It is this reaction to bichromate that gave rise to the term *chromaffine tissue*.

Extramedullary Chromaffine Tissue

Chromaffine tissue is not confined to the adrenal gland but is found in many regions of the body in close association with the sympathetic nervous system, in fact the cells of the chromaffine tissues originate as neurones that have migrated from the spinal cord along the course of the sympathetic nerves. Some migrate to the dorsal abdominal wall to form the adrenal medulla; other prominent aggregates are associated with the sympathetic ganglia, that on the ventral surface of the aorta being called the *organ of Zuckerkandl*; other chromaffine cells are distributed in relation to the gonads and in the dermis of the skin. In the adult mammal, however, the hormone secreted by these extramedullary chromaffine tissues is negligible compared with that secreted by the adrenal medulla.

Phylogeny. As indicated above, the association of the chromaffine tissue with the adrenal cortical tissue is a development in phylogeny. Thus, in fishes the two tissues are not juxtaposed; in amphibians groups of chromaffine cells are interspersed among steroid-producing cells, both being buried in the mesonephros, i.e. the amphibian analogue of the mammalian kidney. In reptiles there is a dual distribution of chromaffine tissue, part being a band applied to the outside surface of the gland and a part distributed as small islets in the gland. In birds, both types of cell are distributed apparently at random within the tissue, and it is only in mammals that the chromaffine cells form a compact mass in the middle of the gland.

Noradrenaline and Adrenaline Cells. The chromaffine cells contain the hormones adrenaline and noradrenaline within membrane-bound vesicles or granules, as in adrenergic neurones. In the latter,

however, the only neurohumour is noradrenaline, whereas the cells of
the adrenal medulla contain either noradrenaline or adrenaline, and
the development of techniques for revealing the presence of one or
other hormone specifically has allowed the histological differentiation
of the two types of cell. Thus the tissue may be treated with the fixative
glutaraldehyde and osmium tetroxide; osmium binds to the cells that

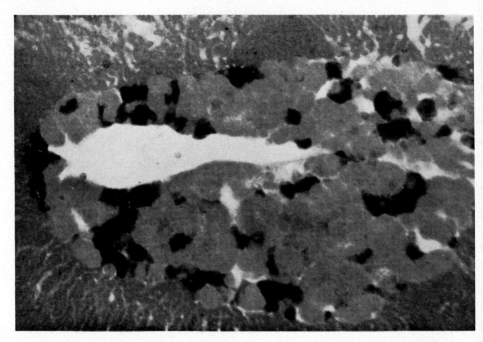

Fig. 2.21. The histological differentiation of noradrenaline and adrenaline.
The tissue is fixed with glutaraldehyde and osmium tetroxide, the osmium
binds preferentially to the cells that store noradrenaline and these appear
dark in relation to those that are pale and contain adrenaline. (Coupland
et al., Nature, 1964, **201**, 1241.)

store noradrenaline and so these cells appear dark in relation to the
pale adrenaline-containing cells (Fig. 2.21). The proportions of the
two types of cell vary with the species amongst the mammals; in man
noradrenaline constitutes some 9–22 per cent of the total catecholamine
and this correlates with the proportions of the cell-types as counted
histologically. The cells come into close relation with the sinusoidal-
type of blood vessels in the tissue and, when activated by their nervous
supply, the granules empty into the extracellular space by a process of
exocytosis.

Sympathetic Activation

The cells of the adrenal medulla are synaptically related to nerve endings derived from the splanchnic nerve. These endings contain typical cholinergic synaptic vesicles of about 350 Å diameter; thus stimulation of the splanchnic nerve causes release of acetylcholine at the cell's membrane, and this causes emptying of the medullary hormones into the blood stream. In a similar way the extramedullary chromaffin cells are activated by the sympathetic outflow from the cord. It will be recalled that sympathetically innervated organs are

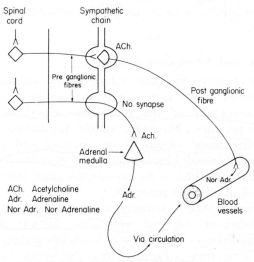

Fig. 2.22. The adrenal medulla. The adrenal medulla is analogous with a sympathetic ganglion; the upper figure shows the normal sympathetic pathway and the lower shows the adrenal pathway.

activated after the outflow from the cord has relayed in a ganglion, i.e. by postganglionic fibres, and these postganglionic fibres usually liberate noradrenaline at their terminals. Thus the preganglionic fibres release acetylcholine, which activates the postganglionic fibre which releases, at its ending, noradrenaline.

Analogy with Ganglion. The chromaffin cells are thus the analogues of sympathetic ganglion cells, being activated by the cholinergic neurones in the spinal cord and releasing their neuro-humour, this time mainly adrenaline, into the general blood circulation instead of in close relation to an effector cell such as the smooth muscle fibre of a blood vessel. The analogy is illustrated in Fig. 2.22.

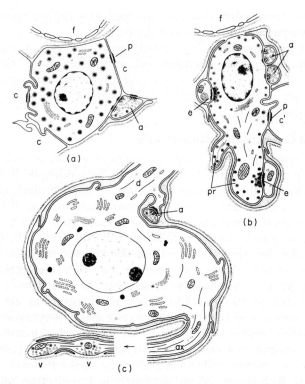

Fig. 2.23. Diagram comparing some features of an adrenal medullary chromaffine cell (a), a small granule-containing cell (b) and a principal sympathetic neuron (c). In the series a to c the covering of satellite cytoplasm (fine stippling) becomes progressively more extensive, whilst the distribution of intracytoplasmic dense-cored vesicles is progressively more restricted. Cell a, which secretes into the bloodstream, is freely related across basement membrane (coarse stippling) to fenestrated capillaries (f); and cell c, which directs the release of transmitter substance to its axon terminals, has a complete covering of satellite cytoplasm. Cell b, with efferent synapses (e) and cytoplasmic prolongations (pr) in addition to areas of cell surface free of satellite covering, appears to represent an intermediate cell type, exhibiting some of the features both of the neuron and the chromaffine cell. a: afferent synapses; p: attachment plaques; c: chromaffine cells adjacent to cell a; c′: small granule-containing cell adjacent to cell b; d: base of dendrite; ax: origin of axon; v: terminal varicosities of axon of cell c. (Matthews and Raisman, *J. Anal.* 1969, **105,** 255.)

to the blood, revealing its endocrine action, whilst the neurone, which directs its transmitter exclusively to the synaptic region, is completely ensheathed. The small cell has some regions free from ensheathing satellite cytoplasm, revealing its similarity to the chromaffine cell.

Once again, then, adrenaline may be seen as a reinforcement for the primary sympathetic outflow from the cord.

Stimuli to Secretion. The stimuli provoking sympathetic activation, with consequent liberation of adrenaline from chromaffin tissue, are all forms of emotional and physical stress—fear, anger, haemorrhage, a fall in blood-sugar (hypoglycaemia), cold, asphyxia and muscular exercise.

The Small Granule-Containing Cells

The technique for identifying adrenergic neurones or cells by virtue of their fluorescence after treatment with formaldehyde has brought into prominence the existence of a class of small granule-containing cells within the ganglia of the autonomic system, e.g. the superior cervical ganglion. These are interesting because they may be regarded as the "missing link" between neurone and endocrine cell, since they not only, like the chromaffin cells of the adrenal medulla, receive a synaptic innervation from one neurone but they also make a post-synaptic type of connection with another neurone; both of these neurones being in the ganglion. They thus appear to act as inter-neurones, intercalated between pre-synaptic and post-synaptic neurones of the ganglion; and it is interesting that the electrical events recorded from post-synaptic neurones in the ganglion led Libet to postulate the existence of adrenergic influences giving rise to the P-wave.

Synaptic Relations. When examined in the electron microscope, these small cells of 6–12 μ diameter were seen to contain granular vesicles of 650–1200 Å diameter, concentrated in the peripheral cytoplasm. Often the cells gave rise to short processes only a few microns long containing high concentrations of the vesicles and these would make efferent synapses with adjacent cells. Sometimes there would be no process, the synapse being a junction between the cell body, or soma, and an adjacent cell—the *somatic efferent synapse*. In some cases it was possible to identify the post-synaptic cell as a principal sympathetic neurone of the ganglion. The afferent synapse, presumably formed by a cholinergic preganglionic nerve terminal, was revealed as a process containing many clear small vesicles in contact with the small cell.

Satellite Cell Enclosure. The similarities and differences between small cell (b), chromaffin cells of the adrenal medulla (a), and principal sympathetic neurone (c), are illustrated by Fig. 2.23. The interesting feature is the progressive increase in the degree to which the cell is enclosed by satellite-cell cytoplasm as we pass from the chromaffine cell (a) to the neurone (c), so that the chromaffin cell's surface has relatively unrestricted access to the extracellular space and thence

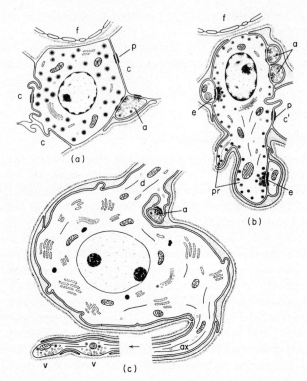

Fig. 2.23. Diagram comparing some features of an adrenal medullary chromaffin cell (a), a small granule-containing cell (b) and a principal sympathetic neuron (c). In the series a to c the covering of satellite cytoplasm (fine stippling) becomes progressively more extensive, whilst the distribution of intracytoplasmic dense-cored vesicles is progressively more restricted. Cell a, which secretes into the bloodstream, is freely related across basement membrane (coarse stippling) to fenestrated capillaries (f); and cell c, which directs the release of transmitter substance to its axon terminals, has a complete covering of satellite cytoplasm. Cell b, with efferent synapses (e) and cytoplasmic prolongations (pr) in addition to areas of cell surface free of satellite covering, appears to represent an intermediate cell type, exhibiting some of the features both of the neuron and the chromaffin cell. a: afferent synapses; p: attachment plaques; c: chromaffin cells adjacent to cell a; c': small granule-containing cell adjacent to cell b; d: base of dendrite; ax: origin of axon; v: terminal varicosities of axon of cell c. (Matthews and Raisman, *J. Anal.* 1969, **105,** 255.)

to the blood, revealing its endocrine action, whilst the neurone, which directs its transmitter exclusively to the synaptic region, is completely ensheathed. The small cell has some regions free from ensheathing satellite cytoplasm, revealing its similarity to the chromaffin cell.

Sympathetic Activation

The cells of the adrenal medulla are synaptically related to nerve endings derived from the splanchnic nerve. These endings contain typical cholinergic synaptic vesicles of about 350 Å diameter; thus stimulation of the splanchnic nerve causes release of acetylcholine at the cell's membrane, and this causes emptying of the medullary hormones into the blood stream. In a similar way the extramedullary chromaffine cells are activated by the sympathetic outflow from the cord. It will be recalled that sympathetically innervated organs are

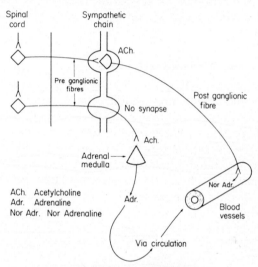

Fig. 2.22. The adrenal medulla. The adrenal medulla is analogous with a sympathetic ganglion; the upper figure shows the normal sympathetic pathway and the lower shows the adrenal pathway.

activated after the outflow from the cord has relayed in a ganglion, i.e. by postganglionic fibres, and these postganglionic fibres usually liberate noradrenaline at their terminals. Thus the preganglionic fibres release acetylcholine, which activates the postganglionic fibre which releases, at its ending, noradrenaline.

Analogy with Ganglion. The chromaffine cells are thus the analogues of sympathetic ganglion cells, being activated by the cholinergic neurones in the spinal cord and releasing their neurohumour, this time mainly adrenaline, into the general blood circulation instead of in close relation to an effector cell such as the smooth muscle fibre of a blood vessel. The analogy is illustrated in Fig. 2.22.

Neural and Hormonal Cooperation

Adrenaline is very similar to noradrenaline in its actions, and in fact it was the strong analogy between the action of adrenaline on its target tissues with that of sympathetic stimulation that led Elliott to formulate the hypothesis of humoral transmission of nervous influences, suggesting that adrenaline was liberated at sympathetic nerve terminals. This similarity in action provides the mechanism whereby the effects of neural stimulation may be reinforced and sustained by hormonal action. In a situation demanding "fight or flight" a generalized stimulation of the sympathetic system includes the sympathetic supply to the adrenal medulla, with its consequent outpouring of its hormones into the blood.

Noradrenaline and Adrenaline Actions

The actions of adrenaline and noradrenaline are not identical, so that the hormonal action may modify the nervous; thus adrenaline causes vasoconstriction of the splanchnic blood supply, thereby raising blood pressure. However, unlike noradrenaline, it causes dilatation of the blood vessels of the muscles and brain, thereby permitting the increased blood-flow in the muscles required during exercise. Where the actions of the two are the same, moreover, adrenaline is some 4–8 times more powerful.

Glycogenolysis. Again, noradrenaline has little or no effect on glycogen metabolism, whereas adrenaline favours breakdown to glucose—glycogenolysis—so that there is an immediate rise in blood-glucose when adrenaline is liberated into the blood. The action is on both liver and muscle glycogen, but in the latter case the glucose-6-phosphate formed is not hydrolysed to glucose but enters directly into the metabolic pathways. Thus the hormonal release following sympathetic stimulation ensures that additional energy supplies are available to sustain the muscular events.

Muscle. Adrenaline does not activate or inhibit skeletal muscle, by contrast with smooth muscle; however it considerably increases the force of contraction, an action that is probably exerted through its influence on carbohydrate metabolism, promoting the regeneration of phosphorylase required for glycogenolysis in the muscle fibre.

Central Nervous System. The effects of adrenaline extend to the nervous system. Thus injections of adrenaline produce a condition of cortical arousal (Vol. 5), that leads to facilitation of spinal and brain-stem reflexes; it also facilitates transmission in sympathetic ganglia, thereby reinforcing the direct nervous influences on effector organs.

Adrenal Cortex

ACTH Activation

More prolonged stresses of the same kind as those which excite medullary secretion cause activation of the cortical tissue; this is not brought about by direct innervation but, as indicated earlier, through the secretion by the pituitary of the adrenocorticotrophic hormone— ACTH—which itself is released in response to the liberation by hypothalamic neurones of the appropriate releasing factor.

Structure

The cortex, or outer rind, of the adrenal gland is divided into three zones (Fig. 2.20, p. 172) according to the arrangements of blood vessels and cells; these are, from outside inwards, the *zona glomerulosa*, leading through a transitional zone to the *zona fasciculata* and the *zona reticularis*. The columnar cells of the zona glomerulosa are arranged in arcades while the cells of the zona fasciculata, which make up most of the thickness of the cortex, are arranged as nearly straight cords, one cell thick, and separated from adjacent cords by vascular spaces. The zona reticularis is a thin zone adjacent to the medulla, composed of an irregular array of darker-staining cells. The blood capillaries, separated from the cortical cells by a basement membrane, are of the fenestrated type and have been classified as sinusoids rather than true capillaries, although their inclusion in the reticulo-endothelial system (p. 292) may be incorrect as no phagocytic activity of their cells has been observed.

Lipid Droplets. The characteristic feature of the cortical cell is the presence of lipid droplets, or liposomes, presumably containing the lipid cortical secretions or their metabolic precursors, such as cholesterol. In the electron microscope the most prominent feature, especially in the cells of the zona fasciculata, is the highly developed smooth-surfaced endoplasmic reticulum made up of an anastomosing system of tubular elements that seems to fill most of the cell. Lipid droplets are associated with the Golgi zone which may well be responsible for hormone storage and/or synthesis. Presumably because of the lipid nature of the hormones of the adrenal cortex, well-developed secretory granules are not observed, nor yet is there morphological evidence for the emptying of vesicles by exocytosis into the extracellular space during activity. A factor militating against observations of this sort, however, is the very low concentrations of hormones in the gland, which relies on synthesis of the hormones before significant secretion into the blood.

Ascorbic Acid. The cortical cells contain a very high concentration of ascorbic acid which diminishes when the gland is thrown into activity, so that the concentration in the gland is often used as a measure of activity.

Function of the Adrenal Cortex

The adrenal medulla is not essential for life, whereas the cortex is, so that its removal from an animal leads to a variety of signs, including fall in blood pressure, failure of renal function, and a fall in blood sugar that may lead to hypoglycaemic convulsions. The defects occur more rapidly if the animal is submitted to stress, and it is customary to regard the adrenal cortex as the endocrine organ most closely concerned in the animal's reaction to stresses of various sorts, such as haemorrhage and hunger. Thus a surgical operation is usually fatal in a human subject if his adrenal cortex is deficient.

Hormones

The hormones of the cortex fall into two classes, namely the *mineral corticoids*, e.q. aldosterone (controlling salt and water secretion), the action of which will be discussed in Vol. 3, and the *glucocorticoids*, so described because of their influence on carbohydrate metabolism; these glucocorticoids are *cortisol* and *corticosterone*. Other steroids found in the gland are cortisone and deoxycorticosterone. The sex hormones—oestrogens, androgens and progesterone—although present in, and synthesized by, the gland, are not secreted into the blood.

Carrier Proteins. The glucocorticoids form the largest part of the adrenal cortical secretion. Like thyroxine, they are carried in the blood bound to carrier protein in a reversible association, mainly with a globulin, namely *transcortin* or *corticosteroid binding globulin* (*CBG*). In this way a considerable store of the hormones is carried in the blood, the target organs competing with the carrier protein for the free material. Normally the carrier protein is about 50 per cent saturated with hormone, and it requires only a small rise in secretion for the whole to be saturated; in consequence, relatively small amounts of steroid hormone added to the blood increase the concentration of free hormone out of all proportion.

Gluconeogenesis. A prominent action of the glucocorticoids, such as cortisol, is to promote gluconeogenesis, i.e. the synthesis of glucose from non-carbohydrate sources, such as amino acids and fatty acids. Associated with this there is inhibition of fat synthesis, so that the concentration of free fatty acids in adipose tissue rises. As reactions to sustained stress these events are understandable. In a similar way many other actions of the hormones are intelligible in terms of making available metabolites that are necessary during stress. Thus the disappearance of lymphocytes from the blood accompanied by a decreased weight of the thymus and lymph nodes may well lead to the availability of nucleic acids, whilst the protein made free could be broken down to amino acids for gluconeogenesis.

Anti-inflammatory Action. A feature of the glucocorticoids is their anti-inflammatory action. In general, inflammation must be regarded as a defence mechanism in response to some form of injury (p. 311) and the increased blood supply and accumulation of leucocytes at the site of injury represent the steps taken to counter the source of damage and to initiate the processes of repair. A feature of the repair process is the destruction of dead and dying cells—achieved by phagocytosis—and subsequent hydrolysis of the phagocytosed material through liberation of enzymes by way of the lysosome system. That a hormone secreted naturally should antagonize this essentially beneficial process is surprising, and we may presume that it does not operate usually. However, inflammation is not always beneficial, as in rheumatic and arthritic conditions, and in practice it has been found that injections of corticosteroids, by antagonizing several features of the inflammatory process, exert a remarkably beneficial effect. In general their action is to antagonize the body's immune responses, and if, as is indeed thought, rheumatic conditions are expressions of an autoimmune response, their effectiveness is understandable. A complication in their use, however, is this "immunosuppressive" action, since it makes the subject more vulnerable to infectious diseases.

Stress Response Mechanism. According to Schayer, the anti-inflammatory action of the glucocorticoids is the key to their action in stress; thus the blood-flow in muscle and other tissues is accurately adjusted to the metabolic needs through an intrinsic mechanism involving probably the continuous production of dilator substances. This action is antagonized by the glucocorticoids, and a balance is normally maintained between the intrinsic vasodilators and the effective vasoconstrictor action of the glucocorticoids. Under stress the extra glucocorticoids secreted antagonize the vasodilatation that accompanies stress, and so allow a balance to be struck. If the animal is adrenalectomized, however, no such compensation occurs, and stress produces a variety of effects attributable to a primary preponderance of vasodilatation.

Permissive Action of Corticosteroids

Although the cortical steroids are secreted during stress in larger amounts than normally, the release of the hormones into the blood seems not to be the primary cause of the physiological responses, such as gluconeogenesis. Thus in the absence of adrenal glands the responses fail and the animal succumbs to stress, but if this adrenalectomized animal is merely given injections of cortical hormones to maintain a normal basic level, it is able to respond to stress in spite of the fact that it has no gland with which to respond by producing *extra* circulating hormone. The hormone is said to have a *permissive action*, enabling the animal to bring into action adaptive responses to stress, rather than activating these responses itself. The manner in which this permissive action may be exerted is illustrated by the cortical control of adrenaline synthesis.

Cortical–Adrenal Relations

Migration of Chromaffine Tissue to Adrenals

The main hormone of the adrenal medulla is adrenaline whereas that of extramedullary chromaffine tissue is noradrenaline, and it was surmised that the migration of chromaffine tissue to the adrenal gland in phylogenetic development represented an adaptation to permit the adrenal gland to methylate the noradrenaline synthesized in its cells. Thus in the fish the main hormone is adrenaline, the chromaffine tissue being completely separate from the steroid-producing adrenal tissue. In reptiles, where the chromaffine tissue is partly in a band outside the gland and partly distributed through the gland as small islets, it is found that there is no adrenaline in the outside band, whilst the inside tissue contains mainly adrenaline; moreover the outside band has no PNMT, the enzyme catalysing the methylation of nor-adrenaline, whilst the enzyme activity in the gland, proper, is very high.

Induction of PNMT Synthesis

We may assume that the close relation between steroid-secreting cells and chromaffine tissue in some way induces the synthesis of the methylating enzyme, PNMT, in the chromaffine cells, and in this way we may account for the intramural circulation referred to earlier, the chromaffine cells being bathed with blood that has passed through the cortex and presumably containing high concentrations of steroid hormones. Hypophysectomy, which abolishes the secretion of ACTH and therefore inhibits secretion of cortical hormones, causes a decline in the amount of adrenaline in the adrenal glands with a decrease in the adrenaline: noradrenaline ratio; administration of ACTH causes a return to normal, as do cortical steroids—aldosterone producing a 50 per cent increase in adrenaline concentration and the synthetic glucocorticoid dexamethasone causing approximately a 200 per cent increase. Figure 2.24 shows the increase in PNMT activity with time during treatment of hypophysectomized rats with dexamethasone; the slow time-course is consistent with the induction of synthesis of the enzyme, and this is supported by the failure of PNMT activity to

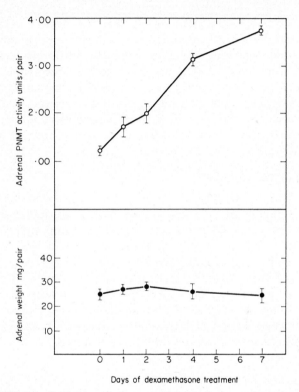

Fig. 2.24. Effect of dexamethasone treatment on adrenal weight and phenylethenolamine-N-methyl transferase activity (PNMT) in the hypophysectomized rat. Animals were given dexamethasone (1 mg intraperitoneally per day) for various periods and killed 17 days after hypophysectomy. (Wurtman and Axelrod, *J. biol. Chem.* 1966, **241**, 2301.)

appear if the animals are treated with actinomycin D or puromycin, inhibitors of protein synthesis (Vol. 1).

Induced Synthesis of Adrenaline. The direct proof that corticosteroids promote synthesis of adrenaline by chromaffin tissue was provided by Coupland who cultured the pre-aortic chromaffin bodies of 2-day-old rabbits, extramedullary tissue that contains greater than 90 per cent noradrenaline. When corticosterone was added to the medium the proportion fell to about 65 per cent, with a corresponding increase in the percentage of adrenaline, from a control value of about 10, to 35 per cent.

Intramural Circulation

It seems likely, then, that the medullary tissue contains a uniform population of cells whose synthetic activities in respect to the methylation of noradrenaline are under the continuous influence of the cortical steroids reaching them through the intramural circulation. Thus, with any given level of steroids reaching the tissue, a certain proportion of the cells has synthesized the methylating enzyme, PNMT, with the result that all their noradrenaline is converted to adrenaline. The adrenal cortex may be said to exert a permissive influence on the animal because it enables it to maintain adequate stores of adrenaline in its medullary tissue and thereby to be in a position to react to stress.

Activation of Key Enzymes

This, of course, is only one aspect of corticosteroid influence; its powers of inducing the synthesis, or of activating, metabolically key enzymes is not restricted to PNMT. Thus the promotion of glycogen deposition in the liver is due to the activation of the key enzyme *glycogen synthetase*, which catalyses the transfer of glucosyl units from UDPG to glycogen. Again, the glucocorticoids cause inhibition of lipogenesis with mobilization of free fatty acids in adipose tissue; this may be effected by reducing the availability of glycerophosphate required for esterification of fatty acids, a reduced availability caused by the simultaneously observed inhibition of glucose metabolism.

CHAPTER 3

The Effector Systems

Skeletal Muscle

Most of the activities with which we are concerned are brought about by the reversible shortening or lengthening of muscle. We have seen that in the voluntary—striated—muscles the shortening is brought about by the arrival of a nervous impulse at the junction, or synapse, between it and the muscle fibre, called the *neuromuscular junction*; this impulse ultimately gives rise to a wave of electrical activity that spreads over the whole fibre causing it to shorten. Between the two electrical events there is the liberation of transmitter; the liberation is caused by the arrival of the electrical impulse at the nerve ending, and the initiation of the muscle action potential results from the presence of this transmitter at the junction.

Smooth and Cardiac Muscle

The muscles concerned with involuntary activity, such as the constriction of blood vessels and movements of the gastro-intestinal tract, are controlled by the autonomic nervous system. Their structure is fundamentally different from that of the voluntary muscle, usually lacking the orderly array of relatively long fibres with their regularly arranged cross-striations, and so they are described as *smooth*, or *unstriated*. Occupying an intermediate position with regard to structure and behaviour is *cardiac muscle*. With these autonomically controlled muscles we find that contraction need not necessarily depend on the arrival of a nervous impulse; instead, both smooth and cardiac muscle are capable of spontaneous shortening and relaxation, whilst nervous activity can modify this by inhibition or potentiation.

In this chapter we shall be concerned with the intimate mechanism of the shortening of muscle that permits it to do work, and some aspects of the control of this shortening process.

CONTRACTION OF SKELETAL MUSCLE

Structure

The unit of voluntary, or skeletal, muscle is the fibre, some 10–100 μ thick and with a length that varies with the muscle; embryologically it is formed by the fusion of many cells, called *myoblasts*, and thus it contains many nuclei. The fibres are arranged in bundles held together by connective tissue; most are continued at both ends into tendinous

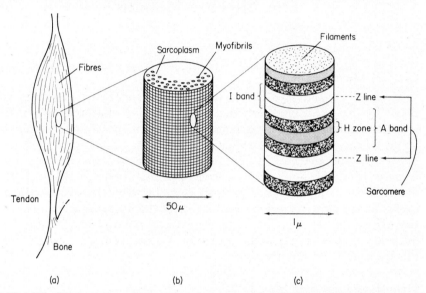

Fig. 3.1. Skeletal muscle and its elements. (a) Whole muscle; (b) part of a single fibre; (c) part of a myofibril.

bands that become attached to the bone or other structure that the muscle operates; they do not usually run the whole length of the muscle, so that they act both in series and in parallel. A portion of a fibre is illustrated in Fig. 3.1 (b), and the most prominent feature at this light-microscopical level of magnification is the horizontal striation. There is also a longitudinal striation and this is a reflexion of the fundamentally fibrous structure of the cell which consists of bundles of *myofibrils*, some 1–2 μ thick, embedded in a medium called the *sarcoplasm* (Fig. 3.1(c)).

Cross-striations

The cross-striations are due to the alternation of the optical and staining properties of the myofibrils along their axes, so that the whole fibre appears to be made up of a series of discs, the *A-* or *anisotropic* discs alternating with the I- or *isotropic* discs; the former appearing dark, with the usual staining methods, and the latter light. In polarized light the A-discs are highly birefringent and this suggests a more highly ordered ultrastructure than that in the I-discs. The thin black lines traversing the I-discs are called Z-lines. From an ultrastructural point of view, the unit of contraction in the myofibril is the sarcomere, measured from one Z-line to the next, thus embracing two half-I-bands and one A-band.

Electron Microscopy

In the electron microscope the myofibrils are seen to be made up, themselves, of large numbers of fine fibres called *myofilaments*. These are arranged closely together in groups separated from each other by a thick layer of sarcoplasm, whilst much thinner sheets of sarcoplasm separate the individual myofilaments. As Fig. 3.2 shows, the cross-striations are manifest as differences in electron-density of the tissue; particularly striking is the Z-line.

Mitochondria. The mitochondria are wedged between myofibrils. We have seen that in their electrical properties voluntary muscle fibres fall into two main classes, fast and slow; and morphologically this difference is manifest in the numbers of mitochondria within them—the fast white fibres having relatively few and the slow red fibres having very many, these being arranged along the myofibrils in a characteristic manner.

Sarcotubular System

A striking feature of the skeletal muscle fibre is the sarcotubular system, a series of tubules and cisterns equivalent to a modified endoplasmic reticulum. In general, this system of tubules has a dual character and may be divided into a *transverse T-system*, organized in relation to the Z-band,* and a *longitudinal system*, consisting of a series of tubules closely applied to the surface of the myofibrils. The arrangement is illustrated by the three-dimensional diagram of Fig. 3.3, and it can be seen that the longitudinal system is a series of tubules and cisterns surrounding the myofibril. From one Z-line to the next the longitudinal system is a continuous structure with both transversely and longitudinally arranged elements, whilst at the Z-line the transverse, or T-system, intrudes between the two terminal sacs of the longitudinal system.

---

* The triad is not always associated with the Z-band; thus in the very fast cricothyroid muscle of the bat it occurs at the junction between the A- and I-bands.

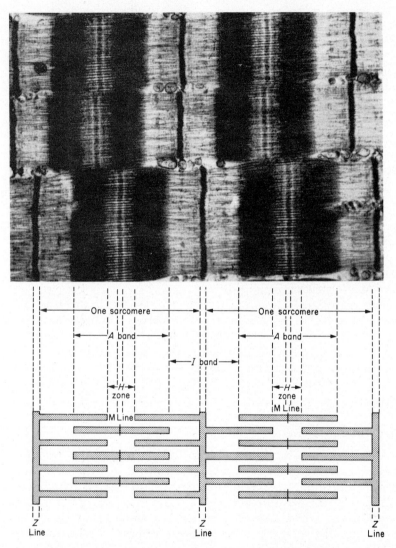

Fig. 3.2. A longitudinal electron micrograph of frog muscle fibrils to show the arrangement of actin (fine filaments) and myosin (dark thicker filaments). Distance between the Z-lines (dense cross bands) is about 2·5 μ. Vesicles of the sarcoplasmic reticulum can be seen at the Z-line level. (Courtesy of Dr. H. E. Huxley.)

Triad. Where the two systems come together there is apparently no connection, but the respective membranes come in close apposition to give the appearance, in section, of a *triad*. These triads are illustrated in the electron micrograph of Fig. 3.4, and their mode of formation is illustrated schematically in Fig. 3.5. It would seem that the longitudinal system of tubules is the strict analogue of the endoplasmic reticulum of other cells, whilst the transverse T-system is a development connected with the activation process of muscular contraction. Thus

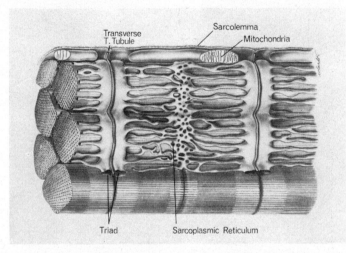

Fig. 3.3. A drawing depicting the T-tubules and sarcoplasmic reticulum in relation to several myofibrils of amphibian skeletal muscle. There are discrete myofibrils of uniform size, each ensheathed by sarcoplasmic reticulum, with pairs of terminal cisternae associated at each Z-line with a slender T-tubule to form a "triad". The localization of the triads at the Z-line of amphibian muscle makes it more comparable to mammalian cardiac muscle. (Fawcett and McNutt, *J. Cell Biol.* 1969, **42,** 1.)

there is little doubt that the T-system opens on to the surface of the muscle fibre, its wall being continuous with the sarcolemma, and is thus in direct connection with the extracellular fluid of the tissue; this is in contrast with the longitudinal L-system. We shall see that it is through the transverse T-system that the individual myofilaments are activated rapidly during the contractile process.

The Sarcolemma

This is the outermost coat of the muscle cell and was revealed as a definite structure by the classical histologists during the formation of a "retraction clot", the internal structures of the fibre contracting locally and leaving a clear translucent membrane bridging the gap. In the light-microscope it appears structureless, but in the electron microscope it appears as a complex, containing the plasma membrane, similar to that of other cells. Outside the plasma membrane there is a 200–300 Å thick zone presumably consisting of "basement membrane material"; and outside this there is a thin feltwork of fine collagen

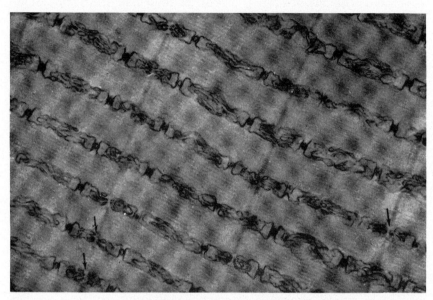

Fig. 3.4. Illustrating the sarcoplasmic reticulum. A small area of a muscle fibre has been cut longitudinally; the triads consist of a slender intermediate tube flanked by two larger lateral channels; these run across the broad face of the myofibrils in planes perpendicular to the page. The longitudinally orientated tributaries of the triads form tight networks parallel to the myofibrils. The branches of the two triads in the same sarcomere are continuous in the region of the H-band, but often appear to be discontinuous at the level of the Z-line (arrows). (Fawcett and Revel, *J. biophys. biochem. Cytol.* 1969, **10,** Suppl. 89.)

fibrils. The myofibrils immediately under the plasma membrane appear to be connected to the latter in the Z-band region to give a scalloped effect. When a muscle fibre atrophies, the plasma membrane and its contents shrink away from the basement membrane layer, which retains the shape of the unatrophied fibre. Again, the Japanese worker Natori showed that a single muscle fibre could be "skinned" by pulling off the sarcolemma and underlying plasma membrane.

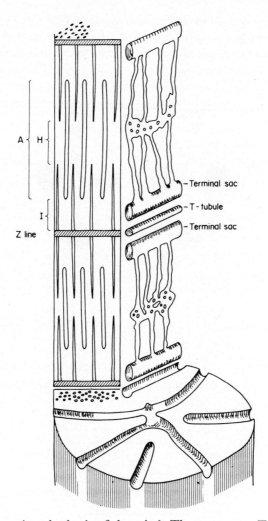

A

H

I

Z line

Terminal sac

T - tubule

Terminal sac

Fig. 3.5. Illustrating the basis of the triad. The transverse T-tubule comes into close relation with terminal sacs of the longitudinal system.

The A- and I-Bands

We have seen that the most striking feature of the histology of the muscle fibre is the cross-striation; in the electron microscope this is revealed as regions of greater and less electron-density, due to the presence of what was called the A-substance in the A-bands Extraction of the protein, *myosin*, from the muscle fibre destroyed this periodicity, so that the accumulations are due to the presence of this protein. When longitudinal sections of myofibrils are examined at very high resolution, it can be seen that they are made up of both thick and thin filaments; in the A-band both types of filaments could be seen as an interdigitated array, whilst in the I-band there were only thin filaments (Fig. 3.2).

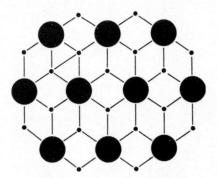

Fig. 3.6. Transverse section of the myofibril showing each thick filament surrounded by six thin filaments.

On cross-section the A-band showed a primary array of thick filaments some 100 Å in diameter, packed hexagonally some 300–350 Å apart, and between these were the thin filaments, some 30 Å in diameter, located such that each was associated with three thick filaments (Fig. 3.6). In the I-bands the cross-section consisted only of an array

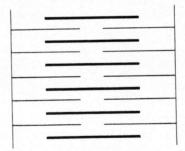

Fig. 3.7. The interdigitation of thin and thick filaments.

of the thin filaments. H. E. Huxley concluded from his electron micro-scopical and X-ray diffraction studies that the thin filaments of the I-band were continuous with those in the A-band, and suggested the structure for the whole sarcomere illustrated schematically in Fig. 3.7, the thin filaments being attached to the Z-line substance and inter-digitating with the thick, myosin, filaments.

Effects of Contraction on Sarcomere: Shortening of I-band

It was shown by A. F. Huxley that contraction of muscle was definitely associated with a shrinking of the I-band, whilst the A-band retained the same length; stretching the muscle caused a lengthening of only the I-band. It was argued that contraction of the muscle

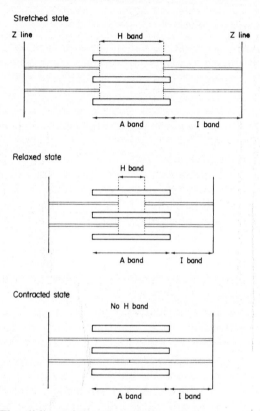

Fig. 3.8. The sliding of the filaments in relation to each other.

represented the sliding of the thin filaments between the thick filaments, a process that was brought about by the formation and breaking of chemical linkages between the two types of filaments. In the electron microscopic picture of Fig. 3.2, it is seen that the dense A-band has a less dense portion, called by the classical histologists the *H-band*; this is clearly the region where there has been no overlap between A- and I-filaments; when the sarcomere shortens the H-band disappears, as illustrated schematically in Fig. 3.8, which shows that at about 90 per cent of resting length the I-filaments attached to adjacent Z-bands have met in the A-band. Further shortening is associated with shrinking of the I-bands until they disappear at about 65 per cent of resting length. Shortening beyond this point, which certainly occurs experimentally, may be associated with a buckling of the filaments in some way.

Constant Filament Length

It was originally considered that the filaments making up a muscle fibre shortened during contraction, so that an important test of the sliding filament theory is that the myofilaments themselves do not change in length. By extracting muscle with glycerol the fibrillar elements remain intact and the muscle is able to contract under appropriate treatment. Such a preparation can be mechanically disrupted, in which case individual filaments can be separated and examined in the electron microscope; these are both thin and thick, the thin ones being often isolated in groups attached to a band of dense material corresponding to the Z-line. The thick filaments were $1 \cdot 5 \, \mu$ long and the thin filaments $1 \, \mu$ long, and these lengths were independent of the state of contraction of the muscle before extraction.

Cross-linkages

The structural relations between the thick and thin filaments in the region of overlap are of the utmost interest, since it is here that chemical changes that cause the thin filaments to slide over the thick filaments must occur. When examined at sufficiently high magnification these thick fibres can be seen to have lateral projections, or cross-bridges, connecting them apparently with the I-filaments, and this gives rise to a definite periodicity along the fibril of about 133 Å, since each thin filament is connected with its three surrounding thick filaments once every 400 Å along its length, these links being spaced fairly uniformly along its length.

Z-line

Of special interest is the structure of the Z-line since this seems to be the anchor for the I-filaments of adjacent sarcomeres; unfortunately it is not easy to resolve its structure. It seems definite that the I-filaments are not continuous across the Z-line, but some sort of looping of the filaments about each other to permit the transfer of tension from one set to another has been postulated.

Force of Contraction

Experimental Measurement

The force of contraction of a muscle may be easily measured by attaching its tendon to a lever, as illustrated in Fig. 3.9a; the muscle may be caused to lift a weight, and during the process it shortens. Alternatively the shortening may be prevented by connecting the tendon of the muscle to a strain-gauge, a device that consists of wire which alters its electrical resistance when stretched; by the use of a Wheatstone-bridge circuit the very small displacement of a stiff

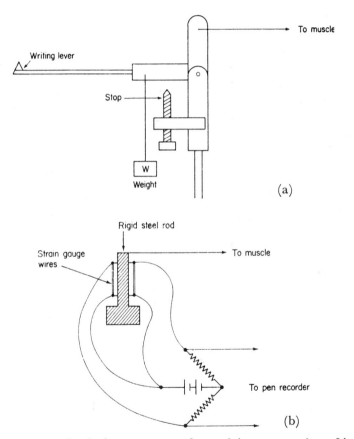

Fig. 3.9. The mechanical arrangement for studying contraction of isolated muscle. (a) Isotonic contraction. The muscle is allowed to shorten. (b) Isometric contraction. The muscle is held rigid by the steel bar and can develop tension without shortening. The tension developed is detected by means of the strain gauge, bridge, and a pen recorder.

isometric lever is converted into a change in voltage, which operates a pen-recorder (Fig. 3.9b). The actual movement required to produce a significant change is so small that the contraction is virtually *isometric*. When the muscle is allowed to shorten and lift a weight the contraction is called *isotonic*, since it maintains the same tension during the whole process of lifting. By applying a single shock to the muscle directly

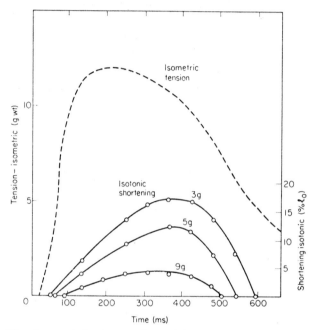

Fig. 3.10. The form of the isometric and isotonic twitch (frog sartorius at 0°C). Note how the isotonic twitches, under various loads, have died away several hundreds of millisecs before the tension has declined to zero. (Bendall, "Muscles, Molecules and Movement", Heinemann, 1969.)

the muscle may be caused to "twitch", and this will be recorded as an increase and fall of tension under isometric conditions, or as a shortening followed by return to initial length under isotonic conditions (Fig. 3.10).

Recruitment

When successively higher and higher shocks are applied to a muscle the tension developed increases until at a certain stimulus-strength, maximal tension is developed. The increase is essentially the result of the recruitment of more and more fibres into the contraction process, the thresholds for the individual fibres being different. On this basis, then, the contraction of a single fibre is all-or-none, in the sense that when contraction has been initiated it develops its maximum tension. Consequently, isolated single fibres should show a single maximal tension on stimulation at suprathreshold strength. For single shocks this statement is essentially true, in the sense that increasing the strength of the stimulus above threshold does not produce any increase in developed tension. *⇒ contraction of syge fiber is all or none*

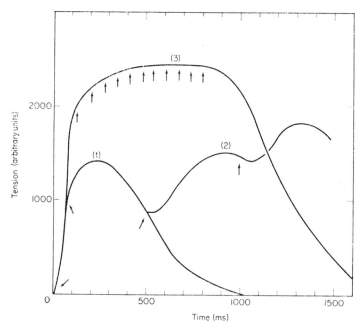

Fig. 3.11. The summation of single twitches. Curve 1—single shock. Curve 2—two shocks separated by a 500 msec interval. Curve 3—15 shocks/sec. Note steady build-up and maintenance of tension. (After Bendall, "Muscles, Molecules and Movement", Heinemann, 1969.)

Summation and Tetanus

Nevertheless, a single fibre may be caused to develop differen tensions in response to stimulation by appropriate variation of the conditions. Thus two shocks applied in rapid succession, such that the second one falls later than the absolute refractory period of the muscle, will give a larger response than that produced by the single shock; three suitably spaced shocks will give a still larger one, and as this repetitive stimulation is continued a maximum *tetanus-tension* is developed (Fig. 3.11). Essentially, what we are seeing is *summation* of the successive *refering to* responses. The frequency of stimulation required to develop the smooth tetanic tension varies with the muscle, depending on its contraction-time, i.e. the time from the beginning of the action potential to the point of maximum tension; as Fig. 3.12 illustrates, this may vary considerably, and muscles may be characterized as fast or slow by this measurement. The faster the muscle the sooner must the next stimulus occur if it is to produce an effect that will add with the previous one, hence the tetanus fusion frequency will be high with a fast muscle. If a muscle has a very long refractory period, extending into the relaxation period, then clearly a tetanus is impossible, the essential feature of the tetanus being the arrival of a new effective stimulus before relaxation has begun.

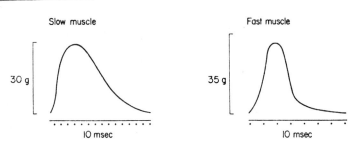

Fig. 3.12. Slow and fast myograms of single isometric twitches. (After Close, *J. Physiol.* 1967, **193**, 45.)

Control

The two phenomena just described, namely the increasing response of a whole muscle with increasing intensity of stimulus, and the increasing responses of single fibres with increasing frequency of repetitive stimuli, form the basis for the control of vertebrate muscle action. A single nerve fibre supplies a limited number of muscle fibres, varying from about 6 in the extraocular muscles to 150 or more in a thigh muscle; a discharge down a single nerve fibre will thus activate a limited number of muscle fibres, and the number is described as a *muscle unit*. The force of contraction of a muscle may be graded by the number of units brought into activity by the central nervous system, i.e. by the recruitment, or dropping out, of more and more units. The second phenomenon, namely the summation of successive stimuli, provides an additional mode of varying the strength of contraction. Thus a weak contraction of the whole muscle may be the result of single twitches of motor units; if these occur asynchronously in the different units making up a muscle the effect will be an apparently smooth, but weak, contraction. Increasing strength can be achieved by increasing the frequency of nervous discharge to the individual units, until finally all are tetanically innervated giving a smooth and maximal contraction of the whole muscle. By inserting a needle electrode into a human muscle, and recording the spike activity in the fibres in the immediate neighbourhood of the electrode, the magnitude of the activity can be estimated from the consequent record, which is described as an *electromyogram* (EMG) (Fig. 3.13).

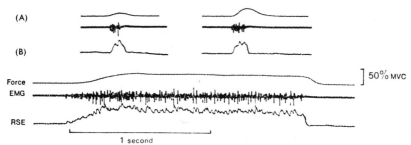

Fig. 3.13. The electromyogram. The upper trace of each record is the force developed as a percentage of the maximum voluntary contraction (MVC). The middle trace is the unmodified electrical activity recorded from surface electrodes on the skin above the contracting muscle—the electromyogram (EMG). The lower trace is the rectified smoothed EMG with a time constant of 10 msec. (RSE) (A) shows two records of a single twitch, the right hand record being of a greater force than that on the left. (B) Shows the response of a sustained contraction. (Courtesy of F. W. J. Cody.)

All-or-None Activity

The basis for the all-or-none response of a single muscle fibre is the spread of action potential. So long as the action potential does, indeed, spread over the whole fibre, the response is maximal for this particular condition of the fibre. If small, localized, electrical stimuli are applied to a fibre, however, such that the action potential does not rise to the required height for propagation, then the contraction remains local. Under these conditions, the contraction is graded, increasing depolarization causing increased force of contraction.

Development of Tension

T-System and Activation

The importance of the Z-line in conducting the effects of electrical change to the interior of the fibre was demonstrated by Huxley and

Taylor. They showed that, if precisely localized electrical stimuli were applied to the A-band, there was no local contraction; applied to the I-band contraction occurred, and this was symmetrical about the Z-line, the two halves of the I-band contracting to equal extents. Thus it appeared that, in the frog, the activation occurred through the Z-line, and in this species the Z-line is where the T-system of the sarco-tubular system is located, i.e. it is here that there is access from the surface of the fibre to its depths. That this is the true significance was shown by similar studies on crab and lizard muscles, where the T-system occurs at the junction of the A- and I-bands; when a local contraction was produced in these muscles, by stimuli applied to this region, the Z-line was pulled over to the half of the I-band to which the microelectrode was applied until it came in contact with the A-band, the other half of the I-band never taking part in the contraction. The important conclusion can be drawn, then, that activation of the muscle fibre occurs through the openings of the T-system on to the exterior.

Depolarization as Stimulus

That depolarization of the fibre membrane is, indeed, a primary cause of contraction may be shown by many experiments. Thus blocking of contraction of muscle, when stimulated through the nerve with curare, fatigue, or any other cause, is always associated with failure of a muscle action potential to develop. Again, we may de-polarize the muscle gradually, instead of in the all-or-none fashion involved in the spike; and in this case we may obtain degrees of muscular contraction, as measured by the tension. This is shown in Fig. 3.14, where the depolarization, caused by placing the muscle fibre in solutions of increasing concentration of K^+, has been plotted against the developed tension. As the concentration is raised, tension develops until a maximum value is reached at a depolarization equivalent to a membrane potential of 25 mV. Thus, when the action potential spreads over the muscle fibre, it is more than adequate to evoke maximal contractile activity since it constitutes a complete depolariza-tion leading to a reversal of potential.

Structural Basis of Summation

We must now enquire why we may develop greater tension in a single muscle fibre by repetitive stimulation than by single shocks. The answer is given by the anatomy of the fibre, which may be considered to be made up of a *contractile machinery*—the sliding myofilaments—and an elastic component in series with it, i.e. the tendon and the sarco-lemma through which the shortening contractile machinery must exert its pull on the load. A single shock, applied to the muscle, may well cause the contractile machinery to exert its maximum capabilities for its given condition, but in order to show these it must pull against the lever to which it is attached experimentally; thus the transmission of its contractile force is delayed, while it shortens the elastic component. If the duration of this "active state" of the contractile machinery is short, a great deal of the potential contractile strength is wasted while

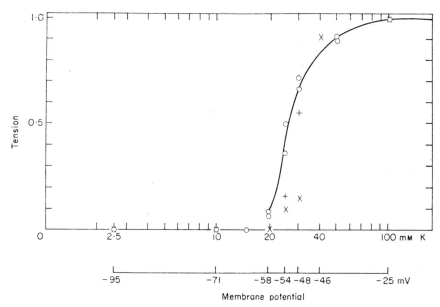

Fig. 3.14. Relation between peak tension and potassium concentration or membrane potential. Circles and plus signs (O, +) refer to a fibre where tension only was measured, whilst crosses (×) refer to a fibre in which both tension and membrane potential were measured. (Hodgkin and Horowicz, *J. Physiol.* 1960, **153**, 386.)

the elastic elements are taking up the strain. A simple model will illustrate this; we may exert a sharp short pull on a tension-bar through an inextensible string, as in Fig. 3.15; the result is an immediate development of tension with an immediate fall to zero at the end of the pull. Alternatively we may exert the same sharp pull on the string, connected to the tension-bar through a spring; now the transmission of the pull to the tension-bar is delayed while the spring is extended, and because of the limited time for which the pull is applied, the maximum tension developed is smaller, and the course of development follows a curve like that of Fig. 3.16, being governed essentially by the elastic

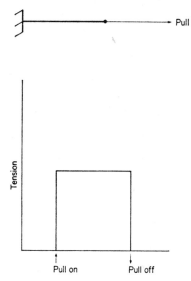

Fig. 3.15. Sharp rise and fall of tension on exerting force on inelastic string.

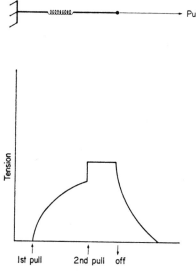

Fig. 3.16. More gradual rise and fall of tension when force is exerted on string connected to a spring.

properties of the spring. If the pull were maintained indefinitely, the tension developed would be exactly the same as in the directly coupled system; and this would be the situation with a tetanus, the contractile machinery being maintained in its active state indefinitely by repetitive activation. If a second pull were applied to the string before the spring had returned to its original state, clearly a greater tension would be developed at the tension-bar, because now the same pull would extend the spring farther. Similarly, if the contractile machinery of muscle were activated for a second time before the elastic component had returned to its original state then it, too, would exert a greater tension on the tension-bar.

Effects of Applied Stretches

This concept of the development of an active state in the contractile machinery for a short period, associated with the transmission of

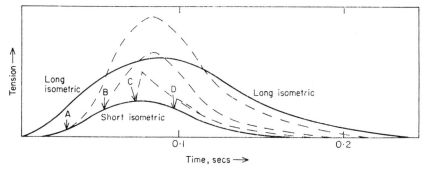

Fig. 3.17. Illustrating the effect on the tension developed, of stretching a muscle at various moments during a twitch. (After Gasser and Hill, *Proc. Roy. Soc. B* 1924, **96,** 398.)

tension to a series elastic component, was derived from A. V. Hill's studies on applying stretches to muscle at different stages during the development of tension in an isometric twitch. The results of an experiment are illustrated in Fig. 3.17. The two full lines show the development of tension of a muscle when stimulated by a single shock at two lengths; in both cases the tension rises to a maximum and falls, but at the greater length the tension developed is greater. Immediately after stimulation of the muscle at its shorter length the muscle is stretched, at intervals, to its greater length; it is found that the tension developed increases well above that which would have been developed at the short length and even, when the stretch is applied early, greater than that developed at the greater length. Clearly, what we are doing by applying stretches is to save the contractile machinery the trouble of pulling out the elastic component; we are doing this for it, and thereby allowing the machinery to exert its pull under conditions when this may be transmitted directly to the tension-measuring apparatus.

Active State. Experiments of this sort led to the concept of the development of an *active state* of the contractile machinery, lasting for quite a short time but coming on virtually instantaneously. This decayed slowly, and the observed tension was the consequence of the interaction of the actively shortening contractile elements with the *series elastic component.* The basis of the observed tension is illustrated in

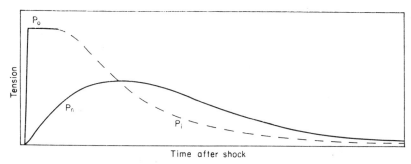

Time after shock

Fig. 3.18. Illustrating the mechanical events in an isometric twitch. P_n represents the actual tension developed, which is less than the tension that the muscle can develop (P_o) when maximally active. P_i represents the intrinsic strength of the contractile elements at any moment, i.e. the tension at which they neither lengthen nor shorten. (Modified from Hill, *Proc. Roy. Soc. B* 1949, **136,** 242.)

Fig. 3.18; here P_o is the maximal tension that the muscle can develop in a tetanus and is equal to the theoretical tension developable by the contractile elements with a single stimulus, i.e. it is a measure of the active state. P_n is the observed tension, and P_i represents the intrinsic state of the contractile elements, which decreases from P_o at the onset of the process to zero when relaxation begins.

Length–Tension Diagram

Figure 3.17 illustrates that, in a twitch, a muscle can develop a greater tension if its length is greater. Does this mean that stretching a muscle permits a greater development of force in the contractile machinery? Or is the greater tension merely the expression of a mechanical advantage in starting the contraction with the elastic elements already stretched? The answer will be given by examining the tension developed in an isometric tetanus; under these conditions we are measuring the maximum effort of the contractile machinery when the elastic elements are fully stretched. When this is done we obtain the length–tension diagram of Fig. 3.19, and it is seen that the maximum tension developed occurs at resting length; here the tension is the difference between the resting tension and that during tetanic stimulation, so that the increased tension that develops when the muscle is passively stretched is allowed for.

Interdigitation of Filaments. This decrease in tension with stretch conforms well with the sliding-filament hypothesis, since

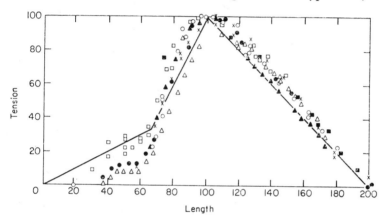

Fig. 3.19. Length–tension diagram for isolated muscle fibres. Ordinates: tension developed (total minus resting) in per cent of maximum developed. Abscissae: length in per cent of resting length. The various symbols represent different experiments. (Ramsey, "Medical Physics", Year Book Publishers, Chicago.)

stretching the muscle occurs at the expense of the interdigitation of the I-filaments with the A-filaments, so that the possibility of formation of cross-linkages is reduced. Ultimately, when the I-filaments have completely come away from the A-filaments, no tension can theoretically be developed. In frog muscle the point where no overlap occurs is at a sarcomere-length of $3 \cdot 5 \, \mu$ $(1 \cdot 5 + 2 \cdot 0 \, \mu)$, and this is the region where the developed tension is very low. It does not fall to zero, however, because when a muscle contracts isometrically, sarcomeres tend to shorten at the expense of a lengthening of others, so that unless special conditions are applied, it is impossible to achieve a state when there is no overlap in any sarcomere. By an ingenious device Gordon, Huxley and Julian were able to reduce this shortening of sarcomeres at the expense of the lengthening of others, and they extrapolated the line relating tension to sarcomere length to zero tension, giving a sarcomere length of 3·65 μ, very close to the theoretical value of 3·5 μ mentioned above.

Effects of Shortening. Thus the sliding filament theory explains the right-hand side of the length–tension diagram sufficiently well. What, then, about the left-hand side? As the sarcomere is shortened

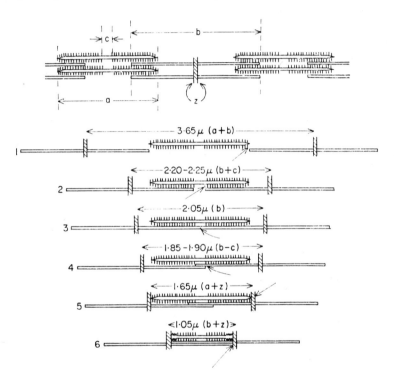

Fig. 3.20. *Below*: Illustrating the critical stages in the increase of overlap between thick and thin filaments as a sarcomere shortens. *Above*: Schematic diagram of filaments, indicating nomenclature for the relevant dimensions. (Gordon, Huxley and Julian, *J. Physiol.* 1966, **184**, 143.)

beyond the point of maximal overlap, the I-filaments tend to overlap, as illustrated in Fig. 3.20, and it seems that it is this overlap, interfering with formation of cross-linkages between I- and A-filaments, that reduces the force of contraction at the shorter lengths. It is certainly interesting that there is a point on the length–tension diagram where the slope of tension versus length becomes very sharp, and this corresponds exactly with the point where the I-filaments meet each other.

Excitation–Contraction Coupling

Activation of the Contractile Machinery

The period during which the action potential of muscle is above the threshold for causing contraction is only some 2 msec, whilst the active state of the contractile machinery lasts much longer. Thus depolarization is only the *trigger* for the contractile process, activating some intermediate process that lasts longer, and it is this process of *"excitation–contraction coupling"* that has attracted attention in recent years. The limited role of depolarization is also revealed by the finding that a fast muscle, depolarized in high-K^+, soon relaxes, so that we must postulate a relaxation process, or reversal of the activation process. Again, the condition of *contracture*, where a muscle contracts without the development of action potentials, also indicates the partial independence of the electrical and mechanical events. Thus caffeine, veratrine and quinine are contracture agents; at lower concentrations they potentiate a contraction, allowing the muscle to develop a greater and more prolonged tension in response to a depolarizing stimulus, as though they prolonged the active state.

Calcium

It has been recognized for many years, especially in respect to heart muscle, that raising the concentration of Ca^{2+} in the external medium increases the force of contraction, but since Ca^{2+} also affects excitability it was not easy to separate an effect mediated through this from one acting directly on the contractile machinery. However, modern techniques of injection into the muscle fibre have demonstrated unequivocally the importance of this ion in activating the contractile machinery. Thus Niederkerke introduced a micropipette into a muscle fibre and released Ca^{2+} from it with pulses of electricity (iontophoresis); local reversible contractions occurred. As more Ca^{2+} was injected, the duration of contraction increased indicating that the mechanism for *removing* Ca^{2+}, upon which relaxation must depend, was being overloaded.

Skinned Fibre. A useful preparation for the study of the effects of Ca^{2+} is the skinned fibre, first prepared by Natori. The sarcolemma is removed so that activation of the fibrillar system can be achieved without interference from electrical changes, whilst ready diffusion of applied chemicals is assured. Podolski showed that the threshold concentration of Ca^{2+} required in the medium in order to develop force was ca. $3 \cdot 10^{-8}$ M whilst maximum force was reached at a concentration of 10^{-6} M or a pCa of 6·0.

Internal Concentration of Ca^{2+}. The actual concentration of ionized Ca^{2+} within the sarcoplasm of resting muscle may be estimated to be remarkably small (i.e. around $10^{-9}M$), this low concentration being the combined result of an active accumulation of Ca^{2+} into the cisterns of the sarcoplasmic reticulum, where it is stored or sequestered,* and an active pump that extrudes the ion into the extracellular fluid, thereby holding to a minimum the influx down the large gradient of concentration and electrical potential, both favouring influx.

Release from Cisterns. Thus if the action potential caused either an influx of Ca^{2+} from the medium or allowed the stored Ca^{2+} to be suddenly released so as to bring the internal concentration to the point where the contractile machinery was activated, we should have the basis for the excitation–contraction coupling. Since Ca^{2+} increases the activity of the enzyme, ATPase, that is involved in the reactions between actin and myosin, the theory is altogether plausible.

In fact, stimulation of muscle does cause a rise in internal concentration of Ca^{2+} ions by a factor of a thousand, a process that precedes tension-development and splitting of ATP in an artificial system. According to the autoradiographic studies of Winegrad, the increase in Ca^{2+} is due to a shift from the cisterns at the centre of the I-band towards the A-band; more precise studies involving localized application of Ca^{2+} and measuring local contraction indicate that the Ca^{2+} is required in the region of overlap of the I- and A-filaments (Gillis).

Relaxing Factor. It may be asked whether the action potential causes an influx of Ca^{2+}-ions into the muscle fibre, say at the Z-line and along the T-system. Alternatively, the action potential could release Ca^{2+} from some bound, or sequestered, state within the fibre. So far as skeletal muscle is concerned this latter hypothesis seems to be correct, the extra influx of Ca^{2+} in the action potential being quantitatively inadequate to account for the process. This concept of sequestered Ca^{2+} grew out of the studies of what was called the "relaxing factor". Thus it is possible to cause glycerol-extracted muscle, which contains the contractile skeleton of the fibre, to contract by treating it with ATP, Mg^{2+} and Ca^{2+}. However, relaxation required the presence of a factor which turned out to be in the microsome fraction of homogenized muscle, i.e. it was apparently made up of broken up sarcoplasmic reticulum; the vesicles isolated by ultracentrifugation were shown to be capable of actively accumulating Ca^{2+} from the medium,

---

* In the electron microscope it is possible to demonstrate regions of high local concentration of Ca^{2+} by treatment of the tissue with oxalate; to ensure penetration of the oxalate into the muscle fibre it is "skinned". Constantin, Franzini-Armstrong and Podolsky found the precipitate concentrated in the terminal sacs with none in the T-system.

and it was in this way that they behaved as "relaxation granules". These microsomes were able to reduce the concentration of Ca^{2+} in the medium to below 0·01 μM, a concentration that is known to be sufficient to prevent the ATPase activity of actomyosin, the complex between actin and myosin.

Basic Scheme

The hypothetical scheme for contraction and relaxation is illustrated by Fig. 3.21. It was calculated by Hill that the onset of tension after the appearance of the action potential on the muscle fibre was far too rapid to be accounted for by the diffusion of a substance from the surface of the fibre into the interior, so that we must postulate the conduction of the electrical change into the depths of the fibre along the transverse T-system, which comes into close approximation with the terminal cisterns at the triads. The Ca^{2+} released by the electrical change causes a reaction between the actin of the thin filaments and myosin of the thick filaments, catalysed by the enzyme ATPase, and presumably involving ATP as a substrate. The reaction is equivalent to the formation of links between the two types of filament, links that, by successive formation and breakage, result in the sliding of the fine filaments over the thick ones. Relaxation is brought about by the taking up of the Ca^{2+} by the terminal cisterns, either directly, or more probably by a preliminary binding in the longitudinal cisterns and ultimate transport to the terminal cisterns where it is ready for further use.

Caffeine. We have seen that caffeine prolongs the contraction of muscle, and this may be due to an inhibition of the relaxation process since the uptake of Ca^{2+} by a microsome preparation is reduced by this drug. Furthermore, if the microsomes have accumulated Ca^{2+} maximally, addition of caffeine causes the liberation of some of the Ca^{2+}, and it is this property of caffeine that may well be at the basis for the contracture induced by high concentrations of the drug.

Transverse T-system

Finally we may ask how the depolarization of muscle causes release of Ca^{2+}; on this point little can be said. The importance of the transverse T-system has been emphasized by many experiments involving local application of current or of Ca^{2+}, whilst destruction of the T-system, which can be brought about by appropriate changes of osmolality of the medium, breaks the link between depolarization and contraction, so that although action potentials may be evoked, no

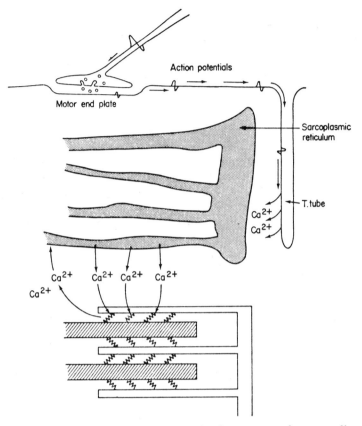

Fig. 3.21. Illustrating the basis of excitation–contraction coupling. The propagated action potential at the nerve ending causes release of transmitter. The new action potential in the muscle is propagated along the T system into the depth of the myofibril. Ca^{2+} is released from its storage sites in the sarcoplasmic reticulum to produce a rise in concentration sufficient to activate the contractile mechanism. Relaxation involves sequestration of the extra Ca^{2+} by the sarcoplasmic reticulum.

twitch follows. There is little doubt that the electrical characteristics of the muscle fibre as a whole are altered by the presence of the transverse T-system so that the simple electrical model, applicable to the axon, of a capacity and series in parallel, will not fit the facts. It has been suggested that the membrane of the T-system, along which the electrical effect of the action potential is transmitted into the interior of the fibre, is different in its permeability characteristics from that of the surface of the fibre, the former being highly permeable to K^+ and the latter to Cl⁻. Thus both sustain a membrane potential, but the one is strongly susceptible to altered K^+-concentration of the medium whilst the latter is sensitive to Cl⁻, and accounts for the overall sensitivity of the muscle's resting potential to Cl⁻. The question has arisen as to whether the action potential spreads as a regenerative spike along the transverse T-system as well as over the plasma membrane proper, or whether the spread of depolarization to the interior of the fibre is purely passive, i.e. electrotonic (p. 26).

Spread to Interior. The spread of the electrical depolarization into the interior of the muscle fibre can be assessed by applying controlled depolarizations to the surface and examining the threshold required to cause microscopically visible contraction in the outermost and innermost myofibrils. The development of action potentials in the muscle fibre was prevented by treatment with tetrodotoxin, which abolishes regenerative spike activity dependent on Na^+-permeability. Under these conditions Adrian found that there was a decay of the applied depolarization, and it was computed that if the spread relied on a mere passive electrotonic process, as opposed to a conducted action potential along the T-system, then only a full-sized action potential on the surface of the fibre would be adequate to activate the innermost fibrils, so that the "safety factor" would be very low, if the process of spread had no regenerative characteristics.

Release of Ca^{2+}. This scheme still leaves unresolved the manner in which the conducted effects of the action potential up the T-tubular system bring about release of Ca^{2+} from the terminal cisterns. The discovery by Ford and Podolsky that Ca^{2+} causes release of labelled $^{45}Ca^{2+}$, previously introduced into the muscle fibre, brings us one step farther. It is easy to show that the amount that could be carried in, during an action potential, would of itself be only one hundredth of that required to activate the contractile machinery. However, if the small amount that enters induces the release of much larger quantities from the terminal cisterns, the Ca^{2+}-release acquires a regenerative character similar to the action potential, a small release of Ca^{2+} provoking greater and ever greater releases until the concentration around the myofilaments required for development of mechanical tension is reached. In this way we can explain the discovery by Adrian that a series of subthreshold potentials carried along the T-system will eventually evoke a contraction of the fibre even when this is treated with tetrodotoxin, which blocks the action potential. This view, moreover, provides the link between the fast striated muscle fibre, where entry of Ca^{2+} is very small, and cardiac and smooth muscles where entry from outside is considerably greater in quantity.

Slow Amphibian Muscle

Amphibian slow muscle differs from the fast twitch fibres in its mode of innervation, the individual fibre receiving multiple endings over its surface, by contrast with the localized end-plate of the fast, or twitch, fibre (p. 53). When twitch fibres are depolarized by placing in a high-K^+ medium we have seen that they develop tension, but that this soon terminates in relaxation in spite of the maintained depolarization. Presumably the Ca^{2+} liberated by the depolarization is resequestered, whilst further release ceases. Slow muscle, on the other hand, maintains its tension indefinitely when depolarized, whether this is by high-K^+ or by treatment with acetylcholine, but this sustained tension relies on the presence of adequate Ca^{2+} in the medium. It has been postulated, therefore, that the excitation–contraction coupling of slow muscle is achieved largely by the penetration of Ca^{2+} into the muscle fibre during the depolarization; during a propagated spike this might be due to an inward Ca^{2+}-current analogous with the Na^+-current of nerve or twitch muscle, or, during sustained depolarization, to an increased Ca^{2+}-permeability caused by the depolarization. In general it seems that the slow fibre lies between the twitch-fibre, relying almost exclusively on release of Ca^{2+} from stores for activation, and smooth muscle, relying very strongly on influx from the outside for its activation.

Relaxation. Correspondingly, relaxation relies almost exclusively on re-accumulation of Ca^{2+} by the sarcoplasmic reticulum in twitch-muscle and to varying degrees on active extrusion from the muscle cell by slow skeletal and smooth muscle. If relaxing activity is measured in terms of the amount of sarcoplasmic reticulum in unit weight of muscle, and the rate of accumulation of Ca^{2+} by unit weight of sarcoplasmic reticulum, then the relaxing activity of slow muscle is only one-sixth of that of twitch muscle.

ENERGY ASPECTS OF MUSCLE CONTRACTION

We have now built up a picture of the basic mechanism of contraction of skeletal muscle, and before passing to the study of other types of muscle we must consider some aspects concerned with the supply of energy for the performance of the mechanical work, which is clearly the function of muscle. The energy of contraction is ultimately derived from the oxidation of carbohydrate—glycogen—to CO_2 and H_2O. The fact that a muscle can be caused to contract vigorously for some time in the absence of oxygen suggests that the prime supply of energy is independent of an oxidative reaction, so that the use of oxygen is rather for restitution processes.

Oxygen Debt

Thus, after a brief burst of very severe exercise, the O_2-consumption of the animal remains at a high level, and it would seem that the organism has gone into *"oxygen debt"*, the increased rate of oxygen consumption after the exercise representing the repayment of this debt. This debt is partly due to the use of oxygen stores held by the muscle on its myoglobin but also to the fact that the fundamental energy-giving reactions are anaerobic, relying on oxygen for restitution of metabolites rather than direct participation in the chemical reaction of contraction.

Chemical Reactions

The generally held view of the chain of chemical reactions associated with contraction is as follows:

(1) $ATP + H_2O \rightarrow ADP + H_3PO_4$
(2) Restitution Process (a):
    $ADP + $ Phosphoryl creatine $\rightarrow$ Creatine $+$ ATP
(3) Restitution Process (b):
    Rephosphorylation of creatine.

Phosphorylcreatine Breakdown. The breakdown of ATP, which is considered to be the prime event in muscular contraction, is apparently obligatorily connected with its resynthesis from ADP and phosphorylcreatine, so that the splitting of phosphorylcreatine may be regarded as the evidence for the previous splitting of ATP. Thus Fig. 3.22 shows the total energy liberated by a muscle under different conditions plotted against the corresponding amount of phosphorylcreatine split.

Aerobic and Anaerobic Processes. The rephosphorylation of creatine is an endergonic reaction, and occurs in association with the utilization of glycogen; this may occur anaerobically, in which case the final product is lactic acid, or more usually (since muscle is well aerated during most activities) aerobically, in which case the pyruvate formed enters the citric acid cycle (Vol. 1) and no lactate is formed. When lactate is formed, oxidative reactions are required to convert a part of it to CO_2 and H_2O, and the remainder is used for resynthesis of glycogen.

$$1/5 \ (2C_3H_6O_3 + 6O_2) \rightarrow 6CO_2 + 6H_2O$$
$$4/5 \ (2C_3H_6O_3) \rightarrow C_6H_{10}O_5 + H_2O$$

In general, rapidly acting muscles, such as those required in running, are adapted for anaerobic restitution processes, whilst muscles utilized in sustained activity are adapted for aerobic processes. The latter have large stores of O_2 in the form of myoglobin, and they are rich in mito-chondria which, as we have seen, are the power-houses of the cell in oxidative activity. The enzymes of glycolysis are not in the mitochondria but distributed through the cytoplasm.

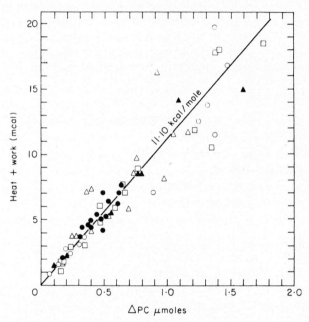

Fig. 3.22. The heat + work (enthalpy) of muscle plotted against the splitting of phosphorylcreatine (Δ PC). The different symbols refer to different modes of contraction. (Carlson, Hardy and Wilkie *et al.*, *J. Physiol.* 1967, **189**, 209.)

Heat Production

The expenditure of energy during contraction, like any other chemical reaction, results in exchanges of heat with the environment. In general, we may divide the heat production of a contracting muscle into two main phases, the *initial* and *delayed* heat. The former is an indication of the chemical events causing contraction as well as of the frictional losses of energy during contraction; whilst the delayed heat, which lasts for a considerably longer time, represents the heat liberated during the restitutive chemical reactions restoring the substrates utilized during contraction. However, since all the ATP of muscle would be used up during 0·5 sec of stimulation, we must conclude that, in any protracted contraction, the restitutive processes would be going on at the same time as contraction.

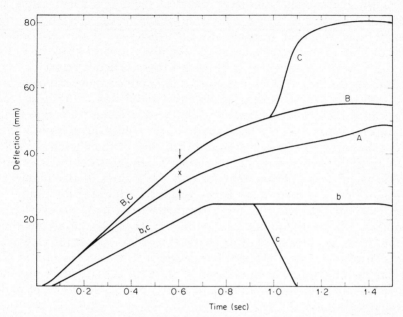

Fig. 3.23. Relaxation heat in isometric and isotonic contractions. A, B and C, heat production in 0·6 sec tetanus at 0°C with initial load of 3·6 g. A, isometric; B, isotonic, after-load 38·6 g, held up so that it cannot fall during relaxation; C, isotonic, same after-load, but free so that load falls during relaxation. When the muscle lengthens under the load, the energy of the load (the work done by the muscle on it) appears as heat, hence the rapid upstroke in C during relaxation. Mechanical records below with corresponding small letters. Note the small relaxation hump on the heat record, A, of the isometric contraction. X, end of stimulus. (Hill, *Proc. Roy. Soc.* 1938, **126**, 136.)

Initial Heat

Hill analysed the initial heat liberated during tetani and twitches and concluded that it could be divided into a rapid burst of what he called *activation heat*; if the muscle was allowed to shorten, it was followed by further liberation of heat, which was proportional to the degree of shortening; this he called *shortening heat* (Fig. 3.23). At the end of contraction, the muscle relaxes and liberates a certain amount of *relaxation heat*; the amount depends on whether the muscle is permitted to lower its load during relaxation, in which case there is a sharp upstroke on the record indicating liberation of heat.

Heat of Relaxation. Essentially the relaxation heat is the expression of the degradation of elastic tension in the muscle to heat. Even when the contraction has been isometric there is a small hump of relaxation heat, due to the relaxation of the elastic elements in the muscle, and the heat is essentially an expression of the *thermoelastic effect* of stretching a material, namely the absorption of heat when, for example, a wire is stretched, and the liberation when it relaxes.

Activation Heat. When a muscle is maintained in a tetanus, there is a sustained liberation of heat after the initial shortening heat, and this, called the *maintenance heat*, is really the summated activation heats following each stimulus. The activation heat comes on so rapidly that it is considered to represent the outward sign of the chemical events leading to the active state or, more specifically, to the formation and breakage of cross-linkages that lead to the sliding of the filaments. Certainly the activation heat is considerably reduced if the muscle is previously stretched to the point that there is virtually no overlap of filaments before stimulation. According to Hill, the heat comes on before there are any signs of mechanical tension, and in his view it is the sign of a chemical process that develops its maximum rate at the beginning and puts the muscle in a state of activity that may be regarded as a readiness to shorten, to exert a mechanical force, or to do mechanical work.

The Fenn Effect

The fact that more heat is liberated from stimulated muscle if it is allowed to shorten, and the more the shortening the more the heat, suggests that the muscle liberates more energy when it is shortening than when it is not, but this is by no means proved, since the energy liberated by a contraction is compounded of the mechanical work done plus the heat. When a muscle shortens, a great deal this means, in effect, that it is lifting a relatively small weight compared with when it shortens a little, in which case it carries a large weight. Thus the work term may well be larger with the smaller shortening, and the sum of heat-plus-work may be the same for all conditions. In fact, however, as Fenn showed, the amount of energy liberated by a stimulated muscle is adjusted to the load it must carry (the Fenn effect).

Force–Velocity Relation

If we appreciate that when a muscle lifts a small load its velocity of shortening is high, and *vice versa*, there will be a certain relationship between tension developed by the muscle, which equals the weight it lifts, and the velocity of shortening. The greater the velocity the smaller the tension developed. The actual relationship is given by the Force–Velocity curve of Fig. 3.24, which is a rectangular hyperbola governed by the equation:

$$(P + a) (V + b) = \text{constant.}$$

Energy Liberation and Velocity. The interesting question is how the energy liberated is related to the velocity of contraction, and this may be simply computed to give the curve of Fig. 3.25, where the

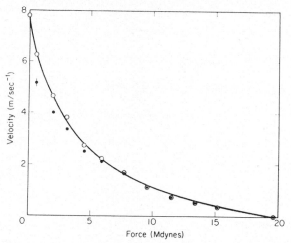

Fig. 3.24. Experimental relationship between force and velocity of contraction of muscles of human arm. ●, Means of 30 determinations of velocity. ○, Experimental points after correction for inertia. (Wilkie, *J. Physiol.* 1949, **110**, 249.)

shaded portion indicates mechanical work and the unshaded part (Q) equals the heat liberated during contraction. It will be seen that the work term passes through a maximum at intermediate velocities, i.e. intermediate loads, and becomes zero when there is either no load or when the load is too heavy to lift. The total energy liberated becomes maximal with very small loads on the basis of this calculation. This is not strictly true,* but the important point to appreciate is that, in some way, the rate of liberation of energy is related to the velocity of shortening. This presumably indicates a link between the two processes,

* Thus according to Fenn's original studies, maximum energy is liberated at intermediate loads; more recent studies, in which the splitting of phosphorylcreatine is used as an index to liberation of energy, also show that maximal energy liberation occurs at intermediate loads.

and must be taken into account when formulating any theoretical model of the process of contraction (p. 229).

Role of ATP

To return to the chemical events during contraction and restitution, we may discuss the role of ATP. Whilst there is no doubt that the restitution processes described above take place, there has been a great

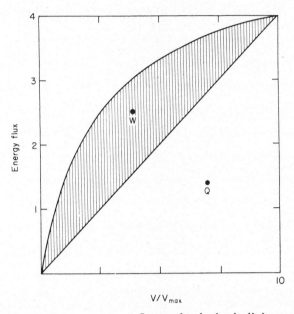

Fig. 3.25. Relation between energy flux and velocity in living muscle. Open region, rate of heat production; shaded region, rate of work production. The unit for the ordinate is the rate of heat production during isometric contraction (the maintenance heat). (Podolksy, "Biophysics of Physiological and Pharmacological Actions", American Association for the Advancement of Science.)

deal of discussion as to the manner in which ATP enters the contractile process, since the linkage of breakdown of phosphorylcreatine with synthesis of ATP means that, normally, it is not easy to demonstrate any breakdown of ATP in working muscle. However, fluorodinitrobenzene (FDNB) is a specific poison of the enzyme concerned in resynthesis of ATP (creatine-ATP phosphoryltransferase); when a muscle is treated with this it will contract in response to stimulation, and this causes a loss of its ATP stores. Thus this type of experiment indicates that ATP is, indeed, concerned in muscular contraction, but of course it begs the question as to how its reaction with the chemical constituents of the muscle fibre brings about a sliding of the muscle filaments. From a thermodynamic point of view, too, a question that has been repeatedly asked is whether the cost of contraction, in energy terms, can be estimated in terms of the free energy of hydrolysis of ATP:

$$ATP + H_2O \rightarrow ADP + H_3PO_4$$

In the normal muscle the net result of contraction and performance of work is the utilization of O_2 in the oxidation of carbohydrate. The heat and work performed can, indeed, be both theoretically and experimentally equated with the free energy made available by the O_2 utilized and carbohydrate consumed.

Free Energy of Hydrolysis. We are not, however, equating the free energy of hydrolysis of ATP with the work and heat liberated, because we are ignorant of the chemical reactions involved in the processes in which ATP enters. As we shall see below, there is no doubt that ATP, added to an artificial contractile system, can cause it to perform work and, during the process, the ATP is converted to ADP and H_3PO_4. In this sense it may be said to have provided the energy for contraction, but even here we are using a loose form of expressing ourselves; the source of energy was the chemical reaction involving ATP as a substrate; the ATP did not simply react with water because, if it did, it could not have provided the energy for contraction. No, the ATP reacted with the chemical constituents of the model system, and as a result it contracted and performed work, and it was the *chemical reaction* that produced the energy.

Mammalian Twitch and Slow Fibres

We have seen that amphibian and other sub-mammalian skeletal muscles consist of two main types according as they are innervated by end-plates or grape terminations, these differences being associated with a fast twitch or a slow sustained type of contraction. In mammals this difference in innervation is not present, but it is possible to classify muscles according to whether they are fast or slow, as judged by the time-course of an isometric twitch. The fast fibres predominate in the typically white muscles by comparison with the red muscles that contain predominantly slow fibres; these latter are red because of the high concentration of the protein, myoglobin, which is present and which acts as an oxygen-carrier supplementing the haemoglobin of the blood vessels; as we should expect, these muscles are concerned in sustained activity whereas the white muscles are concerned with rapid contractions. Histologically the slow fibre is characterized by large numbers of mitochondria, which disturb the regular array of myofibrils, to give what Krüger called the *Felderstruktur*. This type of fibre relies on oxidative metabolism for its supplies of energy by contrast with the fast white type that relies on the anaerobic glycolytic mechanism. This mechanism apparently meets the needs of a muscle when working intensively and going into oxygen-debt, but is unsuitable for the sustained activities involved in maintaining posture for long periods when the much more efficient metabolic utilization of glucose through the citric acid cycle is preferable.

STRUCTURAL BASIS OF CONTRACTION

The Proteins of Muscle

The main components of the fibrillar system of muscle are the proteins myosin and actin, and these form the basis for the thick and thin filaments respectively. Under appropriate conditions they may be extracted from muscle, after removal of the soluble sarcoplasmic components.

Myosin

Myosin has a molecular weight of some 500,000 and, as illustrated by Fig. 3.26, is a rod-shaped molecule, some 1400 Å long, with a

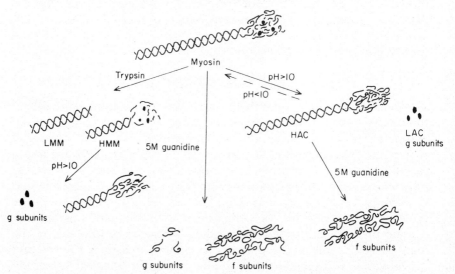

Fig. 3.26. A schematic diagram of the myosin molecule. (Modified from Dreizen *et al.*, *J. gen. Physiol.* 1967, **50**, 85.)

globular portion at one end. The long rod-like portion consists of a double-alpha helix. Attempts to split the molecule into subunits by breaking hydrogen-bond links have not been successful, so that more drastic treatments, designed to break covalent links, have been employed. Thus treatment with trypsin gives rise to two components, called *heavy meromyosin (HMM)* and *light meromyosin (LMM)* with molecular weights of 340,000 and 150,000 respectively. The heavy meromyosin contains the ATPase activity of the protein (p. 223) and this is further localized by treatment of heavy meromyosin with the proteolytic enzyme, papain, in which case heavy meromyosin can be broken into two subfragments apparently identical, called $HMMS_1$

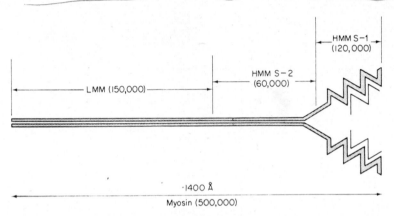

Fig. 3.27. Illustrating the myosin molecule and the basis for the different components isolated from it. LMM: light meromyosin; $HMMS_2$ and $HMMS_1$ are two fractions of heavy meromyosin. (Lowey *et al.*, *J. mol. Biol.* 1969, **42**, 1.)

and a single one called $HMMS_2$. Thus, as indicated in Fig. 3.27, heavy meromyosin may be split into a fibrous portion, made up of a double-helix which continues into two relatively globular components $HMMS_1$, and, as just indicated, it is these globular components that contain the ATPase activity of the myosin molecule.

Actin

Actin is the basis of the thin filaments of muscle and is formed by the linear aggregation of globular subunits—called G-actin—to form fibril-like molecules called F-actin. As indicated by Fig. 3.28 the fibrous F-actin molecule consists of a double-helix of G-actin units, the double-helix having a coiled-coil structure with approximately 13 subunits in six turns of a genetic helix; the pitch of the genetic helix is 59 Å and the near-axial repeat is 385 Å.

G-actin contains a molecule of ATP as a prosthetic group, and, when polymerization to F-actin takes place, a molecule of inorganic phosphate is liberated, so that the F-actin contains ADP:

$$G.ATP \rightarrow F.ADP + P_i$$

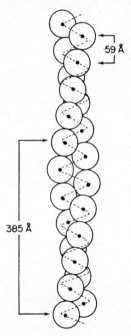

Fig. 3.28. Diagrammatic representation of the actin helix, assuming there are exactly 13 subunits in six turns of the genetic helix. The genetic helix of pitch 59 Å is indicated by the dotted lines. (After Rome, *Cold Spr. Harb. Symp. quant. Biol.* 1972, **37,** 331.)

It seems unlikely that the reversible polymerization of G-actin to F-actin is of any physiological significance, the internal conditions of the muscle cell being such as to maintain the F form, in which it constitutes the thin filaments.

Actomyosin

Actin and myosin, prepared as pure solutions, react together to form a complex—*actomyosin*—and there is now little doubt that the reaction leading to the formation of this complex is the basis of the sliding of the actin and myosin filaments during contraction. In this case the actin and myosin react through the cross-bridges in a reversible and repetitive fashion, and we may regard the actomyosin, prepared artificially from actin and myosin, or extracted from the intact muscle, as the "frozen" state of this reversible interaction.

Myosin as ATPase

A very significant discovery was that myosin had enzymatic qualities, catalysing the hydrolysis of ATP, i.e. it is an ATPase, this enzymatic activity being a feature of the heavy meromyosin component of the molecule.

In fact, as we have just seen, it belongs to the $HMMS_1$ globular component. When the myosin has reacted with actin to form acto-myosin it retains its ATPase activity but now this is greatly increased and its character is different, being activated by Mg^{2+} whereas myosin is activated by low concentrations of Ca^{2+}. Thus we may speak of an actin-activated ATPase of the myosin molecule. ATP is closely con-nected, as we have seen, with contraction, and therefore it is of great interest that a protein with which it can react is part of the contractile machinery; furthermore, it seems to be associated with that part of the myosin molecule that contains the cross-bridges (heavy meromyosin). Thus, whatever brings about the approximation of the actin and myosin filaments, through the cross-bridges, also causes the activation of the enzyme most intimately concerned with releasing the energy required for the contractile process.

It must be appreciated, as Szent-Györgyi pointed out, that it is probably wrong to describe myosin as an enzyme, catalysing the hydro-lysis of ATP, since this hydrolysis is what must be avoided if the ATP in muscle is to carry out its function in promoting the interaction of actin and myosin. The ATPase activity is a reflection of its power to react with ATP in what may be a complex reaction between several components of the fibrillar system.

Actin–Myosin Interaction

The interaction between actin and myosin, when the muscle contracts normally, may be investigated by X-ray diffraction. The sliding-filament theory of muscle contraction was put forward largely because of the absence of serious changes in X-ray diffraction of the myosin or actin component. Nevertheless the movement of the cross-bridges during contraction, and perhaps more subtle alterations involving other

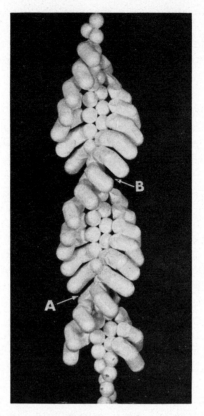

Fig. 3.29. Photographs of models illustrating appearance of a double-helical filament of actin subunits which has been decorated with myosin subfragment-1. The subfragment molecules are both tilted with respect to the long axis of the F-actin filament and also slewed. Points marked A and B are successive "cross over" points in the actin helix; between them the polar, unsymmetrical variation in the projected view of the subfragment-1 units can be readily seen. It is believed that this is largely responsible for the characteristic arrowhead appearance. (Moore, Huxley and De Rosier, *J. mol. Biol.* 1970, **50,** 279.)

protein components, may be expected to produce changes, provided the resolution of the analysing system is adequate to show them up. In general, the most obvious change was a loss in the intensity of the X-ray diffraction diagram indicating a loss of order in the arrangement of the cross-bridges, i.e. in the 143 Å repeat. This would be expected of a system showing dynamic changes, such as the asynchronous movement of the cross-bridges during activity as each went through their individual contractile cycles of attachment and ATP breakdown. X-ray analysis was able, moreover, to picture, with the aid of electron microscopy, the probable manner of attachment of the actin filament with the myosin cross-bridges. This was made possible by studying actin "decorated" with the subunit of myosin containing the ATPase activity, namely $HMMS_1$. Treatment of purified actin with these subunits alters the appearance of the actin filaments in a characteristic manner, producing an arrow-head appearance, one S_1 molecule being attached to each G-actin subunit in the double-helical actin structure, as illustrated by Fig. 3.29.

Models of the Contractile System

Rigor

Actomyosin, extracted from muscle, may be drawn into threads, and when treated with ATP and Mg^{2+} these threads will contract and develop tension. Again, muscle extracted with glycerol—a procedure that leaves the fibrillar system intact but removes most of the sarcoplasmic material—contracts in response to ATP and Mg^{2+}, developing as much tension as a normal muscle. One important feature of these models is that they fail to relax after contraction, in fact when all the ATP has been used up the model is similar to a muscle in rigor, when the force required to extend it is some ten times that required to extend a normal muscle.

ATP as Plasticizer

The development of rigor in muscle is accompanied by loss of its stores of ATP, and this finding emphasizes a second characteristic of ATP, namely its *plasticizing action* on muscle, which permits it to extend in response to passive tension, or to relax after contraction. Thus we may dissociate the *contractile* characteristic of ATP from its *plasticizing* characteristic by inhibiting the ATPase activity of the actomyosin; under these conditions the model does not develop tension with ATP but it does remain plastic. We can conclude from these model studies that when ATP is present, and the conditions are favourable for its breakdown through the muscle ATPase, contraction will occur; relaxation requires, first, the cessation of the chemical reaction but also the presence of ATP to act as a plasticizer.

Relaxing Factor. If this artificial system really has analogies with the living muscle we may ask how relaxation can occur in a muscle that contains ATP in its fibres. The answer is given by the presence of "relaxing factor" in the fibre. Thus we have seen that the contractile process is activated by Ca^{2+}; this presumably activates the myosin ATPase and, as a result, cross-linkages between actin and myosin are formed leading to sliding of filaments and shortening of the myofibrils as a whole. Removal of Ca^{2+} by the sarcoplasmic reticulum blocks this myosin ATPase activity, but the remaining ATP exerts its other role, namely as a plasticizer, and thus permits the muscle to relax.

Dynamic State of Cross-linkages. In terms of reactions between cross-linkages we may say that, in the absence of ATP, the cross-linkages are "frozen" and the muscle is in rigor; in the presence of ATP, cross-linkages are in a dynamic state, being broken and made continuously; this gives rise to a plastic state in which the filaments can be drawn away from each other, but something is lacking to cause the active sliding that leads to shortening of the fibre. In the presence of Ca^{2+} this "something" is present, and formation and breakage of cross-linkages leads to shortening.

Tropomyosin and Troponin

These are two proteins that are associated with the I-filaments, i.e. with the actin of the muscle fibre, and exert an important influence on the ability of actin and myosin to react reversibly. When actin and myosin are very highly purified it is found that they react to form an actomyosin that cannot be converted back to actin and myosin by merely removing Ca^{2+} with EDTA, although this was possible with the less highly purified preparations and constituted the basis of actin-myosin models of muscular contraction.

Native Tropomyosin. Ebashi and Ebashi showed that, during preparation of these proteins, material had been lost, and they called it *native tropomyosin* since it resembled the protein *tropomyosin* that had been isolated from muscle some time before by Bailey. On addition of native tropomyosin to the mixture of purified actin and myosin the system became sensitive to Ca^{2+}; and subsequent studies showed that native tropomyosin consisted of two proteins, tropomyosin proper and *troponin*, that react together and with actin to give the Ca^{2+}-sensitive system. Tropomyosin is a fibrous protein consisting of a two-chain coiled-coil α-helical structure some 490 Å × 20 Å, of molecular weight 74,000.

Tropomyosin–Troponin Control System

Thus the interaction of actin and myosin is controlled by the co-operative actions of two additional proteins—tropomyosin and troponin. The troponin acts as the calcium-sensor, permitting the actin-myosin system to react to altered changes in ionized Ca^{2+} in the sarcoplasm. As the matter is pictured today, in the absence of Ca^{2+}, troponin, in collaboration with tropomyosin, exerts a special effect on actin, inhibiting its interaction with the myosin of the thick filaments. Ca^{2+}, by reacting with troponin, removes this depressing action and permits the actin–myosin reaction that leads to the sliding of the filaments. Ca^{2+} may be regarded as a de-repressor. By employing fluorescein-labelled antibodies to the proteins, tropomyosin and troponin, these could be shown to be located on the I-filaments, and a variety of X-ray and other studies suggest that the long tropomyosin molecule lies in grooves between the actin double strands, a single tropomyosin molecule covering seven actin molecules (monomers). The troponin does not cover the complete I-band but is revealed as two strongly fluorescent lines on either side of the Z-line in the I-band; its points of attachment are some 400 Å apart.

Subunits of Troponin

Troponin has been separated into three subunits, which may be called *troponin-I* with a molecular weight of about 24,000; *troponin-T*

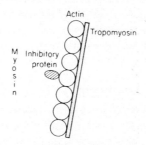

Fig. 3.30. Diagrammatic representation of possible arrangement of the inhibitory protein in relation to the actin and tropomyosin in the I-filament. The scheme shown represents the inhibitory protein acting directly on an actin monomer, and its effect being transmitted to neighbouring actin monomers by the tropomyosin molecule lying alongside them. (Perry *et al.*, *Cold Spr. Harb. Symp. quant. Biol.* 1972, **37**, 251.)

(37,000) and *troponin-C* (20,000). Troponin-C is the component that binds Ca^{2+}, whilst Troponin-I inhibits the Mg^{2+}-activated ATPase of the actin–myosin complex. It will be recalled that the ATPase activity of the myofilament increases enormously during the actin–myosin interaction, becoming Mg^{2+}-sensitive by contrast with the Ca^{2+}-sensitivity of the myosin ATPase in the resting state. Troponin-I is a powerful inhibitor of this actomyosin ATPase, an inhibition that is assisted by tropomyosin; and it has been suggested that a function of tropomyosin is to cooperate with troponin in extending the inhibition of one molecule of troponin to some seven actin molecules, as indicated by Fig. 3.30. At any rate, troponin does not react directly with actin, so that tropomyosin must be the intermediary link.

Troponin as Ca^{2+}-Sensor

To summarize, then, troponin senses the level of Ca^{2+} in the sarcoplasm, and the actin molecules in the thin filament respond either by being "turned on" and permitting reaction between myosin and actin in the presence of ATP (acting as "plasticizer") or "turned off" by becoming inaccessible to the ATP-activated myosin so that the actin and myosin filaments remain dissociated from each other.

The manner in which the troponin–tropomyosin system controls the interaction between the actin and myosin filaments is not completely elucidated. X-ray measurements of resting and contracting muscle suggest that, in the resting condition, tropomyosin lies on the edge of the helical grooves in the actin double-helix, whilst during contraction it moves deeper in, perhaps thereby removing a steric obstruction that prevented the myosin cross-links from reacting with the actin molecule. When the concentration of ATP in the muscle fibre is very low, then the troponin–tropomyosin system is unable to inhibit the myosin–actin interaction regardless of the level of Ca^{2+}, so that rigor occurs even in a Ca^{2+}-free medium.

Control Through Thin Filaments

It will be clear that control over contraction is exerted through actin thin filaments, so that the cross linkages between the S_1 subunit of myosin and actin come into play when these subunits "discover" that the actin filaments have been switched on, e.g. by removal of tropomyosin deeper into the helical groove and thus ceasing to obstruct the interaction, which occurs at specific points. As we shall see, this form of control differs from that in many invertebrate muscles, such as those of molluscs, where the Ca^{2+}-sensitive system is the myosin portion of the contractile system, and where there is no troponin present on either actin or myosin. In evolution it is clear that the troponin-regulator represents a later development. The arthropods likewise have a troponin-activated system working on the actin filaments, but this may well be an example of convergent evolution.

Huxley's Model

A. F. Huxley developed a mechanical model based on the formation of cross-linkages between filaments that predicts remarkably well the basic features of muscular contraction, such as the length–tension diagram (p. 205), the force–velocity relation, the Fenn effect and some thermal phenomena. The model is illustrated by Fig. 3.31 which shows a region of overlap of a thick and thin filament, the Z-line belonging to the thin filament lying on the right. Shortening of the sarcomere thus represents a movement of the thin filament to the left. On the thick filament there is a chemical grouping, M, capable of reacting with another grouping, A, on the thin filament, a reaction that is supposed to occur spontaneously. M is imagined to oscillate about a mean position, O, and the probability of reaction depends on the closeness of M to A at any moment during its oscillations. When the link is formed, the tension in the spring will pull the thin filament

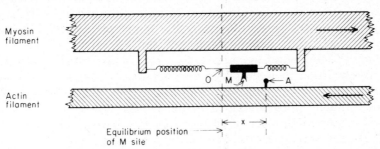

Fig. 3.31. Diagram illustrating the mechanism by which it is assumed that tension is generated. The part of a fibril that is shown is in the right-hand half of an A band so that the actin filament is attached to a Z-line which is out of the picture to the right, the arrows give the direction of the relative motion between the filaments when the muscle shortens. (A. F. Huxley, *Progr. Biophys.* 1957, **7**, 255.)

towards O, thereby causing shortening. If it is postulated that the chance of M forming a link becomes zero when it is on the left of its mean position we impart a one-way character to the pull caused by a given link. For a progressive sliding of the filament, the link must be broken to permit oscillation to a new position that will allow reaction with another A-grouping. It is postulated that the breaking is brought about by an endergenic chemical reaction involving a phosphate compound, such as ATP, uniting with a site near A. The probability of the link being broken depends on the position of M in its linked state, increasing as M approaches its mean position; thus the chance of breaking increases as shortening occurs.

Mathematical analysis of this model showed that it could account for the principal features of muscular contraction, namely the length–tension (p. 205), the force–velocity relation (p. 216), the Fenn effect, by which is meant that the energy made available increases with the work done, and finally that the heat of shortening is independent of contraction-speed, so that the rate of liberation of heat increases linearly with shortening.

ACTIVATION AND CONTRACTION OF CARDIAC MUSCLE

We have seen, in our brief analysis of the actions of the mammalian heart, that its contraction takes place spontaneously, albeit the frequency and strength of the contraction are controllable through nerves and hormones. Associated with the spontaneous activity there is a spread of electrical change over the surfaces of atria and ventricles, indicating that the muscular masses constituting atria and ventricles behave as *syncytia*, an impulse generated at one point being conducted as a wave of action potential over and throughout the whole. Direct spread of conduction from atria to ventricles is prevented, however, by the interposition of a fibrous connective-tissue ring, so that a more orderly and effective spread is achieved by a specialized *Purkinje-type* of cardiac muscle fibre contained in the bundle of His. We must now examine the structural and electrophysiological basis of this spontaneous activity and spread, so different from that of the normal vertebrate skeletal muscle.*

Structure

The Muscle Fibre

The structural basis for contraction of the cardiac muscle fibre is very similar to that of the skeletal muscle fibre, both having the characteristic cross-striations that divide the fibre into sarcomeres, and longitudinal striations indicating the existence of bundles of myofibrils. The similarity persists down to the ultrastructural basis as revealed in the electron microscope, although some differences emerge. Thus the skeletal muscle fibre is a true syncytium resulting from the fusion of many cells,† so effective being the fusion that there is no indication of any separations by individual plasma membranes. This perfect fusion allows of a very regular arrangement of myofibrils running the length of the muscle fibre without interruptions, and in

---

* When comparisons between skeletal and cardiac muscle are made it is implied that the skeletal muscle is of the white or fast type, exhibiting the *Fibrillenstruktur* of Krüger. The slow red muscle, with its *Felderstruktur*, containing large numbers of mitochondria, does not contrast with cardiac muscle nearly so strongly.

† It will be recalled that the skeletal muscle fibre has many nuclei revealing the fact that it is the result of fusion of myoblasts during embryonic development.

the fast or twitch type of muscle this regularity of myofibrillar arrangement is striking.

Intercalated Discs. In cardiac muscle the individual muscle cells retain their individuality, so that the myofibrils belonging to a single muscle fibre are not continuous for long lengths but end at the plasma membranes of the individual cells. The junctions between individual cells are characterized by densely staining regions called by the light-microscopists *intercalated discs*. It was considered, to account for the

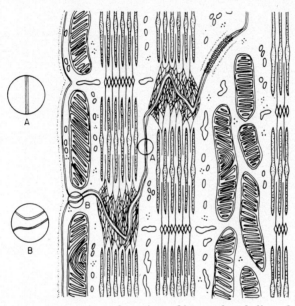

Fig. 3.32. Schematic drawing of portion of intercalated disc of mammalian cardiac muscle. A shows nexus along intersarcoplasmic portion of the inter-calated disc and B shows the region of gap in continuity with the extra-cellular space along the lateral margin of the fibre. In the upper right a desmosome is illustrated in an intersarcoplasmic portion of the disc. (Dewey, "Comparative Physiology of the Heart: Current Trends", Birkhauser Verlag.)

syncytial behaviour of the cardiac muscle, that these represented regions of cytological continuity. In the electron microscope, however, it was seen that the cells retained their individuality, the respective plasma membranes remaining separate, so that the myofibrils did not pass from one to the next. Thus, as Fig. 3.32 illustrates, the inter-calated disc is essentially a region where the plasma membranes of end-to-end apposed cells come quite close, whilst the insertions of the myofibrils in the plasma membranes are accompanied by accumulations

of electron-dense material. They do not represent points of cytoplasmic continuity between cells.

Mitochondria. The large numbers of mitochondria, necessary in a
tissue working continuously, cause the bundles of myofibrils to branch

Fig. 3.33. Electron micrograph of cardiac muscle. The cells are joined end
to end by the step-like intercalated discs (InD). Rows of mitochondria (Mt)
appear to divide the contractile substance into myofibril-like units, but
unlike true myofibrils of skeletal muscle these branch and rejoin and are
quite variable in width. Lipid droplets (Lp), somewhat distorted in the
fixation, are found between the ends of the mitochondria. × 15,000 (Fawcett
and McNutt, *J. Cell Biol.* 1969, **42,** 1.)

and rejoin, and the structure is much more reminiscent of the *Felderstruktur* of certain muscles concerned with sustained contractions by
comparison with the *Fibrillenstruktur* of the more rapid twitch fibres
(p. 219) (Fig. 3.33).

Junctions. Cardiac muscle behaves functionally as a syncytium not
only in respect to a single fibre but in respect to the whole muscle, a
contraction initiated at one point spreading throughout the whole

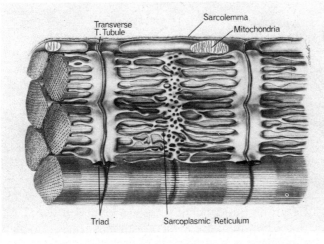

(a)

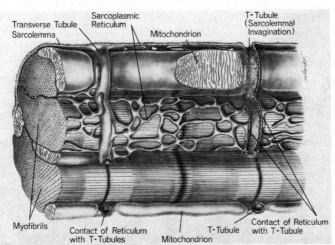

(b)

Fig. 3.34. (a) A repeat of Fig. 3.3, depicting the T-tubules and sarcoplasmic reticulum relation to several myofibrils of amphibian skeletal muscle. There are discrete myofibrils of uniform size, each ensheathed by sarcoplasmic reticulum, with pairs of terminal cisternae associated at each Z-line with a slender T-tubule to form a "triad". The localization of the triads at the Z-line of amphibian muscle makes it more comparable to mammalian cardiac muscle. (b) A drawing of the T-tubules and sarcoplasmic reticulum of mammalian cardiac muscle. Notice the large size of the T-tubules, the simple pattern of the reticulum, and the absence of terminal cisternae. Instead of terminal cisternae small saccular expansions of the reticulum, called subsarcolemmal cisternae, are in close contact with the T-tubes or with the sarcolemma at the periphery of the fibre. The myofilament mass is partially subdivided into irregular myofibril-like areas by clefts that are penetrated by T-tubules. (Fawcett and McNutt, after Peachey, *J. Cell Biol.* 1969, **42**, 1.)

tissue by virtue of the spread of the action potential that precedes this. Thus the *skeletal* muscle fibre is anatomically a syncytium because of fusion of its constituent cells to form a large polynucleate cell, but the *muscle as a whole* is not a syncytium, either histologically or functionally, an action potential initiated in one fibre being confined to this and restricting contraction to this. The cardiac muscle is built up of single cells that seem all to be separate from each other, yet its electrical behaviour is syncytial. The contradiction has been resolved by Sjöstrand's careful examination of the intercalated disc where he found a junctional complex containing a region that he called a *longitudinal connection* which was considered to be the same as the zonula occludens of Farquhar and Palade, i.e. a region of fusion of the outer laminae of the adjacent plasma membranes (Fig. 3.32). Subsequent work has shown that the basis for intercellular connection is a junction of the *nexus-* or *gap-type*, permitting passage of material between the cells and also from one cell to the next so that a dye, injected into one cell diffuses rapidly into an adjacent one, or a depolarization of one is reflected in a spread of electrical charge to the next, the so-called *electrical coupling*. In this way, then, we may explain the contrasting behaviour of cardiac and skeletal muscle, the syncytial arrangement of the cardiac muscle extending throughout the whole muscle, by contrast with the skeletal muscle where it is confined to the single fibre.

Tubular System. Cardiac muscle possesses a sarcotubular system, but this is by no means so elaborately organized in relation to the individual myofibril as in skeletal muscle. The sarcoplasmic reticulum has no terminal cisterns coming into relation with the transverse tubules to give, on section, the triads of the skeletal muscle. There is, indeed, a transverse tubular system quite clearly open to the extracellular space, but it makes relations with the sarcotubular system in a simpler fashion, flattened saccular expansions of this sarcotubular system immediately under the plasma membrane coming into close relation with T-tubules to form "dyads". We may assume that these subsarcolemmal cisterns are regions of storage of calcium, which is released by the conducted effects of the action potential along the transverse T-system. Figure 3.34 illustrates schematically the relation between the tubular system and the myofibrils in cardiac muscle and this should be compared with Fig. 3.4 (p. 190).

Experimental Methods

Isolated Perfused Heart

The natural tendency for the heart to contract spontaneously in a coordinated fashion is easily demonstrated by removing it from the body and perfusing the coronary system by simply tying a cannula into the aorta and allowing a nutrient medium to flow through this under a suitable pressure-head; the nutrient medium passes through the coronary arteries which are branches from the aorta: the Langendorff preparation (Fig. 3.35). In this way a cold-blooded heart may beat for

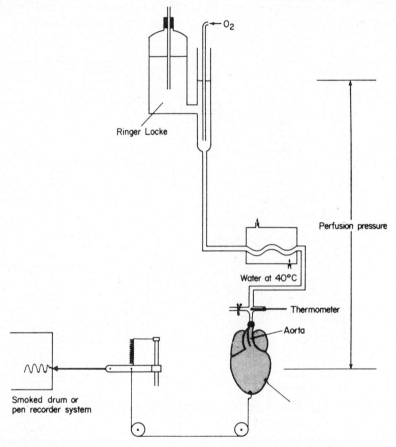

Fig. 3.35. Technique for perfusion of the isolated heart through the aorta.

many hours, and the same is true of the warm-blooded heart provided adequate precautions are taken. A more satisfactory method of studying the heart of the warm-blooded animal is Starling's heart-lung preparation, illustrated in Fig. 3.36; here the heart, separated from the body, is perfused by a pump supplying blood which is circulated through an aerating device to permit reoxygenation and removal of CO_2.

Isolated Muscle

When it is required to study the mechanical properties of cardiac muscle its inherent tendency to contract may be a nuisance experimentally, so that ventricular muscle, with its much lower intrinsic rhythmicity, is most often employed, especially the fine papillary muscles controlling the valves. In general, the muscle studied in this way broadly exhibits the same electrical and mechanical behaviour as

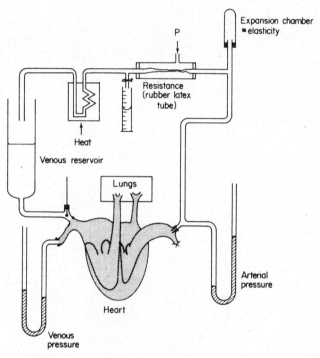

Fig. 3.36. The Starling heart–lung preparation.

that of skeletal muscle, although its syncytical character means that a single suprathreshold stimulus will produce a maximal contraction, since there is no possibility of recruitment of individual fibres, as in skeletal muscle.

Summation

The force of contraction of a skeletal muscle fibre in response to a stimulus can be increased if the stimulus follows a first stimulus within a short enough period, i.e. the second stimulus can be made to summate

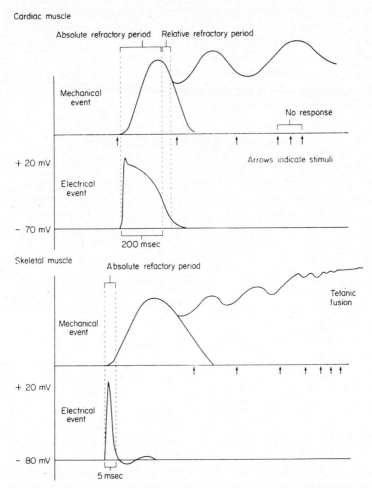

Fig. 3.37. A comparison of the duration of the electrical and mechanical events in cardiac and skeletal muscle. Because the electrical event, and hence the refractory period, in cardiac muscle are of similar duration to the mechanical event, fusion of responses to repetitive stimuli to give a tetanus does not occur. The lower figure shows the tetanic fusion of skeletal muscle.

with the first; and a maximal tension can be developed during a tetanus when successive stimuli arrive before the muscle has had time to relax from the previous one. The refractory period of cardiac muscle extends into its relaxation period, so that only a limited amount of summation is possible, and certainly the muscle cannot be tetanized (Fig. 3.37). Variations in strength of contraction of cardiac muscle, which can be quite large, thus depend on a different mechanism than that of summation. Furthermore, the fact that the muscle is functionally a syncytium means that another method available to skeletal muscle, namely recruitment of individual fibres, is not available to cardiac muscle. The main methods available are through changes in muscle fibre length and through a changed "contractility", of the muscle fibre manifest in the "staircase phenomenon".

Mechanical Aspects of Contraction

Length–Tension Diagram

We have seen that in skeletal muscle the tension developed in a tetanus depends critically on the length, to give the length–tension diagram of Fig. 3.19 (p. 205); cardiac muscle exhibits similar properties. However, although the contractile force increases to a maximum

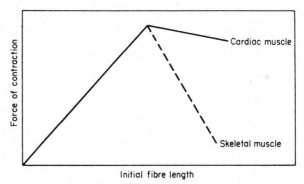

Fig. 3.38. The length–tension diagrams of cardiac and skeletal muscle.

of some six times the unstretched value at twice the unstretched length, further increases in length cause only a gradual decrease in tension, by contrast with the rapid falling off in skeletal muscle once the maximum has been reached (Fig. 3.38). Starling, employing his heart–lung preparation, showed that the force with which the ventricle contracted increased with the increasing size of the ventricle before contracting, i.e. as the chamber was better and better filled. This provides a mechanism through which the heart can automatically adjust its power output to meet its need, a well filled ventricle requiring a greater force to expel its contents than a less well filled one. The length–tension diagram of Fig. 3.38 is an expression of Starling's Law of the Heart. It must be emphasized, however, that variations in contractile power are not normally brought about through changed size of the heart, but rather by a change in the intrinsic power of the muscle to contract independently of its length, a characteristic described as its *contractility*.

Staircase Phenomenon

By the staircase phenomenon we mean the increased tension developed in cardiac muscle when successive suprathreshold shocks are applied to it. Clearly, the muscle becomes more responsive to a stimulus after several contractions, and this is considered to be due to the failure of the relaxation machinery, which sequesters Ca^{2+} after each activation of the contractile machinery, to sequester all the extra Ca^{2+} "let loose".

This staircase phenomenon may be regarded as just one of several ways in which cardiac muscle reveals a greater variability in its "contractility" than skeletal muscle, variability that is necessary if adequate control is to be exerted by neural and hormonal influences, since as just indicated, the fine graduations of activity brought about by recruitment of individual all-or-none fibre responses, and the gradual summation leading to a tetanus, are not possible in this syncytial type of muscle.

Basis of Pacemaker Activity

Action Potentials

When microelectrodes are inserted into the heart in the pacemaker region, the spontaneous activity of the muscle cells is revealed as a series of action potentials; Fig. 3.39 shows some records taken by Hutter and Trautwein from the pacemaker region of the frog's heart (the sinus venosus) and also from the atrium. There is a strong contrast between the action potentials according as they are taken from the pacemaker region or not. In the latter case (c of Fig. 3.39) the spike rises rapidly from the baseline, which is the resting potential. By contrast, the record from the pacemaker region shows an initial slow depolarization which passes into the rapid spike; at the end of the spike a new phase of slow depolarization occurs (a and b of Fig. 3.39).

Unstable Resting Potential

Thus the essential feature of the pacemaker is the instability of its "resting potential" which, in fact, is never at rest; no sooner has the potential reached its maximum value after a spike than it starts to fall (depolarize) until the depolarization has reached a critical value, in which case the spike is fired off. The normal absence of this membrane instability in the atrial fibres indicates a reliance on direct excitation, presumably by spread from the pacemaker cells. The fibres constituting the AV-bundle, or bundle of His, are often described as *Purkinje fibres*, being large and easily penetrated by microelectrodes in some species. Records of spontaneous activity in the Purkinje fibres reveal the same rhythmical slow depolarization—the *pacemaker potential*—followed by the spike.

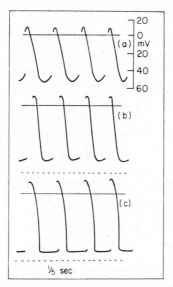

Fig. 3.39. Action potentials from the frog's heart. a and b are records from different fibres in the sinus venosus. c is a record from an auricular fibre. In each case a line is drawn through zero potential. Note absence of preliminary depolarization in auricular record; also that the depolarization is smaller in record b than in a. (Hutter and Trautwein, *J. gen. Physiol.* 1956, **39,** 715.)

Ionic Basis of Action Potential

The mechanism for the development of the pacemaker potential has attracted a great deal of experimental study along the lines developed by Hodgkin and Huxley in their study of the axon spike. In general, the action potential is, indeed, governed by an increase in Na^+-permeability, so that a characteristic "overshoot", depending on the external concentration of Na^+, can be measured.

Repolarization. The phase of repolarization is also due to a phase of increased K^+-permeability, but this is more complex in its development than that observed in the axon. In general, it is doubtless the more complex factors involved in repolarizing the membrane that also lead to the development of the pacemaker potential, or membrane depolarization, that begins the new cycle. Thus rhythmicity is essentially a failure to maintain the repolarized condition immediately following the spike, and this may be partly due to a finite Na^+-permeability that holds the membrane potential at a level different from the K^+-potential, i.e. it tends to reduce this; but this is by no means certain, and the slow depolarization may be a result of rather complex changes in K^+ and Cl^- permeabilities. Perhaps the most important point to appreciate is that the stable membrane potential, as typically seen in the axon and the striated muscle fibre, may well be regarded as the exception, resulting from the powerful repolarizing K^+-current that follows the reversal of the membrane potential due to increased Na^+-permeability. As Huxley showed in his study of the effects of reduced external Ca^{2+}-concentration on the squid axon, this stability can be easily upset, leading to repetitive discharge.

Excitation–Contraction Coupling

The action potential of the cardiac muscle is, in general, slower and more prolonged than that of fast skeletal muscle. This prolongation,

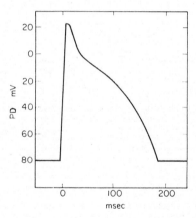

Fig. 3.40. The action potential of a ventricular muscle fibre.

moreover, is very pronounced with ventricular muscle, a characteristic plateau occurring during the declining phase indicating a slow rate of repolarization (Fig. 3.40). The various features of the action potential may be modified by nervous influences, and since there is no doubt that, not only the frequency of the heart-beat, but also its strength, are governed by the nature of the action potential, we see at once how nervous activity may modify both aspects—*chronotropic* and *inotropic*.

Duration of Action Potential

Many observations suggest that the duration of the action potential governs the duration of tension-development in cardiac muscle, a situation quite different from that in skeletal muscle where the action

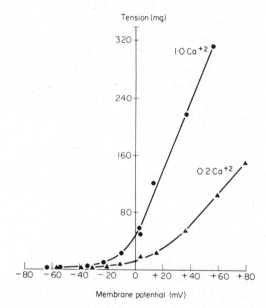

Fig. 3.41. The tension developed in cardiac muscle fibre during sustained degrees of depolarization applied by voltage clamp. Note how the tension depends on the external concentration of Ca^{2+}. (Morad and Orkand, *J. Physiol.* 1971, **219**, 167.)

potential is usually over before measurable tension develops. Thus we may apply a voltage-clamp to frog heart muscle to maintain a sustained depolarization, and in this way we may maintain a sustained contraction for as long as 30 sec, as illustrated by Fig. 3.41, the tension developed being governed by the degree of depolarization. In mammalian muscle the position is not so simple, since the muscle relaxes after a period of about 100 msec of sustained depolarization, and it must be repolarized before a second contraction can be brought about, hence it is more similar to skeletal muscle.

Penetration of Ca^{2+}

As with skeletal muscle, there is good evidence that contraction is mediated by the appearance of free Ca^{2+} in the fibrillar spaces of the muscle fibre. The effectiveness of Ca^{2+} can be demonstrated easily by placing functionally "skinned" cardiac muscle fibres in solutions containing increasing concentrations of free Ca^{2+}; the functional skinning consists of destroying the selective permeability of the fibre membrane by pre-treatment with EDTA, so that free Ca^{2+}-ions in the medium rapidly come into equilibrium with the insides of the muscle cells. When this is done it is found that tension develops when the concentration in the medium is as low as 10^{-8} M and becomes maximal at 10^{-5} M; relaxation is brought about by a medium containing less than 10^{-8} M. An important feature of cardiac muscle contraction, recognized by the earliest investigators, was its dependence on the concentration of Ca^{2+} in the external medium. Thus replacement of Ca^{2+} in a Ringer's solution by Mg^{2+} completely blocks the spontaneous heart beat, or the ability to respond to depolarization with tension-development, whereas skeletal muscle is largely independent of the external concentration. This suggests that cardiac muscle depends to a greater extent than skeletal muscle on the influx of Ca^{2+} from outside the fibre for activating the contractile machinery, and Fig. 3.41, showing the much smaller effects of depolarizing currents on muscle tension when the concentration of Ca^{2+} in the medium is low, tends to confirm this viewpoint.

Inward Ca^{2+} Current. There is some evidence that a part of the inward current of the cardiac action potential is carried by Ca^{2+}-ions, and this would produce a net influx during the rising phase of the spike. Moreover, it has been shown that depolarized cardiac muscle has a higher passive permeability to Ca^{2+}-ions, and this would favour influx during the plateau phase of the action potential. As Fig. 3.42 shows for the guinea pig heart, the measured influx per beat is proportional to the tension developed.

Release from Stores. However, there is a great deal of evidence indicating that release of Ca^{2+} from internal storage sites, mediated by conduction of the depolarization process along the T-system, is also an important event in excitation–contraction coupling. Thus, as in skeletal muscle, it is possible to identify stores of Ca^{2+} in the lateral cisterns of the sarcoplasmic reticulum, and after contraction some of this Ca^{2+} is seen to have moved into the region of overlap of A- and I-filaments. It is likely that the Ca^{2+}, entering during the action potential, is taken up into preferred storage sites where it is ready to be released rapidly in response to a stimulus. This view is demanded by the extraordinary effects of previous depolarization of the mammalian ventricular muscle on its subsequent power to contract in response to a new stimulus, i.e. on its state of inotropy.

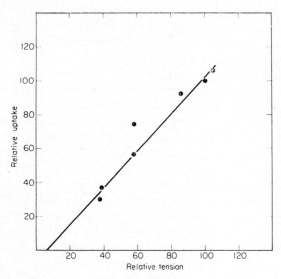

Fig. 3.42. The relative calcium uptake per beat of guinea pig left atrial appendages as a function of the tension developed. Different tensions were obtained by varying beat-rate and external concentration of Ca^{2+}. (Winegrad, *Circulation Res.* 1961, **24**, 523.)

Potentiation of Muscular Contraction

Effects of Depolarization on Tension

The effects of depolarization of the muscle are at the basis of the staircase phenomenon described above, namely the successive increase in strength of contraction with repeated stimuli. If, by a voltage-clamp technique, the muscle is held depolarized for various periods, increases in inotropy amounting to an eight-fold increase in contractility can be achieved. If the muscle is left unstimulated after this potentiation, the increased inotropy lasts for a long time, decaying with a half-life of some 100 sec. If the heart is stimulated during this period, however, the return to normal inotropy is much more rapid.

Figure 3.43 illustrates some of these effects. Here the tension developed by the muscle in response to a standard stimulus is plotted as ordinate against the time after the potentiating treatment. The top curve shows that the tension, immediately after treatment with a depolarizing current of 5·5 μamp for 2·7 sec, was some 8 times that of the control, indicated by the broken line. This positive inotropy decays with a half-life of about 100 sec. The next curve shows the smaller potentiation due to a smaller depolarization of 3·7 μamp for 6 beats; the lowest curve shows a small negative inotropic effect due to application of a hyperpolarizing current.

Rapidly Released Store of Ca^{2+}. The most satisfactory explanation for these phenomena is based on the presence of a special storage site for Ca^{2+} in the fibre whence it is rapidly released in response to an

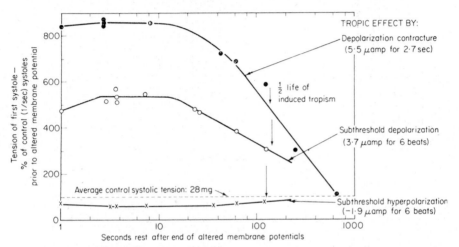

Fig. 3.43. Illustrating the potentiation of cardiac muscle contraction by a preliminary treatment with depolarizing currents. For further details see text. (Wood *et al.*, *Circulation Res.* 1969, **24**, 409.)

action potential. Potentiation, of the sort described above, consists in a build-up of this "rapidly-released" store, possibly on the sarcoplasmic reticulum. Once in this special site the Ca^{2+}, entering the fibre in consequence of depolarization, is only slowly removed into other storage sites or extruded out of the cell altogether, and this accounts for the slow decay of potentiation at rest. However, if the muscle is excited, then the action potential releases this Ca^{2+} and, after about 8 stimuli, all potentiation is lost.

Cause of Variable Inotropy. It is in this way that we may account for the remarkable capacity cardiac muscle has for variation in its inotropy or contractility. Thus the basis for an increase in contractile power of a fast skeletal muscle fibre is the summation of successive contractions, which, because of the time required to stretch the series elastic element, are unable to develop this increased power when occurring alone. The long refractory period of cardiac muscle precludes the development of large increases in tension through this summation process. The basis for an augmentation of cardiac muscle contraction is therefore different, and it consists in the building up of a readily releasable store of ionizable Ca^{2+} through successive depolarizations.

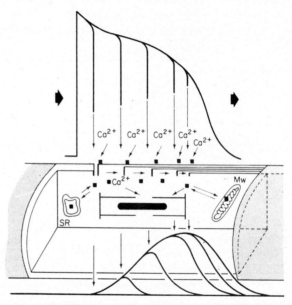

Fig. 3.44. Schematic representation of control of contraction by the action potential superimposed on a diagram of a myocardial cell. At the vertical arrows, the action potential is repolarized and contraction is terminated. The "latches" in the membrane withdraw with depolarization (opening the "gate") for various times (horizontal arrows). Calcium (squares) is either released from the membrane or is bound and then released (indicated by short and heavy arrows). Mw: mitochondria; SR: sarcoplasmic reticulum. (Morad and Orkand, *J. Physiol.* 1971, **219**, 167.)

The mere building up of a store of ionized Ca^{2+} in the cytoplasm of the muscle fibre would not be a practicable method of potentiation since contraction occurs once the concentration rises above the basic level of about 10^{-7} M, and the essential feature of potentiation is that the muscle can remain relaxed while potentiated, the potentiation only showing itself when the muscle has been stimulated to contract. Hence the establishment of a readily releasable store provides the simplest basis for permitting the potentiation that is necessary if large variations in contractility are to be achieved.

Relaxation during Depolarization

As with skeletal muscle, sustained depolarization leads to relaxation, and this is presumably due to the re-accumulation in storage sites of Ca^{2+}, both the readily releasable and mitochondrial, whilst active extrusion may be accelerated. Thus *in vitro* studies with microsomes, i.e. fragmented sarcoplasmic reticulum and plasma membrane, show that these, as well as mitochondria, are able to accumulate Ca^{2+} from the medium. Ultimately, with this sustained depolarization, a steady state is reached, with the level of free ionized Ca^{2+} in the sarcoplasm below the threshold of 10^{-7} M required for contraction. The muscle, however, is in a highly potentiated condition because the store of readily releasable Ca^{2+} is maximal and it will remain in this condition for several hundreds of seconds unless the extra stores of this Ca^{2+} are dissipated by subsequent contractions. A basic scheme for the cycle of contraction and relaxation is illustrated in Fig. 3.44.

Nervous Control of Beat

Chronotropy

The heart beats spontaneously so that nervous activity is only required to modify the frequency and force of its contraction. Since the magnitude and duration of the action potential have strong influences on both the force and duration of the contraction, it is reasonable to expect the influence to be exerted largely, if not exclusively, through the electrical characteristics of the tissue. So far as the rate of beating—*chronotropy*—is concerned, the influence must be exerted at the pacemaker zones, notably the S.A. and A.V.-nodes, whilst the specialized conducting pathway, the bundle of His, may also be expected to be influenced. In fact it is these regions that are densely innervated by inhibitory fibres from the vagus, and acceleratory sympathetic fibres. Stimulation of the vagus nerve slows and, if continued, finally stops the heart from beating; eventually, in spite of continued stimulation, the beat recommences—*vagus escape*. The action of the vagus can be mimicked by acetylcholine and abolished by atropine. Stimulation of the sympathetic supply to the heart increases the rate and force of contraction, an effect that can be mimicked, in the isolated heart, by adrenaline, or noradrenaline, the sympathetic transmitter.

Mechanism of Inhibition

It will be recalled that inhibition can be brought about by stabilizing the resting potential of the excitable tissue. Thus, since excitation consists in a preliminary depolarization, or reduction of the resting potential, of the cell membrane, anything that favours the maintenance of the existing potential should counteract excitation. A method of doing this is to increase the cell's permeability to K^+. We have seen, in the Goldman analysis of the resting potential, that it depends on the difference in concentration of K^+ inside and outside the cell *and* on the relative permeabilities of the membrane to the K^+ and Na^+ ions; the higher the permeability to K^+, and the lower the permeability to Na^+, the nearer the potential comes to its maximum theoretical value, E_K, given by the Nernst Equation. The initial depolarizing, or pacemaker, phase of the cardiac action potential consists in a slow decrease in the resting potential, and is most probably due to an increased permeability to Na^+ possibly accompanied by a decreased permeability to K^+. Clearly, if the inhibitory nerve impulse, or acetylcholine, caused an increased permeability to K^+ it would counteract this depolarizing phase and might altogether inhibit the development of an action potential. If the resting potential of the cardiac muscle is less than the theoretical K^+-potential, then the increased permeability should be manifest not only in a slower depolarizing phase, but in an increase in resting potential, i.e. the maximum potential developed between spikes.

Effects on Rate. These points will be clearer from a study of Fig. 3.45. In (a) we have the development of two spikes in the uninhibited condition; when E_{Th} is reached, the slow depolarizing phase leads to the abrupt spike followed by the repolarizing phase, which depends to some extent on an increased permeability to K^+, so that at the end of repolarization the resting potential is high, E_{max}. In (b) we imagine that the increased K^+-permeability, due to inhibition, results in a slowing of the depolarizing phase with no change in E_{max}, because this is already the K^+-potential. It will be seen that there is an increase in the pause between beats due to this cause alone. In (c) we imagine that the inhibitory action has led to an increase in E_{max} and no other change; this is sufficient to increase the pause between beats, since the change in potential required to reach threshold is larger. In (d) we imagine that the threshold depolarization required to set off the spike has been increased, with no other change. Once again, there has been a lengthening of the pause between beats.

Experimental studies of inhibition show that certainly an increased

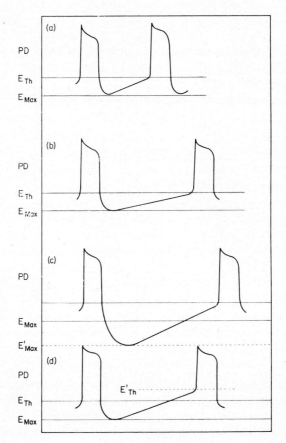

Fig. 3.45. Showing how the rate of beating may be modified. (a) Uninhibited condition. (b) Slowed depolarization phase. (c) Increased E_{MAX}, the maximum value of the membrane potential during a cycle. (d) The threshold depolarization required to fire the spike has increased. E_{Th}: Threshold membrane potential. E_{MAX} = maximum value of membrane potential. (Modified from Hecht, *Ann. N.Y. Acad. Sci.* 1965, **127,** 149.)

resting potential between beats (Fig. 3.45c), and a slowed depolarization phase (Fig. 3.45b), are important in the frog's heart. In the dog's atrium, because the resting potential is close to the maximum theoretical K^+-potential, vagal stimulation exerts its slowing action largely through slowing the depolarizing phase; it is interesting that it actually shortens the duration of the action potential by increasing the speed of repolarization, since this apparently depends on increased K^+-permeability (Fig. 3.46). Studies on the actual rate of movement of

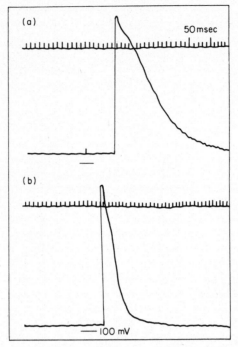

Fig. 3.46. (a) Control action potential recorded from a single fibre of the isolated dog atrium. (b) Same atrium in presence of $5 \cdot 5 \times 10^{-4}$ M acetylcholine. Note absence of any decrease in amplitude of resting or action potentials. (Hoffman and Suckling, *Am. J. Physiol.* **173**, 312.)

isotopically labelled K^+-ions confirm that inhibition is accompanied by increased permeability.

Acceleration

The action of adrenaline, or sympathetic stimulation, is to shorten the diastolic pause; and this is accompanied by an increased force of beat. The positive chronotropic effect is due to a more rapid depolarizing phase, i.e. to an acceleration of the pacemaker, and the actual mechanism seems to be an alteration in the dependence of K^+-permeability on the membrane potential, so that for a given membrane potential the K^+-permeability is lower, thus favouring depolarization.

Positive Inotropy

The increased power of the beat—*positive inotropic effect*—may be unrelated to changes in the action potential but rather to an increased penetration of Ca^{2+} or release from stores.

ACTIVATION AND CONTRACTION OF SMOOTH MUSCLE

The muscle lining the vertebrate viscera, such as the stomach, intestine and uterus, and forming the contractile basis of the blood vessels, is described as *smooth*, or *unstriated*, because of the absence of the characteristic cross-striations seen in skeletal and cardiac muscle. It is called *involuntary muscle* because it is brought into play either spontaneously or through activity of the autonomic division of the nervous system. Smooth muscle varies considerably in structure and behaviour so that this account must be drawn largely from the behaviour of the smooth muscle lining gut and uterus, the most commonly studied. The main variable in behaviour is the degree of spontaneity in contraction, and the requirements for innervation to bring this about. At the one extreme we have the smooth muscle of gut with pronounced spontaneous activity, and at the other the smooth muscle lining the seminal vesicles or constituting the nictitating membrane of the eye, these last requiring nervous or humoral excitation for their contraction, and thus resembling striated muscle.

Structure

Cells

The muscle is composed of cells that are small by comparison with the fibres of skeletal muscle, and they are not usually arranged in the parallel alignment characteristic of the latter. The cells are spindle-shaped, varying in length from 0·02 mm in arterioles to about 0·5 mm in the pregnant uterus. In the electron microscope the cytoplasm is seen to be filled with myofilaments, which contrast with those of striated muscle by their absence of cross-striations and their irregular arrangement. Essentially, then, the cell consists of a bundle of filaments, in the clefts of which are contained the nucleus, mitochondria and endoplasmic reticulum.

Contractile Units

The relations of the individual muscle cells with each other vary according to the type of muscle; in some muscles cells are closely apposed to each other over most of their areas, but in others they may be separated by collagen fibres (Fig. 3.47). In general, the cells are linked in an end-to-end fashion, as with cardiac muscle cells, to give a fibrous arrangement consisting of bundles of these chains of cells. This is an important feature, since the unit of contraction, be it caused by nervous

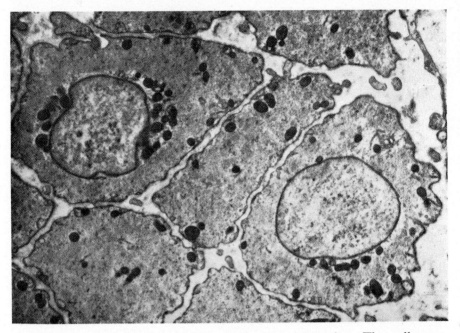

Fig. 3.47. Longitudinal intestinal muscle in cross section. The cells are loosely arranged and touch each other over broad planar areas. × 7000 ca. (Lane and Rhodin, *J. Ultrastr. Res.* **10,** 470.)

discharge or occurring spontaneously, is probably the bundle rather than the single cell, in the sense that it is virtually impossible to initiate a contraction or action potential in a single cell; the stimulus must be applied to a group making up a bundle. This does not mean that the bundles are electrically separate, so that it is quite possible for an action potential to spread from one to the next, and in this way large parts of a muscle are brought into activity. However, the arrangement in bundles leads to a preferential mode of transmission parallel with

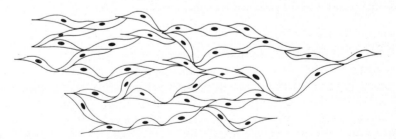

Fig. 3.48. Smooth muscle cells.

the bundles' axis, the spread of excitation at right angles being very much smaller (Fig. 3.48).

Mechanical Aspects

Myofilaments

Contraction of smooth muscle is associated with a widening of the cell and a crumpling of its plasma membrane; the mechanism by which this shortening of the cell is achieved is still not clear. The filaments observable in the electron microscope are predominantly of the actin type, of diameter about 50–80 Å, and these may often be seen in cross-section as regular arrays. Myosin is certainly present in smooth muscle, but its identification in the form of thick filaments has not been easy, in fact it has been more common to deny their presence than to affirm it. However, in vascular smooth muscle well-defined filaments some 180 Å in diameter surrounded by thinner filaments have been described, the lowest ratio of thin to thick being some 12:1 (Fig. 3.49). Again, in intestinal smooth muscle Lowy and Small have identified ribbons that are apparently made up of myosin filaments, these are some 80 Å thick and 350 Å wide, extending for considerable lengths along the axis of the cell; and these authors consider that a sliding filament hypothesis would be applicable here, the thin filaments sliding over the ribbons which might well be connected to each other in line so as to stretch from one end of the cell to another.* A constituent of the ribbon, in addition to myosin, is tropomyosin, which is involved in the control of skeletal muscle actin–myosin interaction. A third type of filament, with diameter of about 100 Å, is called an *intermediate filament*, and seems to be neither actin nor myosin.

Longitudinal and Circular Muscles

The muscle surrounding a hollow viscus, such as the intestine or uterus, can usually be divided into groups of fibres running longitudinally and circularly, in which case it is customary to speak of the *longitudinal*, or *circular* muscle respectively. The relation between the two groups is functionally close so that activity taking place in one can often be transmitted to the other. Nevertheless much of the coordinated activity of this muscle indicates that the two may be controlled independently.

---

* Dense bodies is the name given to darkly staining regions of about 4000 Å by 700 Å found in the cytoplasm, and it has been argued that they take the place of Z-lines; Lowy and Small consider they are artefacts due to destruction of the regular array of thin filaments locally.

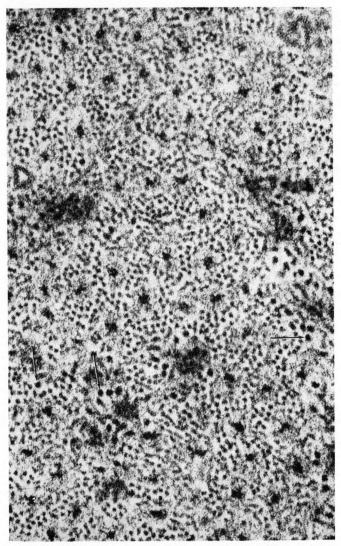

Fig. 3.49. High magnification view of transversely-sectioned thick and thin filaments. The closest centre-to-centre thick and thin filament spacing is approximately 15 nm, but usually there is an amorphous electron-opaque area around each thick filament where no thin filaments are present. The centre-to-centre spacing between thin filaments is approximately 8–11 nm. At the regions of high filament density, the ratio of thin to thick filaments is 12:1. Rabbit portal-anterior mesenteric vein, 30 min incubation, stretch, **glutar**aldehyde-sucrose. Arrows point to thick filaments. × 186,000. (Devine and Somlyo, *J. Cell Biol.* 1971, **49,** 636.)

Cell Contacts

The cells of smooth muscle retain their individuality, in the sense that there is no microscopically visible continuity of cytoplasm from one cell to the next, each being surrounded by its plasma membrane. Because smooth muscle, like cardiac muscle, behaves as a syncytium, a contraction initiated at one point spreading through large numbers of cells, the presence of specialized contacts between muscle cells has been sought, and Dewey and Barr described regions of very close membrane approximation which they called the *nexus*, the membranes appearing to have fused. In fact, the cell contact is of the gap-junction type, and one that permits coupling of adjacent cells similar to that between cardiac muscle fibres.

Absence of T-system

The muscle cells contain an endoplasmic reticulum but there is no transverse tubular system so that activation of the myofilaments probably takes place by diffusion of Ca^{2+} from the surface rather than release through a special conducting mechanism.

Electrical Basis of Spontaneous Activity

A portion of intestine placed in a suitable nutrient medium will contract and relax spontaneously for long periods of time, an activity that will take place when all possibilities of nervous action are abolished by, say, the application of a neurotoxin like tetrodotoxin. Thus smooth muscle is like cardiac muscle in giving *myogenic* contractions and, as with cardiac muscle, the force and frequency can be modified by nervous and hormonal influences.

Resting Potential

The smooth muscle cell has a resting potential of the order of 50 mV, which is less than that encountered in skeletal muscle or nerve. Nevertheless the same basic mechanism operates in its production, namely the maintenance of gradients of concentration of K^+ and Cl^- resulting from continuous pump activity. The generally low values of the potential are due to a relatively high Na^+-permeability, and recent work indicates that the Na^+ pump, operating to extrude Na^+ from the cell, is not electrically neutral, i.e. it tends to expel Na^+ faster than K^+ can enter, giving rise to an internal negativity on this account. This is best demonstrated when the muscle is placed in a K^+-free medium, when the increased pumping activity causes a rise in internal negativity—

hyperpolarization—which may be counteracted by ouabain, which inhibits the pump.

Spontaneous Depolarization

The question arises as to whether, as with cardiac muscle, the spontaneous contractions are preceded by a depolarization of the membrane; until the development of intracellular recording techniques it was not easy to say whether or not this was the case, although Bozler's classical studies, using extracellular recordings, strongly suggested this. Bozler concluded that a muscle such as the longitudinal or circular muscle of gut behaved essentially as a single giant fibre or syncytium, an action potential initiated at a given point spreading with a characteristic velocity over all, or a large part, of it, the extent of propagation being governed by a variable excitability of the tissue from point to point. So far as the ureter was concerned, the spread of electrical activity was apparently myogenic, in the sense that it did not require nervous impulses for its propagation, in spite of the well coordinated nature of the wave of contraction that propelled fluid in one direction only. In general, Bozler and later workers observed two types of propagated activity, namely *slow waves* and *spikes*, the latter occurring in bursts and being accompanied by muscular contraction, the greater frequency of the burst the more powerful the contraction. The rate of propagation in the ureter was some 3–4 cm/sec, and in the uterus it was 0·26–6·0 cm/sec.

Pacemakers. With intracellular recording the spike activity has been shown to be the result of depolarization and reversal of the resting potential. As we shall see, the basis for the rising phase is probably not an inward flow of Na^+-ions but is due to influx of Ca^{2+}. The spike potentials usually occurred in association with slow waves of depolarization that appeared to act as a pacemaker, but this was not always true; so that it is necessary to postulate that, whilst all or most muscle cells give rise to rhythmic slow potentials, only certain cells act as *pacemakers*. This pacemaker activity not only governs the appearance of spikes in the cell giving rise to the slow potential but it also determines the spikes in neighbouring muscle cells by virtue of a spread of pacemaker action. In this way we can account for the different time-relations of slow potential and spike; in the pacemaker cells the spike arises from the slow depolarization (Fig. 3.50), as with cardiac muscle, but in the other cells, called "driven" cells, the spike originates at a relatively high membrane potential without a slow depolarization leading up to this. According to Bennett, the slow potentials recorded from many cells are simply the electrotonically propagated pacemaker activity occurring in relatively few true pacemaker cells. Again, the spikes in the driven cells are the result of electrotonic spread of depolarization from the spikes occurring in the pacemaker cells.

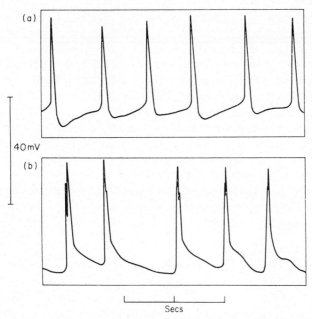

Fig. 3.50. Two contrasting types of activity recorded in the smooth muscle cells of the taenia coli. (a) Action potentials preceded by slow depolarizations ("pacemaker-like" activity). (b) Action potentials with slow repolarization phases ("driven" activity). (Bennett, Burnstock and Holman, *J. Physiol.* 1966, **182,** 527.)

Unit of Conduction

The cells of visceral smooth muscle are very small—some 50–100 μ— so that the propagation over long distances requires some coupling between the cells, and this is presumably provided by the nexuses described earlier. Thus treatment of muscle with hypertonic solutions will break these junctions, and this results in the failure of electrical change to propagate. In general, the behaviour of intestinal smooth muscle is best described in terms of "units" made up of numbers of muscle cells linked electrically, so that an impulse originating at one part spreads over the whole unit. Thus, usually, stimulation of a single cell fails to bring about propagated activity, and only when a certain minimum width of tissue is stimulated does this happen; hence propagation over large distances requires that at least one group, or unit, of cells be activated, and then transmission occurs from one unit to the next. For example, we may reduce the width of a piece of smooth muscle step by step, and at a critical width (100 μ) propagation ceases.*

Sucrose Gap. Perhaps the best demonstration of cell-to-cell functional continuity is given by the "sucrose-gap" technique; a portion of a strip of muscle is soaked in isotonic sucrose solution, and this, by removal of salt, raises the electrical resistance of this part of the strip. A spike arising on either side of the gap is not propagated across it because of this high resistance. However, by shunting the gap, as in Fig. 3.51a, transmission across it occurred, and this would not have been possible without flow of current through the muscle tissue in the gap, i.e. the tissue was behaving like a single cell. The situation is analogous with one demonstrated many years ago by Osterhout on a large single cell; a portion of the surface was damaged and, as a result, a wave of action potential was extinguished in the damaged region. By a salt-bridge shunt the action potential could be carried across the damaged gap (Fig. 3.51b).

Slow-waves and Spikes

In general, then, we may differentiate a slow-wave activity from spike-activity. In a genuine pacemaker cell this slow-wave builds up to a spike which is then propagated through many cells along the muscle, each cell developing a regenerative spike. In many cells a slow-wave activity will be manifest that is not due to pacemaker activity in these cells but to electronically propagated activity in nearby spike-producing cells; so that we may speak of a "propagated wave" of slow-potential change passing along a smooth muscle, but the mode of propagation is through the spike potentials, whose effects spread electrotonically. A special form of slow-wave activity, accompanied by spikes, described as *Type III*, may be observed in intestinal muscle. Here the waves are abolished by nerve toxins or atropine, and consequently we must assume that the depolarizations are due to the spontaneous release of transmitter—acetylcholine—from the nerve endings belonging to the plexus of ganglia and nerve fibres within the tissue—*Auerbach's plexus.*

---

* When a microelectrode is placed inside a single smooth muscle cell, and the membrane is depolarized by passing a current through the electrode, it is rare for a spike to be initiated, so that electrical stimulation must usually be carried out with a large electrode covering many cells. As Tomita showed, the reason for this may be sought in analogous studies on the neurone where a depolarizing stimulus, confined to a very small area of membrane, fails to initiate a propagated spike. In the smooth muscle, because of its syncytial connections which ramify in all three dimensions, the highly localized depolarizing current is dissipated before it can generate the depolarization required for spike propagation.

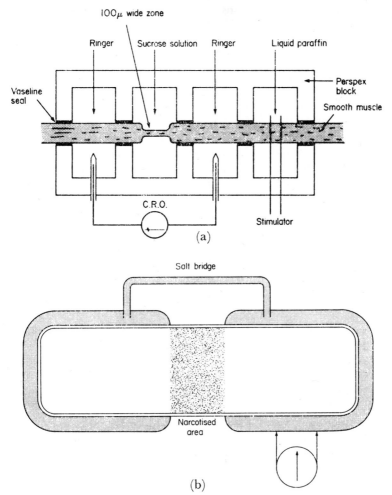

Fig. 3.51. (a) Salt bridge across a "sucrose gap", i.e. a portion of the tissue soaked in isotonic sucrose solution to increase the external resistance. (b) Salt bridge across a narcotised area on a giant plant cell.

Effects of Stretch. Smooth muscle of gut contracts more vigorously if it is distended, e.g. by the presence of an inflated balloon, or bolus of chyme; the increased activity is associated with a decrease in resting potential and an increase in frequency of spontaneous spikes. Thus, to some extent at any rate, the basis of the response to distension of the gut is inherent in the characteristics of the muscle cells. However, the presence of nervous plexuses, containing both sensory and motor neurones, in the tissue means that responses to stretch can be, and indeed are, mediated reflexly. Thus peristalsis (Vol. 3) is abolished by cocainization of the mucosa, which blocks the sensory neurones that are excited by stretch when the bolus passes along the gut.

Single- and Multi-Unit Types of Smooth Muscle

Bozler classified vertebrate smooth muscle as single-unit and multi-unit, according to the way in which electrical activity was propagated. Thus the muscle lining the gut and uterus was described as *single-unit* or *visceral-type* muscle, behaving as a syncytium. The multiple-unit type was analogous in its behaviour with skeletal muscle in that the individual fibres apparently had to be activated separately, and showed little or no spontaneous activity; this type is illustrated by the nictitating membrane of the eye. Bozler included the musculature of the arteries and veins in the latter category, but there is little doubt that they are capable of spontaneous activity and propagation of electrical activity from one cell to another. However, as we should expect of muscles that are employed in the control of blood-flow, spontaneous activity is not prominent, whilst the responses to nervous stimuli are.

In general the basis of Bozler's classification is not sound; all vertebrate smooth muscles are, in fact, syncytial in so far as nexus-type junctions between cells are found in them; and the difference between the "syncytial" and "multi-unit" types resides solely in the ability to generate pacemaker activity. Thus gut and uterine muscle can do this and develop tension independently of nervous activity; the nictitating membrane does not do so and relies on the sympathetic nerve supply for its activation. Even when a single type of smooth muscle is considered, variations in behaviour are encountered, not only between species, but in the same animal; thus the muscle of vein may or may not show spontaneous activity according to which vein is studied.

Electrical and Mechanical Activities

When all the cells of a piece of smooth muscle are excited simultaneously, the development of tension follows a slow course of rise and fall, as illustrated by Fig. 3.52, the tension curve beginning after the action potential is over. When the muscle is stimulated repetitively, the tension increases in proportion to the frequency of stimulation. In a similar way, when observing spontaneously developing spike activity, Bülbring found that the higher the spike frequency in individual cells the greater the tension developed in the muscle. The smooth muscle of gut and uterus will also develop tension independently of spike activity, this tension being related to the degree of membrane depolarization. In this respect it is similar to amphibian slow muscle which develops and maintains tension when the membrane is depolarized, as for example, in solutions of high K^+ (p. 212). This contrasts with the fast muscle which only develops tension for a short time, and subsequently relaxes during sustained depolarization.

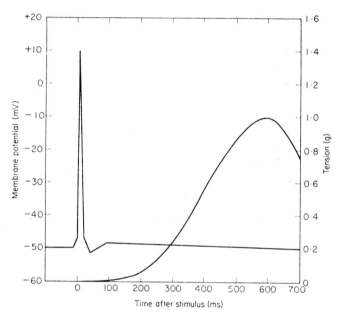

Fig. 3.52. Illustrating the slow development of tension resulting from electrical stimulation of all the cells of a piece of rat uterus. (Bennett, from Mountcastle's "Medical Physiology", Mosby, 1968.)

Excitation–Contraction Coupling

Thus, in analysing the relation between electrical activity and tension we must consider both frequency of spikes and the level of the membrane potential. As with other types of muscle studied, the question arises as to how the electrical changes bring about tension development, i.e. the problem of excitation–contraction coupling. The limited amount of endoplasmic reticulum and the absence of a T-system suggest that activation of the myofibrils of the smooth muscle cell depends on the influx of Ca^{2+} from the extracellular medium, rather than its liberation from storage sites within the cell; and a great deal of evidence has accrued emphasizing the much greater importance

at the of A.P.

of extracellular Ca^{2+} to contraction than with skeletal and even cardiac muscle. The very slow time-relations of the tension curve probably reflect the time required for the Ca^{2+}, entering the cell, to react with the contractile proteins.

Ca^{2+}-Current as Basis of Spike. The spike recorded intracellularly is similar in many respects to those of skeletal muscle and nerve. However, a striking feature is the dependence on external Ca^{2+} so that it may be abolished by removal of this ion from the medium, and this also abolishes muscular contraction. Again, the external concentration of Na^+ can be reduced to zero without abolishing the spike, suggesting that the inward current of the rising phase is carried by some other ion than Na^+, and in fact it is very likely that Ca^{2+} is the carrier of current. If this is, indeed, true it is possible to calculate how much Ca^{2+} would be carried into the cell with a spike; this comes to 4 picomoles per mg. of muscle, which would change the internal concentration by 7.10^{-6} M, sufficient to induce contraction. The fact that tetrodotoxin, which blocks spikes dependent on an inward Na^+-current, does not affect spike activity in the smooth muscle of the intestine also suggests that the normal spike, and not only that taking place in a Na^+-free medium, is dependent on Ca^{2+}.

Release of Ca^{2+} from Stores. Thus qualitatively it might be possible to account for contraction of smooth muscle by the influx of Ca^{2+} occurring during the spike, whilst its relaxation would be governed by either a direct extrusion across the plasma membrane, or by accumulation in a store with subsequent extrusion. The effects of a sustained depolarization could be due to the increased permeability to Ca^{2+} caused by the depolarization, with consequent increased influx down the gradient of electrochemical potential. In fact, the situation is more complex, and it is likely that the difference between smooth and skeletal muscle is quantitative rather than qualitative, the release from stores being less important than the gain from the medium. Thus the contraction that develops when the muscle is depolarized in high-K^+ medium consists of two components, a rapid "spike-phase" and a following sustained tonic contraction—the "tonic phase". The spike phase is abolished by lowering the external concentration of Ca^{2+} below 10^{-7} M, whilst the tonic phase can still be elicited. It may be that the tonic phase is sustained by stores of Ca^{2+} that are released in proportion to the degree of depolarization of the cell membrane, as well as by continued influx from the medium.

Lanthanum. A useful technique that permits the investigator to distinguish between activation through influx of Ca^{2+} and activation through release of stores is provided by the lanthanum ion, La^{3+}, which apparently blocks Ca^{2+}-permeability by competing for the membrane sites that Ca^{2+} uses for penetration. When a smooth muscle, such as a strip of aorta, is held in a Ca^{2+}-free medium, depolarization in high K^+ solution fails to produce contraction; when Ca^{2+} is added, however, contraction occurs. When La^{3+} is added before adding Ca^{2+}, the contraction fails, indicating the importance of Ca^{2+}-influx for this contraction. It is interesting that La^{3+} fails to inhibit the activation by noradrenaline, indicating that noradrenaline can mobilize internal stores of Ca^{2+}. The same is true of histamine and angiotensin, two other activators of vascular smooth muscle. However, it should be noted that under these conditions only a single contraction could be evoked, so that repeated activity requires the replacement of the mobilized Ca^{2+}.

Nervous Influences on Smooth Muscle

Myogenic and Neurogenic Activity

Although smooth vertebrate muscle possesses the powers of automatic myogenic contraction, the wealth of autonomic innervation from both parasympathetic and sympathetic divisions indicates that a great deal of control is exerted on its activity by nervous means. It is, indeed, exceedingly difficult to separate purely myogenic activity from that initiated or modified by nervous activity. For example we have seen that electrical activity in gut or uterine muscle takes the form predominantly of slow waves and spikes. The slow waves of gut, classed as Type III, are intimately associated with the development of tension, and propagate for long distances; they may be abolished by treating the muscle with tetrodotoxin, suggesting that they result from the rhythmic release of transmitter from nerve terminals in the muscle, even when the muscle has been separated from its extrinsic nervous supply. Treatment of the muscle with atropine, which inhibits the effects of acetylcholine, usually abolishes the slow-wave activity. Under other conditions, or in other muscles, however, the slow wave may be a spontaneous pacemaker depolarization, leading up to a spike. Thus, when working with excised muscle, such as gut, the presence of an *intramural plexus of nerve ganglia and fibres* makes it difficult to separate myogenic from neurally mediated activity.

The details of the nervous supply to the alimentary tract will be considered in Vol. 3 when dealing with control of digestive function; here it is important to know the mode of termination of the nerve fibres with a view to interpreting the phenomena of neuromuscular transmission in this form of muscle.

Nerve Endings on Smooth Muscle

Varicosities

The postganglionic autonomic fibres give rise to a branching system of terminal axons ramifying in the smooth muscle. These terminal axons, as studied in the electron microscope in intestinal muscle, have numerous varicosities filled with vesicles and thus appear as a string of beads with thick portions, $0 \cdot 5 – 1 \cdot 0 \mu$ in diameter, separated from each other by narrow regions of $0 \cdot 1 – 0 \cdot 2 \mu$ in diameter, the varicosities occurring at a frequency of about 20 per 100 μ. Within the varicosities there are numerous vesicles, and these are undoubtedly filled with the transmitter substance. Thus in adrenergic nerves the fluorescence-test of Falck and Hillarp enables the identification within the nerve endings of noradrenaline, and this may be confirmed by homogenization of the tissue and separation of the vesicles when the noradrenaline may be identified chemically, or after the incorporation of ^{3}H-noradrenaline.

Vesicles

Altogether three types of vesicle have been identified in autonomic neurones: small, of 300–600 Å diameter containing a dense granule; similar sized vesicles without a dense granule; and large granular vesicles of 600–1500 Å. Adrenergic neurones contain the vesicles with dense granules, those in the perikaryon usually being of the large kind, and since the vesicles are synthesized in the perikaryon, and are carried to the terminal, it seems that there is a reduction in size at some stage. The small agranular vesicles probably belong to cholinergic neurones, containing acetylcholine, but there are also large granular vesicles present in these neurones (Fig. 3.53).

Vesicles as Stores. The vesicles are essentially storage depots for the transmitters that have been synthesized within the neurone, most probably at the nerve terminals rather than in the perikaryon, since the precursors (tyrosine and choline) are actively taken up by the nerve terminal membrane whilst the enzymes responsible for the final synthesis (dopamine β-hydroxylase, and choline acetyltransferase) are transported from the perikaryon to the terminals. Within the axoplasm of the terminals, enzymes that break down the transmitters are present, namely monoamine oxidase and acetyl cholinesterase, and we may presume that the transmitters are safe from destruction within the storage vesicles. The accumulation of large quantities of material with relatively low molecular weight within a vesicle raises problems of internal osmolality, and it is likely that the transmitter is bound in some osmotically inactive complex within the vesicle. The latter contains a high proportion of protein, called *chromogranins*, and it is considered that this acts as a matrix for a complex between noradrenaline, ATP and Ca^{2+} in the granular core of the adrenergic vesicle.

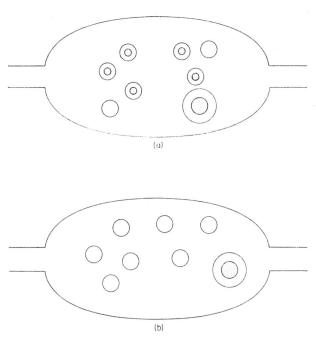

Fig. 3.53. Diagram illustrating the types of vesicles to be found in autonomic nerve terminals. (a) Sympathetic adrenergic nerve terminal varicosity; present in this varicosity are small granular vesicles which contain noradrenaline, small agranular vesicles and a large granular vesicle. (b) Parasympathetic cholinergic nerve terminal varicosity; present in this varicosity are small agranular vesicles which contain acetylcholine and a large granular vesicle. (Bennett, "Autonomic Neuromuscular Transmission", C.U.P.)

Relation to Muscle Cells

The axons are covered by Schwann cells until close to their termination, so that the varicosities are usually covered, either wholly or partially, by these cells. The way in which these terminal axons come into relation with the effector cells, namely the muscle fibres, varies with the muscle, and falls roughly into two categories, as illustrated in extreme form in Fig. 3.54. In (A) the terminal bundles of axons remain in the extracellular space between bundles of muscle fibres, and usually the axons fail to make a synaptic type of close contact with the muscle cells; this is typical of intestinal muscle. In Fig. 3.54 (B) we see a more intimate type of innervation, the terminal axons penetrating the bundles, pushing their way through the intercellular spaces and making close contacts through the varicosities, varying in separation from 0·1 μ to 200 Å. Functionally this difference may well be related to a difference in behaviour. Thus the Type B, or *close-contact varicosity*, form of termination is found in muscles that exhibit little

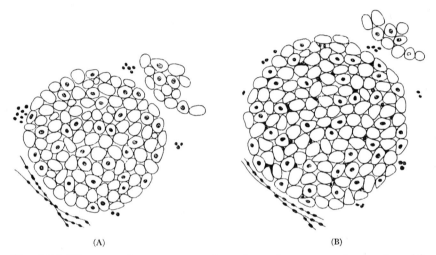

(A)   (B)

Fig. 3.54. Diagram of transverse sections through two smooth muscles with contrasting patterns of innervation. (A) Terminal axons, shown in cross-section as black dots and in longitudinal section as a group of varicose fibres (lower, left-hand corner), are confined to the extracellular space surrounding the bundle. (B) Terminal axons penetrate the bundle of smooth muscle cells and can be seen lying in some of the spaces between the tightly packed smooth muscle cells. (Holman, *In* "Smooth Muscle", E. Bulbring Ed., Arnold.)

spontaneous activity, such as those in the vas deferens and the blood vessels, which respond rapidly to nervous stimuli as in the ejection of semen or vasoconstriction. The Type A, or *axon-bundle type*, is found in intestinal and uterine muscle, characterized by spontaneous activity and generally slower responses to nervous stimuli.

Effects of Nervous Stimulation

Tension and Junctional Potentials

Stimulation of the excitatory nerve to a smooth muscle causes it to develop tension; usually this requires repetitive stimuli, a single shock being inadequate to evoke measurable tension. As frequency of stimulation increases, tension increases, but a limit is reached by the long refractory period, which may be of the order of 500 msec or more. Examination of the muscle cell during excitatory stimulation shows the development of a junctional potential, similar to the end-plate potential of fast skeletal muscle but with much slower time-characteristics. The potential is graded, and repetitive stimulation leads to a build-up of membrane depolarization that finally, at about a resting potential of

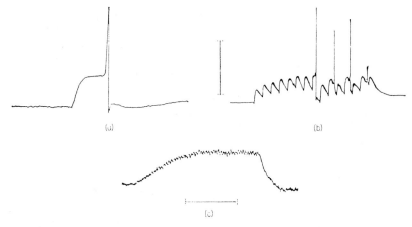

(a)   (b)

(c)

Fig. 3.55. The membrane potential changes in smooth muscle due to excitatory junction potentials (e.j.p.'s). (a) The initiation of an action potential by an e.j.p.; (b) Repetitive nerve stimulation at 2 Hz leading to the summation of e.j.p.'s and action potential firing. (c) High frequency nerve stimulation (10 Hz) leading to the summation of e.j.p.'s and maintained depolarization. Sympathetic nerves to the guinea pig vas deferens. Calibrations: (a) 40mV and 300 ms; (b) 40 mV and 2 s; (c) 20 mV and 2 s. (Bennett, "Autonomic Neuromuscular Transmission", C.U.P.)

−40 mV, leads to the development of a spike (Fig. 3.55), which may be propagated over the whole of the muscle. Thus, at low frequency of stimulation, before development of a spike, we may have only localized depolarization; this is accompanied by tension development, which remains local. On increasing the frequency of stimulation the frequency of spike-discharge in the muscle increases, whilst the steady level of membrane potential, from which the spikes arise, decreases still further, until finally a point is reached when the membrane remains continuously depolarized at about −30 mV without spike activity. The tension developed, as the frequency of stimulation is increased, is proportional to the degree of depolarization, and reaches its maximum as spike firing ceases and the steady level of depolarization is maximal.

Fast and Slow Junctional Potentials

The junctional potentials may be relatively slow, rising to a peak in 100–200 msec. These are associated with the type of contact between nerve and muscle cell called *axonal-bundle type*, and we may presume that the slowness with which the potential develops is the consequence of the long diffusion-path for transmitter to muscle cell. At the other extreme there are junctional potentials with time-to-peak of the order of 20 msec, and these are associated with the *close-contact varicosity type*, with a much shorter diffusion path. Muscles that have mixtures of these two types of innervation give junctional potentials of a more complex type. The junctional potential is electrically similar to the neuromuscular end-plate potential in that it is the consequence of an increased permeability to ions, which destroys the K^+-selectivity that is the basis for the normal resting potential.

Quantal Units

We have seen that in resting skeletal muscle there is a continuous background of miniature end-plate potentials due to release of "quantal units" of acetylcholine at the end-plate. In a similar way, spontaneous miniature excitatory junctional potentials can be recorded from those smooth muscle cells that have the close-contact varicosities.

Inhibition

When an inhibitory nerve is stimulated, this produces a *hyperpolarizing junctional potential* that tends to bring the resting potential to its theoretical K^+-potential. When both excitatory and inhibitory impulses reach the muscle, the effects are predictable on the basis of an interaction between the two effects on membrane permeability, the inhibitory impulses tending to stabilize the membrane potential and so reduce the depolarizing action of the excitatory impulse.

Transmitter Release

As with transmission in skeletal muscle, it is considered that the nerve impulse causes an inward movement of Ca^{2+} at the nerve terminal, and this leads to release of transmitter, probably by a process of exocytosis from vesicles.

Removal of Transmitter

In fast skeletal muscle destruction of acetylcholine, liberated at the end-plate, is necessary to bring about rapid relaxation; and this is achieved by the concentration of cholinesterase at the junction. Inhibiting the enzyme with eserine or DFP prolongs the end-plate potential and may lead to repetitive firing (eserine-twitching). Cholinesterase is present in smooth muscle, but the evidence indicates that it does not play a significant role in bringing the junctional potential to a stop, so that the diffusion of transmitter away from the terminal, or re-uptake into the terminal, may well be the manner in which the potential decays. In adrenergically innervated tissue there are two enzymes capable of altering noradrenaline, monoamine oxidase (MAO) and catechol-*o*-methyl transferase (COMT). There is also, however, a powerful method of recapturing the liberated transmitter by active transport across the terminal axonal membrane, so that it is considered that this *re-uptake mechanism* is important for the immediate removal of sufficient of the transmitter to allow decay of the junctional potential. This active uptake may be inhibited by cocaine or phenoxybenzamine, which can therefore prolong the action of the transmitter. Experiments in which smooth muscle has been incubated with ^{3}H-labelled noradrenaline have shown, moreover, that the *muscle cells* can also accumulate the transmitter.

Function of Breakdown Enzymes. The function of the enzymes catalysing the breakdown of noradrenaline in smooth muscle is not clear; the enzymes are present, both within and without the nerve terminals, and we may assume that, within the terminals, they tend to act as a brake on the accumulation of too much transmitter. As Bennett has emphasized, we must distinguish between two situations, namely the removal of the transmitter released in response to a single nervous impulse and that released in response to a train of impulses. According to him, the immediate decay of the junctional potential results from diffusion away from the site of liberation, and this applies to both adrenergic and cholinergic stimulation. When transmitter accumulates as a result of repetitive stimulation, then diffusion away from the terminals plays the same role, but the re-uptake process, and metabolic alteration, now become significant.

MECHANICAL BASIS OF MUSCLE TONE

Facilitation and Depression

By tone is meant a sustained maintenance of tension in the muscle; there is no performance of external work so that the existence of tone is revealed most easily as an increased resistance to stretch. Its significance in muscles concerned with the maintenance of posture is obvious, and it is also clear that this type of contraction, sustained for long periods of time, must be carried out with considerable economy of energy.

Skeletal Muscle

Where skeletal muscle is concerned, tone results from sustained nervous activity and disappears with denervation. As we shall see (Vol. 4) this sustained nervous activity is brought about through a reflex, the stretching of the muscle bringing about a contraction that resists its lengthening. The tone of skeletal muscle consists in alternating activities of different muscle units, so that at a given moment many are in the relaxed condition whilst others may be developing tension, which may vary from a twitch to a tetanus. As we have seen, skeletal muscles in which tonic activity is a prominent feature are of the red type exhibiting a slow rate of contraction, by contrast with the fast or twitch-type concerned with phasic types of movement.

Speed versus Economy

Thus, as a general rule, sustained tonic activity and slowness of contraction run parallel in skeletal muscle. Moreover, as might be predicted, the tonic type of muscle, besides being slow, is also highly economical, where economy may be measured by the time during which unit tension can be maintained by the energy of 1 gm wt in 1 cm^3 of muscle. Thus the fast twitch sartorious muscle of the frog has an economy of 1·2 sec and contraction time of 0·04 sec, by contrast with the slower tortoise skeletal muscle with an economy of 10 sec and a contraction time of 1–2 sec.

Facilitation and Depression

As with skeletal muscle, the size of the junctional potential in response to a nerve stimulus may be used as a measurement of the output of transmitter due to this impulse. Using this as a criterion, Bennett showed that the release of transmitter in response to nerve stimulation had similar characteristics to those at an end-plate. With successive stimuli, increasing outputs-per-impulse occur—*facilitation*—but if the repetitive stimulation is maintained, a steady level of release per impulse is reached (Fig. 3.56). At this point, we may presume that synthesis of new transmitter just keeps pace with release. If the frequency of stimulation is increased, the steady level of output per impulse declines, and, with a sufficiently high rate, it falls below the output at the first impulse of the train. This *depression*, or *fatigue*, may be attributed to failure of the synthetic machinery to keep pace with the high rate of liberation, so that a steady level of output is eventually reached

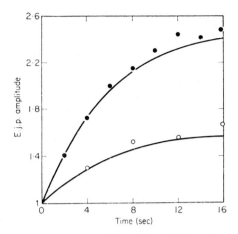

Fig. 3.56. Changes in amplitude of the e.j.p. during short trains of impulses at different frequencies of sympathetic nerve stimulation. Filled circles stimulation rate is 0·5/sec. Open circles, 0·25/sec. (Bennett, *J. Physiol.* 1973, **229,** 515.)

with lower output-per-stimulus. This is illustrated by Fig. 3.57 where the black circles indicate the output-per-impulse at each plateau for different frequencies of stimulation, from one to ten per second. The open circles show the output in unit time and it will be seen that the output measured in this way remains fairly constant, the increased

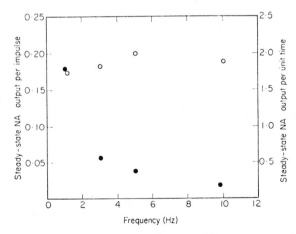

Fig. 3.57. The dependence of the steady-state NA output-per-impulse and per-unit-time, reached during long trains of impulses, on the frequency of nerve stimulation. Filled circles give the output-per-impulse, and open circles give the output-per-unit-time. (Bennett, *J. Physiol.* 1973, **229,** 515.)

number of stimuli in a given period just compensating for the reduced output of transmitter at each stimulus.

Storage and Release of Transmitter. The connection between release of transmitter and its replacement by synthesis is by no means direct. In other words, the increased release during the early facilitation is not an indication of increased synthesis, whilst the decreased release, as a high frequency of stimulation is maintained, is not due to a decreased rate of synthesis. The basic feature is the existence of a store,

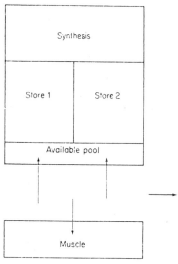

Fig. 3.58. Model of the uptake, storage and release of noradrenaline (NA) at a sympathetic nerve terminal. NA is released from a pool in the axon varicosity which is principally replenished by the uptake of the transmitter released by the immediately preceding impulses in the train. This pool is also replenished by the mobilization of NA from two stores, which are maintained to some extent by newly synthesized NA. (Bennett, *J. Physiol.* 1973, **229,** 515.)

or perhaps stores, of transmitter, which supply an "available pool"; the amount released by a stimulus from this pool varies, either increasing or decreasing. The major factor governing release seems to be the size of the available pool at the moment, and this itself is governed mainly by the ability of the neurone to recapture its lost transmitter—the re-uptake process. As soon as a strain is placed on the available pool, more is made available from the stores—vesicles—and these stores are, in turn, "topped up" by synthesis. The scheme suggested by Bennett (Fig. 3.58) contains two stores, to account for the complex features of the decrease in amplitude of the junctional potential with time of repetitive stimulation; as he suggests, the double store may correspond with the small and large granular vesicles in the nerve terminals. The uptake takes place by nerve terminals and muscle cells as the transmitter diffuses away; thus the nerve terminals that capture the liberated transmitter may not be those that liberated it.

Speed versus Force

Not only is the slow tonic muscle more economical but it is also capable of exerting greater forces, or resisting greater pulls, than is fast muscle. Thus the maximal tension that the frog's sartorius can develop is $2 \cdot 3$ kg/cm^2 of cross-section, whilst the byssus retractor muscle of the clam, *Mytilus*, can develop 14 kg/cm^2. The special features of this tonic muscle will be discussed later. For the moment we must try to interpret these basic features of contraction, namely the inverse relation between economy and speed, and between maximal tension and speed.

Speed versus ATPase Activity

Let us consider the requirements of a fast muscle. This will depend on the rapidity with which actin–myosin linkages can be made and broken, in accordance with the sliding-filament theory. Since a fundamental step in this make-and-break of links is the interaction of ATP with the myosin, catalysed by the myosin ATPase, we may expect to find a correlation between speed of contraction and muscle ATPase activity. Studies of different muscles do, in fact, reveal considerable differences in ATPase activity of their isolated myosin; for example the fast frog's sartorius has one of $8 \cdot 3$ moles/sec split by one mole of myosin, compared with $0 \cdot 4$ for the slow muscle of the tortoise. The generally much slower activity of many mammalian smooth muscles, such as the uterus, is reflected in a low ATPase activity ($0 \cdot 1$ for mammalian uterus for example). However, many muscles have similar ATPase activity but greatly different speeds and economies, so that at least one further factor must be invoked.

Sarcomere Length. This is a structural one, as illustrated by Fig. 3.59 where portions of two muscle fibrils are shown, the upper having half the sarcomere-, or thick-filament length of the lower. The cross-links are indicated by the short vertical lines, and it is assumed that the rate of turnover of these linkages governs the speed of shortening. It will be clear that, because of the series arrangement in the upper figure, a given rate of sliding or cross-bridge turnover will cause twice as much shortening as with the parallel arrangement in the lower figure. Thus sarcomere, or filament, length will be an important feature, the shorter the length the more rapid the muscle. If we consider the two parameters together, namely sarcomere-length and ATPase activity, we may prophesy that the speed of shortening, v, in lengths/sec, will be given by:

$$v = k.e.l^{-1}$$

where e is the ATPase activity and l the sarcomere length. Fig. 3.60 illustrates the validity of this conclusion.

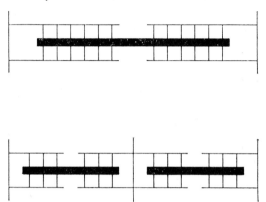

Fig. 3.59. Diagram illustrating effect of sarcomere- or filament-length on number of cross-bridges acting in series or in parallel in sliding-filament contractile systems with the same number of cross-bridges. With a given rate of sliding (cross-bridge turnover) muscles with short filaments will shorten faster than long filament muscle. But slow muscle has a larger fraction of cross-bridges acting in parallel and it will therefore maintain a given tension with fewer cross-bridges and hence more economically than fast muscle. (Ruegg, *Physiol. Rev.* 1971, **51,** 201.)

To choose an example, the fast frog sartorius and the slow skeletal muscle of the tortoise have very similar sarcomere lengths, the difference in speed being due almost entirely to the difference in ATPase activity. To return to Fig. 3.59, it will be clear, too, that the fibre with the long sarcomere will be able to resist a greater tension for the same number of linkages, and thus it will be more economical, maintaining an equal tension with a smaller number of cross-linkages. Thus the sliding-filament hypothesis provides a reasonable basis for interpreting the mutual exclusiveness of speed with economy.

Smooth Muscle Tone

Smooth muscle exhibits tone to a very high degree. This may be electrogenic in origin, as with certain smooth muscles that behave rather similarly to skeletal muscle, such as nictitating membrane, the vas deferens and some vascular muscle. Hence denervation of these causes loss of tone. With the smooth muscle of the gut or uterus, on the other hand, the capacity for spontaneous activity on the part of the individual muscle cells is reflected in a myogenic state of tone. So far as comparative studies between vertebrate smooth and skeletal muscles have been made, it seems that there is no serious hiatus in behaviour, the slowness of the smooth muscle, revealed by its long contraction-time and low frequency of tetanus (about 1/sec in intestinal muscle) is correlated with a low ATPase activity of its extracted myosin.

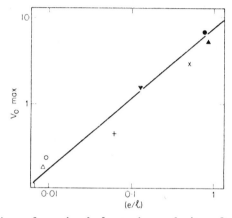

Fig. 3.60. Relation of maximal shortening velocity of muscle to myosin activity (e) divided by filament length (l). ●: Frog sartorius; +: tortoise rectus femoris; ○: bovine heart; □: guinea pig smooth muscle; △: oyster tonic adductor; ▲: pecten striated adductor; ×: squid mantle. (Ruegg, *Physiol. Rev.* 1971, **51**, 201.)

Comparisons of filament length are difficult to make since only the thin filaments are unequivocally demonstrable, but if invertebrate smooth muscles, with well defined thick and thin filaments are examined, it is found that their speed of shortening is related to filament-length and ATP-splitting as shown by the straight line of Fig. 3.60.

The Catch Mechanism

Certain smooth muscles of invertebrates, notably those that maintain closure of the shells of bivalves such as the mussel or oyster, are peculiar in that they exhibit a very high degree of holding economy (so that a sustained contraction can be maintained for over a week without fatigue). The evocation of this form of activity, described as "catch", depends on the mode of stimulation; thus tetanic stimulation leads to a fairly economical tetanic contraction, relaxing quickly and completely after cessation of the stimuli; but direct-current stimulation, or treatment with acetylcholine, gives rise to a sustained contraction with little expenditure of energy, a state from which it relaxes very slowly. It has been postulated that, in some way, the linkages have been "frozen" and therefore require no energy-expenditure for maintenance, just as in rigor due to loss of ATP; however, the situation with the catch type of contraction is reversible, and ATP is present. When the active state is estimated, e.g. by Ritchie's quick-release method the ATP seems to be absent, the muscle tension being held by some sort of passive holding process. The catch mechanism can be inhibited by serotonin (5-HT).

Thick Filament Interaction. Probably the most satisfactory hypothesis to account for the facts is that two types of contractile linkages are formed, according as a "classical" and "catch" type of contraction is brought about. If the classical type depends on an actin–myosin interaction, the catch type might result from interaction between thick filaments. Thus ATPase activity in the muscle during catch can be inhibited by treatment with thiourea or by washing out Ca^{2+}, yet the tension is sustained. It is difficult to say whether or not linkages comparable with those between actin and myosin occur between myosin filaments in the catch condition. It may be that mere steric interactions between thick filaments that have not been held in strict register during contraction are sufficient, as in skeletal muscle. At any rate, when catch muscle is contracted and the fibre is examined in the electron microscope, the thick filaments appear packed together in a central core of the myofibril, surrounded by a cortex of thin filaments. This condition is reminiscent of the appearance of supercontracted skeletal muscle when the muscle has shortened well beyond the point where the thin filaments have been drawn between thick filaments to give maximum overlap.

Control System

A fundamental difference between molluscan and vertebrate muscles is the role of troponin and tropomyosin, and the site of exertion of the control. As we have seen, in vertebrate skeletal muscle the control through Ca^{2+}, troponin and tropomyosin is exerted on the actin filament, so that binding of Ca^{2+}, for example, is a property of the thin filament rather than of myosin. In molluscan muscles Ca^{2+}-binding is certainly involved in activation, but the binding is exerted by myosin, whilst troponin is absent and tropomyosin, although representing a prominent feature of the molluscan fibre, apparently plays no role in control. Experimentally we may prepare a purified molluscan myosin and combine this with purified actin from rabbit muscle; in this case the ATPase activity of the actomyosin is Ca^{2+}-sensitive, and the force of contraction, i.e. the degree of interaction of the actin and myosin, is governed by the concentration of this ion free in the sarcoplasm. By contrast, a mixture of pure rabbit myosin and pure rabbit actin would not give rise to a Ca^{2+}-sensitive system because the actin has been robbed of its troponin and tropomyosin, the system that confers the Ca^{2+}-sensitivity to the combination. The converse experiment may be made, namely preparation of purified rabbit myosin and combination with purified molluscan actin: once again no Ca^{2+}-sensitivity is brought about since the rabbit *myosin* has no Ca^{2+}-binding capacity, whilst the molluscan *actin* also lacks this. Whether or not the Ca^{2+}-binding activity of the molluscan myosin belongs to a troponin-like component has not been proved; such a component would be covalently bound to the myosin molecule since it resists the methods of separation that are adequate for separating troponin from vertebrate actin.

Phylogeny. According to Lehman, Kendrick-Jones and Szent-Györgyi, the troponin–tropomyosin system represents a late development in phylogeny; it is present in arthropod muscles, too, but this may be an example of convergent evolution. Thus at some stage troponin began to be synthesized. This would have been adequate, without any fundamental change in the character of the actin molecule, to confer on it the regulatory power. Thus molluscan actin will complex with rabbit troponin and tropomyosin, and will then react with rabbit myosin, conferring on the system a Ca^{2+}-sensitive activation of the myosin ATPase. Again, molluscan tropomyosin, which is present on the thin filaments and apparently exerts no regulatory role, will substitute for rabbit tropomyosin in regulation, so that rabbit actin plus troponin plus molluscan tropomyosin combine to form a Ca^{2+}-sensitive system which reacts with rabbit myosin. Thus the troponin-binding sites on actin preceded the appearance of troponin in phylogeny, and it is clear that actin has remained evolutionarily invariant in structure, whereas myosin has undergone considerable changes. Such comparative studies on the properties of actin and myosin in different phyla are illustrated in Fig. 3.61; an interesting feature is the occurrence of both types of control in polychaetes, but since the studies were on homogenates of the whole animal it is not possible to state whether the two types were segregated in different muscles or not.

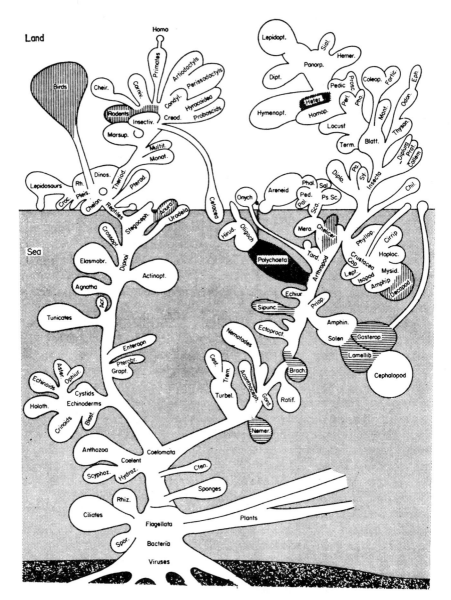

Fig. 3.61. Evolution of regulatory systems. Phylogenetic tree: vertical lines indicate the presence of troponin, horizontal lines the presence of myosin-linked regulatory systems. Note that both regulatory systems are found in annelids and insects. (Lehman *et al.*, *Cold Spr. Harb. Symp. quant. Biol.* 1972, **37,** 319.)

THE SECRETORY CELL

The more obvious functions of the body are fulfilled by the muscular system, so that it is reasonable that a great deal of study has been paid to the mechanisms of action of these classes of effector. Another class of effectors is constituted by the glands of internal and external secretion.

Nervous and Hormonal Control

As with muscles, their activity—the synthesis and elimination of specific substances—is provoked by nerve impulses which transmit their effects by means of a neurohumour, or transmitter, such as acetylcholine or, less frequently, noradrenaline. Thus the secretion of the adrenal gland, adrenaline, is liberated in response to a cholinergic nerve, and the secretion may be provoked experimentally by perfusion of the gland with acetylcholine. In a similar way the exocrine secretions of the salivary gland or the pancreas may be provoked by acetylcholine or other parasympatheticomimetic drugs, such as pilocarpine. The pancreatic gland illustrates the dual character of the control over secretion since not only will a nervous impulse, or its equivalent neurohumour, acetylcholine, provoke secretion, but also the intestinal hormone, pancreozymin. In this case pancreozymin may be considered to be analogous with adrenaline which, in mammals at any rate, is not a neurohumour but a hormone. Since the effects of acetylcholine on promoting secretion are inhibited by atropine, whilst those of pancreozymin are not, we may say that there are separate "receptors" on the secretory cell's membrane responsive to different agents.

Exocytosis of Granules

The secretions of the exocrine cells into acini, and of the endocrine cells into the interstitial spaces of the gland, are apparently contained in secretory granules, and it would seem that the mechanism of elimination is by the process of exocytosis. This was clearly demonstrated by Palade's electron-microscopical studies of the pancreatic acinar cell. Since then, similar studies on secretion of milk (p. 429), the liberation of catecholamines from the chromaffin cells of the adrenal gland (p. 174), and the liberation of the neurosecretory products of the posterior pituitary, etc. have confirmed that this is probably the universal mechanism for elimination of the contents of cytoplasmic granules which are, in effect, membrane-bound vesicles containing the secretion.

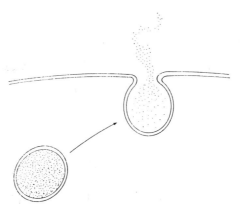

Fig. 3.62. Exocytosis. The vesicle's membrane becomes incorporated in the plasma membrane of the cell. (Modified from Douglas, *Br. J. Pharmacol.* 1968, **34,** 451.)

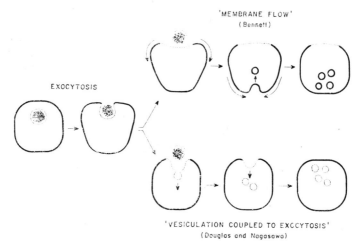

Fig. 3.63. Illustrating the formation of empty vesicles by vesiculation of the plasma membrane. (After Douglas, *Biochem. Soc. Symp.* 1974, 39.)

Vesiculation. One problem concerning the fate of the vesicle's membrane after exocytosis has been recently solved; thus exocytosis, as illustrated in Fig. 3.62, consists in the incorporation of the vesicle membrane with the plasma membrane of the cell. Clearly, if this process continued, the cell's membrane would become larger and larger. In fact the presence of numerous empty vesicles in the secreting cell shows that the fusion has been only temporary, and in the electron microscope Douglas and Nagasawa have shown that these empty vesicles are re-formed by a process of "vesiculation" of the plasma membrane. The process begins with formation of a caveola which becomes a vesicle by pinching off, as illustrated in Fig. 3.63. Clusters of small vesicles, presumably formed in this way, can be seen closely apposed to the inside of the plasma membrane. If a particulate suspension was added to the medium surrounding the cells, e.g. the isolated adrenal medulla, the particles could be seen within the small

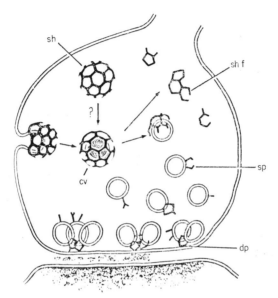

Fig. 3.64. The possible pinching off of the plasma membrane by the presynaptic terminal to form complex synaptic vesicles (cv) with subsequent alterations. Sh: shell of complex vesicles; Shf: shell fragments; Sp: material thought to be shell fragments; dp: dense projection. In more recent work Gray (*J. Neurocytol.* 1972, **1**, 363, and *Brain Res.* 1973, **62**, 329) has suggested alternative interpretations on the nature of the vesicle coats and dense projections. (Gray and Willis, *Brain Res.* 1970, **24**, 149.)

vesicles. When freshly formed, the vesicles are coated, having carried extracellular material into the cell during invagination. With time the coat disappears and the surface becomes smooth.

Central Nervous Synapse. It may well be that a comparable mechanism exists in the synapses of the central nervous system. Gray and Willis have described "complex" synaptic vesicles that could be the result of a primary pinching off of membrane, the latter carrying on its outside a shell of smaller bodies which are subsequently lost to give the typical smooth vesicle (Fig. 3.64).

Excitation–Secretion Coupling

Penetration of Ca^{2+}

It seems very likely that the synaptic vesicles of a neurone, e.g. in the terminals of a motor neurone at the end-plate, or in the endings of an adrenergic nerve on smooth muscle, likewise empty their contents by exocytosis. In this case, of course, the emptying is provoked by a wave of action potential. It has been argued by Katz and Miledi, as we have seen, that the link between the action potential and release of transmitter is the penetration of ionized Ca^{2+} into the terminal, so that it may well be, as Douglas and Rubin argued, that the common feature in all processes involving exocytosis, be it the release of hormones or neurotransmitters, the release of enzymes from phagocytic cells (p. 330) or of histamine from mast cells (p. 334), is the penetration, or release from internal stores, of Ca^{2+}. Thus excitation–contraction and excitation–secretion coupling would have a common basis.

The importance of Ca^{2+} in the external medium for the release of granular secretions has been established in a variety of tissues, and examples have already been quoted. For example, the secretion of amylase by the isolated pancreas, in response to acetylcholine or to the hormone pancreozymin, is abolished in a Ca^{2+}-free medium.

Depolarization of the Secretory Cell

The release of enzymes by many secretory cells is accompanied by depolarization, in the sense that there is a decrease in the membrane potential as measured with a microelectrode impaling the cell. Thus numerous "secretogogues" promote secretion of adrenaline from chromaffine cells of the medulla, e.g. acetylcholine, nicotine, pilocarpine, histamine, 5-HT, angiotensin and bradykinin, and all these reduce the membrane potential of isolated chromaffine cells by factors ranging from 54 per cent for acetylcholine to 24 per cent for angiotensin.

When the cell is depolarized by increasing the concentration of K^+ in the medium, secretion is also provoked. However, whilst there is no doubt that the stimulus to secretion, e.g. with acetylcholine, does provoke depolarization, the observation that the depolarization caused by high K^+ causes secretion, must be viewed with caution, since it was shown that the effect of high K^+ on secretion of amylase by the pancreas could be abolished by atropine, indicating that the effect was actually being mediated by cholinergic nerves within the tissue, excited by the high K^+.

Resting Potential. The secretion of amylase by the pancreatic acinar cell has been studied more thoroughly by modern electrophysiological techniques than other processes, so we may profitably concentrate on this. The mean membrane potential of the rat acinar cell is 39 mV, the inside negative; this is low by comparison with conducting cells such as nerve and skeletal muscle, and is due to the lower internal concentration of K^+ and probably to a higher resting permeability to Na^+.

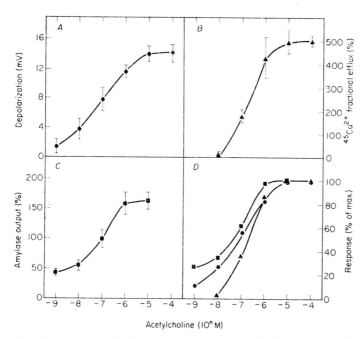

Acetylcholine $(10^n M)$

Fig. 3.65. Effect of acetylcholine on pancreatic depolarization, $^{45}Ca^{2+}$ efflux and amylase release. A, depolarization in mV. B, increase in $^{45}Ca^{2+}$ efflux (%). C, increase in amylase release (%). D, curves from A, B and C superimposed for comparison. Each curve is plotted as a percentage of the maximum response. (Matthews *et al.*, *J. Physiol.* 1973, **234**, 689.)

$^{45}Ca^{2+}$**-Flux.** Both acetylcholine and pancreozymin depolarize the cell in a dose-dependent manner, the maximal depolarization being 15 mV. The corresponding effects on depolarization and amylase release are indicated in Fig. 3.65A and C. The depolarization depends on the external concentration of Na^+, decreasing as this is increased. but it cannot be abolished in a Na^+-free medium so that the depolarization is not due to influx of Na^+ only, and it is likely that, as with smooth muscle, a part of the depolarizing current is carried by Ca^{2+}. If glands were incubated with isotopic $^{45}Ca^{2+}$ until the internal Ca^{2+}

had been well labelled, acetylcholine treatment of the gland, placed in a non-labelled medium, was accompanied by an increased efflux of $^{45}Ca^{2+}$, as measured by the increase in radioactivity of the medium. The excellent correlation between Ca^{2+} efflux, depolarization, and amylase release is indicated in Fig. 3.65. This increased efflux of $^{45}Ca^{2+}$ may simply reflect an increase in permeability of the cell membrane, or it may reflect a release from stores. Since, however, secretion depends on the presence of external Ca^{2+}, mere release from stores cannot be a sufficient stimulus to secrete.

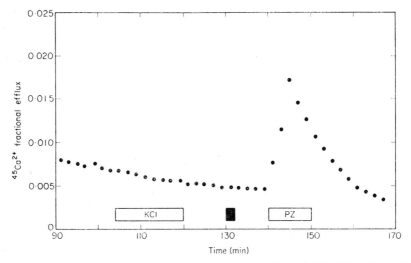

Fig. 3.66. The failure of KCl depolarization to affect Ca^{2+} efflux from the pancreas and the strong effect of pancrozymin (PZ). The preparation was treated with atropine so acetylcholine (black bar) had no effect. (Matthews *et al.*, *J. Physiol.* 1973, **234,** 689.)

The Sufficient Stimulus

Depolarization alone is insufficient to cause secretion; thus simply placing the gland in a medium of high K^+ in the presence of atropine (to prevent activation of nerves), does not provoke secretion, although it depolarizes. This is presumably because, in the acinar cell, depolarization does not cause increased concentration of Ca^{2+}; at any rate, as Fig. 3.66 shows, KCl-depolarization produces no increase in $^{45}Ca^{2+}$-efflux, whereas pancreozymin does. In other instances a high external K^+ does provoke secretion, e.g. excess K^+ provokes catecholamine secretion from the adrenal medulla, but this is due to the fact that excess K^+ causes influx of Ca^{2+} into the medulla. Thus depolarization can be an *adequate* stimulus, but by itself it is not a *sufficient* stimulus, so that if we omit Ca^{2+} from the medium, excess K^+ does not cause secretion. Again, we may reduce the depolarization of a chromaffin cell, due to acetylcholine, by reducing the external Na^+ yet the secretory response may be actually increased. Thus depolarization is to be regarded as an outward sign of other events, particularly the influx of Ca^{2+}, this latter being the link between excitation and secretion.

Mechanical and Chemical Events

Role of Microtubules

The release of material by exocytosis is a mechanical event involving structural alterations in the cell, and it has been argued that, as with so many structural changes within the cell, exocytosis might be mediated through microtubule formation and dissolution. It will be recalled that colchicine specifically inhibits assembly of microtubules and correspondingly inhibits several morphological changes, such as cytokinesis, migration of chromosomes, and formation of the spindle. Lacy showed that colchicine inhibits the release of insulin by the β-cells of the pancreas, whilst Poisner showed that adrenaline-release from the chromaffin cells was likewise inhibited. But this is not universal, since the secretions of the adenohypophyseal (anterior pituitary) hormones is not affected, nor yet is the release of amylase from the pancreatic acinar cells. It may be, then, that the effects of colchicine, and perhaps of other agents, vary according to the secretory system considered. Thus colchicine has no effect on the secretions of the adeno-hypophysis and the pancreas but does influence the secretions of the neurohypophysis and adrenal medulla; these last have a different embryological origin, being derived from the neuroectoderm.

Microfilaments

It will be recalled that these actin-like filaments, with diameters in the region of 50–70 Å, are present in the cytoplasm of many cells that exhibit marked changes in shape, e.g. in platelets, elongating nerve axons, and so on. Phenomena depending on their involvement are typically inhibited by the alkaloid extracted from the fungus, *Helminthosporium dematioideum*, called cytochalasin B (Vol. 1). Release of growth hormone from the adenohypophysis is inhibited by cytochalasin B as well as the release of noradrenaline from sympathetic nerves, both depending on exocytosis. In this connection, we must emphasize the similarity between the material extracted from microfilament-containing cells, e.g. from the slime mould or from platelets, and actin derived from vertebrate muscle. Thus we have referred to the "decorating" of actin filaments with heavy meromyosin or its S1 subunits (p. 225); according to Nachmias, the material from the slime mould forms similar arrow-headed complexes with heavy meromyosin from muscle.

Cyclic AMP

This "second messenger" has been implicated in the release of enzymes, and where this release does not involve liberation from granules, as with the thyroid and adrenal cortex, the evidence is strong; with the granular type of secretion the evidence is contradictory and on balance weighs against involvement of cAMP (Benz *et al.*)

Involvement of ATP

The analogy between excitation–contraction coupling and the corresponding secretory process has been strengthened by the demonstration that ATP promotes the release of adrenaline from isolated adrenal granules. ATP is undoubtedly an important constituent of the adrenal chromaffin granules, perhaps functioning along with protein— *chromogranin*—to form an osmotically inactive complex. When secretion is provoked, ATP and its metabolites, AMP, ADP, etc., are released. The evidence indicates, however, that the exocytosis of secretion does not involve breakdown of ATP, which is released from the granule with the secretion. The enzyme, ATPase, is a structural component of the chromaffin granule and of the granule membranes of many other cells, e.g. the mast cell containing histamine, the insulin-containing granules of β-cells, and so on. The mere interaction of the ATP *in* the granule with an ATPase on its surface is unlikely to affect its power of fusing with the plasma membrane, so it may be that the ATPase of the granule membrane promotes a reaction with ATP which is either in the cytoplasm or in the plasma membrane. Thus Ca^{2+} might facilitate a reaction between ATP in the plasma membrane catalysed by ATPase on the granule membrane, the reaction leading to membrane-fusion and exocytosis.

CHAPTER 4

The Cells of the Blood and the Response to Injury

PROTECTIVE MECHANISMS

When the complex organism is injured, several mechanisms are brought into play to limit the injury and to initiate repair. Principal among these are: the *clotting mechanism* that converts the fluid blood into a gel and so restricts bleeding; the *inflammatory response* that increases the local blood supply and at the same time mobilizes the phagocytic cells necessary for combatting invasive organisms and clearing up damaged tissue; and finally the *immune response*. This last takes many forms and would require a book of its own for an adequate description; essentially it consists in the production of specific proteins called *antibodies* that antagonize in one or more ways the invasion of foreign material, such as viruses or bacteria, or their products, toxins, and so combat infection. The reaction between the antibody and the foreign material, called an *antigen*, is such as to neutralize the damaging effects of the foreign material. Neutralization is achieved through a number of mechanisms, which may include the inflammatory reaction, the activation of phagocytic leucocytes, and the raising of the body temperature by the release of *pyrogens* into the blood circulation.* In all these mechanisms cellular elements of the blood, i.e. the platelets and white cells, or leucocytes, play a dominant role, so that it is appropriate to begin with a brief description of the types of blood cell, in addition to the erythrocyte, and their site of origin in the haemopoietic tissues.

THE BLOOD CELLS
The Erythrocyte
Biconcave Shape

The functions of this cell as a transporter of the blood gases and as a buffering system whose ionic exchanges cooperate with its gas-

---

* The fever of an infectious disease may well be accidental, however, with no beneficial effect on the sufferer (Vol. 3).

carrying functions, have already been described. The significance of its biconcave shape (Fig. 4.1a) has also been discussed in relation to the rheological characteristics of the blood as well as the closely related phenomenon, the tendency to form rouleaux. The actual mechanism whereby the biconcave shape is maintained has been the subject of discussion for many decades and no clear cut explanation has been reached. Thus it has been argued that the surface tension forces might well impose this shape on a cell which, in effect, has a membrane too large for the spherical shape.

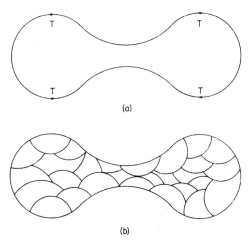

(a)

(b)

Fig. 4.1. (a) Biconcave erythrocyte. (b) Postulated internal structure of erythrocyte required to maintain biconcave shape. T = Tension forces.

Disk–Sphere Transformation. In support of any theory based on the importance of surface characteristics we find that the shape of the erythrocyte is very sensitive to small changes in the environment; thus when a drop of cell suspension in saline is placed on a microscope slide and a glass coverslip is placed on top, the cells assume a spherical shape—the so-called *slide-coverslip transformation*. This may be prevented by addition of a little plasma, or may be reversed if it has already taken place by the same treatment. There is little doubt that the transformation results from alteration in the surface forces, and a similar transformation can be induced by a variety of chemical agents, such as saponin, that probably act by accumulating in the membrane or at its surface.

Surface and Structural Forces. It is by no means easy, however, to envisage the maintenance of this dumb-bell shape by the operation of forces acting solely in the surface, and it has been argued, in consequence, that the cell contents, consisting as they do of a highly concentrated haemoglobin solution, contribute through their rigidity to the maintenance of the structure (Fig. 4.1b). There is no doubt that slight alterations in the haemoglobin of the erythrocyte can modify its shape, as in sickle-cell anaemia where the cell acquires a sickle shape in consequence of a slight genetically induced change in the nature of the haemoglobin. Again, rat erythrocytes, treated with citrate solution, cease to haemolyse even when placed in distilled water, indicating that the whole cell has acquired a structural rigidity that enables it to oppose the very large difference of osmotic pressure across the cell membrane that must subsist under these conditions. It would seem

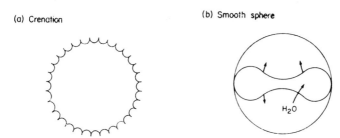

(a) Crenation   (b) Smooth sphere

Fig. 4.2. (a) Crenated shape of erythrocyte that has lost its biconcave disk shape without increasing its volume. (b) Smooth sphere resulting from uptake of water.

therefore that both surface tension and internal structural factors operate to maintain the normal disk shape. The balance of forces is obviously very delicate, so that small changes in the environment of the cell can upset the balance leading to the acquisition of a spherical shape. When the spherical shape is acquired without any increase in cell volume then clearly the cell's membrane is too large for its volume, and as a result it appears "crenated". (Fig. 4.2a) When the spherical shape is reached through osmotic swelling, on the other hand, the membrane is smooth (Fig. 4.2b).

The Leucocytes or White Cells

Differential Count

The white cells of the blood are concerned in the body's response to injury and infection. When whole blood is centrifuged, the erythrocytes form a densely packed layer at the bottom of the tube, above which is a very much thinner layer—called the buffy coat—containing the white cells and platelets, these latter being pieces of cytoplasm broken off from large megakaryocytes. The leucocytes belong to three main groups (Fig. 4.3), i.e. *polymorphonuclear leucocytes* (or *granulocytes*), *lymphocytes* and *monocytes*, and their relative numbers, the *differential count*, are given as follows:

Cells	% of Total	Thousands/mm^3
Granulocytes		
Neutrophils	40–75	2·5–7·5
Eosinophils	1–6	0·04–0·44
Basophils	1	0·015–0·1
Lymphocytes	20–50	1·5–3·5
Monocytes	2–10	0·2–0·8

Granulocytes

It will be seen that the granulocytes are subdivided in accordance with their staining characteristics into *neutrophils, eosinophils* and *basophils*; of these, the neutrophils are the great majority. They are amoeboid and actively phagocytic, and are the cells first mobilized to deal with any injury or bacterial invasion, rapidly leaving the capillaries or venules at the site of inflammation and phagocytosing bacteria and broken down cells.

Eosinophils and Basophils

The functions of eosinophils and basophils are not so clear. The immediate response to invasion by bacteria, or local tissue damage, is mobilization of the neutrophils at the inflammatory site; at later stages eosinophils predominate. Again, allergic conditions, or chronic infections, are associated with eosinophilia. It has been argued by Litt that the unifying feature of eosinophilic mobilization is the attraction of antibody–antigen complexes, formed in the immune reaction (p. 340), for the eosinophils which phagocytose them. Since these complexes are usually short-lived it is much more likely that they would be present in sufficient amount to give a detectable eosinophilia in chronic diseases, or in an allergic response, than in the acute phase which usually lasts for a short time. Eosinopenia, i.e. a reduced eosinophil blood-count, is part of the stress syndrome and may be produced by administration of ACTH or adrenal cortical steroids. The basophils have been likened to mast cells of the tissues, in that they contain a large amount of histamine. In stress they are reduced in amount.

(a) Granulocytes

Basophil leucocyte 8–10 μ Eosinophil leucocyte 10–14 μ Neutrophil 9–12 μ

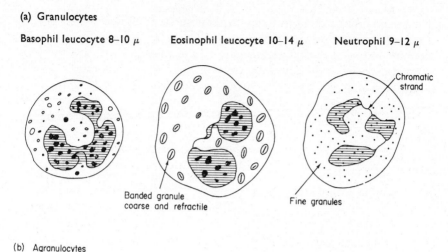

Banded granule
coarse and refractile

Fine granules

Chromatic
strand

(b) Agranulocytes

Lymphocyte 6-10 μ Monocyte 12 - 15 μ

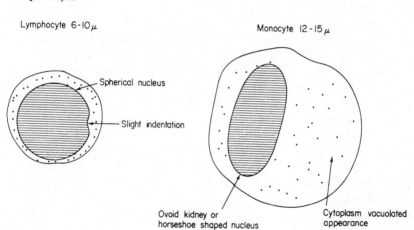

Spherical nucleus

Slight indentation

Ovoid kidney or
horseshoe shaped nucleus

Cytoplasm vacuolated
appearance

Fig. 4.3. Diagrammatic illustrations of leucocytes.

Lymphocytes

These small cells with little to distinguish them cytologically are present in the blood and lymph; they multiply in the lymph nodes, bone marrow, thymus and spleen, the tissues where they are concentrated being described as *lymphoid*. Although morphologically alike, they are actually a functionally heterogeneous group of cells. For example, some are capable of producing antibodies—they are said to be immunologically competent—whilst others are not; some are short-lived with a span of a few days, others long-lived with a span of years; some have theta antigen on their surface, and so on. In general the lymphocytes, by virtue of their own capacity to produce antibodies and by virtue of their transformation into plasma cells, are the most important cells in the immune reaction to antigen. They are the cells, too, that are at the basis of delayed hypersensitivity (p. 363), invading the site of antigen-intrusion and being, in fact, the cells primarily responsible for rejection of grafted tissues. As we shall see, certain "lymphoid cells" or large lymphocytes are probably stem cells capable of giving rise, by division, to cells that ultimately produce erythrocytes, granulocytes, or megakaryocytes as well as to small lymphocytes.

Macrophages and Monocytes

The macrophages may be grouped with the monocytes proper, from which they are derived. They are, as their name indicates, large phagocytic cells, those in the blood representing only a very small proportion of the total. Many are fixed in the tissues of the *reticulo-endothelial system*, where they are given different names.

The Reticulo-endothelial System. This is the name given to a widely distributed system containing phagocytic cells, both fixed and motile. Its distribution is revealed by giving the animal an injection of radioactive colloidal gold. This is ingested by the macrophages throughout the system and a scan of the body reveals the main sites of uptake; as Fig. 4.4 shows, the blood-forming regions of the bones, as well as the liver, spleen, and lungs are the main sites of uptake. The reticular tissue will be discussed in detail later, and it suffices to say here that the cells forming the reticular fibres—called reticular cells—are phagocytic and may be described as fixed macrophages. Similarly the blood sinuses of the reticulo-endothelial system, e.g. the liver or spleen sinuses, contain as their "endothelial cells" fixed macrophages which are often called *mural* cells or *littoral* cells to distinguish them from true endothelial cells. The cells in the liver sinuses are called Kupffer cells and are easily distinguished by their capacity to engulf colloidal iron. Other tissue-located macrophages are called *adventitial cells*, being located in the adventitia of blood vessels; *interstitial cells* of the lung alveolus; *histiocytes* of connective tissue, and so on. Thus the dominant cell of the reticulo-endothelial cell is the macrophage, the whole forming an exceedingly efficient system for entrapping and engulfing foreign particles.

The Macrophage

As indicated above, the macrophage of the blood is a phagocytic cell derived from the monocyte. It is a large cell, some 15–20 μ in diameter and its most striking characteristics are its motility and its

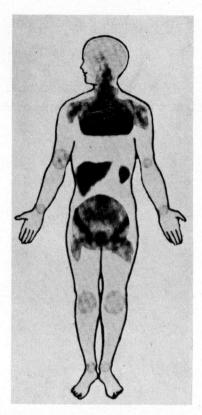

Fig. 4.4. The blood-forming regions of the body demonstrated by the ingestion of radioactive colloid and subsequent scanning. The colloid is taken up by the phagocytes of the body, X-rays are then taken and, super-imposed upon them is a record of the disposition of the radioactivity as detected by a scanning device which passes over the body. A composite photograph is then made, revealing the layout of the reticulo-endothelial system. Note that the location and form of the liver, spleen and bone marrow are shown. (L. Weiss, "The Cells and Tissues of the Immune System", Prentice-Hall.)

ability to engulf particulate matter; this latter characteristic is illustrated by Fig. 4.5 which shows a macrophage engulfing erythrocytes. The process is that of endocytosis described earlier, the object being engulfed in plasma membrane which is then pinched off to form what is, in effect, a phagosome (p. 329).

Derivation from Monocytes. Macrophages may be formed from pre-existing macrophages in tissue or they may be derived from monocytes that originate in the bone marrow. This may be proved by labelling the nuclei of monocytes by giving the animal tritiated

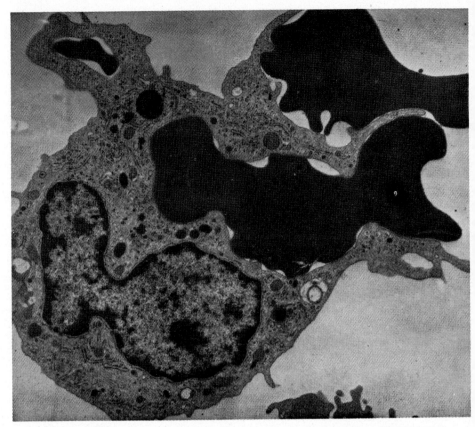

Fig. 4.5. Human macrophage. This cell, in the process of phagocytizing erythrocytes, was found in the thoracic duct lymph. Note the variegated lysosomes and segments of rough ER. × 9000. (Original micrograph provided by Dr. Dorothea Zucker-Franklin. L. Weiss, "The Cells and Tissues of the Immune System", Prentice-Hall.)

thymidine, which becomes incorporated into their DNA when the cells divide. These labelled monocytes can be transferred to another animal whose blood-forming capacity has been destroyed by irradiation, and it is found that the macrophages become labelled.

This derivation of free macrophages from monocytes extends to the fixed macrophages of the reticulo-endothelial system. Thus, injected labelled monocytes may be seen later in the liver acting as Kupffer cells and absorbing colloidal iron from the blood. Within the reticulo-endothelial system the fixed macrophages are, however, able to re-produce by mitotic division, and this may be the main mode of replacement when this is actively stimulated, as in oestradiol treatment. However, the normal turnover, e.g. of Kupffer cells, may well be the replenishment through marrow-derived monocytes.

Monocyte

The monocytes are smaller cells, 12–15 μ in diameter; those circulating in the blood constitute some 10% of the leucocytes. Only in circumstances where flow of blood is sluggish will transformation of monocytes to macrophages occur within the blood vessels, the process occurring predominantly in connective tissue spaces. This transformation becomes especially prominent in the inflammatory response to injury, so that the monocyte is to be regarded as the *transport precursor* of the macrophages that are mobilized at the site of injury. In general, the monocyte–macrophage is involved in the long-term response to injury, the immediate response being the invasion by granulocytes. Although they do not produce antibodies in the immune reaction they nevertheless co-operate in the process with lymphocytes (p. 353). Finally, the macrophage produces interferon, the protein whose production is stimulated by viruses and which inhibits their multiplication.

Plasma Cells

These free cells, of 8–20 μ diameter, are mainly concentrated in lymphatic tissues and certain tissues likely to be exposed to foreign substances, such as the lamina propria of the intestine. In the electron microscope the dominant feature is the extensive rough-surfaced endoplasmic reticulum denoting high protein synthetic ability, the synthesized material being antibody. They almost certainly represent the terminal stage in development from lymphocytes when these are stimulated by antigen to form antibodies (p. 349).

The Platelet

The platelet, or *thrombocyte*, is a cell fragment derived from the megakaryocyte, one of the lines of blood cells produced in the bone-marrow. It is normally disk-shaped, with a longitudinal dimension of 1·5–5 μ and a transverse dimension of 0·5–2 μ, and is enclosed by a plasma membrane about 70 to 90 Å thick. Outside this there is an outer amorphous coat with the chemical reactions of a sulphated mucopolysaccharide. This "fluffy coat" is presumably important for aggregation during formation of the "platelet plug" (p. 317).

Granulocytes. An obvious cytoplasmic feature is the presence of many granules some of which may well contain one or more of the platelet factors that are concerned with the blood-clotting mechanism (p. 320), since "degranulation" occurs in association with the clumping of platelets in a region of tissue injury. The platelet contains a high concentration of serotonin, or 5-hydroxytryptamine (5HT) which is almost certainly contained within very electron-dense granules, which may also contain the ADP and ATP of the platelet. The 5HT is accumulated from the blood by an active transport mechanism. It is released from the platelets in tissue injury, and its powerful vasoconstrictor activity competes with the vasodilator activity of the histamine and kinins that are liberated in the tissue at the same time. Other granules seem to be lysosomal in character and may be concerned with the digestion of material phagocytosed by the platelet.

HAEMOPOIESIS

Marrow Stem Cells

The prime source of the blood cells is the bone marrow. Many of the white cells, e.g. the lymphocytes, are produced within the lymphoid tissue, e.g. the lymph nodes, but it could well be that in the first instance this tissue was colonized by certain stem cells derived from the marrow. By a haemopoietic stem cell we mean a cell that does not possess any signs of differentiation, in its cytoplasm or nucleus, but it is nevertheless capable of differentiating into an erythrocyte, granulocyte, monocyte or megakaryocyte. Thus we may expose an animal to a lethal dose of radiation, as a result of which its power to produce new blood cells is destroyed. Death may be avoided, however, if the animal is injected with a suspension of marrow-cells. By labelling these cells before injection it is found that the new blood-forming centres which appear, e.g. in the spleen, are derived from these marrow-cells. It is profitable, then, to think of the marrow as the ultimate source of all types of blood cell, producing many within its own tissue and "colonizing" other tissues by providing them with "stem cells" from which more specialized cells may be derived. An actual scheme relating the stem cells to the more differentiated blood cells is described later (p. 299).

The Reticulum

The basic structure of the blood-forming tissues is that of a reticulum, or fine net, which acts as a support for the parent cells and provides a temporary home for their progeny. It also contains in its meshes phagocytic cells—macrophages—required to break down and digest unwanted cells and residues. In certain situations this network also acts as a filter, as in the lymph-nodes where it filters the lymph, or in the spleen where it submits the blood to an analogous process. In general, the reticulum is made up of fine reticulin fibres secreted by the *reticular cells*, which are large branching bodies, the cytoplasmic branches following the branching of the reticulin fibres, so that to a large extent the meshwork of protoplasmic processes overlaps with the meshwork of reticulin fibres. Reticulin is a protein, similar to collagen, synthesized by these reticular cells, whereas collagen is synthesized by fibroblasts. The main function of the reticular cells is undoubtedly to synthesize reticulin, but many of them are phagocytic and are classed as fixed macrophages and thus form part of the reticulo-endothelial system.

Bone-Marrow

In foetal life haemopoiesis occurs at several sites, including the liver, but in man by the time of parturition the bone-marrow has become the sole source of erythrocytes, granulocytes, platelets, monocytes, and the source of many lymphocytes, these last being produced in so-called lymphoid tissues, such as lymph nodes, Peyer's patches, etc. At birth the bone-marrow is entirely haemopoietic but with time the haemopoietic—red—marrow becomes restricted to the bones of the torso and head, and in the long bones it becomes restricted to the regions close to the axial skeleton. As Fig. 4.6 indicates, the main basis of the marrow is a sinusoidal arrangement of blood vessels surrounded by the reticular blood-forming spaces. The sinusoids are endothelium-lined vessels, across the walls of which blood cells are able to migrate. The outer adventitial layer of the sinus is cellular, its cells being phagocytic and thus constituting a part of the reticulo-endothelial system (p. 292). One of their functions is to digest the nuclei extruded by the normoblasts during their transformation into erythrocytes.

Blast Transformation

It is now generally agreed that the erythrocytes, leucocytes and megakaryocytes are derived from pluripotent stem cells of a single type in the bone-marrow. This is a self-perpetuating population from which are derived, by division, stem cells that are committed to produce one of the three types just enumerated (Fig. 4.7). These "committed" stem cells undergo "blast transformation", leading to a series of proliferative divisions, under the influence of hormones called *poietins*, e.g. *haemopoietin* for erythrocytes; *thrombopoietin* for platelets and *leucopoietin* for leucocytes, although little is known about the last two agents. The newly formed *pronormoblasts*, leading to erythrocytes, and

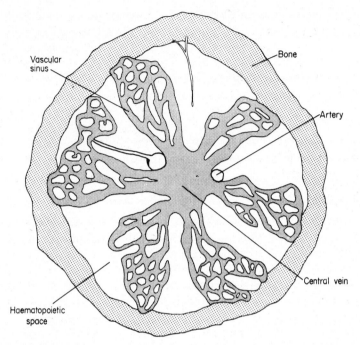

Fig. 4.6. Cross section of bone marrow. The central longitudinal vein receives vascular sinuses as tributaries. The sinuses are large thin-walled vessels which form anastomosing complexes and run radially toward the central vein. Some of the sinuses originate in channels in the surrounding bone. The haemopoietic spaces lie between sinuses. The central longitudinal artery (CA) is cut in cross-section. Several of its tributaries are present. (L. Weiss,"The Cells and Tissues of the Immune System", Prentice-Hall.)

myeloblasts, leading to leucocytes, undergo three to five mitotic divisions, leading to an 8- to 32-fold multiplication, and giving rise to more and more differentiated cells. The megakaryoblast, i.e. the ancestor of the megakaryocyte, undergoes a similar number of nuclear mitotic divisions, but without cytoplasmic division, so that we are left with a few huge cells with multilobed nuclei.

Lineage of Erythrocyte

The lineage of the erythrocyte is as follows: a *haemocytoblast* or *pronormoblast* gives rise, on division, to *proerythroblasts*; these give rise to *basophilic erythroblasts*, the basophilia being a reflection of the large amounts of nucleic acids that will be required for haemoglobin synthesis.

The next step is the *polychromatophilic erythroblast*, containing haemoglobin, which differentiates into *normoblasts*, cells that have lost their
basophilia and have pyknotic nuclei. Ultimately the nucleus is extruded
and the normoblast has become a *reticulocyte* which "matures" to an
erythrocyte, the reticulocyte containing sufficient ribonucleoprotein to
confer some basophilic or polychromatic colour on staining with
Romanovsky stain. When erythrocytes are produced in large numbers
in response, say, to haemorrhage, the number of reticulocytes in the
blood increases.

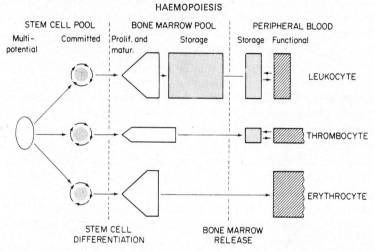

Fig. 4.7. Model of haemopoiesis. (Erslev, *Am. J. Pathol.* 1971, **65**, 629.)

Lineage of Granulocyte

The corresponding stages in the formation of polymorphonuclear
leucocytes, or granulocytes, consist in the formation of *myelocytes* of
three types to give ultimately the neutrophil, eosinophil and basophil
types. The myelocytes are derived by division from *promyelocytes*, which
give rise to *heterophil myelocytes* and these, after probably several
divisions, give rise ultimately to the *metamyelocyte* which matures
without further division to the mature granulocyte.

Monocytes

So far as the monocytes are concerned, it would seem that their
ancestry is much more closely related to that of the granulocytes than
that of the lymphocytes, and this doubtless explains the frequent association of monocytes and granulocytes in leukaemia—*myelomonocytic
leukaemia*.

Platelets

The cells from which the platelets are derived are the megakaryo-cytes, formed within the bone-marrow. These lie close upon the outside surface of the blood-sinuses and discharge platelets into the lumen through gaps in the wall.

The Lymphocytes

Lymphocytes are formed in so-called lymphoid tissue. The bone-marrow is described as being made up of predominantly *myeloid* tissue; but it does contain some lymphoid tissue from which lymphocytes are derived, these representing some 10–20% of the nucleated cells of the marrow. The lymph nodes constitute the main bulk of the lymphoid tissue and are arranged along the course of the lymph vessels, whilst additional elements are found in the spleen and in peripheral lymph nodules scattered in the mucous membrane of the alimentary canal, respiratory passages, conjunctiva, etc. When grouped in the alimentary canal they are described as Peyer's patches. The lymph nodes act as filters for the lymph flowing through them and also as sources of lymphocytes that find their way into the blood, either by way of the lymph vessels or more directly into the blood vessels supplying the node. The nodes are clustered in certain strategic regions, notably the inguinal and axillary nodes at the junctions of the limbs with the trunk, whilst the supply of lymph from the head and neck is filtered, by nodes at the base of the neck.

Lymph Node

The basic unit of the node is a body some 30 mm in largest diameter, many of these being clustered together to form a much larger body. It is enclosed in a connective-tissue capsule penetrated by afferent lymphatic channels which open into what is essentially a large lake, or *subcapsular sinus*, concentric with the capsule. This space is criss-crossed by very fine reticulin-fibres secreted by reticular cells lying amongst them; larger trabeculae, formed by chains of cells, also cross the space (Fig. 4.8). From the sinus, channels run deeper and converge at the hilum of the node on to one or more efferent lymph vessels. On their way these radial sinuses run close to large nodular masses of lympho-cytes—the primary and secondary nodules; in the deeper medullary region the lymphocytes are grouped as medullary cords (Fig. 4.8).

The reticulin fibres not only fill the lumina of the sinuses, thereby constituting a filter that entraps foreign particulate matter such as bacteria, but also pervade the tissue, as a support for the numerous

Fig. 4.8. Three views of a lymph node. On the right, the reticulum of the node is depicted, the reticular cells in nucleated outline and the fibres in stipple. Afferent lymphatics penetrate the capsule emptying into the subcapsular sinus. This sinus is virtually coextensive with the capsule and is criss-crossed by reticular fibres. Trabeculae interrupt it at places. Radial sinuses, also criss-crossed, run from the subcapsular sinus, irregularly, toward the hilus, where they converge into large efferent vessels. The reticular meshwork is specialized to form the follicles and peri-follicular zones of cortex, the deep cortical zone and medullary cords. In the central panel, the distribution of veins is shown, closely drawn after the work and illustrations of Guy St. Marie. Note how post-capillary venules, the terminal twigs, originate about the cortical follicles as well as deep to the follicles. In the remaining panel the arrangement of the reticulum together with lymphocytes and other free cells is presented. The reticulum becomes masked by the crowds of lymphocytes. Nodules are present in the cortex, many of them containing germinal centres. The tertiary portion of the cortex, that part deep to the nodules separating them from the medulla, is not large here. Note that when sinuses become crowded with lymphocytes the lines of demarcation between the sinus and contiguous tissue are not clear. The endothelium of the sinuses is incomplete on that aspect of the vessels which abut lymphatic masses. (L. Weiss, "The Cells and Tissues of the Immune System", Prentice-Hall.)

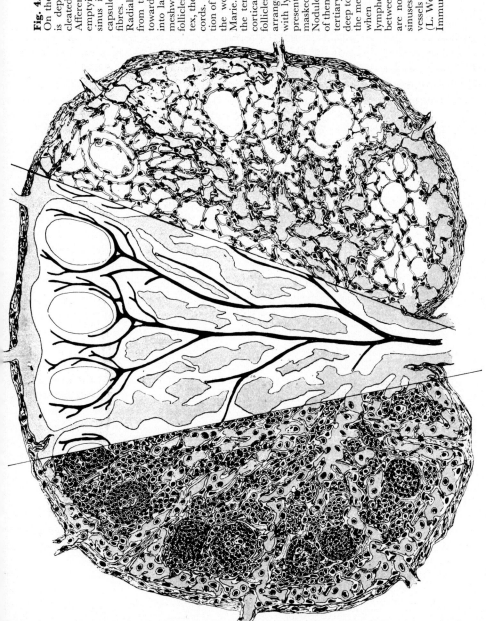

cells either produced within the node or that have been brought to it from, for example, the thymus or marrow. Thus blood vessels enter the node at the hilus and break up into capillaries and post-capillary venules; from here small lymphocytes can be seen either passing through the endothelial cells or between them.

Germinal Centre. The nodules indicated in Fig. 4.8 are called *secondary* if they contain a *germinal centre*, i.e. a mass of large or medium-sized lymphocytes together with some plasma cells and macrophages surrounded by the smallest lymphocytes of the nodule. As its name implies, the germinal centre is the site of rapid multiplication, so that if a single injection of ^{3}H-thymidine (a DNA-label) is given to the animal, the nuclei of these cells rapidly become labelled. They become prominent during an immune response and there is little doubt that they are antibody-producing centres. They occur not only in lymph nodes but in spleen, tonsils, Peyer's patches in the walls of the intestine, and pulmonary, genital and urinary lymphatic tissue, i.e. at virtually any antibody-producing site.

The Spleen

The spleen is the blood-vascular analogue of the lymph node. Just as the lymph node acts as a filter for lymph, as a storage and multiplication site for white cells and as a theatre in which these cells may exert their phagocytic and immune functions, so is the spleen a corresponding filter for the blood-borne material, its reticular meshwork acting as a labyrinth through which the blood cells must pass and undergo "scrutiny" so that if they are defective they are removed by phagocytosis. Like the lymph node, the spleen acts as a storehouse for lymphocytes which are, indeed, formed here in typical *germinal centres* along with plasma cells. In the spleen these lymphocytes participate in immune reactions, capturing antigen and synthesizing antibody which has ready access to the blood stream. In some species, such as the mouse, the spleen is haemopoietic, producing granulocytes and erythrocytes, a feature shared by the human embryo. Finally, because of its large capacity, the spleen may be considered to act as a storehouse for blood cells. Certainly, in species like the cat and dog, where the organ is enclosed in a muscular capsule, activation of this muscle by sympathetic stimulation, or by adrenaline, causes a powerful contraction driving a cell-rich blood into the general circulation.

Structure

The spleen is a large organ, constituting some 0·5% of the body-weight (i.e. weighing about 400 g in man) and is situated high under the diaphragm on the left side. It is enclosed in a connective-tissue capsule from which radiate trabeculae, which divide it into lobes. In a histological section the tissue, so divided, appears as islands of *white pulp* in a sea of *red pulp*, with *marginal zones* representing the transition between white and red pulp. The difference in colour is due to the concentration of blood sinuses and red blood cells in the red pulp, otherwise their fundamental structure is the same, being based on a reticulum, constituted by reticular cells and their secreted reticular fibres, the meshes of this network being stuffed with cells of the various types.

Blood Supply. The splenic artery divides into a series of trabecular arteries which course along the trabeculae which divide the body of the spleen into its lobes. Branches of the trabecular arteries plunge into the tissue as *central arteries* (Fig. 4.9), acquiring an outer "cuff" of tissue—the *periarterial lymphatic sheath* (PALS)—stuffed with lymphocytes and other free cells, and criss-crossed with reticulin fibres derived from reticular cells similar to those constituting the reticular cells of the lymph node.

White Pulp. It is these cuffs that constitute the white pulp. Like the lymph node they contain nodules, primary and secondary, the latter containing germinal centres and representing sites of lymphocyte multiplication and plasma cell formation. The central artery sends out branches through its cuff, which end in the marginal zone, the region constituting the transition between the cuff—or white pulp—and the red pulp.

Marginal Zone. This marginal tissue is characterized by a dense meshwork into which many of the branches of the central arteries empty their blood, and it is here that the first processing of the blood takes place so that carbon particles, injected into the blood, are found in this marginal zone first, being phagocytosed by the fixed reticular cells and free macrophages of the tissue, which, as we have seen, constitute a part of the reticulo-endothelial system (p. 292).

Immune Response. The importance of the spleen in immune responses is revealed by the early accumulation of antigens, injected into the blood-stream, in the marginal zone. It thus acts as a trap for antigen and promotes antibody formation.

Red Pulp. The red pulp is a reticular meshwork, made up of branching cords of tissue—*the splenic cords*—enclosing a honeycomb of anastomosing venous sinuses; these thin-walled vessels collect the blood from the marginal zone after it has been processed there. There is a more direct communication through the central arteries; these arteries lose their cuffs of PALS and enter the red pulp as *arteries of the red pulp*, and branch into slenderer vessels called *penicilli* which open into the meshwork of the pulp, whence the blood is collected in the venous sinuses. The walls of the sinuses are not made up of a true endothelium, but of reticular cells which are actually fixed macrophages similar to those in the cords, but not so actively phagocytic. As indicated above, the basic reticular structure of the white pulp continues into the red pulp. This reticulum is crammed with cells of various types including erythrocytes, lymphocytes (mainly derived from the white

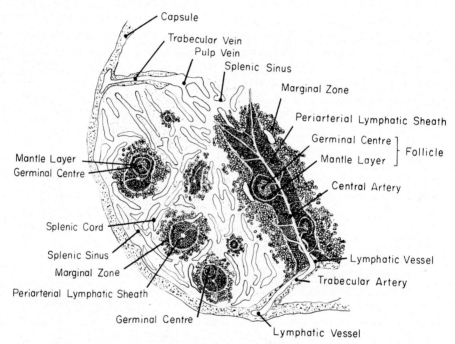

Fig. 4.9. A schematic view of spleen. (L. Weiss, "The Cells and Tissues of the Immune System", Prentice-Hall.)

pulp and migrating to the red), free macrophages, granular leucocytes, platelets etc. so that the cords are in effect conglomerates of these various cells held by the reticular fibres.

Blood Circulation

The main physiological problem concerned with the spleen is the mode of blood circulation, as there is some uncertainty as to whether the circulation is closed, in the sense that blood has to pass through a system of tubes separated morphologically from an extravascular space, or whether, in the marginal zone and red pulp, the blood escapes into non-vascular spaces to be re-collected in the venous sinuses. Studies on the passage of labelled cells indicate that there are a slow and rapid route for circulation. The slow route is taken by damaged cells, which are in some way shunted out of the more rapid route, so that it may well be that there are both closed and open parts of the circuit.

Spherocytosis. This selection of unsound cells is remarkable. In the congenital disease of spherocytosis, the erythrocytes are small and spherical and are characterized by a higher-than-normal osmotic fragility (Vol. 1). The spleen recognizes them as defective and destroys them to the point that the sufferer has an anaemia, a condition that can be rectified by removal of the spleen.*

The Nature of the Haemopoietic Stem Cell

We have defined the haemopoietic stem cell as an undifferentiated cell that has the capacity to multiply, and in so doing gives rise to other cells that are committed to a definite line of development through further divisions. Thus we may speak of the *stem cell proper*, the ancestor of all the blood cells, and the *committed stem cell*, which, although not showing any obvious sign of differentiation, will give rise to one of the classes of cells of the blood—erythrocyte, granulocyte, etc.

Stimulation of Haemopoiesis

The search for the stem cell has occupied the attention of haematologists for a long time, and an unequivocal demonstration of its existence has yet to be made. The basic mode of study is to stimulate blood cell formation and to examine the blood-forming tissues in an attempt to define the primary event in proliferation of new cells, since we may presume that an increased requirement for cells, e.g. erythrocytes, will provoke an early multiplication of its ancestors. The formation of blood cells may be provoked by damage to the blood-forming tissues, e.g. by X-irradiation, or where erythroid cells are concerned by exposure of an animal to hypoxia. The results of modern studies have permitted the exclusion of two types of cell, namely the reticulum cells of the marrow and the sinusoidal endothelial cells.

Haemopoiesis. Yoffey's scheme for haemopoiesis is illustrated in Fig. 4.10.

---

* There are considerable species variations in the structure of the spleen. As indicated, in mice and rats the spleen is a site of erythrocyte and granulocyte formation. The description given here is essentially that of the human spleen.

Sinusoid	Pachychromatic small lymphocytes	Pale transitionals	Basophilic transitionals	Blast cells

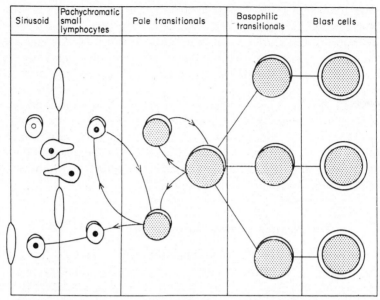

Fig. 4.10. Scheme of haemopoiesis. The most undifferentiated cells are the pale transitional cells. These may either undergo proliferation or leave the compartment. When they proliferate, small transitional cells grow into large ones, which then divide. When they leave the compartment, they may either develop basophilia and then become blast cells, or else they may divide to give rise to small lymphocytes, which can leave the marrow by traversing the sinusoidal endothelium in the opposite direction, i.e. from blood to marrow. Transitional cells can also enter the blood-stream from the marrow (not shown in the scheme). They do so in much smaller numbers than lymphocytes. (Yoffey, *In* "Haemopoietic Stem Cells", CIBA Symp. Elsevier.)

Transitional Cell

The basic element in this scheme is a lymphocyte-type of cell called the *pale transitional cell*; it is called a transitional cell because it occupies a stage in transition from lymphocyte, proper, to the blast cell that is committed to form one or other type of blood cell. Because this transitional cell undergoes change, the compartment containing it is not uniform but represents a spectrum ranging from the large pale transitional, about to develop protein-synthesizing capacity (basophilia) and become a blast cell, down to the small "pachychromatic" lymphocyte derived by division from transitional cells proper. According to this scheme, blast formation results from, first, the growth of a transitional cell; at a certain size it divides giving rise to cells that leave the compartment to become blast cells. The scheme indicates also the formation of small lymphocytes from the transitional cell, and these can leave the marrow by traversing the sinusoidal endothelium, thus entering the blood-stream. The scheme also suggests that the small pachychromatic lymphocytes may grow to become transitional cells, so that these small lymphocytes could be regarded as a reserve of transitional cells to meet extraordinary requirements.

Colony Forming Units. If the stem cells are formed in the bone-marrow, then stimulation of haemopoiesis demands that stem cells pass from the marrow to the spleen, since this is another haemopoietic tissue. In fact, the blood of an animal exposed to X-irradiation contained an increased number of "colony forming units" i.e. cells that, on incubation in a culture medium, were capable of giving rise to colonies of blood cells.

Stem Cell Competition

If all the blood cells are derived from a common ancestor, it is to be expected that the different groups will compete for the stem cells in existence at any moment. Hence, provoking erythropoiesis might be expected to depress production of granulocytes, or sustained stimulation of granulopoiesis might cause anaemia through diversion of stem cells from erythropoiesis. These phenomena have, in fact, been described.

More Primitive Cell?

The existence of a stem cell, which is probably the transitional cell, is reasonably well established, and the remaining problem in blood cell heritage is whether there is an even more primitive cell—an *immuno-haemopoietic stem cell*—that can be diverted into either haemopoiesis or immune reactions. So far nothing definite on this point can be stated.

Control of Erythropoiesis

Erythropoietin

When animals are exposed to low oxygen tension, for example by maintaining them in a low pressure chamber—*hypobaric*—they respond by increased erythrocyte production—the *polycythaemia* of high altitude. This is recognized by an increase in proportion of erythrocytes to plasma when the blood is centrifuged in a haematocrit tube. The stimulus to erythropoiesis is the anoxia, so that the "cobalt polycythaemia" obtained by feeding animals with cobalt is due to the interference with cellular metabolism by this metal, producing cellular anoxia. The sensitive tissue in this reaction is the kidney; the involvement of this organ in the control of erythropoiesis had long been suspected because of the common occurrence of anaemia in kidney disease and the occurrence of polycythaemia in cases of tumour of the kidney. By perfusing the isolated kidney it is possible to isolate a factor, or hormone, called *erythropoiesis-stimulating-factor* (*ESF*) or *erythropoietin*, in the perfusate. This factor is present in the plasma of normal animals, and the amount is increased under conditions that provoke increased erythrocyte formation, such as anaemia and the early stages of exposure to high altitudes.

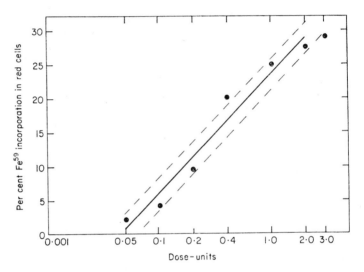

Fig. 4.11. Illustrating the haemopoiesis stimulating action of haemopoietin, as measured by incorporation of ^{59}Fe into erythrocytes of mice. (After Fisher *et al. In* "Kidney Hormones", Academic Press, 1971.)

Assay. It is a polypeptide hormone that has so far not been isolated in the pure form, and the activity of a preparation from plasma is estimated commonly by injecting into mice and measuring the rate of incorporation of ^{59}Fe into the animal's blood cells. In order to have animals with a minimum amount of erythropoietin in their blood to act as suitable tests, the mice are maintained in a hypobaric chamber at a pressure of about 350 mm Hg for two weeks. At the end of this period, when they are brought back to normal pressure, the endogenous haemopoietin in their blood is minimal, and injections of haemopoietin preparations produce an increase in rate of incorporation of ^{59}Fe into the blood in a dose-dependent fashion (Fig. 4.11).

When normal animals are injected with large amounts of erythropoietin a polycythaemia develops, and there is also macrocytosis, i.e. larger than normal erythrocytes. In addition to this, *reticulocytosis* occurs, which is the appearance of immature forms of erythrocytes in the blood, a condition associated with enhanced production of blood, as for example after haemorrhage. By preparing an antiserum to erythropoietin and injecting this into animals, the concentration in the blood may be reduced to zero, in which case erythropoiesis is almost or completely brought to a halt.

Renal Erythropoietin Factor. Just as angiotensin is produced by an enzymatic breakdown of plasma protein through the action of renin, so is erythropoietin produced by incubation of plasma a-globulin with an extract of kidney, the factor responsible being called *renal erythropoietin factor (REF)*. The REF seems to be diffusely distributed in the kidney tissue and is found in both nuclear and light mitochondrial fractions of kidney homogenates.

Effects of Drugs and Hormones

The rate of erythropoiesis, as measured by the rate of incorporation of radioactive iron into the blood, is increased by a great variety of drugs and hormones, such as the adrenal cortical steroids or ACTH, thyroid hormones or TSH, angiotensin, norepinephrine, 5-HT, testosterone, prolactin, and so on. According to Fisher, all these actions are mediated largely through increased erythropoietin production, so that they may be counteracted by injections of an antiserum to erythropoietin. The factor common to many of these actions is probably an induced renal anoxia brought about either by increased utilization of O_2—by decreased blood-flow—or by interference with utilization of O_2 to produce a histotoxic hypoxia.*

Mode of Action of Erythropoietin. As to the site of action of the hormone, it seems that its principal attack is on the precursor cell that is committed to formation of erythrocytes, accelerating the differentiation into haemoglobin-synthesizing cells; this is achieved by inducing synthesis of RNA. The hormone also has a direct action on the cells, inducing and stimulating synthesis of haemoglobin. Thus, although the stem cell is committed to erythropoiesis, in the absence of erythropoietin it fails to synthesize haemoglobin. Since large doses of erythropoietin will induce macrocytic erythrocytes, it is reasonable to assume that the hormone also accelerates haemoglobin synthesis in cells that are already synthesizing it, i.e. in the early normoblasts—polychromatophilic.

* The mechanisms of action of testosterone and prolactin are not known, however.

Inhibition of Erythropoiesis

It has been suggested that erythropoiesis is governed by both an accelerating factor (erythropoietin) and an inhibitory factor. There is a great deal of evidence indicating that the plasma of polycythaemic animals will inhibit erythropoiesis, whether the polycythaemia is produced by exposure to high altitudes or by simple injection of large numbers of erythrocytes from another animal (*hypertransfusion*). It is uncertain, however, whether the hypothetical factor inhibits the formation of erythropoietin, inactivates a pre-formed erythropoietin, or directly inhibits the formation of blood cells and haemoglobin synthesis.

Platelets

Since the total number of platelets in the circulation is kept quite constant under normal conditions, we may postulate some homeostatic mechanism that adjusts the rate of production of megakaryocytes to the circulating volume of platelets. At any rate, an experimentally induced thrombocytopenia results in accelerated production leading to thrombocytosis. A humoral factor, extracted from thrombocytopenic serum, which causes increased platelet production, has been called *thrombopoietin*.

Leucocytes

Knowledge of the control of release and multiplication of leucocytes is also vague; adrenal corticosteroids and bacterial endotoxins cause increased release from stores, but probably do not directly influence multiplication. Recently a factor in neutropenic blood has been found, by Stohlman, to stimulate reproduction of a colony of leucocytes *in vitro*; this may be appropriately called *granulopoietin*.

Lymphocytes

The lymphocytes are concerned with the production of antibody, and since the stimulus to production is also the stimulus to multiplication, the production of lymphocytes is essentially variable. The stem cells from which they are derived are in the bone marrow since, if an animal is lethally irradiated, it is only a suspension of marrow cells that will restore to the animal the capacity to regenerate its lymphocyte population. As we shall see, however, multiplication takes place in all the lymphoid tissues, e.g. the thymus, spleen, etc.

Circulating Lymphocytes

The blood and lymph contain many lymphocytes, and these represent a store of circulating cells. Thus we may place a cannula in the large thoracic duct and collect the lymph that flows continually. The number of cells collected in a given time indicates that the whole population would have to be replaced several times a day if the concentration in the blood were to remain constant in spite of this drain; in fact no such replacement occurs so that robbing the animal of its lymph in this manner robs it of its stores of lymphocytes. By injecting lymphocytes, with their RNA labelled by previous incubation with ^{3}H-adenosine, it was possible to show that these cells passed out of the blood, in the lymph nodes, and made their way into the lymph vessels whence they were carried back to the blood by way of the large lymphatic ducts. These *circulating lymphocytes* are presumably ready to engage in the first immune response to foreign antigen, which they would probably meet in the reticular tissue of the lymph nodes and spleen, the antigen-trapping region.

THE RESPONSE TO INJURY

The Inflammatory Response

The obvious response to local injury, such as that caused by a burn, is a reddening and warming of the skin, due primarily to a dilatation of the arterioles and collecting venules. The initial increase in blood-flow through the arterioles causes a dilatation of the capillaries, which may well be largely passive. Further changes, depending on the degree of injury, consist in: the exudation of a plasma filtrate from the capillaries and venules, due to an abnormal increase in endothelial permeability—oedema or turgor; a "stickiness" of the endothelial linings of the small vessels, manifest in a tendency of platelets and leucocytes to adhere and so cause plugging of small vessels; and finally a tendency for leucocytes, mainly polymorphs, to leave the circulation by diapedesis from the capillaries and venules. The increase in blood-flow may be only temporary, and may be followed by actual stasis leading to necrosis of the tissue. The functions of this increased blood-flow are various and usually obvious; one, that is often overlooked, is the washing of infectious organisms away from their site of aggregation in the tissue into the general bloodstream, where they are immediately brought against the various defensive mechanisms in the spleen and lymph nodes. Thus, usually, intravenous injections of bacteria are remarkably ineffective in causing disease, since this requires a site for multiplication of the organisms, e.g. the lung tissue.

Triple Response

Some of the basic features of the skin reaction are illustrated by Lewis's description of the *triple response* to, say, a scratch. This consists in: (1) a local vasodilatation, occurring independently of the nerves; (2) a more widespread vasodilatation of arterioles occurring through an axon-reflex, i.e. the afferent nerve terminal is excited and transmits its excitation down an antidromic branch to a blood vessel (Fig. 4.12); this effect can be blocked by local anaesthetics. Finally, (3) an increased permeability of the small blood vessels leading to local oedema, and due apparently to the local release of a chemical agent which is considered to be histamine or a similar "H-substance".

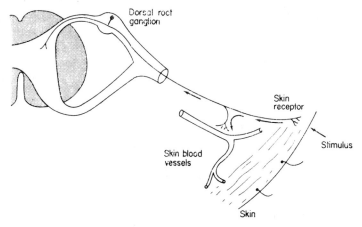

Fig. 4.12. Illustrating an axon-reflex. A stimulus to a sensory nerve-ending in the skin initiates a response in the sensory axon which not only is transmitted to the cord but also passes "antidromically" down a branch innervating a blood vessel.

More Severe Injuries

The inflammatory responses in more severe injuries, such as burns, are to be viewed as extensions of these basic processes. Thus, the first reaction in acute damage is actually a short period of arteriolar constriction, and this can be demonstrated by mechanical stroking or the skin giving rise to a pallid area. Subsequently, blood-flow is increased as much as tenfold; this is achieved by flow through direct arteriolar–venular shunts, whereby the terminal capillary bed may tend to be bypassed but, as the precapillary sphincters are opened, there is increased capillary flow. Up to this point the reaction is similar to the *reactive hyperaemia*, when the blood-flow to a limb is re-established after a period of ischaemia, and it is a phase that can be blocked by antihistamine drugs. Subsequently, the loss of fluid into the tissue spaces, the changed reactivity of the blood vessels, and the tendency of capillaries and venules to become plugged, all contribute to reduce the actual blood flow, with stasis in many of the channels. Not only may leucocytes migrate but also red cells, giving rise to petechial haemorrhages.

Oedema

It was originally thought that the escape of proteins into the tissue was from the capillaries, but studies with the electron microscope have shown that it is the post-capillary venules that are the weakest point, the increased permeability being accompanied by a tendency of the endothelial cells to separate. Only at a later stage does the leakage extend to the capillaries. The actual concentration of protein in the oedema fluid is initially less than in plasma but eventually it becomes equal to this, indicating an exudation into the tissue rather than a filtration process.

Dyed Protein. Experimentally, the increased vascular permeability to proteins may be measured by injecting a dyed protein into the blood stream. The dye, Evans blue, attaches itself strongly to serum albumin so that the mere intravenous injection of the dye is sufficient to label the protein. If, now, some active principle is injected into the skin, the increased vascular permeability is revealed as a patch of blue in the tissue.

"Sludging." The loss of plasma from the capillaries and venules, if extreme, may lead to *stasis*, i.e. the cessation of flow through loss of fluidity of the blood, the small vessels being stuffed with erythrocytes. This may well be the basis of "sludging", the aggregation of clumps of erythrocytes that are ultimately driven back into circulation. It is very likely that some change in the erythrocyte surface takes place, allowing a close aggregation (or agglutination) and it is interesting that often masses of platelets are also associated with the clumps.

Diapedesis

The increased permeability of capillary and venule may frequently be seen to be accompanied by a separation of the endothelial cells, and through these gaps erythrocytes may pass to give small petechial haemorrhages. We may consider the increased "stickiness" of the endothelium, manifest as a tendency of leucocytes and platelets to stick to the endothelial wall, as an adaptation to permit the plugging by the platelets of these endothelial holes, whilst adhesion to the wall of the vessel by the leucocyte is the first and necessary step in its migration into the subendothelial space. This migration takes place *between* the endothelial cells of the post-capillary venule, in the case of the polymorphonuclear leucocyte; by contrast, the lymphocyte apparently takes a route *through* the endothelial cells. The two methods are illustrated in Fig. 4.13.

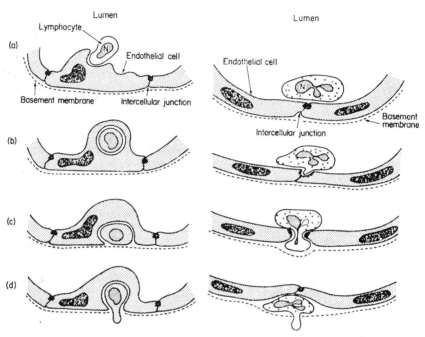

Fig. 4.13. Comparing the passage of a lymphocyte and a polymorphonuclear leucocyte through the endothelial wall. The lymphocyte (left) is engulfed by the cell cytoplasm whereas the polymorphonuclear leucocyte passes through the intercellular junction. (Marchesi and Gowans, *Proc. Roy. Soc. B*, 1963, **159**, 283.)

Immune Reactions

It must be appreciated that inflammation is usually accompanied, or caused, by infection, i.e. the invasion of foreign organisms. Consequently, the *immune response*, involving antigen–antibody complex formation and cellular immune reactions, is brought into play so that it is not easy to discuss the basic features of inflammation without referring to many of the features of an immune response. This is especially manifest, say, in the behaviour of the leucocytes of the blood. A sterile injury of any sort, or even the injection of sterile isotonic saline, will cause a local emigration of neutrophils into the tissue. However, if the injected material is antigenic, provoking an immune reaction, the emigration is on a vastly larger scale and is usually accompanied by the liberation of pharmacologically active materials, *kinins*, that greatly enhance the other features of inflammation, notably the tone of the small blood vessels and their permeability to proteins. Furthermore, experimentally, some of the inflammatory manifestations that are most easily evoked under controlled conditions are immune reactions, e.g. the Arthus and Schwartzman reactions, so that a great deal of our knowledge is derived from these, rather than from the sterile type of damage caused by a burn or cut.

Antigen and Antibody

The detailed discussion of immune reactions will be left to the last part of this chapter, but it would be convenient to summarize very briefly the basic features now. Essentially we are concerned with the body's reaction to foreign material—*antigen*, a reaction that involves the production of antibodies that tend to neutralize the invasive material. Once the organism has been "infected" with this foreign material it acquires a "sensitivity" or "hypersensitivity" to the same antigenic material, so that its response to a second infection is more exaggerated; antibodies are produced in larger quantities, and more rapidly, whilst local or generalized inflammatory reactions are usual.

Anaphylaxis. The inflammatory response is seen in its most extreme form in *anaphylaxis*, when an animal (say, a guinea pig) is injected with the serum protein of another species, and after an appropriate interval a second injection is given. By correct timing and dosages it is possible to cause the animal to die as a result of the second injection, there being a widespread vasodilatation with a severe constriction of the smooth muscle of the bronchioles, so that the cause of death is actually the asthma due to this.

Allergy. Allergic manifestations are similar examples of sensitivity but are usually less severe, and in this case the sensitivity may be inherited or have been acquired long ago.

Arthus Reaction

The state of hypersensitivity induced by previous sensitization with an antigen is simply revealed by the *Arthus reaction*. Thus we may sensitize an animal by injecting it *intravenously* with a suitable antigen; and after a period of some days a second injection may be given *into the skin*. The result is an immediate local inflammation, accompanied by massive escape of leucocytes into the tissue. The reaction is due to the meeting between antigen and antibodies, which form complexes in the vascular walls.

Activation of Leucocytes

How the antibody–antigen reaction induces the response is not clear, but the primary event seems to be the activation of the leucocytes, predominantly polymorphs, since it may be largely prevented if these have been destroyed, e.g. by preliminary irradiation of the animal. Thus the escape of leucocytes into the tissue, itself, leads to inflammation, i.e. increased vascular permeability with dilatation of small vessels, and this is probably achieved by the liberation from the leucocytes of their hydrolytic enzymes into the tissue spaces, these enzymes producing *kinins*, such as bradykinin.

Anaphylotoxins

In addition, the reaction of complement* with the antigen–antibody complex can lead to the formation of vaso-active peptides, called *anaphylotoxins*. These aspects will be considered in a little more detail later, but here it is sufficient to appreciate that inflammation is a very essential feature of most reactions to invasions by foreign material, and since injury without invasion is a rare event, we must treat the immune inflammatory response as a usual feature of tissue damage.

HAEMOSTASIS

Before the healing process may begin, the loss of blood through any damaged vessels must be stopped; and this is achieved primarily by the mechanical plugging of the holes with aggregates of platelets—*white bodies*—associated with a solidification of the shed blood by the process of *clotting*. The basic protein-scaffolding of this clot—namely *fibrin*—contributes to strengthen the platelet plug which would otherwise be washed away by the current of blood. Where large arteries are damaged, the plugging mechanism is usually inadequate and artificial aids will be necessary, although the tendency for a damaged or cut artery to constrict may, of itself, be adequate to prevent exsanguination; a further, mechanical, aid to loss of blood may be the tendency for the pressure in the tissue to rise.

---

* The function of complement will be discussed later (p. 365); it consists of protein material in normal plasma that co-operates in the neutralization and removal of foreign material after the antibody–antigen complex has been formed.

The Platelet Plug

When a small artery is cut, the platelets aggregate to form a rim round the edge, accumulating in the subendothelial space. This ring grows to form a capsule, and the accumulation extends into the lumen and so finally blocks the vessel completely. As seen in the light-microscope, the platelets are clumped into a mass, undergoing what is called "viscous metamorphosis"; but in the electron microscope it is seen that the platelets do not fuse, retaining their individual identities. Their cytoplasmic granules tend to disappear (*degranulation*) and in the surrounding spaces typical lipid micelles are seen, obviously related to the lipid- or lipoprotein material constituting the granules. It is this *platelet factor* that is presumably concerned in clotting (p. 320). The factors causing aggregation of the platelets have not been un-equivocally established, but an important one seems to be the exposure of the blood to the subendothelial tissue of the blood vessel, i.e. to the basement membrane and adjacent connective tissue. Thus, so long as the endothelium is intact, the tendency to aggregate is absent, and it is probably the contact with the collagenous material that alters the platelet's surface, permitting it to stick to the collagenous basement membrane and also to stick to other platelets. Certainly, preparations of collagen have these effects. Another factor favouring aggregation and degranulation is thrombin, which is formed under the same conditions of vascular damage (p. 319).

Aggregation of Platelets

Experimentally, platelets may be prepared from blood by the simple expedient of centrifuging the blood relatively slowly, in which case the heavy erythrocytes and leucocytes settle out, leaving the platelets still in suspension. After removal of the former cells, the platelets may be caused to form a "pellet" by centrifuging at a much higher speed; this pellet may be resuspended in saline, and the tendency to aggregate may be measured quite simply by the scattering of light by the sus-pension, the clumping into larger particles reducing the light-scattering. Figure 4.14 shows the effects of adding ADP to such a suspension. There is a very striking increase in clumping, an effect that may be abolished by removal of Ca^{2+}; and it has been suggested that *in vivo* damage in some way causes the platelets themselves to release ADP, which then alters their surface to favour aggregation. The fact that Ca^{2+} is necessary suggests that the aggregation is brought about by the for-mation of a Ca^{2+}–ADP complex that links the two surfaces of opposing platelets, the ADP molecule combining with a positive amino-group in the surface of the platelet. If thrombin (p. 319) caused the platelet to release ADP, we could explain its action.

It may well be, however, that the picture of an ADP–Ca^{2+}-linked aggregation system is too simple; for example, it has been argued that ADP reacts with the contractile protein, thrombosthenin (p. 324), and in this way affects its aggregating powers. Additional factors that favour aggregation are preparations of fibrinogen and adrenaline and noradrenaline. The action of these adrenergic mediators may well be secondary to a liberation of ADP by the platelets. Serotonin is contained in granules within the platelets and released during aggregation, the vasoconstrictor action doubtless being important in the haemostatic mechanism. Serotonin, when added to platelets, causes aggregation.

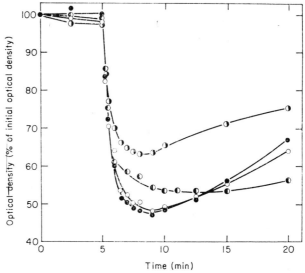

Fig. 4.14. Effects of adding ADP to a suspension of platelets in plasma; clumping causes a reduction in the optical density of the suspension. ● : Normal platelet-rich plasma; ○ : unwashed platelets in platelet-free plasma : ◑ unwashed platelets in platelet-free plasma with ADP added at 5 min; ◔ unwashed platelets in plasma which has been preheated to 100°C for 10 min. (Born and Cross, *J. Physiol.* 1964, **170**, 397.)

The Blood Clot

The mere formation of the platelet plug is inadequate to stop bleeding through a damaged artery. The plug must be reinforced by the formation of a fibrin gel or clot, brought about by the enzymatic conversion of fibrinogen, a soluble protein of the blood, into fibrin, an insoluble derivative. The individual fibrin molecules have a tendency to aggregate in an end-to-end fashion, like those of tropo-collagen, to form fibrils which constitute a scaffolding in which the remaining constituents of the blood are held suspended.

Clotting Time

The process of coagulation, or clot-formation, is easily observed; freshly drawn blood may be placed in a tube and, within a matter of seconds (the *clotting time*) it becomes a solid lump. The process may be delayed by keeping the blood in a wax- or silicone-covered tube, so that contact with glass is a powerful initiator of the process. It may be prevented indefinitely by removal of calcium, with oxalate, or by sequestering the ion by formation of a complex with citrate or EDTA.

Thrombin

The factor responsible for the clotting is described as an enzyme, *thrombin*, which, in the presence of calcium, converts the inactive prothrombin of the blood into thrombin. It was early found that an extract of tissue would accelerate the clotting process, and it was assumed that a "tissue factor" was liberated at the site of damage. Thus the clotting process was described as:

$$\text{Prothrombin} \xrightarrow[\text{Ca}^{2+}\text{-ions}]{\text{Tissue Factor}} \text{Thrombin}$$

$$\text{Fibrinogen} + \text{Thrombin} \xrightarrow{\hspace{1.5cm}} \text{Fibrin}$$

Morphological Changes. In the electron microscope the process of aggregation, and its reversal, deaggregation, may be followed; at first the platelets do not fuse but come to within about 200 to 600 Å of each other, so that adhesion must be through the coating of sulphated mucopolysaccharide. The coming together is preceded by the formation of blebs and pseudopods on the surface; adhesion is associated with the platelets' acquiring a more spherical shape with increase in size of the pseudopods. During deaggregation the platelets separate, the pseudopods become smaller and finally the cells return to their disk shape. In later stages of agglutination there is fusion of cell membranes of adjacent platelets, with disintegration of the lysosomes and other granules, a process called *thrombocytorrhexia*.

Prothrombin Time

According to the above formulation, the important factor in blood required for clotting was the prothrombin concentration, so that the time required for a decalcified specimen of blood to clot when Ca^{2+} and a tissue extract were added (called the *prothrombin time*) was used as a measure of the prothrombin concentration in the blood. The discovery that in certain haemophiliac conditions, i.e. in conditions where clotting was unusually delayed, the actual concentration of prothrombin was normal, has limited the value of the test.

The Fibrinogen–Fibrin Transformation

The fibrinogen molecule has a weight of some 330,000 to 340,000 and is a rod-shaped molecule about 475 Å long. Actually its molecules have a tendency to aggregate end-to-end to produce fibrils, so that fibrinogen itself can form gels. However, the enzymatic splitting off of two small peptides from the fibrinogen molecule—*fibrinopeptides*— allows a much firmer linkage of the molecules, which are now called fibrin. This linkage is made even more stable by a chemical reaction, catalysed by *fibrin-stabilizing factor* (*FSF*), or *fibrinase*, the chemical reaction being a transpeptidation as illustrated in Fig. 4.15.

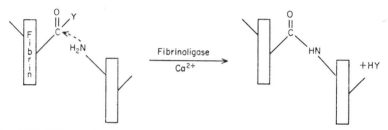

Fig. 4.15. Illustrating the transpeptidation that stabilizes the end-to-end linkage in fibrin. The thrombin-activated FSF is described here as fibrinoligase. (Lorand, "Dynamics of Thrombus Formation and Dissolution", Lippincott, & Co.)

Mechanism of Thrombin Formation

We may ask the questions: What is there about shed blood that allows thrombin to be formed from prothrombin? or, What is the factor in the circulating blood that prevents this conversion? The finding that removal of platelets from blood delays clotting suggested that these bodies, when damaged or altered during aggregation at the site of bleeding, released a "platelet factor" that remained inactive so long as it was within the platelets. Again, the finding that the surface of the vessel holding shed blood was important suggested that mere contact of shed blood with a surface different from the endothelial lining of the blood vessel was sufficient to activate either the platelets or some other factor.

The Various Factors. As indicated above, the process of conversion of prothrombin to thrombin has, in fact, been shown to be dependent on several factors. Thus the condition of haemophilia in which clotting is considerably delayed could not be attributed to any lack of prothrombin in the blood, but was in fact due to the absence of a protein in plasma called the *antihaemophiliac factor* (Factor VIII). This was later shown to be necessary in a reaction between platelets and normal plasma globulin that was necessary for prothrombin conversion, a reaction that did not occur in haemophiliac plasma.

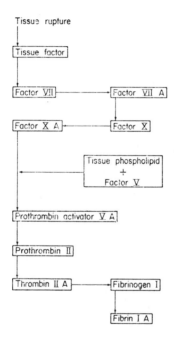

Fig. 4.16. Sequence of changes in extrinsic mechanism of blood clotting. (After Macfarlane, *In* "The Inflammatory Process", Ed. B. W. Zweijach *et al*. Academic Press.)

As indicated in Fig. 4.16, tissue rupture is thought to release a factor that activates Factor VII; the active form of this, indicated by VIIA, reacts with Factor X; the product of this reaction, XA, reacts with Factor V and phospholipid (which may be derived from the tissue) to activate, finally, prothrombin, which has been called Factor II.

Reaction Sequence. The important point to appreciate is that all these reactions probably occur in sequence, rather than simultaneously, so that it is the product of the reaction between a given pair that proceeds to react with the next factor, and so on, just as the product between prothrombin and its ultimate activator, Factor VA, converts this to an active proteolytic enzyme (thrombin) that reacts with fibrinogen.

Amplification. There is thus what Macfarlane calls a *cascade* of reactions leading to an explosive production of thrombin which then rapidly converts fibrinogen into fibrin. This explosive type of reaction, rather than a slow accumulation, is necessary if clot-formation is to be effective in stopping bleeding since it is found that very slow clotting, as in haemophilia, leads to serious haemorrhage with the slightest damage. Macfarlane likens the succession of chemical events to the successive steps in an electronic amplification process, so that the initial release of only a small amount of tissue-factor finally results in the production of large amounts of thrombin.

Extrinsic and Intrinsic Mechanisms

The second main step in describing clotting was the separation into an *extrinsic* and an *intrinsic* process. Thus, blood withdrawn with great care to avoid tissue damage, and kept in a glass tube, soon clots, so that the blood contains an intrinsic mechanism for clotting apart from the extrinsic one just described; extrinsic because it involves tissue (non-blood) factors. The intrinsic process may be delayed by covering the glass with a layer of wax or silicone, and it is the contact of the blood with the glass surface that initiates the reaction, this contact having a twofold effect. First, it activates a plasma protein, Factor XII or Hageman factor, probably causing it to unfold; secondly, the intrinsic process is dependent on the platelets, clotting time in a glass tube being prolonged in their absence, and contact apparently causing them to release the phospholipid that is necessary in the activation of Factor X.

Factor X. The chain of reactions is indicated in Fig. 4.17, and it will be seen that Factors X and V are common to the two processes; furthermore, purified phospholipid, phosphatidyl ethanolamine and phosphatidyl serine, will substitute for tissue or platelet phospholipid in both extrinsic and intrinsic systems. The central role of Factor X in both mechanisms is illustrated by Fig. 4.18, which also illustrates the manner in which Russell viper venom, a powerful activator of the clotting mechanism, acts by stimulating Factor X to produce activated X or XA.

Safety Factor

These remarkable series of reactions are regarded as an adaptation

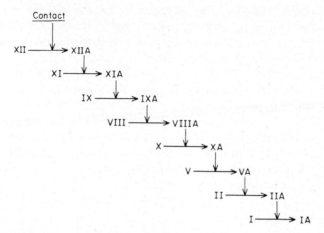

Fig. 4.17. The sequence of changes in the intrinsic mechanism of blood clotting. (Macfarlane, *In* "The Inflammatory Process", Ed. B. W. Zweifach *et al.* Acadmic Press.)

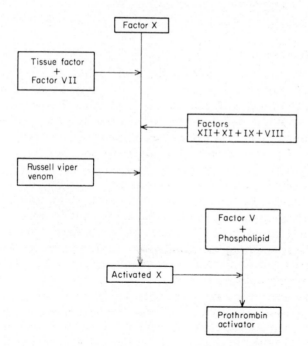

Fig. 4.18. Illustrating the central role of Factor X in the extrinsic and intrinsic clotting mechanisms. (Macfarlane, *In* "The Inflammatory Process", Ed. B. W. Zweifach *et al.* Acadmic Press.)

to ensure safety inasmuch as the complexity makes a fortuitous production of a clot more difficult. Thus, there are not only activating processes for the various factors but also inactivating processes, and it is the predominance of the activation process at any step that ensures that the clotting process will take place. It is considered that at earlier stages in evolution the process was much simpler, involving just one or two stages. The complex system, revealed in man, is thus the result of "plugging in" new stages in the amplification process, steps that are possible if the different factors are essentially enzymatic products of the factor that preceded them in the succession of events; thus fibrin is the enzymatic fission product of fibrinogen, thrombin is the enzymatic product of prothrombin, and so on.*

Vitamin K

Deficiency of vitamin K leads to delayed blood-clotting revealed by, say, a lengthened prothrombin time, and this is because the vitamin is necessary for the synthesis of prothrombin and Factors V and VII in the liver. The antagonist to vitamin K, bishydroxycoumarin (Dicumarol) is used clinically to delay clotting in the treatment of thrombosis.

Clot-Retraction

When a blood-clot is allowed to stand it tends to shrink, extruding a clear fluid, which is now called *serum* to denote its loss of fibrinogen. This retraction is greatly delayed if the platelets are removed prior to allowing coagulation. It has been argued that it is the tendency for the platelets to contract that causes the shrinkage of the fibrin scaffolding leading to extrusion of serum. It must be appreciated that the tendency for a gel to contract and express its fluid component—called *syneresis*—is a general phenomenon and results from a tendency of the fibrillar elements to aggregate, due to some progressive alterations in the forces favouring aggregation or separation of the fibrillar material. It does not depend on a specifically contractile component, so that it seems more likely that the platelet releases materials that influence the aggregating tendency of fibrin rather than that it causes clot-shrinkage by a mechanical pull.

Thrombosthenin. Nevertheless, the platelet does seem to be capable of shape-changes, and the extraction of an actomyosin-like protein from platelets, called *thrombosthenin*, which is sensitive to ATP and Mg^{2+}, has led to the hypothesis that the shrinkage of the fibrin

---

* In primitive organisms, the cellular plug is the only mechanism for haemostasis, the fibrinogen–fibrin conversion being a feature of higher vertebrates.

clot, and the tendency for the platelet-plug to consolidate, are the result of a mechanical shortening of actomyosin-like fibrils within the platelets. Normally the only microfibrils visible in the cytoplasm are a ring of microtubules, similar in basic structure to those seen in nucleated erythrocytes and spermatozoa and apparently responsible for the asymmetrical shape of these bodies. It seems that these, in the platelet, do not participate in any contractile process, but when the platelets are submitted to stress, such as spreading on glass, fine fibrils become visible, and it has been suggested that it is these *microfilaments* that constitute the basis for contraction. As indicated above, however, a contractile force, developed from without, is an unnecessary postulate and certainly begs the question as to how the shortening of individual platelets can give rise to this contractile force on the clot.* It may be that the contraction of platelet fibrils is concerned with the morphological changes in these bodies during the earlier phase of "viscous metamorphosis".

Thrombosthenin and Actomyosin. When thrombosthenin was fractionated, myosin and actin were separated, whilst the myosin could be split into two portions corresponding to the head and tail parts, the former containing the ATPase activity. The actin was similar to that extracted from rabbit skeletal muscle, with a molecular weight of 46,000, and it could combine with troponin and tropomyosin and then react with rabbit myosin to give a Ca^{2+}-sensitive system. The myosin, however, was not completely identical with that from skeletal fast muscle.

Anticoagulants

As indicated, removal of Ca^{2+} blocks coagulation, and this is because Ca^{2+}-ions are necessary at several steps in both intrinsic and extrinsic mechanisms. Of great practical use is heparin, a natural substituted glucose polymer secreted by most cells; in high concentrations it inhibits the thrombin-fibrinogen interaction; in lower concentrations its actions are more complex, and lead to a slowing down, or inhibition, of the mechanisms of prothrombin activation.

Dissolution of the Clot

The blood clot must be regarded as a temporary structure, wound-healing requiring its eventual dissolution. This is brought about by the blood's proteolytic enzyme, *plasmin*, which is derived from an inactive precursor, *plasminogen*, by a series of reactions probably as complex as

---

* It has been argued that the thrombosthenin leaks out of the platelet forming an extracellular continuum that undergoes contraction.

those involved in the activation of prothrombin. The activating factor, when produced in serum, is called *fibrinokinase*; certain bacteria are able to promote dissolution by virtue of their kinases, e.g. staphylo-kinase, streptokinase, etc.

Behaviour of Leucocytes

An early response to tissue damage or infection is the tendency of leucocytes to adhere to the blood vessel wall and to move out of the vessel into the tissue spaces. Usually the first cells to exhibit this behaviour, and to accumulate in the damaged area, are the poly-morphonuclear leucocytes, especially the neutrophils, but these are replaced in the later stages of tissue repair, or in chronic conditions, by monocytes (macrophages); like the polymorphs these are phagocytic, being concerned largely with digesting damaged cells and debris.

Release of Granule Enzymes

Although phagocytosis is the primary activity of these leucocytes, there is little doubt that, by contrast with the more specific immune reactions of lymphocytes, which also emigrate into damaged or other-wise invaded tissue, these phagocytic cells can also provoke vascular changes by virtue of materials secreted by them, probably the hydro-lytic enzymes that are employed in intracellular digestion in the phagolysosomes (p. 329). If these react with blood proteins to produce, say, bradykinin, they may cause local dilatation of blood vessels and increased permeability. In addition, the leucocytes contain histamine in granules, which is released during immune responses. A striking example of this aspect of leucocyte function is shown in the Arthus reaction, characterized by a massive infiltration of leucocytes in the inflamed area. If the leucocytes of an animal are destroyed, by irradi-ation or with nitrogen mustard, then the inflammatory reaction is either abolished or very much diminished. Again, a preparation of leucocyte granules, injected into a tissue, will provoke inflammation.

Chemotaxis

By chemotaxis we mean the conversion, by a chemical agent, of a random movement of cells to one directed towards the origin of the chemical agent; the phenomenon is illustrated by Fig. 4.19a and b, which shows the random tracks of polymorphonuclear leucocytes (a) and the tracks in the presence of a clump of staphylococci (b). The hypothetical chemotactic agents, liberated either by damaged tissue

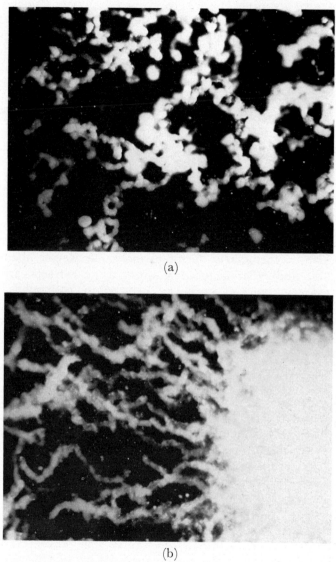

(a)

(b)

Fig. 4.19. (a) Migration pattern of polymorphonuclear leucocytes moving at random as recorded by the dark-ground trace technique. (b) Effect of a clump of *Staphylococcus epidermidis* (*Staphylococcus albus*) on the migration pattern of polymorphonuclear leucocytes. The clump of bacteria is on the right; the leucocytes moved directly toward it. (Harris, *Bact. Rev.*, 1960, **24,** 3.)

or by invasive organisms, have been given a variety of names, such as *leucotaxin, phlogistin,* and so on. *In vitro,* chemotaxis may be studied by separating a chamber containing the migrant cells from one containing the chemotactic agent by a membrane with pores large enough to allow the cells to pass through. In the absence of a chemotactic stimulus there is virtually no passage, but the presence of the agent in the other chamber will provoke leucocytes to worm their way through the pores. We may presume that it is the gradient of concentration of the agent that dictates the direction of movement.

Chemotactic Agents. *In vitro* studies of this sort have established beyond doubt that certain substances are chemotactic. Thus, a fragment of the C3 component of complement (p. 365), called C3a, not only behaves as an anaphylotoxin, increasing vascular permeability through the release of histamine, but also is chemotactic; C3a is a cleavage product of C3 and has a molecular weight in the region of 7000; in a similar way it is possible to prepare from C5, by treatment with trypsin, a chemotactic factor of molecular weight about 8500. When these and other factors, e.g. from tissue extracts, are tested against different types of leucocyte (neutrophils, eosinophils, monocytes), the responses do not differ, so that if chemotaxis is an important factor *in vivo,* the preferential aggregation of one type is due to other factors than the nature of the chemotactic agent.

Preferential Retention. It may be, however, that the migration of the leucocyte out of the blood vessel is governed by other factors than chemotactic agents, these last being concerned with movement within the tissue after the cells have left the blood vascular system. Thus the observation that usually the initial accumulation of polymorphonuclear leucocytes is followed by one of mononuclear cells may well be due to altered conditions in the tissue that favour the retention of one type rather than the preferential migration at any given time.

Increased Permeability. It is generally agreed that the increase in vascular permeability that usually accompanies the inflammatory reaction is not the cause of leucocyte emigration. However, the actual escape of protein may well be a factor since Hurley has shown that injection of the animal's own serum into its skin provokes a massive emigration of leucocytes; this occurs after a delay of some hours and so may be the result of a chemical reaction leading to the production of kinins (p. 336).

Phagocytosis

The ingestion and subsequent destruction of bacteria constitute one mode of defence against them, and to a large extent this may be described as a non-specific mode, by contrast with the agglutination and subsequent destruction brought about by the formation of antibody–antigen complexes. However, in many cases, invasive organisms seem to be "primed" for phagocytosis by adsorbing antibodies, specifically directed against them, on their surfaces; these priming agents were called by Wright and Douglas *opsonins*. To this extent, then, phago-

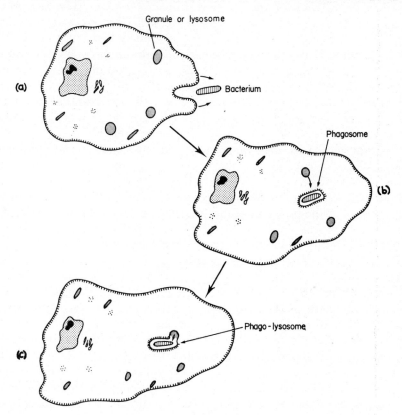

Fig. 4.20. (a) Engulfment of bacterium by phagocyte to form phagosome. (b) Fusion of phagosome with granule, or lysosome, to form (c) phagolysosome.

cytosis is also a specific reaction. Phagocytosis of a bacterium does not always result in its destruction, however, so that with tuberculosis, brucellosis and diphtheria, for example, the infective organisms, although readily ingested, multiply within the phagocytes, and the body's defences rely on specific immune reactions rather than simple ingestion and destruction.

Phagolysosome. The basic mechanisms by which a cell may either engulf a particle or extrude material from within its cytoplasm have been described earlier. In the former instance the process is called endocytosis and represents the engulfment of the particle into an invagination of the plasma membrane followed by pinching off, so that the engulfed particle is surrounded by a portion of the cell's membrane. In this state the whole is called a *phagosome*. The process is illustrated in Fig. 4.20. If we are dealing with a phagocytic cell, the engulfment is followed by intracellular digestion by hydrolytic enzymes. Such enzymes, if allowed free in the cytoplasm, might well destroy the phagocyte, and this is avoided by the sequestration of the enzymes in granules, a very characteristic feature of the polymorphonuclear leucocyte which, on this account, is also called a granulocyte. The granules are membrane-bound vesicles, and are called more generally lysosomes. These lysosomes migrate towards the engulfed particle, i.e. the phagosome, and their membranes fuse to form a *phagolysosome*, containing both particle and the enzymes required for its digestion.* Thus both storage of the enzymes, and their liberation, are carried out in such a way as to prevent escape into the cytoplasm. The subsequent fate of the phagolysosome, after digestion has been completed, varies with the cell. The residue is described as a residual body and may finally empty its contents out of the cell by exocytosis.

Pseudopods. The forces governing these processes, notably the initial coming together of leucocyte and particle leading to endocytosis and the subsequent fusion of the granule with phagosome, are not well understood. The subject of cell contact has been discussed earlier where it was seen that the surface potential (zeta-potential) must be important, a potential that tends to oppose contact because of the repulsion of opposite charges. Only if the particles can approach to within some 5 Å is the really close approximation required for engulfment possible. It may be that this requirement is made possible, as argued by Bangham, by the initial formation of pseudopods, a process that reduces the charge-density in the region of contact (Fig. 4.21).

Opsonins. The importance of the surfaces of both leucocyte and ingested particle is revealed by the effects of *leucokinin* and of opsonins and related substances. Leucokinin is the name given to a γ-globulin in plasma which binds to the leucocyte and favours phagocytosis of bacteria. The name *opsonin* was given by Wright and Douglas to

---

* In response to some bacterial toxins the degranulation or release of enzymes from lysosomes may not be so orderly; thus streptolysin causes leakage into the phagocyte's cytoplasm, thereby killing it.

immune bodies that were produced by the animal and became adsorbed on to the antigen, e.g. bacteria, thereby encouraging phagocytosis by leucocytes. An example of the necessity for opsonization is given by the encapsulated pneumococcus, which owes its virulence to its outer capsule which provides the bacterium with a "non-wettable" surface that inhibits close surface approximation with the leucocyte.

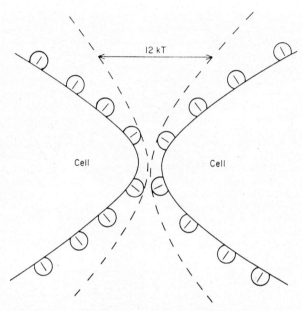

Fig. 4.21. Fusion of two cells requires the overcoming of the mutual repulsion caused by their net electrical charges. The energy for this may be considerably reduced if the cells form minute villous projections. Thus the cells depicted in the figure could approach to within 5 Å, if their projections had a radius of curvature of 0·1 μ, as a result of Brownian movement which could provide an interaction energy of 12 kT, T being the absolute temperature and k the Boltzmann constant. (Bangham, *Ann. N. Y. Acad. Sci.* 1964, **116,** 945.)

When studied in cell suspensions *in vitro*, it is found that encapsulated pneumococci are not phagocytosed by leucocytes, although non-encapsulated ones are. Thus *in vivo* the opsonins, probably composed not only of antibody but also of complement, since they may usually be inactivated by treatment at 56°C, modify the surface of the particle, permitting the close association with the leucocyte's surface required for endocytosis. Where artificial particles are concerned, e.g. latex beads, some sort of "opsonization" is almost invariably required; thus it was found by Fenn that if such particles were placed in blood plasma they became phagocytosable, but not otherwise.

Surface Tension. An additional and very important factor is the interfacial tension; if this is low the surfaces are said to be "wettable" and contact is favoured. The reason for this is understood when it is

Fig. 4.22. Scanning electron micrograph of polymorphonuclear leucocyte, incubated for 1 hour with zymosan. Arrows indicate phagocytic cups. These cups have an inside diameter of approximately 2 μ and a wall thickness of 0·4 to 0·6 μ; each cell has several. (Weismann *et al.*, *Am. J. Path.*, 1972, **68**, 539.

remembered that a system tends to adopt a state with a minimal energy; if the interfacial tension is high the energy of the surface of contact is high and the two bodies tend to restrict their area of contact. With a low interfacial tension, just the opposite takes place. It is reasonable to assume that the opsonins act in this way.

Formation of Cups. We may assume that contact is the stimulus for invagination of the cell membrane to form a cup; this process may be followed in the scanning electron microscope and is illustrated in Fig. 4.22. Here the several cups on a single leucocyte are shown; during fixation the granular material to which the leucocyte was exposed has fallen out of the cups. The tremendous deformation of the cell that takes place during formation of these cups indicates the action of contractile protein within the cytoplasm, and this may be why cytochalasin B, a bacterial product, reduces phagocytosis of bacteria, inhibiting the intracellular contractile mechanism.

Immobilization. Wood observed in the lungs of infected rats that many encapsulated bacteria were, in fact, phagocytosed in the alveoli in spite of the fact that antibodies had not yet been formed, so that opsonization was unlikely to have occurred. He deduced that it was the crowding of the leucocytes in the individual alveoli that improved their chances of phagocytosis, and he proved this by preparing dense suspensions of leucocytes, which were able to phagocytose bacteria without any extraneous opsonins. Thus an important step in phagocytosis seems to be the immobilization of the leucocyte; this can be achieved by tight packing, so that the particles are engulfed in the sparse intercellular spaces between the engulfing cells. A second line of defence is provided by the lymph nodes; when bacteria escape from the original lesion into the blood in appreciable quantities the lymph nodes become stuffed with phagocytic cells, and this favours engulfment. Finally, within blood vessels themselves, infection may be accompanied by stickiness of the endothelial wall, revealed by the tendency for leucocytes to adhere; in this condition they can be seen, *in vivo*, to phagocytose encapsulated bacilli without the help of antibodies (opsonins), the organisms being first trapped against the wall of the vessel or against adjacent leucocytes. A further factor favouring phagocytosis is the immobilization of the leucocytes with strands of fibrin when inflammation has been accompanied by blood-clotting.

The Humoral Inflammatory Agents

Histamine

Lewis described the humoral agent in the tissue responsible for the local vasodilatation and increased capillary permeability as H-substance, which he identified with histamine.

This amine which, when injected into the skin, causes a dilatation of the small blood vessels and local oedema, is synthesized within most tissues of the body by decarboxylation of the amino acid histidine:

$$
\begin{array}{cc}
\underset{\text{Histidine}}{\text{HOOCCHCH}_2}\overset{\displaystyle NH_2}{\big|}
\;\underset{\text{Histidine}}{\overbrace{\substack{H\\N\\HC\quad CH\\C\;—\;N}}}
&
\underset{\text{Histamine}}{NH_2CH_2CH_2}\;\underset{\text{Histamine}}{\overbrace{\substack{H\\N\\HC\quad CH\\C\;—\;N}}}
\end{array}
$$

Mast Cells. A well established site of accumulation of histamine is within the mast cells.* These free connective-tissue cells are closely associated with the blood vessels of a tissue, and their striking feature is the large number of granules within their cytoplasm. When an animal is treated with the histamine-releasing compound, Compound 48–80, there is a striking reduction in the number of granules within the mast cells—"degranulation"—so that they appear much smaller. Recovery is associated with increasing numbers of granules, and possibly with reproduction of the cells by mitotic division, since Fawcett observed many pairs of cells during the recovery phase. It has been customary to consider the mast cells as the sites of release of histamine at the time that it exerts its physiological functions, so that during an anaphylactic response, for example, it is considered that in some way the mast cells are induced to release their stores.

Histamine Forming Capacity. Modern work, pioneered by Kahlson and Schayer, however, has drawn attention to the capacity of tissues to synthesize histamine locally through the action of histidine carboxylase—the *histamine forming capacity* or *HFC*. On this view, histamine exerts its main functions—whatever these may be—largely in consequence of a stimulus to synthesis, so that Kahlson speaks of "nascent histamine" as the likely functional material, the large accumulations in mast cells representing a clearing up process that maintains the tissues relatively free of this highly active material. However, the histamine involved in anaphylactic responses does come from the mast cells, since these show degranulation; nevertheless, the anaphylactic responses outlive the period of histamine release, and it has been argued that the more prolonged responses are due to the activation of synthesis of nascent histamine. This is shown by measuring the ability of the individual tissues to synthesize histamine from histidine. As Fig. 4.23 shows, in respect to the tuberculin reaction, there is a very large increase in HFC some 12 hours after the challenge. The figure shows,

---

* The platelets of some species contain histamine as well as serotonin; the histamine is released spontaneously from platelets suspended in a balanced saline medium, a process that can be inhibited by removal of Ca^{2+}. The anticoagulant, heparin, opposes release, perhaps by reducing the amount of ionized Ca^{2+}.

incidentally, that the actual histamine content of the skin is reduced. In this way we can explain the poor effectiveness of antihistamine agents in immune reactions; they are able to alleviate the initial effects of mast cell release but are unable to attack the nascent histamine formed within the other cells of the body.

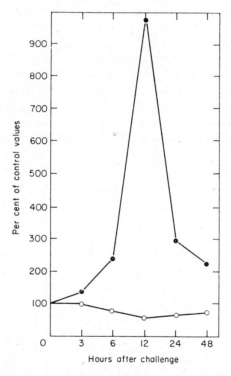

Fig. 4.23. Histamine-forming capacity (HFC) (●) and histamine content (○) of tuberculin skin reactions expressed as percentage of control. (Graham and Schild, *Immunology*, 1967, **12**, 125).

Permeability Increase. The actual mechanism of oedema formation by histamine is twofold, namely through increased vascular pressures in small vessels leading to increased filtration and also through increased permeability of the small vessels allowing an escape of protein into the interstitial spaces. It was originally thought that the capillaries were the site of increased protein leak, but the electron microscopical studies of Majno and Palade have shown that it is the venules that show the first signs of escape of large molecular weight material, and only later, when the reaction is more severe, do the capillaries, proper, become involved.

Other Functions. It is probably true to say that the immune response is the only physiological reaction in which histamine has been unequivocally proved to play a part, but this may be because this involves predominantly preformed histamine liberated from mast cells, whilst other involvements of histamine may be through alterations in synthesis within the cells of the organ concerned. Thus the secretion of acid by the stomach may be provoked by histamine and in fact this is the usual way of doing so experimentally. As we shall see in Vol. 3, the involvement in physiologically induced secretion is by no means certain, but if it is involved, it is through alterations in histamine forming capacity. Histamine is present in the pituitary gland and hypothalamus. Since there are no mast cells in the hypothalamus it is presumably within the neurones or glial cells, and may well be concerned in synaptic transmission; at any rate the brain tissue is capable of synthesizing histamine; and its distribution within the brain is remarkably similar to that of 5-HT, another amine concentrated in mast cells.

Kinins

Whether or not histamine is an important chemical mediator in inflammation as argued by Schayer, there is little doubt that other agents may also contribute, in particular the kinins. Thus examination of the fluid exudates in inflammatory loci reveals the presence of non-histamine substances that cause vasodilatation and increased vascular permeability.

Bradykinins. Of these, the kinins are peptides derived by enzymatic splitting from an α-globulin of the blood plasma. Thus *bradykinin* has been prepared by the action of trypsin on plasma. It is a nona-peptide:

$$\text{Arg.Pro.Pro.Gly.Phe.Ser.Pro.Phe.Arg}$$

whilst the product formed by the enzyme *kallikrein*, is a decapeptide, *lysyl-bradykinin*. A third active substance contains a further amino acid, and is *methionyl-lysyl-bradykinin*. All these substances have physiological actions that may well implicate them in inflammation, and the close involvement of the formation of kinins with the clotting and plasmin systems, as indicated by Fig. 4.24, makes this very likely.

Thus the active enzyme forming kinins in blood, is kallikrein; this has to be activated from an inactive precursor, and this activation can be achieved apparently by either Hageman factor, or plasmin. Kinin formation occurs when plasma comes into contact with glass; this activates the Hageman factor which then activates the kallikrein precursor, which has been called *kallikreinogen*. In the saliva and urine the enzyme is already active, and it is customary to call the product of kallikrein on plasma, *kallidin*, which is identical with lysyl-bradykinin.

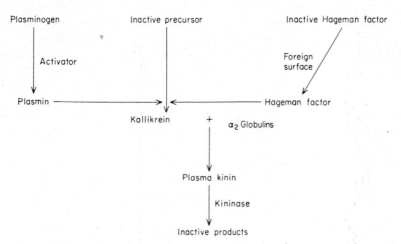

Fig. 4.24. The plasma kinin system, emphasizing the relation to the clotting mechanism. (Lewis, *Ann. N.Y. Acad. Sci.*, 1964, **116**, 847.)

Venoms

The venoms of insects, snakes, etc. are mixtures of highly pharmacologically active substances such as 5-HT, histamine, acetylcholine, etc. and as a result produce severe local reactions consisting of vasodilatation and tissue oedema. Amongst the potent compounds are peptides, such as the nonapeptide, bradykinin, illustrated above. The undecapeptide elesoidin:

Pyr–Pro–Ser–Lys–Asp–Ala–Phe–Ileu–Gly–Leu–Met NH$_2$

is a constituent of the salivary secretions of molluscan octapods, whilst the kinin from the wasp, *Polistes*, is a chain of 18 amino acids, the terminal nine being bradykinin. *Cerulein* is a higher molecular weight compound extracted from the skins of some Australian amphibians. Like bradykinin and elesoidin, it has a potent and long-lasting hypotensive effect due to its powerful vasodilator activity. It is of special interest since it has the same C-terminal pentapeptide as that of the digestive hormones gastrin and CCK-pancreozymin, i.e. (Vol. 3)

Gly–Try–Met–Asp–Phe NH$_2$.

Neurotoxins. The lethal effects of most snake venoms are due to so-called neurotoxins, which are curare-like, producing flaccid paralysis and respiratory failure. These are peptides of considerably higher molecular weight, so that some fall into the class of proteins, such as β-bungarotoxin and crotoxin, with molecular weights greater than 10,000. The action may be of the curare type, at the neuromuscular junction, preventing development of end-plate potentials and the spike, or the effect may be presynaptic, reducing release of acetylcholine but not affecting sensitivity of the end-plate to applied acetylcholine. Of special interest is the venomous principle of the Japanese puffer fish, *Spheroides rubripes*, which has been named tetrodotoxin; this is non-polypeptide and specifically blocks the activated Na^+-permeability at the basis of the axon or muscle spike. It has proved useful experimentally because it leaves the development of end-plate and synaptic potentials unaffected and so allows a specific block of axonal conduction.

Haemolytic Agents. Some snake venoms cause haemolysis of red cells, an effect attributed to *phospholipase A*, which apparently acts on the blood lecithin splitting off a haemolytic material that subsequently causes haemolysis. The so-called direct lytic factor in venom (DLF) is not phospholipase A but a *cardiotoxin*; by itself it is only weakly haemolytic but it acts synergistically with phospholipase A.

Immune Inflammation

Histamine and plasma kinins may be involved in all forms of immune inflammatory reactions. Thus the *anaphylotoxins* are polypeptides derived from complement in the immune reaction, and they probably act by stimulating histamine release from mast cells. The polymorphonuclear leucocyte, as indicated earlier, may well be involved in the inflammatory response by liberating its hydrolytic enzymes. This might occur during phagocytosis, since Weissmann has described, in the electron microscope, how a granule may pour its contents into the phagosome while it is forming, i.e. before connection with the outside of the phagocyte has been broken, as illustrated in Fig. 4.25. It may well be that in many disease states, e.g. in rheumatism and gout, the large infiltration of granulocytes is accompanied by release of these hydrolytic enzymes.

Effects of Colchicine. It has been argued, on this basis, that the beneficial effects of colchicine in the treatment of gout are due to preventing this release. Thus the migration of a phagocyte granule to the phagosome, to pour its contents into it, is considered to be brought about by microtubular action, and since the processes that apparently depend on this type of mechanism (e.g., mitosis, vesicular transport along nerve axons, etc.) are inhibited by colchicine, this is invoked as an explanation for the beneficial effect. There is no doubt that lysosomal enzymes, when they leak into the tissue matrix, may do damage. Thus, the degradation of tissue cartilage caused by vitamin A is brought about by the release of proteases from the cartilage cell lysosomes.

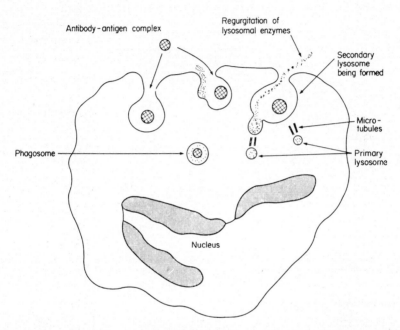

Fig. 4.25. The leucocyte is phagocytosing antibody–antigen complex. Before phagocytosis is complete, a lysosome may fuse with the forming phagosome so that its enzymes can escape into the extracellular medium instead of being confined to the phagolysosome. (After Weissman *et al.*, *Am. J. Path.*, 1972, **68,** 539.)

Frustrated Phagocytosis. This tendency for lysosomes to extrude their enzymes out of the cell may be provoked experimentally by placing an immune complex on a surface that cannot be engulfed, e.g. by entrapping it in the pores of a glass filter. The leucocytes attempt to engulf the complex and, in doing so, regurgitate enzymes into the medium. Since cytoplasmic enzymes, as opposed to those contained in lysosomes, were not regurgitated, it was concluded that the process occurred by exocytosis, as in glandular secretion (Fig. 4.26).

Platelets

Besides leucocytes, platelets have been suspected of releasing inflammatory factors; this is likely since they contain all the serotonin of blood and this may be liberated by thrombin. A large molecular weight factor—a cationic protein—that increases vascular permeability has been extracted from platelets. Its action seems to be through damage to mast cells, however, and so it operates through histamine.

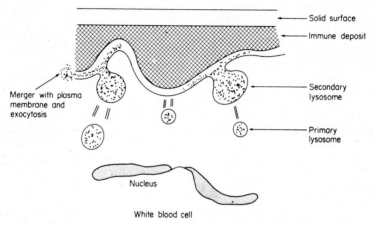

Fig. 4.26. Illustrating reverse endocytosis of lysosomal enzymes from white blood cells engulfing immune deposits on a surface. (After Weissman *et al.*, *Am. J. Path.*, 1972, **68**, 539.)

Anti-Inflammatory Agents

Corticosteroids and their synthetic analogues, e.g. 9 α-chlorhydrocortisone, are used widely to ameliorate inflammation. According to Schayer, their mechanism of action is to alter the balance between vasodilator and vasoconstrictor influences in the tissue by reducing the synthesis of inducible histamine forming capacity (HFC).

THE IMMUNE RESPONSE

Active and Passive Immunity

It is well known that a previous invasion of the body by foreign agents such as viruses and bacteria leads to an acquired resistance to a second invasion. This is due to presence in the blood of special proteins called *antibodies* that have been formed in response to the first attack; some of these remain in the circulation, whilst the antibody-producing mechanism is geared for further rapid production of the same antibodies. The animal so infected is said to have acquired an *active immunity* to the antigen that has invaded it, by contrast with the *passive immunity* that results from merely supplying the animal with antibodies formed by another, immune, animal. Thus it is well known (p. 437) that the newborn child has a temporary immunity to many infections, such as measles and mumps; this is due to its passive immunity obtained through the maternal circulation across the placenta. The passive immunity may be of short length because of the limited life of the antibodies; and without the induction, by an attack of antigen, there are no cells that have been "taught" or specially "geared" to make antibodies to this particular antigen. Thus the difference between active and passive immunity is essentially the possession of cells that are geared to produce antibody to the particular antigen.

Antigens

In general, the ability to call forth an immune reaction depends on the chemical character of the foreign material; proteins make good antigens, as do many polysaccharides, especially those containing amino sugars. Thus the antigenicity of many viruses and bacteria depends on the presence on their surfaces of specific proteins; the antigenicity of erythrocytes, on the other hand, depends on the presence of relatively short chains of polysaccharide comprising hexoses and hexosamines attached to proteins or lipids constituting part of the cell surface, these proteins and lipids acting only as carriers for the antigen. The bacterium *Salmonella* contains its antigenicity in its flagellum, so that extracts of flagella will provoke an immune response.

Active Grouping. Moreover, the antigenicity of a molecule, such as a protein, depends only on quite a small part of it. Thus we may take gastrins from several species, all of which are capable of showing gastrin activity and all with very similar amino acid sequences. Yet we may prepare antibodies to them separately because the antigenic character of the gastrin molecule is not determined by the same sequence of amino acids that determines its enzymatic character, the latter depending on the terminal pentapeptide. It is for this reason that it is possible to make antibodies to the protein hormones, such as growth-hormone, and employ them in the assay of the hormone; human growth-hormone differs slightly in its amino acid sequence from, say, rabbit growth-hormone, so that injection of the human material into a rabbit will produce anti-human growth-hormone antibodies which may be used in radio-immunoassay (p. 149). In a similar way the antigens on erythrocytes determining their compatibility (p. 369) rely on only a few carbohydrate molecules for their specificity, the attached protein being merely a carrier.

Haptens. It is well known that certain substances with quite low molecular weights evoke what appears to be an immune response after previous sensitization. Thus some people respond with an anaphylaxis type of reaction to penicillin; repeated application of many chemicals, such as picryl chloride, to the skin produces a condition of sensitivity so that a single application produces a severe inflammation. In these conditions the foreign chemical reacts with the animal's protein, which acts as a carrier for it, the foreign chemical being described as a *hapten*.

Soluble and Particulate Antigens. It is customary to divide antigens into soluble and particulate types but the difference reflects rather the type of immune response than the fundamental nature of the antigen stimulus. Thus injection of a soluble protein leads to the formation of antibody to this protein, which reacts with it and usually causes it to precipitate—the so-called *precipitin reaction*; in this pre-cipitated condition it can be removed by phagocytic cells, which cooperate in the immune reaction. Particulate antigen, such as bacteria or an engrafted foreign tissue, will also produce soluble antibodies but their reaction with the solid antigen is reflected in a different way; bacteria are usually agglutinated, i.e. forced by a change in their surface characters to come together into clumps. In this agglutinated condition they may be effectively phagocytosed by scavenger cells.

Phagocytosis and Complement

In general the production of antibody, and its reaction with antigen, are the basic features of the immune response; after this reaction other factors may be brought into play, such as phagocytosis and complement, with the result that the reaction product is eliminated.

Complement. This is the name given to a group of some eleven proteins of the globulin class, which, in the presence of the antigen–antibody complex, undergo a series of reactions that, if occurring in the vicinity of the cell membrane, cause damage to it. In addition, the products of these reactions may cause release of factors that contribute to the inflammatory reaction to injury or infection, e.g. the release of histamine from mast cells and the production of kinins that increase vascular permeability and provoke the migration of leucocytes. The action of antibody is best demonstrated by the haemolysis of foreign erythrocytes brought about by an immune serum. Thus we may sensitize a rabbit to sheep's erythrocytes by injecting these into its circulation. The serum, of the rabbit now contains antibodies to the sheep's cells, so that when these cells are mixed with the rabbit's serum, they go into clumps—agglutination—and subsequently they haemolyse, provided the complement, normally in the serum, has not been destroyed. If the serum is heated to 56°C, the complement is destroyed, and the cells do not haemolyse. Haemolysis can be brought about by simply adding serum, that of the guinea pig being used most frequently because of its high complement content. Thus complement is a series of proteins that, when activated by the antigen–antibody reaction, finally produce materials that are damaging to the cell. As with the clotting mechanism it is important that this mechanism be held in check under normal conditions, and, as with the clotting system, this is achieved by the interposition of many reaction stages between the initial activation of the first component in the chain, namely Cl, and the final production of the components C8 and C9. The details of these steps will be briefly reviewed later (p. 365).

Antibodies

Antibodies are gamma-globulins and, like the other gamma-globulins of the blood, they belong to three main classes, indicated by γM, γG and γA. γM has a molecular weight of about one million whilst γG and γA have smaller molecular weights in the region of 160,000. The antibody globulins are indicated by the prefix I, so that we have IγM, IγG and IγA. IγM is typically the first produced in an immune response, and is regarded as the phylogenetically oldest antibody; IγG is usually the dominant class in an immune response.

Light and Heavy Chains

The gamma-globulins are made up of pairs of light and heavy chains (Fig. 4.27). Common to all the classes, M, G and A, are the light chains which are of two kinds, K (kappa) and γ (lambda) whilst the heavy chains are of one type, and thus determine its class, being characterized as γ, a and μ. Thus the formulae, in terms of chains, for the gamma-globulins are:

$$\kappa_2\gamma_2 \text{ or } \lambda_2\gamma_2 \equiv \gamma\text{G}; \ \kappa_2a_2 \text{ or } \lambda_2a_2 = \gamma\text{A}; \ (\kappa_2\mu_2)_n \text{ or } (\lambda_2\mu_2)_n = \gamma\text{M}$$

e.g. $\kappa_2\gamma_2$ means that there are two identical kappa-chains linked with two identical gamma-chains. It is the light chains that confer specificity on the immunoglobulin molecules, so that $\kappa_2\gamma_2$ is immunologically different from $\lambda_2\gamma_2$.

Myeloma Proteins

The light and heavy chains are synthesized separately and joined together within the antibody-producing cell. However, in the patho-logical condition of myeloma, where there is abnormal proliferation of bone-marrow cells, the light and heavy chains appear free in the blood in large amounts; because of their low molecular weight the light chains are excreted in the urine where they are described as *Bence–Jones proteins*, whilst the heavy chains remain in the blood as pathological *myeloma globulins*. In a normal response to antigen, the antibodies produced are very heterogeneous, being not only distributed through the three main classes but through subclasses and variations on these that defy separation into single components, so that the

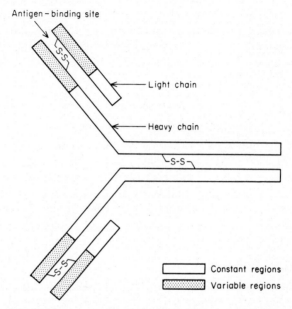

Fig. 4.27. Schematic representation of a gamma globulin molecule. It consists of two light chains and two heavy chains joined by disulphide linkage. The variable regions are indicated in stipple. The antigen-binding sites lie at the end of the variable region and require both light and heavy chain. (Weiss, "The Cells and Tissues of the Immune System", Prentice-Hall.)

determination of the primary structure of the chains, i.e. their amino acid sequences, has not proved feasible. However, the abnormal myeloma proteins are, by contrast, homogeneous, belonging to the γ- and β-classes. Consequently it has been possible to determine the complete sequences of Bence–Jones proteins, i.e. light chains, from different individuals.

Bence–Jones Protein. As indicated above, the light chains fall into two classes, called kappa and lambda, the two from a given subject having different antigenic characters and, corresponding with this, greatly different amino acid sequences. When the light chains of one or other class, kappa or lambda, are examined in a series of individuals it is found that the sequence of amino acids, amounting to some 214, can be divided into two halves, one being invariant in

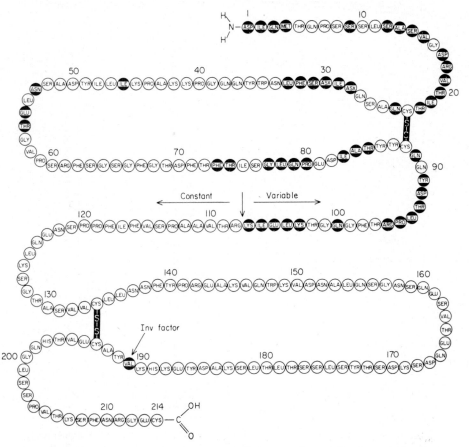

Fig. 4.28. Amino acid sequence of the human κ Bence–Jones protein Ag. The black circles mark variable loci, where different amino acids have been found in other human κ Bence–Jones proteins. Note that the correct sequence of positions 7 and 8 is Ser–Pro. (Putnam *et al.*, *Cold Spring Harb. Symp. quant. Biol.*, 1967, **32**, 9).

respect to sequence and the other showing variations of a random character from one subject to another; this is illustrated in Fig. 4.28 for a human kappa Bence–Jones protein, the black circles marking loci where different amino acids have been found.

Heavy Chains. The heavy chains of the immunoglobulins differ from the light chains not only in molecular weight—they do not share the same antigenic characters of the light chains and they contain carbohydrate. When the amino acid sequences in given lengths of light and heavy chains are compared, there are some remarkable

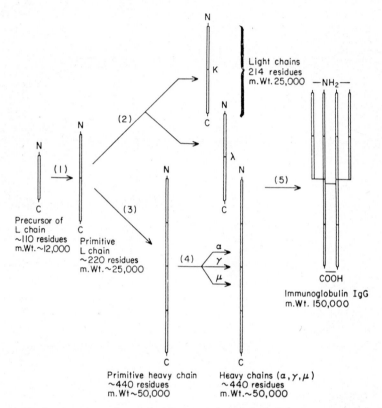

Fig. 4.29. A tentative scheme for the genetic origins of the immunoglobulins. (Putnam *et al.*, *Cold Spring Harb. Symp. quant. Biol.*, 1967, **32**, 9).

coincidences, suggesting a common origin through a more primitive gene that determined the sequence of a primitive chain. This idea is illustrated in Fig. 4.29 where the chains are considered to be derived phylogenetically from a precursor-chain of 110-residues; by doubling, this could become a primitive light chain of 220 residues and thence, by loss of six, it could become the kappa and lambda chains of today or, by doubling yet again, the heavy chains of 440 residues, which were subsequently modified to form the basis for the heavy chains of the M, G and A globulins.

Heterogeneity

As indicated above, the antibodies produced in an animal in response to a single antigen represent a very complex mixture of globulins. This is probably because they are derived from groups of different cells, all responding to the antigen but producing slightly different proteins. In the pathological condition it seems that there has been abnormal proliferation of one type of cell, thereby giving rise to a more uniform production.

Sensitivity

Although the phenomena of immunology are diverse, they can be summarized quite simply in terms of a sensitivity (or hypersensitivity) to the presence of certain, usually foreign, material in the organism. Sensitivity already exists, and is manifest as the primary response to an antigen met for the first time; *hypersensitivity* is revealed by the response to a second meeting, and it is with this aspect of the immune response that we must mainly concern ourselves here.

Hypersensitivity

It is sufficient, then, if we discuss the general phenomena of hypersensitivity and the associated formation of antibodies. Hypersensitivity is divided by immunologists into two classes, namely an *immediate* and *delayed*. Thus we may sensitize an animal to an antigen by giving it a single injection; this, the primary response to antigen, leads to the production of circulating—*humoral*—antibody in the sensitized animal. When, after a period of some days, a second injection of the antigen is given into the skin there is an immediate local inflammation, the so-called *Arthus reaction*, due to the arrival of circulating antibody—this represents *immediate hypersensitivity* and may be transferred to another animal by injections of its plasma. It represents the basis of anaphylaxis and *serum sickness*.

Delayed Hypersensitivity. Delayed hypersensitivity is revealed after a delay of perhaps 6–8 hours after the immediate response has subsided; it appears as a second inflammatory response and may last for days. It differs fundamentally from immediate hypersensitivity in that its manifestations are not dependent on blood-borne "humoral" antibodies but on the migration to the site of injection of lymphoid cells. The hypersensitivity is transferable from one animal to another *only* by transfer of sensitized lymphocytes; apparently these cells carry some "transfer" factor that brings about the skin reaction, a factor that may be isolated experimentally. It is considered that the rejection of a graft is the result of this delayed hypersensitivity response, the prime feature of rejection being the infiltration of the foreign tissue by lymphocytes which secrete their antibodies locally. In some diseases the predominant response to the invading organism is the production of humoral antibodies, and these are sufficient to combat the disease, as in pneumococcal infections; in others, e.g. tuberculosis, delayed hypersensitivity is the main response.

Bursa of Fabricius

The capacity to produce humoral antibody evolved in early vertebrates and represents an efficient means of controlling widely dispersed microorganisms, relatively few cells producing large numbers of immunoglobulin molecules. The cell-mediated immunity, at the basis of the delayed hypersensitivity, is a more primitive reaction evolving in invertebrates; it can deal effectively with localized invasions, as with tubercle bacilli which tend to proliferate locally, but is less efficient against widely distributed invasive material. It is interesting that in birds these two types of immune reaction are controlled by different organs. The *bursa of Fabricius*, which originates as a diverticulum from the posterior cloacal wall, controls antibody production and is therefore concerned in immediate hypersensitivity, whilst the cellular type of immunity, manifest in delayed hypersensitivity, is controlled by the thymus.*

Anaphylaxis and Serum Sickness

Immediate hypersensitivity is the basis for these reactions; anaphylaxis has been described earlier, the vascular and other responses being due to the formation of antigen–antibody complexes after a preliminary sensitization. In serum sickness, only a single, but large, injection of foreign serum is adequate to cause a series of symptoms including swollen joints and urticaria. These are due to the persistence of antigen in the circulation for some days, during which time antibodies are being formed; these form complexes with the still circulating antigen, and it is these complexes that provoke the inflammatory response.

---

* In higher vertebrates, lacking a bursa of Fabricius, the division of function by two types of lymphocyte has been postulated, but the equivalent source of "bursal" lymphocytes remains to be demonstrated.

Tissue Grafting

A piece of tissue, say skin, may be grafted from an individual of the same species to another—the *homograft*. After a time, in spite of an initial blending with the host tissue, the graft is "rejected", due to the migration of antibody-forming cells whose reaction with the graft leads to an eventual sloughing off. Here, the foreign tissue is acting as a continual source of antigen leading to the formation of antibodies that ultimately cause its destruction. As indicated, graft rejection is a manifestation of delayed hypersensitivity, relying on cell migration to the antigenic site.*

Production of Antibodies

The Lymphocyte and Plasma Cell

The cell that produces antibody belongs to the class of lymphocytes, so that when an animal responds to an antigen it is found that the antibody accumulates first of all in the lymph nodes and the white pulp of the spleen. This accumulation of antibodies is associated with the multiplication of cells in the germinal centres with later accumulation in the surrounding zones. The multiplication of lymphocytes is accompanied by a morphological change, i.e. with the appearance of new types of cell probably derived from a "normal" lymphocyte, changes that ultimately lead to the mature *plasma cell*. Faegreus observed that maximum production of antibody occurred when large "transitional" cells were preponderant, and suggested that these cells produced antibody maximally, the mature plasma cell producing less.

Transitional Stages. In the electron microscope, cells probably corresponding to the various stages in transformation from a lymphocytic cell, acting as precursor to the plasma cell, through the "blast" and transitional stages, may be recognized essentially as stages in the development of endoplasmic reticulum or protein-synthesizing capacity, as illustrated in Fig. 4.30. Antibody within the cell can be recognized by use of a suitable antigen that may be recognized in the electron microscope; thus horseradish peroxidase evokes the production of antibodies to it, and if lymphocytes from sensitized animals are treated with this compound it complexes with the antibody within the cell in a histological preparation and may be subsequently visualized. If it is appreciated that very few cells of a population produce antibody to a particular antigen, the chances of finding one for electron microscopy are small, so that it is not easy, by random selection, to assess the types

---

* Tissue grafted from the same subject—the *autograft*—is, on the other hand, successfully retained due to the absence of an immune response.

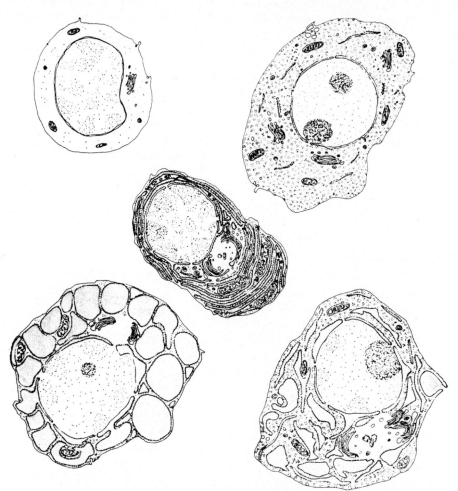

Fig. 4.30. Several stages in the life cycle of plasma cells. At the upper left is a cell, lymphocyte in form, which may be a plasma cell precursor. The upper right hand cell is a "blast" form. It has polyribosomes, segments of RER, nucleoli, nuclear pores, and other cellular elements indicative of protein synthesis. Antibody may be present in the perinuclear space and in the lumen of the RER. The lower cells, right and left, are clearly plasmacytic, of intermediate or transitional character. They have dilated perinuclear spaces and dilated ER both containing antibody. Indeed, the continuity of the outer nuclear membrane and the ER is shown. The cell in the centre is the classic small plasma cell, Marshalko cell, displaying polarized nucleus and cytoplasm, distribution of heterochromatin in chunks along the inner nuclear membrane, prominent cytocentrum including Golgi and centrioles, and deeply basophilic or pyroninophilic (RNA) cytoplasm. This cell is a near terminal form, past the peak of antibody production. The intermediate cells turn out most of the antibody. (Weiss, "The Cells and Tissues of the Immune System", Prentice-Hall.)

of cell that produce antibody and those that do not. This difficulty was avoided by Harris who employed Jerne's haemolytic plaque technique (p. 353) since it had been shown that each plaque contained in its centre a single antibody-producing cell. Thus every cell chosen was an antibody-producer and it was possible to show whether they were all of a particular type. In fact, the lymphocytes, so identified, showed varying degrees of development of the endoplasmic reticulum, corresponding to the successive stages shown in Fig. 4.30. The actual liberation of the antibody into the surrounding medium is probably achieved by exocytosis.

Response in Sensitized Animal

The cellular response to a second injection of the antigen, i.e. when the animal is sensitized, follows the same pattern but more rapidly and vigorously, especially in the germinal centres, which may therefore

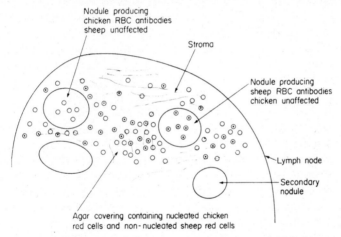

Fig. 4.31. Illustrating the experiment by Young and Friedman. (Young and Friedman, *In* "Germinal Centre in Immune Responses", Ed. C. Cottier *et al.*, 1967, Springer, New York.

be the site of "memory", i.e. the more rapid response, with production of more antibody than in an animal not pre-sensitized. By fragmenting spleen and estimating antibody production of different parts, it is found that the regions showing memory are the germinal centres, which presumably accumulate "memory cells".

Clones. It is considered that the response to a given antigen leaves behind a group, or "clone", of cells that can respond immediately to the same antigen by synthesizing antibodies to it. This was neatly demonstrated by Young and Friedman who examined the production of antibodies by histological sections of lymph nodes from animals sensitized to both sheep and chicken erythrocytes. The section was covered by agar gel containing the two types of erythrocyte, and it was found that antibodies of only one type were released from a given secondary nodule, as revealed by the haemolysis of only one type of red cell (Fig. 4.31).

Cooperation between Cells

The production of antibody in response to antigen is a complex process usually requiring the cooperation of two or three types of cell, which must be in close proximity, or "clusters". In general, we may divide the phenomenon into an "antigen-recognition" process, carried out by one type of cell, and an "antibody-production" process triggered off in another cell by the former. In addition, there may be an "antigen-processing cell", a macrophage which engulfs the antigen and ultimately releases some factor—a modified antigen—that then reacts with the antigen-recognizing cell. It must be emphasized that immune reactions show a wide spectrum of behaviour so that it may well be that one, two or three cells are involved in a given response. The cooperation between cells has been revealed by the use of two main types of experiment. In the one, suspensions of cells may be studied *in vitro*, since it is possible to cause antigen–antibody responses in, say, a suspension of mouse spleen cells containing predominantly lymphocytes and macrophages. In the second type of experiment an animal's powers of immune reaction are destroyed by lethal irradiation; if the dose is strong enough, the dividing stem-cells of the haemopoietic tissues are destroyed* and unless the tissues are repopulated by new cells the animal is incapable of forming antibodies. We may thus inject the irradiated animal with a given type of cell, and see whether it can now respond to antigens by antibody formation.

Haemolytic Plaque Technique. *In vitro* studies are especially valuable since it is possible to identify antibody-forming cells by the consequences of this formation. Thus we may spread a suspension of a mouse's cells, suspected of forming antibody to sheep's erythrocytes, together with these erythrocytes, on a microscope slide; the suspension is caused to solidify by incorporation of agarose in the medium. After a time, if antibodies are being formed and if complement has been added, haemolytic plaques appear, i.e. localized spots where the erythrocytes

---

* Cells are sensitive to X- and γ-radiations when dividing, because the DNA becomes vulnerable under these conditions; thus the tissues likely to suffer most are those containing rapidly dividing cells, such as the gonads, the lens of the eye, and bone-marrow.

are being haemolysed; each plaque contains at its centre a single antibody-producing cell (Fig. 4.32).

Involvement of Macrophages. With this technique Mosier showed that, if the macrophages were separated* from a suspension of mouse spleen cells before exposure to sheep's erythrocytes as antigen, there were no antibody-forming cells. Addition of macrophages which had been exposed to sheep erythrocytes, to a suspension of spleen cells from which the macrophages had been removed, and consisting of

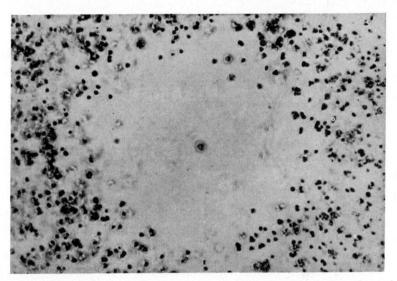

Fig. 4.32. The formation of plaques as a result of antibody reaction with red blood cells in the presence of complement. Each plaque contains at its centre a single antibody-producing cell. (Jerne and Nordin, *Science, N.Y.*, 1963, **140**, 405.)

lymphocytes, resulted in formation of plaques, but it was found that the lymphocytes, and not the macrophages, were producing the antibodies. Indirect evidence was provided suggesting that two lymphocytes had to cooperate with a macrophage in order to produce antibody. Subsequent studies on the same system by Fishman showed that material extracted from the macrophage, after it had ingested the antigen, was adequate to permit activation of the lymphocytes in

* This separation was achieved by observing that certain cells of the suspension stuck to the plastic dish, and these were the macrophages. Another method of fractionation consists in centrifuging the suspension in a gradient of specific gravity, as in the separation of particulate fractions from tissue homogenates. In this case the specific gravity of the medium is increased by adding varying amounts of serum albumin, thereby avoiding the large differences of osmotic pressure that would arise from sucrose gradients.

producing antibodies, and the material extracted appeared to be either pure RNA or a combination of this with protein. Thus the suggestion was made that the macrophage synthesized an "informational RNA", which was subsequently absorbed by the antibody-producing cell, which then synthesized antibody with the aid of this "information". This information either acted as a template for synthesis of the antibody or for synthesis of an enzyme, such as an RNA-polymerase, that would allow the necessary messenger RNA to be formed. The situation is by no means clear, however. There is little doubt that the RNA itself may be attached to protein, which is probably a fragment of the antigen molecule, so that the RNA tends rather to act as a vehicle, or "adjuvant" for the antigen, being very similar chemically to RNA extracted from macrophages that had not been exposed to antigen. Pronase, which splits off the protein from the complex, abolished the activity of the remaining RNA.

The Role of the Thymus

A further example of cellular cooperation in the production of antibody is revealed by the function of *thymus-derived lymphocytes*.

Structure of the Thymus

At this point it is useful to describe the thymus and its role in antibody production. In man it is a bilobar structure in the mediastinum coming into close relation with the trachea, being just below the thyroid gland (Fig. 4.33). Perhaps the most significant aspect of its structure is that it attains its maximum size by puberty and then begins to "involute", being invaded by adipose at the expense of true, thymic tissue. The gland consists of an outer cortex and an inner medulla. The basic structure common to both is that of a reticulum made up of epithelial cells, by contrast with the mesenchyme cells that form the basis of the reticula of lymphatic and splenic tissue; the interstices of the reticulum are crammed with lymphocytes and related free cells (Fig. 4.34). Features of unknown significance are the *Hassall corpuscles* in the medulla, spherical bodies formed by the layering of epithelial cells on each other like the scales of an onion; some of these bodies develop a hollow interior.

Thymic Lymphocytes. The lymphocytes of the thymus are of all sizes, ranging from large (15 μ diameter) to small (5–8 μ diameter). These arise by division of stem cells derived from the bone-marrow, so that after lethal irradiation the thymus can only be repopulated by bone-marrow cells. Some 95 per cent of the cells produced in the thymus are short-lived with a life-span of 3–5 days, being destroyed within the thymus; the remainder are long-lived with life-spans of the order of years in man. These cells are released from the thymus and constitute the circulating thymic cells that pass in and out of certain zones of the spleen and lymphatic tissue and contribute significantly to the population of small lymphocytes circulating and recirculating through blood and lymph. They are described as *T cells*, responsible

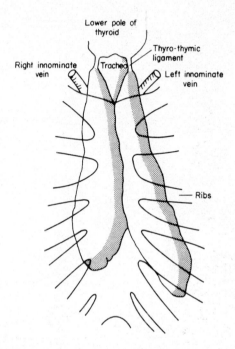

Fig. 4.33. Drawing to show the location of the thymus in the anterior mediastinum and neck. The apices of each thymic lobe are joined to the lower poles of the thyroid gland by the thyrothymic ligaments; the lower thymic poles extend down to the level of the fourth costal cartilages.
(Goldstein and Mackay, "The Human Thymus", Heinemann.)

for delayed hypersensitivity reactions, as in graft rejection (p. 358), and *antigen-sensitive cells* that cooperate with bone-marrow cells in antibody formation.

Bone-Marrow Dependence. Although there is massive division of lymphocytes in the thymus, this organ is dependent on the bone-marrow for a continual supply, and by appropriately marking bone-marrow cells a regular movement can be demonstrated. In the thymus the marrow lymphocytes acquire the power to participate in immune

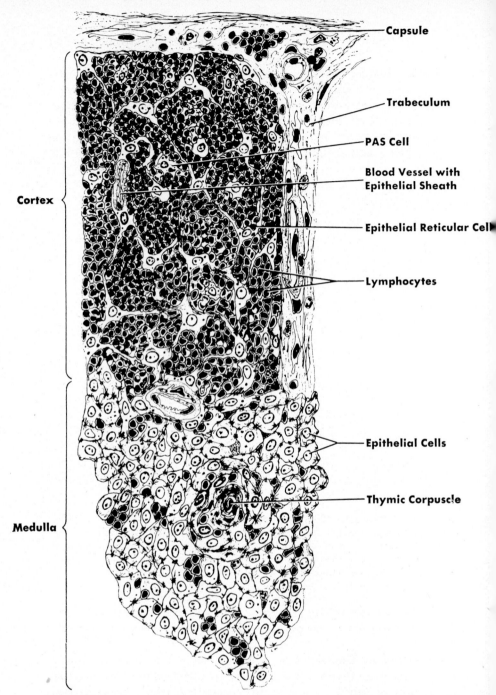

Capsule

Trabeculum

PAS Cell

Blood Vessel with Epithelial Sheath

Epithelial Reticular Cell

Lymphocytes

Epithelial Cells

Thymic Corpuscle

Cortex

Medulla

Fig. 4.34. Portion of a lobule of thymus. The cortex is heavily infiltrated with lymphocytes. (Weiss, "The Cells and Tissues of the Immune System", Prentice-Hall.)

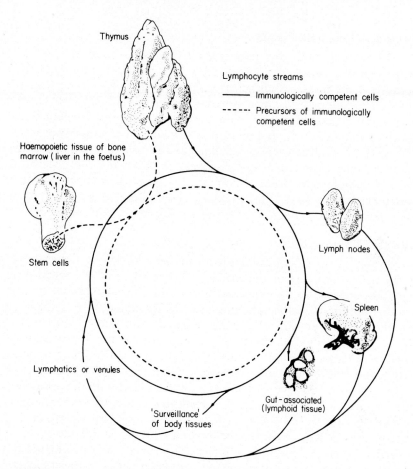

Fig. 4.35. Diagram to show circulation of lymphocytes in the body. Lympho-poietic stem cells arise in the bone marrow and reach the thymus via the blood stream. Within the thymus, stem cells become immunologically competent lymphocytes, emigrate to the blood stream, and circulate between the tissues, lymphatics and blood stream. (Goldstein and Mackay, "The Human Thymus", Heinemann.)

reactions, i.e. they become *competent* cells, a process associated with the acquisition of the theta-antigen on their surface. The basic role of the thymus, then, is illustrated in Fig. 4.35; it receives immunologically incompetent stem cells from the marrow and these, or cells derived from them by division, become, after their residence in the thymus, immunologically competent.

Thymus-dependent Tissue

Cells released from the thymus travel to special thymus-dependent regions of the lymphatic tissue; they are called thymus-dependent because, if the newborn animal is thymectomized, the tissue, which is not fully developed at birth, remains defective. For example, in the spleen the periarterial lymphatic sheaths are poorly developed and poorly populated with lymphocytes; similarly the lymph nodes are defective, a band of cortex just deep to the primary and secondary nodules being depleted of lymphocytes. By following the progress of marked lymphocytes from the thymus, it can be shown that they pass primarily to these *thymic-dependent zones*, and it is here that these immunologically competent cells presumably react with antigen.

Effect of Thymectomy

The role of the thymus remained a mystery for a long time because of the absence of serious deficiencies after removal of the organ from the adult animal. It now appears that by the time the animal is adult it has produced sufficient long-lived immunologically competent lymphocytes to permit it to react normally for some time; it was only when the drastic effects of thymectomy in the newborn were discovered that a clue to the role of the thymus in the immune response was found. Thus a thymectomized newborn animal succumbed to wasting disease and died of generalized infection, due to the absence of any capacity to react to invasive organisms—it was an immunological cripple.

Homograft Rejection. Experimentally this is best demonstrated by studying the animal's ability to reject a homograft of skin, which relies on the migration of immunologically competent cells to the site of the graft (delayed hypersensitivity); animals that had been thymectomized at birth retained the graft by comparison with the normal animal which rejected it after a short period. When the thymus of the adult is removed, the effects are less drastic due to the presence of long-lived T-cells, so that in animals many weeks must elapse before significant deterioration in delayed hypersensitivity, as measured by graft rejection, is demonstrable. If at the same time as thymectomy a non-lethal irradiation of spleen, lymph nodes, bone marrow and remaining lymphatic tissue is given, the animal suffers in the same way as a thymectomized neonate. Thus in adults the thymus has sufficiently stocked the lymphatic system to enable it to function for a long time.

Thymosin. Grafts of thymus allow the neonatally thymectomized animal to survive and to reject skin grafts normally. Since thymus grafts, enclosed by millipore filter, are effective, it has been concluded that the thymus may exert an action in inducing lymphocyte competence through a hormone—*thymosin*—and it has been claimed that injections of extracts of thymus enable thymectomized animals to reject grafts more readily.

Lymphocyte "Rejects"

The interesting feature of the thymus is the rapid, and apparently useless, multiplication of lymphocytes, only some 5 percent leaving the thymus. It has been suggested that there is a protective mechanism that prevents cells from becoming immunoactive against the tissues of the animal's own body; the 95 per cent of cells that die in the thymus are supposed to represent the "rejects", i.e. immunologically competent but reactive against self; in the thymus they are presented with a "library" of the body's antigens and it is argued that the large number of cell-types in the thymus, e.g. the myoid cells, Hassall's corpuscles, are there for this reason.

Marrow and Thymus Cell Cooperation

To return to the matter of cellular cooperation, the importance of thymus-derived lymphocytes in the immune reaction was established by injecting various cell suspensions into lethally irradiated animals, and measuring the recipient's ability to synthesize antibody to sheep erythrocytes or other antigen. Spleen cells or thoracic duct suspensions were able to confer the capacity, but since these are mixtures of several types this tells us little. However, thymic cells alone were unable to confer this capacity nor yet a suspension of bone-marrow cells, but marrow and thymic cells in combination would; thus the thymic cells must cooperate with the marrow cells. Moreover, when the two types of cell are labelled by karyotype marking,* it is found that the antibody-producing cell is derived from the marrow and not the thymus. Thus the thymus-derived cells are responsive to antigen and react in some way on marrow-derived cells, causing them to synthesize and release antibody. This meeting of the two types of cell takes place in the spleen and lymph nodes, the regions where the antigen is trapped.

Lymphocyte Traffic. Thus this type of experiment emphasizes the importance of a traffic of lymphocytes between the various lymphoid tissues. The bone-marrow releases cells which pass directly to the white pulp of spleen and lymph nodes; others pass to the thymus where

---

* By this is meant the choice of an animal strain with some recognizable difference in a chromosome from the normal; cells derived from this animal are recognized whenever they under gomitosis.

they probably act as stem cells producing immunologically competent T-cells which also find their way to the spleen and lymph nodes, and are thus ready to interact with antigen in cooperation with macrophages already present. If not immediately involved in an antigenic reaction these migrating cells pass back into the circulation and represent the long-lived circulating pool of immunologically competent cells that permit the thymectomized adult to take part in immune reactions for years.

Antigen–Cell Reaction

The most fundamental problem in immunology concerns the way in which a cell may be stimulated to produce antibody, a protein with a certain specific amino acid sequence on a part of its light chains that allows it to complex with a complementary region on the antigen molecule. The primary step is the adsorption of the antigen to the recognition cell, and such an attachment is easy to recognize in the electron microscope (Fig. 4.30). It is seen to attach at localized patches, an attachment that seems specific for certain cells since only a small proportion of a population take the antigen up. An important feature of this attachment is that it is apparently mediated by antibody itself, so that treatment of a cell with an "anti-antibody" can block attachment of the antigen. It appears, then, that even when the cell has never "seen" the antigen it has antibody to it that will permit the first stage in the immune reaction that leads to rapid multiplication of antibody-producing cells with its concomitant liberation of large quantities of antibodies into the circulation.

Clonal Selection Theory

This suggests, then, that antibody production in response to antigen is really an enhancement of a process that has been going on before at a very slow rate; and this forms the essential basis of Jerne's and Burnet's selection theories. Thus, as formulated by Burnet in his *Clonal Selection Theory* in 1957, the body contains clones of a large variety of antibody-producing cells, which will be stimulated to reproduce and secrete antibody in response to meeting only one specific type of antigen, or at any rate, a limited number. Thus the organism will have certain genes determining the power to synthesize certain groups of immunoglobulins, and these will be a specific feature common to the organisms of a given species. Burnet suggested that, during mitotic division of the antibody-producing lymphocytes, a large number of minute variations in structure of the basic immunoglobulins would be continuously taking place, comparable with the mutations that govern alterations in heritable characteristics, but taking place in somatic rather than germ cells. Antigen, meeting one of these types of cell that produced a suitable antibody, might then stimulate it to proliferate and thus produce large amounts of this antibody of complementary structure to the antigen.

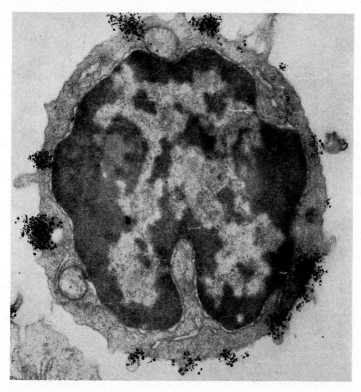

Fig. 4.36. Electron microscope autoradiograph of a spleen lymphocyte labelled with ^{125}I-haemocyanin. The antigen is present as a series of discrete patches scattered around the cell periphery. (Mandel and Byrt, *In* "The Role of the Lymphocyte and Macrophage in the Immune Response", Ed. D. C. Dumonde, 1971, Springer.)

Informational Hypothesis

The alternative "informational hypothesis" suggests that the antigen causes the cell's synthetic machinery to make an immunoglobulin after its own image, perhaps by forcing the basic immunoglobulin molecules into a suitable tertiary conformation. However, it is now recognized that the specificity of an immunoglobulin resides in its primary structure, i.e. its amino acid sequence, so that the antigen would have to modify the cell's synthetic ability at the gene level, since it is known that antibody production occurs in the progeny of the stimulated cells. In fact the stimulus to antibody production may well be the stimulus to cell multiplication. Again, the informational theories would imply that all immunologically competent cells could produce a large variety of different antibodies, according to their "instructions", but the evidence is against this. Thus the haemolytic plaque technique has certainly provided evidence indicating that the power to produce a given antibody resides in only certain cells of a population of lymphocytes. For example, lymphocytes may be sensitized to two species of erythrocytes and when examined by the plaque technique a given plaque-forming cell, i.e. one producing antibody, only produces antibodies against one of the species of erythrocyte (p. 352).

Radioactive Antigen. Again, if a highly radioactive labelled antigen is employed, its emissions may destroy the cells to which it attaches as soon as they begin to divide, since it will be recalled that it is during division that the DNA becomes susceptible to radiation-damage. Thus the antigen, provoking cell division and production of antibody, if radioactive, blocks the cell so provoked and prevents antibody formation to this antigen. By exposing a cell population to two antigens, one of which is radioactive, it was found that antibodies to the non-radioactive antigen were produced, whereas if all the antibody-producing cells had been of the same type, capable of responding to both radioactive and non-radioactive antigens, they would all have been destroyed by the radioactive antigen and so no antibodies would have been produced.

Recognition and Antibody Production

In this discussion we have implied that the recognizing cell is also the one stimulated to reproduce and produce antibody. In fact, the usual condition is cell cooperation, so that some effect of antigen–cell interaction is transmitted to another, antibody-producing, cell. We have seen that an RNA or RNA–antigen complex can be extracted from macrophages exposed to the antigen, and that this material will provoke production of antibody, reactive with the antigen; but whether the material acts in an informational sense, dictating to the antibody-producing cell the type of molecule it should produce, or whether it exerts its specificity by the cell that it chooses to stimulate, is by no means clear. If Burnet's theory is correct, the antibody-producing cell is already differentiated to produce a given type of molecule or molecules, and requires only the external stimulus.

Delayed Hypersensitivity

The essential feature of delayed sensitivity is the circumstance that the response to antigen is the production of a sensitized lymphocyte, rather than the activation of a lymphocyte or plasma cell to produce circulating antibodies. Thus the immediate response to antigen by a sensitized animal is the result of the meeting of antigen with circulating antibodies produced as a result of the first sensitization. The delayed inflammatory response to the same antigen is due to a series of events culminating in the migration of large numbers of lymphocytes from the blood vessels into the tissue at the site of antigen invasion. It is thus a *cell-mediated response*, and we have seen that the sensitivity can only be transmitted from a sensitized animal to a non-sensitized one by transfer of lymphocytes and not by serum.

Sensitized Lymphocytes

We may ask: How are these lymphocytes sensitized to antigen? and, How do the lymphocytes, so sensitized, bring about the inflammatory response, which may be extensive, as with a graft rejection?

The evidence indicates that the production of a sensitized or activated lymphocyte, like the production of one capable of making antibody, requires cooperation between marrow- and thymus-derived lymphocytes, probably involving the formation of clusters of cooperating cells in the lymph nodes. The sensitized lymphocytes join the circulating body of white cells and thus are ready to meet antigen when injected into, say, the skin. As a result of this meeting they activate, or produce many activated, lymphocytes in the regional lymph node, and these are carried in the blood stream to the site of antigen penetration. That the circulating sensitized lymphocytes are not specially mobilized to meet antigen is revealed by using labelled sensitized lymphocytes from another animal in transferring sensitivity to a previously unsensitized animal. When this passively sensitized animal is given antigen, the lymphocytes accumulating at the site of the delayed reaction are mainly the animal's own, so that the foreign lymphocytes have activated the animal's own cells in some way to make them antigen-reactive.

Lymphokines

By collecting the lymphocytes accumulating in a delayed hypersensitive response, and incubating them, several soluble factors have been isolated. These have been called *lymphokines*; they have effects on cells and may well be involved in the interactions between lymphocytes, as well as in the production of the delayed inflammatory response. Four of these factors have been described, namely, those producing inflammation, stimulating mitosis (mitogenic), damaging cells (cyto-toxic) and inhibiting migration of macrophages (MIF). Thus we may sensitize animals to a foreign globulin, for example, and collect the lymphocytes from its peritoneal cavity. These sensitized cells are then incubated with the foreign globulin and they release into the medium one or more of these factors.

Inflammatory Factor. The inflammatory factor is studied by injecting it into an animal that has been previously injected with ^{131}I-labelled plasma proteins. The inflammatory response is revealed by the passage of the labelled material into the tissue, where its presence is detected by an appropriate form of counter.

Mitogenic Factor. Again, the mitogenic factor is assessed by the increased incorporation of labelled DNA precursors, such as thymidine, into lymphocytes. Since, as we have seen, the fundamental basis for the immune response is the multiplication of cells capable of producing antibody, etc., the importance of the mitogenic factor is obvious.

MIF. The delayed migration of macrophages is a characteristic phenomenon in delayed sensitivity reactions, the cells tending to round up in response to the presence of the sensitizing antigen.

Macrophage Activation

An opposite type of response, called macrophage activation, may also take place in delayed hypersensitivity. Here, the formation of lysosomes is increased and the macrophages show a vastly increased tendency to phagocytose foreign material. In fact in some diseases, such as tuberculosis, it is only the macrophages of the infected animal that are able to ingest the tubercle bacilli; interestingly, although the activation may be specific, the macrophages so activated show an unspecific avidity for bacteria, attacking unrelated organisms such as brucellae, listeria and salmonellae.

Thus it would seem that in delayed, or cellular, hypersensitivity, the specific or immune reaction is the production of a population of lymphocytes sensitized to antigen, and this requires some cellular cooperation. Once the lymphocytes become active, most of the remaining activities are unspecific, being dependent on factors that are released from the sensitized cells.

Transfer Factor

The lymphokines are factors that produce a non-specific effect on cells and tissues. The actual transmission of sensitivity from one lymphocyte to another, as in the acquisition of delayed hypersensitivity by an injection of sensitized lymphocytes, is brought about by another factor. Like the lymphokines it has a molecular weight of 22,000 and, when injected into the skin of normal guinea pigs, gives them a delayed hypersensitivity to the antigen.

Complement

We have already mentioned that the completion of the immune response usually requires the intervention of a system called *complement*, which is inactivated at a temperature of 56°C; and it was through this characteristic that it was discovered. Subsequent work has shown that this heat-labile factor actually represents a series of some eleven separate globulin-type proteins with molecular weights from 79,000 to 400,000 and constituting some 10 per cent of the serum globulins in man.

Activation

As a group they are inactive, but when activated, each member of the group, indicated by C1, C2 . . . C9, is able to undergo reactions with others, many of which involve the splitting off of a small fragment. Only with C1, the first member to react, is the combining site normally active, the others requiring previous activation. Thus C1 binds with the antibody–antigen complex; in effect C1 is a complex of three sub-components, indicated by q, r and s, so that, with the usual notation, C1 is described as C1qrs. On combination, the complex becomes activated so that it is able to behave as an enzyme—an esterase— acting on the next component C2, an action which, like that of other esterases, is inhibited by DFP.

Reaction Series. The series of reactions leading to membrane damage is summarized by Fig. 4.37; thus SA, the antigen–antibody complex, reacts with C1 in the presence of Ca^{2+} to give the activated SAC1 complex, the bar over C1 indicating its active form. This complex catalyses the binding of both C4 and C2 to the cell surface and thereby assembles the enzyme called C3 convertase, i.e. the complex SAC1, 4b, 2a is enzymatically active and able to react with C3, a reaction that leads to the fixing of the changed C3, called C3b, on the cell surface. C8 makes a direct attack on the cell surface, when prepared by the previous series of reactions, and this is when a slow breakdown of the cell begins, so that C9 may be considered as a factor enhancing the action of cell-bound C8.

Recognition

This complex series of reactions becomes more intelligible if we consider what is required of a system capable of destroying certain

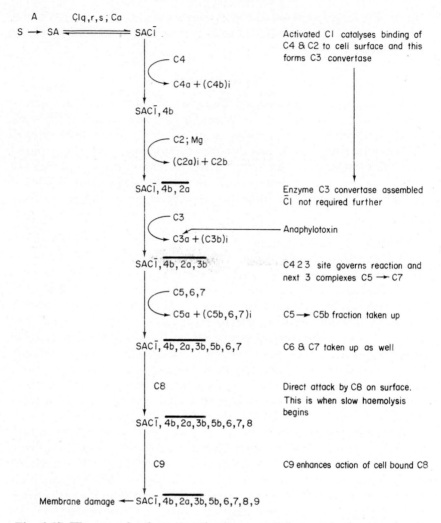

Fig. 4.37. The cascade of reactions leading to cell damage in the complement reaction. (Muller-Eberhard, *A. Rev. Biochem.*, 1969, 407.)

cells within the blood. Just as with the clotting mechanism it is important to prevent clotting of the blood in the vessels, so it is important that the complement system does not attack the normal cells of the body. Hence a first requisite is that the system must be able to *recognize* the immune complex and having done this to organize the attack mechanisms.

Activation and Attack

The problem is to prevent the attack mechanism from acting indiscriminately, and the solution is given by the presence of an additional system called the *activation system*, as illustrated in Fig. 4.38. Thus the recognition system attaches to the antibody–cell complex, AB. It mobilizes the activation system and forces it to attach itself to the cell membrane where it is unable to attack the cell but is able, by virtue of its attachment, to organize or activate the *attack system*. The action of the attack system is confined to the target cell by virtue of its proximity to the activation system and the fact that all factors have a very limited life after activation, due to an inactivation process.

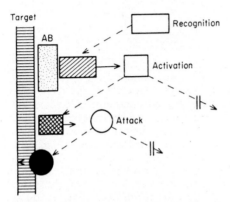

Fig. 4.38. Theoretical model of complement action, consisting of three mechanisms. (Muller-Eberhard, Harvey Lectures, 1972, **66**, 75.)

More specifically, the recognition unit is, in fact, the C1 complex (C1q, C1r, and C1s). While attached to the AB complex it organizes the formation of the activation unit, which has an affinity for cell membranes and attaches to it. Thus in effect the activation unit is C2, C3 and C4, whose reactions lead to the attachment of C3b to the cell surface. The activation unit has become attached to the cell membrane, but it, by itself, is incapable of doing damage; instead it has the power to organize the attack mechanism, C5 to C9. The series of reactions are illustrated schematically in Fig. 4.39.

Anaphylotoxins

It will be seen from the reactions indicated on the right-hand side of each step in Fig. 4.37, that C2, C3 etc. undergo conversion into components indicated by C2a, C2b and so on. These consist of enzymatic

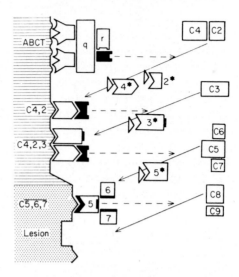

Fig. 4.39. Pictorial diagram summarizing present concept of action of complement on biological membranes. C1, the recognition unit, is depicted in combination with membrane-bound antibody molecules of the 7S variety. On the right-hand side are indicated the inactive precursors of the activation mechanism, C4, C2, C3, and of the attack mechanism, C5, C6, C7, C8 and C9. On the opposite side is depicted the assembly of complement molecules on a membrane surface in sequent of action (from top to bottom). The catalytic site of C1 causes fusion of C2 and C4 into a bimolecular complex and its binding to a membrane receptor. The newly formed enzyme activates C3, allowing its binding to the membrane. Association of C3 with the C4,2 complex modifies this enzyme to enable it to act on C5, thereby initiating fusion of C5 with C6 and C7 and binding of the complex to the membrane. At this stage, through a function of the C5 molecule, the membrane undergoes structural alterations: its diameter increases and the outer surface displays lesions. Functional membrane damage for cell lysis occurs only after binding of C8. The action of C8 is enhanced and accelerated by C9. The blank areas symbolize active sites or activated subunits which are critical for the cytolytic reaction. (Muller-Eberhard, Harvey Lectures, 1972, **66**, 75.)

splitting, giving rise to small and large fragments; thus C3b is the large fragment that is bound to the cell whilst the smaller fragment C3a is a small basic fraction of molecular weight 7000, and is one of the *anaphylotoxins* that cause contraction of bronchial smooth muscle and increased vascular permeability. C3a also has chemotactic activity in relation so leucocytes. Thus the participation of complement may lead to more generalized manifestations of the immune reaction in addition to specific attack on foreign cells.

Inactivation

In general, activation is followed rapidly by an inactivation process so that, for example, only a small proportion of C2a attaches to the cell surface, the remainder remaining in the serum in an inactivated form, indicated by $(C2a)_i$. Thus the generalized sequence of action in any step is indicated by the following:

$$
\begin{array}{lll}
C & C^* & \text{(active in respect of com-} \\
\text{(native} \quad \dashrightarrow \quad \text{(Site I)} & & \text{bining site)} \\
\text{inactive)} & & \\[2ex]
C^* + \text{Acceptor} \dashrightarrow & \begin{array}{l} C_{\text{Bound}} \\ \text{(Site II)} \end{array} & \text{(active in respect of func-} \\
& & \text{tional site)} \\[2ex]
C^* \quad \dashrightarrow C_1 & & \text{(inactive)}
\end{array}
$$

Thus if C^* fails to collide within a short period with its acceptor it becomes inactivated, and because C^* may have to move some distance from the point where it was activated to the point where it exerts its specific activity, inactivation may be very considerable. In this way the activity of complement is confined to the region of the cell–antibody complex.

The Blood Groups

Compatibility

The immune reactions we have considered so far are those provoked by organisms or tissues of a species foreign to the host. The requirement to replace a human subject's blood after haemorrhage with that of a donor naturally led to the study of the reactions of a given subject to infusion of foreign bloods. As we should expect, blood from a different species provoked severe immune reactions leading to the destruction of the foreign blood cells, but when human blood was transfused the reaction could be variable leading sometimes to haemolysis of the transfused corpuscles, with consequent jaundice and haematurea, and at other times to no obvious ill effects, so that bloods could be described as *compatible* or *incompatible*.

ABO System

In 1900 Landsteiner observed that when he mixed the red cells of a given human subject with the serum of another, the cells could go into clumps—*haemagglutination*—and he likened the process to the agglutination of bacteria, i.e. to the reaction of the bacteria with an antibody already present in the recipient blood serum. By studying the reactions between cells of many individuals with the sera of others, it became clear that the phenomena could be explained on the assumption that the red cells contained certain antigens whilst the plasmas contained certain antibodies. It was the reaction of the antigens of the foreign cells with the antibodies in the recipient–plasma that determined incompatibility. Alternatively, the antibody in the foreign plasma reacted with the antigen on the recipient's cells, although, as we shall see, it is the former reaction that is the more important when judging compatibility of blood for transfusion. The bloods examined fell into four classes according to the presence or absence of antigens on the red cells, and of antigens in the plasma, as indicated in Table I.

TABLE I

The ABO system of blood grouping

Type	Antigen on Red Cells	Antibody in Plasma
O	———	Anti-A and Anti-B
A	A	Anti-B
B	B	Anti-A
AB	A and B	None

Thus the red cells of Group O have no antigen. Group A the A-antigen, Group B the B-antigen and Group AB both antigens. These antigens react with antibodies, *Anti-A* and *Anti-B*, present in the plasma. Clearly, if a given subject, e.g. one of Group A, is not to agglutinate his own red cells, the anti-A antibody must be absent from his plasma; one of Group AB must lack both antibodies, and so on. As Table I shows, the serum of Group O, with no antigen, has both antibodies. From the Table, the effects of mixing the cells of a given group with the plasma of another are at once predictable; thus Group O cells are compatible with the plasma of all blood groups but the plasma of this group will agglutinate the cells of the remaining three groups, and so on.

Typing of Blood. Thus from the practical point of view, to decide on whether a given blood is compatible with the prospective recipient, it must be "typed", and ideally one should be chosen that is of the same type. This is often not practicable, and not strictly necessary, since the antibodies present in the donor blood are relatively unimportant compared with those in the recipient blood owing to the great dilution of the antibodies that occurs on transfusion. Thus the usual transfusion of 500 ml of blood corresponds to about 250 ml of plasma, and the antibodies in this volume can easily be taken up by the red cells of the recipient without causing agglutination. If the donor cells are incompatible, however, they are exposed to the antibodies in the entire plasma volume, and will therefore agglutinate. On this basis, then, Group O subjects can receive blood from all four groups; Group A subjects can receive Group O and Group A blood, and so on. On this basis, too, we see that Group O blood can be considered as a *universal donor*, and conversely Group AB subjects can be given blood of any other group, so they could be called *universal recipients*. However, the use of Group O blood as a universal donor can lead to trouble when the serum has an exceptionally high titre of Anti-A and Anti-B, so that a useful precaution is to centrifuge the cells down and replace the supernatant plasma with saline.

TABLE II

The percentages of U.K. subjects in the four blood-groupings based on a study of 190,177 people.

Group	Percentage
O	46·684
A	41·716
B	8·560
AB	3·040

Proportions in the Population. The relative proportions of the four groups in the population vary with the country; in the United Kingdom they are those shown in Table II, and it will be seen that Groups B and AB are the least common.

Inheritance

Bernstein showed that the inheritance of the blood grouping followed the Mendelian pattern and could be described in terms of a gene at a single locus on a chromosome. The gene has three allelic forms, which may be indicated by O, A and B, the child inheriting one allele from each parent. Thus the genotypes are those indicated in Table III, namely OO, AA, AO, BB, BA, AB. In classical terminology, the alleles A and B would be said to be dominant over the allele O, so that O only obtains expression as a phenotype O when it has a "double-dose", OO. Hence genotypes AA and AO have the same phenotype, A; BB and BA have the same phenotype, B, and AB has the phenotype AB. It will be clear from this that merely determining a subject's

TABLE III
Phenotypes and genotypes in the ABO classification

TABLE III
Phenotypes and genotypes in the ABO classification

Phenotype	Genotype	Antigen on Red Cell
O	OO	————
A	AA AO	A
B	BB BO	B
AB	AB	A and B

blood-group does not necessarily determine his genotype, since he could have inherited, say, an A allele from his father and an A from his mother, or he could have inherited an O allele from his mother. In both cases he would belong to Group A, which would be described as his phenotype. Consequently, when blood-grouping is used to exclude paternity, considerably more knowledge is required; and this is usually based on the existence of many more groupings within the main ABO grouping.

TABLE IV
The A_1A_2BO groups

Genotypes	Phenotypes
A_1A_1 A_1A_2 A_1O	A_1
A_2A_2 A_2O	A_2
BB BO	B
A_1B	A_1B
A_2B	A_2B
OO	O

Groups A_1 and A_2. Subjects in Group A may, on the basis of serological tests, be subdivided into A_1 and A_2 and since the distinction is transmitted along Mendelian lines, a fourth allele has been invoked so that the genotypes and phenotypes are those indicated in Table IV, a child receiving from each parent one of the four genes, A_1, A_2, B or O. There are thus 6 phenotypes recognizable by appropriate antisera.

Further Classification

In addition to this subdivision of the A-group a large number of additional groups, falling within the ABO grouping, have been identified by employing several techniques. Thus the *Lutheran, Kell, Lewis, Duffy, Kidd* systems were discovered by finding human sera that reacted with certain red cell samples irrespective of their known antigens, i.e. of the ABO system; clearly there was some new factor in the serum that reacted with an antigen on the red cells of these subjects. Another technique is to use samples of red cells as antigens for an immune reaction in a foreign species, such as the rabbit. The plasma of the rabbit will contain antibodies to the various antigenic groupings on the red cells. If the particular sample of red cells is different from others by possessing a hitherto unrecognized antigen, it should be possible to show this by the fact that it will be agglutinated by this rabbit plasma (whilst other samples are not) after the "usual anti-bodies" i.e. Anti-A, Anti-B, have been removed by appropriate absorption techniques.

MN and P Systems. In this way the MN and P systems were discovered. Thus, so far as the MN system is concerned, all human red cells may be classed as those containing only M, only N, and M and N; features that are determined genetically, as with the ABO system. Usually antibodies to M and N are not present in appreciable amounts in the sera of human subjects, so that incompatibility on this basis is extremely rare.

The Rhesus Factor

The most important development since the recognition of the ABO classification was clearly the discovery of the Rh-factor, owing to its involvement in haemolytic disease of the newborn, or *erythroblastosis foetalis*, as well as in cases of incompatible transfusions taking place when blood of the apparently correct type within the ABO classification was employed.

Isoimmunization. In 1939 Levine and Stetson described the case of a woman having a severe reaction to a transfusion of her husband's apparently compatible blood after she had delivered a still-born macerated foetus, and it was discovered that her serum agglutinated the cells of her husband as well as those of 80 out of 104 donors who were "compatible" on the basis of the ABO classification. Levine and Stetson postulated, therefore, that there was a new, and hitherto undiscovered, antigen on the cells of certain human subjects, including the mother's husband; this antigen was not on the mother's cells but they had been inherited from the father by the foetus, and the mother had developed antibodies to this factor through mixing of the foetal red cells with her circulation—*isoimmunization*.

Rhesus Monkey Cells. Subsequent work showed that the antigen was similar to, or identical with, the Rh-factor discovered by Landsteiner and Wiener in their studies on the antibodies obtained by injecting Rhesus monkey cells into rabbits. These antibodies not only agglutinated monkey red cells but also those of about 85 per cent of human subjects tested, these people being described as *Rh-positive* (Rh+). Thus Rh+ humans apparently possessed antigens on their red cells capable of reacting specifically with this antibody.

Anti-Rh-Factor. Later Wiener and Peters discovered that certain people's sera contained an antibody to the Rh-factor—anti-Rh— apparently the same as that made by the rabbit against monkey cells; the people having this anti-Rh factor were those who gave incompatible reactions to transfusions with blood that was compatible in the ABO classification.

Erythroblastosis Foetalis. In general it has been established that some 85 per cent of white people are Rh-positive, the characteristic being dominant. The proportion varies with different ethnic groups, so that blood-typing on this basis has proved of great anthropological interest. So far as erythroblastosis foetalis is concerned, the original suggestion of Levine and Stetson has been confirmed abundantly; thus, if the hypothesis is correct, mothers of children with erythroblastosis foetalis should be Rh-negative, whilst the infants and fathers should be positive; and in a statistical analysis Levine and his colleagues found that 91 per cent of 111 mothers of erythroblastic infants were Rh— as compared with only 14–15 per cent of Rh— in the population generally, whilst 100 per cent of 66 fathers and 58 affected infants were Rh+ compared with about 85 per cent Rh+ in the general population.

Complexity of Rh-Factor. The Rh-factor has turned out not to be single but to involve several factors, whilst the corresponding antibodies are also multiple. Generally speaking the original Rh-factor has now been called D or Rh_0 and its corresponding antibody, anti-D or anti-Rh_0; two other Rh factors are designated C and E and their corresponding antisera anti-C and anti-E.*

Chemistry of the Antigens

The antigens we have been concerned with in interspecific responses have been mainly proteins, and their antigenic capacity has depended

---

* We may note that the Rh-factor present in human plasma is not identical with that obtained by immunizing rabbits with *Rhesus* blood cells.

on a specific arrangement of a few amino acids in the polypeptide chains constituting the protein. Antigenicity of the blood-group substances, embedded on the surface of the erythrocyte, depends on the presence of relatively short chains of polysaccharide, attached to a backbone of lipid—*sphingosine*—so that they are *lipopolysaccharides*. Experimentally the lipopolysaccharide may be extracted from the red cell ghosts with a lipid solvent, such as ethanol, and its antigenicity measured by determining whether it combines with a known antiserum.

$$CH_3(CH_2)_{12} \text{---} CH == CH \text{---} CH(OH) \text{---} CH(NH_2) \text{---} CH_2 OH$$

Sphingosine

Glycoproteins. The amounts extractable are very small so that the fundamental work of Morgan and Watkins, which laid the foundation for our knowledge of the basic structures of the antigens, was carried out on water-soluble materials of identical antigenic character found in certain secretions or tissues. Thus, amongst the normal secretions, the saliva and gastric juice are rich sources of a water-soluble material, consisting of a polysaccharide attached to a polypeptide—a *glycoprotein*— and it is the successful analysis of the polysaccharides from these materials that has laid the foundations for our knowledge of the basis of antigen specificity. More recent developments in analytical techniques have permitted the isolation and characterization of the lipopolysaccharides from the red blood cells.

Secreted Antigens. Before describing the basic constitution of the blood-group antigens we must say a few words about the material that is obtainable from the secretions, as opposed to the red cells. In general, A and B antigens are only found in the secretions when these are present on the red cells. Some 20 per cent of individuals with A or B antigens on their red cells, however, fail to secrete, and it has been found that the ability to secrete A and B substances is genetically controlled by a pair of allelic genes, Sese, inherited independently of the ABO system; Se in single or double dose, i.e. Sese or SeSe will bring about secretion but se requires a double dose, sese, to bring about non-secretion.

H-Substance. According to the original description of the ABO system, the O-group red cell was characterized by the absence of A- and B-antigens and *not* by the presence of an O-antigen. O-cells do however contain a specific substance, as recognized by their agglutination by certain bovine sera, and when these subjects secrete blood-group substances in their saliva, etc., a similar "O-substance" is found in their secretion, as recognized by its reaction with the bovine serum agglutenins. The evidence makes it very unlikely that this O-substance is synthesized in response to the O-gene, however, and for this reason the substance has been called *H-substance*, with its synthesis controlled by a pair of alleles, H and h, a double dose of h being required for absence of H-substance.

The Lewis System. As we have indicated earlier, a large variety of groupings within the ABO system, have been discovered, and given a variety of names, usually after the person whose blood provided the first evidence for their existence, e.g. Lutheran after a Mr. Luther, and so on. The Lewis system was discovered by Mourant when investigating the blood-grouping of a woman who produced a child with haemolytic anaemia and who turned out not to be Rh-negative, i.e. she had not been immunized by her baby. Mourant found that some 24 out of 96 Group O bloods were agglutinated by the plasma of this woman, and the antigen on the red cells, responsive to the woman's plasma, was called the Lewis antigen, Le. Subsequent studies showed that the Lewis system was defined by two allelic genes, Le and le, inherited independently of the ABO system and of the Hh and Sese genes, but there proved to be a very strong interrelation between them, the specific changes produced by the Le gene being produced on the same molecules as those produced by the Hh and ABO genes. The relation to the Sese alleles became evident when it was found that Le-positive persons were non-secretors of ABH, whilst their saliva strongly inhibited anti-Le antibodies. The secretions of Le-positive persons contain Le-substance in their secretions, so that analytical work has been primarily devoted to A, B, H and Le-substances.

Polysaccharides. The average molecular weights of substances from different individuals range from 3.10^5 to 1.10^6 and it is likely that the material from a single individual contains a family of molecules very closely related in general structure and composition. The basic structure is that of a large number of relatively short polysaccharide chains attached at intervals to a peptide backbone. Each factor, e.g. A-substance, contains the same five sugars, namely D-galactose, L-fucose, N-acetyl-D-glucosamine, N-acetyl-D-galactosamine and the 9-carbon sugar N-acetylneuraminic acid (sialic acid) (Fig. 4.40); the peptide component contains 15 amino acids.

Sugars. The qualitative composition, in terms of sugars, does not determine the distinctive antigenic character of the material, whereas the *proportions* of the various sugars do vary amongst the different antigens.

Specificity. Space will not permit of any detailed description of the results of chemical studies aimed at determining the specificity of a given blood-group substance. Suffice it to say that it soon became clear that it was the polysaccharide moiety, as opposed to the peptide, that was determining, and that the difference between, say, A and B substance resided in quite small changes in order of linking and in the type, e.g. α- or β-. Thus A-substance contains the characteristic series:

α-GalNAc-$(1{\rightarrow}3)$-β-Gal-$(1{\rightarrow}3)\beta$GNAc-$(1{\rightarrow}3)\beta$Gal-$(1{\rightarrow}3)$GNAc-

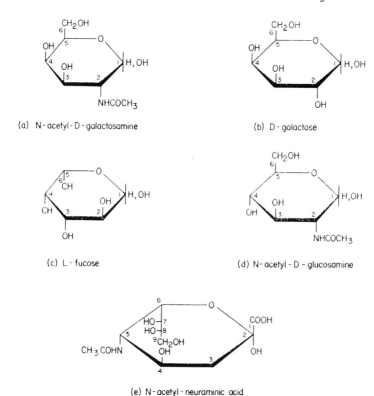

(a) N-acetyl-D-galactosamine

(b) D-galactose

(c) L-fucose

(d) N-acetyl-D-glucosamine

(e) N-acetyl-neuraminic acid

Fig. 4.40. Sugars contained by the carbohydrate portions of the blood group substances.

and the B-substance

a-Gal-$(1\rightarrow3)$-β-Gal-$(1\rightarrow3)$-β-GNAc-$(1\rightarrow3)$-β-Gal-$(1\rightarrow3)$GalNAc*

Phylogeny. In general, the chemical studies suggest that the specific antigens were developed from a common precursor molecule by the addition of one or more sugar molecules. According to this, the H-substance is produced in response to the H-gene which directs the addition of a fucose molecule to the precursor sugar chain; the A-substance results from the addition of N-acetylglucosamine to the H-active chains, directed by the A-gene, and so on. If, as the chemical evidence suggests, H-substance is converted by the A and B genes to A-antigen and B-antigen, it is understandable that O-group individuals will have large amounts of H-substance.

* GalNAc = N-acetyl-D-galactosaminopyranose; Gal, D-galactopyranose; GNAc, N-acetyl-D-glucosaminopyranose.

CHAPTER 5

Reproduction and Lactation

REPRODUCTION

Mitotic Division

The cells of most of the tissues of the body, and the individual cells of the blood, undergo a continuous process of death, and regeneration by division from parent cells. Thus, the epithelial layers of the skin undergo cornification and eventual shedding, the lost cells being replaced from below by division of the cells in the germinative layer; the epithelial cells of the intestinal villus move up to the apex and are cast off, being replaced by division of epithelial cells in the crypt, and so on. In the young growing organism, moreover, the enlargement of the tissues is the result of multiplication of cells by a similar process of division. The manner in which this multiplication takes place has been described earlier, its basis being the separation of the nucleus and cytoplasm into two portions, the nuclear division being preceded by synthesis of new genetic material by replication of the chromosomes before their separation and migration to opposite poles of the cell.

Maintenance of Genetic Potency. Through this—*mitotic*—type of division the complex organism can develop from a single fertilized ovum, or zygote. Because of the replication of the genetic material of the chromosomes, each cell has the same potentialities, in the sense that it has the genetic material—DNA—that can form the basis for synthesis of enzymes and other proteins that could allow it to develop into a neurone, a muscle cell, and so on. Differentiation of the cells means, in effect, an exploitation of some of the genetic material and suppression of other material, but the essential consequence of the exact replication of the genes means that the potentialities are in the cell.

Germ Cells

The reproduction of the organism itself, where this is done sexually, requires something more than mitotic division of an existing cell, since the genetic materials of male and female have to be intermingled. This is achieved by the "setting aside" by the developing organism of certain *germ cells*, whose ultimate task will be to contribute half of their chromosomes to the fertilized zygote, the other half being contributed by the partner in this sexual reproduction.

Reduction Division. Before this intermingling of genetic material takes place, however, the respective male and female germ cells undergo changes leading to the production of the mature *gametes*, i.e. the cells that will ultimately fuse to give the *zygote*. The primary basis of this maturation process is the reduction in the total number of chromosomes by half, to give the *haploid* number, as contrasted with the *diploid* number in the remaining cell types. Thus in man there are 48 chromosomes in cells with the diploid number; these are in homologous pairs, in the sense that one of each was derived from one of the parents. Clearly, if a male and female cell with the diploid number of chromosomes were to fuse, we should be left with a cell containing twice the number of chromosomes of its parents, and to prevent this the germ cell undergoes a *reduction division* during the maturation process.

Meiosis

The germ cells of the organism are concentrated in a special region, the *gonad*, and here they may undergo many divisions to produce more germ cells of the primitive type, called *spermatogonia*, or *öogonia*, according to the sex; these divisions are of the usual mitotic type, so that the diploid number of chromosomes is maintained. At a certain point, a spermatogonium, or öogonium, divides mitotically to produce a *primary spermatocyte* or *öocyte*; thus the genetic material of the primary spermatocyte, or öocyte, is equivalent to that of the spermatogonium or öogonium from which it was derived, but the cell is different in so far as it is now committed to a different form of division, namely *meiosis*, that will lead to the production of the mature gamete, the spermatozöon or ovum.

First Meiotic Division

The stages of the first meiotic division are illustrated in Fig. 5.1; they are essentially similar to those taking place in mitotic division, in that a spindle is formed and that chromosomes pass to opposite poles before cytokinesis. During *mitosis*, however, the individual chromosomes split and are reduplicated prior to the migration to the poles, so that equal numbers of chromosomes are maintained; during the first meiotic division, on the other hand, as illustrated in Fig. 5.1, the homologous chromosomes associate and ultimately separate, one of

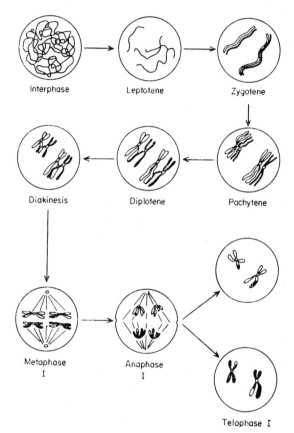

Fig. 5.1. Meiosis first division. The result of this series of changes in the öocyte or spermatocyte is that the daughter cells have half the diploid number of chromosomes, since the individual chromosomes did not split and reduplicate as in mitosis.

each homologous pair passing into the daughter cells. During this period of close association, giving rise to the *diplotene* stage, there is an exchange of genetic material between chromosomes of homologous pairs, so that the individual chromosomes, when they ultimately separate during metaphase and anaphase, are not identical with those of the parent cells.

Stages in Meiosis. The details of meiosis, as illustrated schematically in Fig. 5.1, may be briefly reviewed. *Prophase* is lengthy and is divided into five phases as follows: *Leptotene* (*leptos*, slender), the chromosomes appear as thin threads with beads, the *chromomeres*. *Zygotene*: (*zygosis*, joining), homologous chromosomes undergo pairing, or *synapsis*, to form bivalent chromosome units. Thus the nucleus at this stage contains the haploid number of paired units. *Pachytene*: (*pachys*, thick) the chromosomes contract longitudinally. *Diplotene*: (*diplous*, double) the homologues of each bivalent unit now appear double, as a result of a longitudinal split; each homologous chromosome thus becomes a pair of sister *chromatids*, and the whole unit is called a *tetrad chromosome*. There is a tendency for paired chromosomes to separate, but paired homologues frequently remain in contact at one or more points along their length to give the characteristic X-configuration called *chiasmata*. Each chiasma represents a region where two chromatids of the tetrads are exchanging corresponding segments with each other; as a result, two of the chromatids of the tetrad become structurally reorganized in so far as each contains genetic units that belonged to the other. Hence each homologous chromosome contains two chromatids, one of which remains unchanged and the other is made up of an original and an exchanged component. *Diakinesis*: (*dia*, through, in different directions; *kinesis*, movement). There is a gradual shortening of homologues, with separation, so that at the end of diakinesis homologous pairs are only associated at their ends. Thus, during prophase, replicated homologous chromosomes have paired, exchanged chromatid segments and initiated their longitudinal separation. In subsequent metaphase and anaphase, the homologous pairs complete their separation and their individual units pass to opposite poles of the spindle to form the nuclei of the *secondary spermatocytes* or öocytes.

Second Meiotic Division

As Fig. 5.2 shows, the second meiotic division involves a splitting of the paired chromatids of the individual chromosomes, so that the haploid number of chromosomes is retained in the *spermatid* or *öotid*.

DNA in Nuclei

When the amount of DNA in the nuclei of germ cells during successive stages in production of the gamete is measured, it is found that the amounts in the primary spermatocyte, secondary spermatocyte and spermatid are in the proportions of $4:2:1$. Thus the primary spermatocyte, before entering its first meiotic division, doubles its DNA content and contains twice as much as that in other cells with the diploid number of chromosomes. The *reduction division* produces a cell with the diploid amount of DNA, but half the number of chromosomes, and it is the splitting of these chromosomes into their chromatid pairs and their separation into the spermatids that gives the haploid nucleus of the latter, with half the amount of DNA found in somatic cells.

Sex Difference

Although the processes of formation of the male and female gametes are fundamentally similar, there are some essential differences. Thus in the male mammal the spermatogonium develops through primary and secondary spermatocytes to the *spermatid*, which then undergoes morphological changes to become the *spermatozöon*. In the female the öogonium gives rise to the *primary öocyte* (Fig. 5.3) and this, by meiotic division, gives rise to a *secondary öocyte* and a much smaller cell called

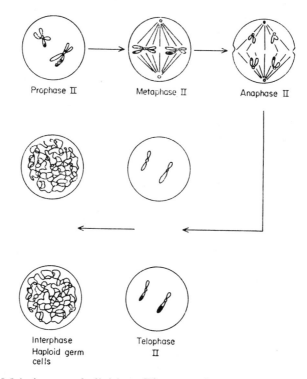

Fig. 5.2. Meiosis second division. The secondary öocyte or spermatocyte goes through changes similar to those in mitosis in so far as the paired chromatids of the individual chromosomes split. The haploid number of chromosomes is retained.

the *first polar body*, which remain in close association. The second meiotic division, which gives rise to an *ootid* and, once again, a much smaller cell, the *second polar body*, only occurs *after fertilization* of the secondary öocyte. Thus, when we speak of a female "ovulating" we mean the discharge into the oviduct of a secondary öocyte. If the ovum is fertilized, then the second meiotic division ensues, preparatory to the union of male and female pronuclei to give the fertilized zygote with the haploid number of chromosomes.

Multiplication of Germ Cells

In both male and female there is rapid multiplication of the primitive germ cells, or *gonia*, but in the human female this ceases in early embryonic life and is not resumed, so that mature ova develop from primary öocytes already formed in embryonic life, amounting to some 5–10 million.

Determination of Sex

In mammals the sex of the progeny is determined by a particular pair of chromosomes on which the relevant genes are carried; in the male the pair is of two types called X and Y whereas in the female both are of one type, Y. Thus the male pair is written XY and the female XX. When the reduction division has occurred, all ova will contain an X chromosome whilst half the sperm will contain an X and half a Y. Thus fertilization of an ovum can lead to a zygote with the XX (female) or XY (male) pair. The X chromosome is similar to the remainder that are not concerned in sex differentiation (the autosomes), whilst the Y chromosome is small and contains, next to the centromere, a special sex determining segment in which no crossing over of genetic material takes place, there being no corresponding part on the X chromosome. There is a short segment which pairs with the X, forming chiasmata. The Y chromosome is almost entirely concerned with sex, containing few other genes. People with only an X and no Y are female; the situation arises abnormally through fertilization of an ovum by a spermatozöon that has lost its Y chromosome. The individual so constituted is a sterile female with poorly developed gonads and secondary sex characteristics.

Fertilization

Fertilization Membrane

Because the invertebrate egg has been so much easier to study, most of our knowledge on the fertilization process is derived from the study of events in the egg of the sea-urchin, star-fish and so on. So far as the egg is concerned, the first change observed microscopically in the egg, following penetration of the sperm, is in the outer coat, the *vitelline membrane*; this elevates from the underlying hyaline plasma layer and plasma membrane, and becomes tougher, being now called the *fertilization membrane*. It is within this fertilization membrane that subsequent divisions of the ovum take place. The elevation proceeds as a wave over the surface of the egg, and is accompanied by a bursting

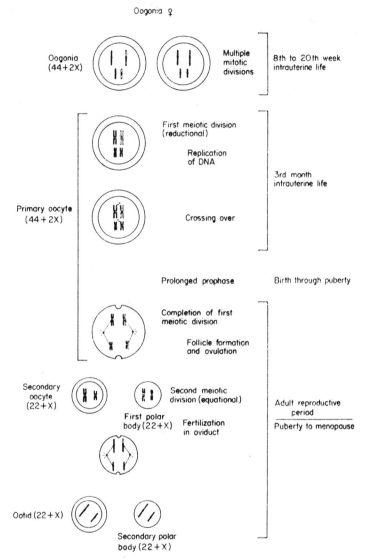

Fig. 5.3. Comparison of male and female gametogenesis. For full details consult text. Note that in the female, the first meiotic division began in the embryo and is not completed until puberty. The "ovum" that passes out of the ovary may or may not be fertilized on its route to the uterus, and is a secondary öocyte, i.e. the second meiotic division has not occurred and will only occur on fertilization. (Odell and Moyer, "Physiology of Reproduction", Mosby Co.. St. Louis.)

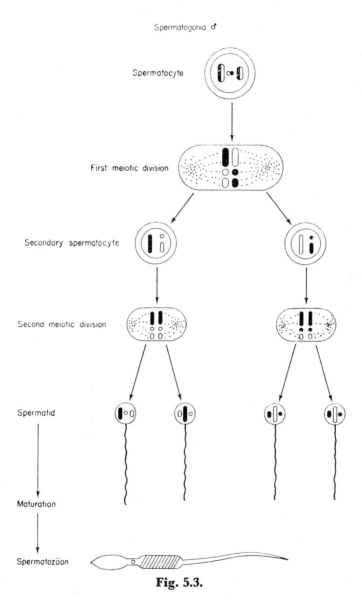

Fig. 5.3.

of special granules which, during maturation, have become concentrated in the cortex. We may presume that these granules contribute to the material of the fertilization membrane and of the hyaline plasma layer, which becomes thicker. The mechanism of the elevation may well be the emptying of the granules under the vitelline membrane;

if these contained colloid, the colloid osmotic pressure in the sub-vitelline space would attract water from the egg and the surrounding medium.

Block to Polyspermy

The changes taking place on the surface of the egg immediately after sperm entry are of considerable interest from the point of view of the block to polyspermy, i.e. the mechanism that prevents the egg from being fertilized by more than one sperm. In many species the eggs are normally polyspermic, several spermatozoa entering the egg, but only the first to enter is effective, the remainder dying off presumably as a result of chemical change due to the entry of the first sperm; this form of inhibition of polyspermy is called Type II by contrast with Type I where only one sperm succeeds in entering owing to a change in the surface after fertilization that prevents entry of further spermatozoa. The sea-urchin belongs to Type I; the lifting of the fertilization membrane requires some 18 sec and is thus too slow to account for the block to polyspermy.

Fertilization Wave. Runnström observed that when the egg was viewed under dark-field illumination immediately after fertilization, a characteristic change in colour took place, beginning at the point of sperm entry and passing as a wave over the whole surface, the process lasting some 4–6 sec. It was considered that this optical effect reflected some chemical change that prevented further sperm from entering. The situation is, however, highly complex, so that we must speak rather of a reduced probability of successful penetration by a sperm rather than an absolute block, so that, in fact, polyspermy may occur within as long a period as 60 sec after penetration of the first sperm, but there is a rapid decrease in probability of a second penetration, the chemical basis for which is not known; it clearly precedes the optical change which may reflect the condition when the probability of a second penetration is zero.

Mechanism of Sperm Entry

It was originally thought that the sperm was engulfed by the ovum after a preliminary fusion of their cell membranes, but the studies of Colwin showed that what really happened was the transfer of the sperm's nucleus and associated organelles—mitochondria and cen-trioles—into the ovum through a tubule—the *acrosome filament*—which is a part of the spermatozöon. By the *acrosome reaction* is meant two processes: first the release of a lysin by the sperm-head that tends to dissolve the egg's vitelline membrane; and, second, the development of the acrosome filament which stretches into the outermost jelly coat and makes contact with the egg surface.

Acrosome. The acrosome is a complex body in the sperm head lying under the plasma membrane and in close relation to the nucleus (Fig. 5.4,A). When the sperm makes contact with the egg there is first a dehiscence of the apex resulting in an opening of both plasma

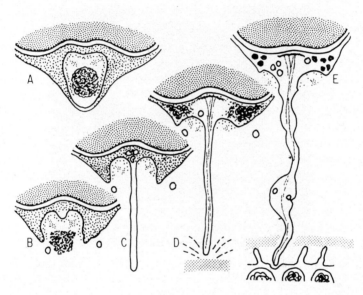

Fig. 5.4. Diagrams of acrosomal region at successive stages at beginning of fertilization. A, unactivated; B to E, activated. For further details see text. (Colwin and Colwin, *J. Cell Biol.* 1963, **19**, 477.)

membrane of the sperm and of the acrosomal membrane; this permits the granule within the acrosome to emerge, and the two membranes fuse to form a rim round this opening (Fig. 5.4,B). Next the acrosomal membrane evaginates to form a tubule which finally makes contact with the plasma membrane of the egg (Fig. 5.4,C-E). Finally the two membranes fuse to form a continuous mosaic membrane and to become adjacent segments of the plasma membrane of the fertilized zygote. The egg part of the zygote undergoes the fertilization reaction—membrane elevation etc.—and the fertilization cone is elevated, whilst the sperm nucleus etc. penetrate the acrosomal filament and enter the egg; and finally the egg cytoplasm penetrates between the internal sperm structures and the part of the zygote plasma membrane that was formerly the sperm membrane.

Pronucleus and Zygote Nucleus. The nuclear material that was formerly the sperm nucleus reorganizes within the egg cytoplasm to

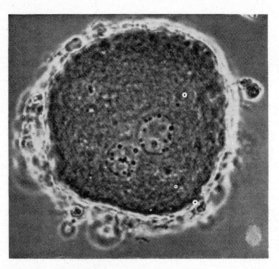

Fig. 5.5. Fertilized ovum showing position of the two pronuclei; later the pronuclei will fuse to form the zygote nucleus. (Dickmann *et al.*, *Anat. Rec.*, 1965, **152**, 293.)

form the *pronucleus*; and this takes up a position beside the egg pronucleus as illustrated in Fig. 5.5. Subsequently the pronuclei fuse to form the zygote nucleus by junction of their membranes over a limited region.

The Female Reproductive System

The primary reproductive apparatus in both male and female consists of tissue in which the mature sperm and ova are produced. The secondary reproductive apparatus in the male is concerned with the transfer of the sperm into the female reproductive tract whilst in the female the secondary apparatus is concerned with the nutrition of the fertilized ovum until birth and for a variable period after.

Structure

The human female reproductive system is illustrated in Fig. 5.6; basically it consists of the pair of ovaries from which mature ova are liberated into the *oviduct*, or *Fallopian tube*, which leads into the *uterus*, the cavity in which the fertilized ovum develops. The oviducts or Fallopian tubes are open at each end; at the fimbriated end the ovum enters and passes to the *isthmus* where it may be retained for some time; eventually it travels on to the uterus. If the ovum is to be fertilized it must meet a spermatozöon in the oviduct within a limited period of its arrival there; if this does not happen, the unfertilized ovum fails to be

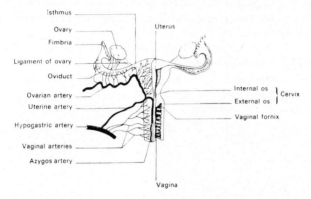

Fig. 5.6. The human female reproductive system. (Odell and Moyer, "Physiology of Reproduction", Mosby Co., St. Louis.)

implanted in the wall of the uterus and is subsequently carried away through the vagina in the menstrual outflow. The sperm are introduced, during the act of copulation, or coitus, into the vagina whence they migrate through the uterus to the Fallopian tubes.

Oestrus Cycle

It is because the ovum has to be fertilized within a short period of its liberation from the ovary that the whole behaviour of male and female has to conform to rules that will permit the spermatozöon to be in the oviduct within a short period of the liberation of the ovum; and it is this mutual behaviour of male and female—the mating behaviour—that represents the mechanism by which the ovum and sperm are enabled to meet within this critical period. In animals lower than primates the basic feature of mating behaviour is the cyclical occurrence of a *breeding season,* during which copulation between male and female takes place. During this period changes take place within the sexual organs of both female and male, and the female is said to be *on heat* or in *oestrus.* The characteristic of the change in the female is its cyclicity, so that the female is said to go into one or more cycles of oestrus, the essential feature of the cycle being the development of the ovum within a follicle, and its release into the oviduct.

Corpus Luteum

The cycle is completed by the development of an organ, the *corpus luteum,* that secretes a hormone principally controlling the events subsequent to fertilization, namely the satisfactory implantation of the fertilized ovum in the womb, or uterus, and its subsequent nutrition during development.

Follicular and Luteal Phases

Thus the cycle has two main periods, the *follicular,* leading to ovulation, and the *luteal,* dominated by the corpus luteum. If fertilization of the ovum does not take place, then the cycle is shortened, the corpus luteum degenerates and the changes in the uterus preparatory to receiving the fertilized ovum regress, and the cycle begins again by initiation of the events leading to the production of a new mature ovum.

Oestrogens and Progestins

As we shall see, the phases are governed by two types of hormone, the *oestrogens,* secreted mainly by the follicle and controlling the follicular phase, and *progestins,* secreted mainly by the corpus luteum, and controlling the subsequent phase, being especially prominent in the control of the state of the uterus during pregnancy. Failure of implantation makes continued progestin secretion unnecessary, and the corpus luteum degenerates, whilst a new follicle begins to develop, introducing the next oestrogen-dominated phase.

Variations among Species

Even if we confine attention to mammals, the features of the mating activity vary widely; some of the variations have obvious significance, such as the timing of the breeding season to coincide with the availability of food for mother and offspring, as, for example, the sheep with a gestation period of 145 days, the season being in the autumn; the mink with a shorter gestation period of 48 days has its breeding season in March, whilst rabbits, guinea pig and rat breed continuously throughout the year, as with man.

Ovulation. Apart from the actual breeding cycle, there are variations in the oestrus cycle, both in the length of a single cycle, which may be 4–5 days in the rat, 17 days in the sheep, and 28 days in the human, and in certain features of it. Some of these have been tabulated in Table I, and it will be seen that in many species the actual release of the ovum into the oviduct—*ovulation*—is not spontaneous but requires some external event, as with copulation in the cat and rabbit, so that until this happens the oestrus cycle remains uncompleted. If the female rabbit or cat is mated with a sterile male it ovulates and enters a stage of *pseudopregnancy*, with formation of a corpus luteum.

Luteinization. Similarly, the development of the corpus luteum—the luteal phase—does not always follow automatically from ovulation,

TABLE I

Differences among species in reproductive cycles
(From Schwartz, "The Hypothalamus", Academic Press.)

Overall Breeding Period	Cycles within Breeding Period	Delays	Ovulation	Luteal Stage	Gestation Period (days)	Example
Seasonal (Jan.-Feb.)	Monoestrous (few days)	None	Spont.	Follows Ovul.	52	Fox
Seasonal (Fall)	Polyoestrous (17 days)	None	Spont.	Follows Ovul.	145	Sheep
Seasonal (Spring to Summer)	Continuous	None	Induced	Follows Ovul.	42	Ferret
Seasonal (Spring and Fall)	Polyoestrous (2 weeks)	None	Induced	Follows Ovul.	62	Cat
Seasonal (March)	Polyoestrous (8–9 days)	Implant- ation	Induced	Follows Ovul.	48	Mink
Seasonal (Cop. in Fall)	Monoestrous (?)	Fertil- ization	Spont. (Spring)	Follows Ovul.	55	Bat
Seasonal	Polyoestrous	Implant. (Dec.-Jan.)	Spont. (Summer)	Follows Ovul.	42	Badger
Continuous	Continuous	None	Induced	Follows Ovul.	31	Rabbit
Continuous	Polyoestrous (16 days)	None	Spont.	Follows Ovul.	68	Guinea Pig
Continuous	Polyoestrous (4–6 days)	None	Spont.	Copulation Induced	22	Rat

so that in the rat, for example, copulation induces it; if there is a sterile mating in the species there is a period of *pseudopregnancy*, with corpus luteum formation which lasts for some 13 days compared with the true pregnancy period of 22 days.

Human. In the human, where we shall examine the cycle in some detail, the essential features are the absence of any breeding period and also the regular cycle of events which, in this species, is described as the *menstrual* cycle if this is completed without fertilization of the ovum and implantation. The obvious feature of the human cycle is the period of bleeding resulting from the breakdown of the structure of the internal lining of the uterus, the *endometrium*; this is associated with regression of the corpus luteum and marks the beginning of a new cycle.

Menstrual Cycle

Thus the uterus is a muscular organ lined internally with a mucosal surface called the *endometrium*, beneath this are three layers of smooth

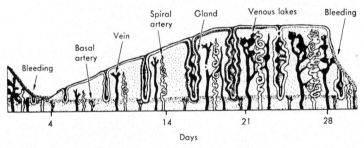

Fig. 5.7. Structural changes of the endometrium during the menstrual cycle; day-zero is taken as the first day of bleeding. (Odell and Moyer, "Physiology of Reproduction", Mosby Co., St. Louis.)

muscle, and the external surface is covered with serosa. As illustrated in Fig. 5.7 the endometrium is a complex glandular structure whose vascular supply is important for the nutrition of the freshly implanted ovum and subsequent development of the placenta. During the events leading to the release of the ovum into the oviduct, i.e. in the first part of the cycle, there is proliferation of the endometrial tissue leading to a large increase in thickness; this is associated with development of the glands whose secretions are apparently important for the implantation of the fertilized ovum. A day or two after ovulation, which occurs at about the 15th day of the cycle, histological changes are observable in the endometrium, mainly characterized by increased secretory activity of the glands; and at the time of implantation of the ovum, if this occurs, the tissue is oedematous and favourable to penetration of the *blastocyst*, as the fertilized ovum is called at this stage. If fertilization and implantation do not occur within the cycle, the endometrium breaks down with bleeding and the cycle starts again. The changes are illustrated in Fig. 5.7, where the first day of menstrual bleeding is arbitrarily called the first day of the cycle. In general, the first, or proliferative, half of the menstrual cycle begins at the end of menstruation and ends at the time of ovulation; since it is dominated by development of the follicle it is called the follicular phase, and, as we shall see, is governed by the secretion of oestrogen by this body. The latter half is called the luteal phase, the physiological reaction being determined largely by the continuing influence of oestrogens but also by the intervention of progestins secreted by the corpus luteum.

Ovulation

The menstrual cycle, and the oestrus cycle in lower animals, are essentially expressions of the ovulatory process, which in the human female occurs in a cyclical fashion with a periodicity of some 28 days. The site of ovulation is the ovary.

Primordial Follicle. During early embryonic development large primordial germ cells migrate to a localized portion of peritoneum in the body of the embryo. Continued multiplication of these, together with that of the contiguous mesenchyme cells with subsequent differentiation, leads ultimately to the mature *ovary* containing about half a million germ cells at different stages of development, some of them being primary öocytes. A covering of mesenchymal cells encloses the primary öocyte to give a cellular unit called the *primordial follicle*, the covering layer of cells being now called *follicular* or *granulosa cells*. It is within the follicle that the primary öocyte will mature to be expelled from the ovary. At birth the number of follicles ranges from 150,000 to 500,000 but by puberty this number has been considerably decreased, as a result of degeneration, or *atresia*.

Structure of Ovary. The structure of the adult ovary is illustrated in Fig. 5.8. In the adult woman they weigh about 4 grammes each, lying on the posterior wall of the pelvis, one on either side of the uterus (Fig. 5.6). The vast majority of the follicles are in the primordial stage, consisting of a primary öocyte (p. 384) surrounded by granulosa or follicular cells. Further in towards the centre there are some much larger follicles, and these represent stages in development leading to the evolution of the mature ovum, which remains, as we have seen (Fig. 5.3), a secondary öocyte.

Mature Graafian Follicle. Thus in the mature ovary the primary follicle consists of a large öocyte covered by a layer of granulosa cells; during each menstrual cycle of a woman, or the oestrus cycle of lower mammals, a certain number of primordial follicles undergo development by multiplication of the outer granulosa cells, with enlargement of the öocyte, to become a *secondary* or *Graafian follicle*; continued enlargement and the development of a fluid-filled cavity, as illustrated in

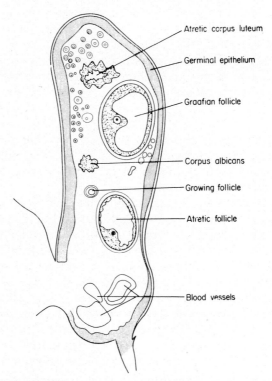

Fig. 5.8. Diagram of a section of an adult ovary.

Fig. 5.9, lead to the mature Graafian follicle with its enclosed öocyte. Development is accompanied by the formation of an outermost connective-tissue layer, the *theca*, consisting of two layers, the *theca interna* and *externa*, the former containing many blood capillaries. Under normal conditions only one of these ten-to-fifteen enlarged follicles extrudes its ovum into the Fallopian tube or oviduct (Fig. 5.6), the remainder undergoing regression, or atresia, so that for the next cycle another set of primordial follicles undergoes development.

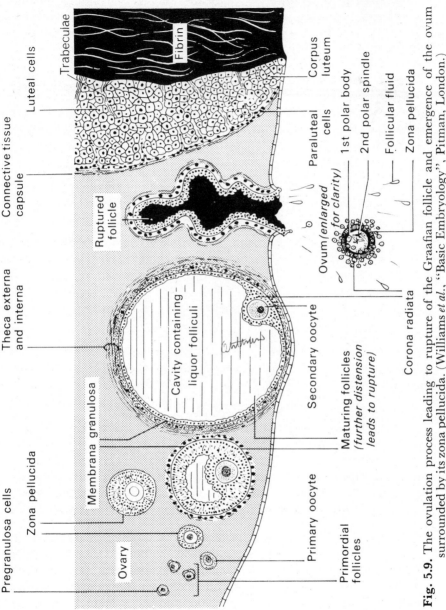

Fig. 5.9. The ovulation process leading to rupture of the Graafian follicle and emergence of the ovum surrounded by its zona pellucida. (Williams *et al.*, "Basic Embryology", Pitman, London.)

Passage into Oviduct. As indicated in Fig. 5.3 the first meiotic, or reduction, division occurs in the mature follicle prior to ovulation, whilst the second maturation division only occurs if the ovum is fertilized. If the ovum does not meet a viable spermatozöon within about 24 hours after ovulation, it begins to degenerate. The ovum expelled from the mature Graafian follicle consists of the secondary öocyte enclosed by its plasma membrane; closely attached to it is the first polar body. The öocyte plus polar body are enclosed by a non-cellular layer—the *zona pellucida*—and the latter is covered by several

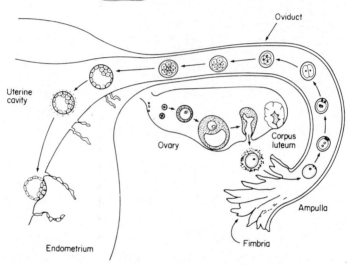

Fig. 5.10. Migration of the ovum from ovary to ampulla of oviduct and along the uterine cavity. (After Hamilton *et al.*, "Human Embryology", Heffer, Cambridge.)

layers of cells, derived from the granulosa cells of the follicle, called the *corona radiata*. The fimbriated end of the oviduct becomes closely applied to the ovary partially covering it, and the ovum passes rapidly into the duct (Fig. 5.10).

Development of Corpus Luteum. Ovulation is followed by further developments in the remainder of the Graafian follicle, which becomes the *corpus luteum*. Following rupture, with escape of the ovum, the follicle wall collapses and the hole left by the escaping ovum is sealed by a coagulum derived from blood from the cavity of the follicle. The granulosa cells multiply by mitotic division, and capillaries sprouting from the theca invade the granulosa layer; the whole body enlarges progressively through growth and multiplication of cells, which exhibit great metabolic activity. If the ovum is not fertilized the implantation in the wall of the uterus (p. 407) does not take place, and the corpus luteum then degenerates at about 9 days after ovulation to become, in about 3 months, a *corpus albicans*. If fertilization occurs, the ovum, after passing along the Fallopian tube into the uterus, eventually, after a latent period of 6–8 days in the uterus, burrows into the endometrium and is said to be implanted. During this period it has undergone development through mitotic division to become a *morula* and thence a *blastocyst* (p. 408), and it is in this latter condition that it is ready for implantation (Fig. 5.10). Successful implantation prevents the regression of the corpus luteum which survives morphologically to the end of pregnancy.

The Male System

The male reproductive organ is the *testis*, the site of production of the spermatozoa and of secretion of sex hormones called androgens. As indicated in Fig. 5.11 there are a number of accessory organs

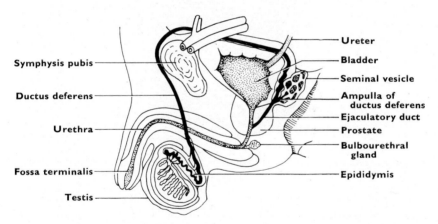

Fig. 5.11. The male reproductive system. (Odell and Moyer, "Physiology of Reproduction", Mosby Co., St. Louis.)

concerned with the storage of the spermatozoa and their subsequent transfer to the female reproductive tract namely the *epididymis* within the scrotal sac, in which sperm are stored, the *seminal vesicle* and *prostate* gland, producing secretions in which the spermatozoa are suspended, and the duct system along which the sperm and its fluid environment are transferred through the penis, the organ that is inserted into the vagina of the female.

Testes

The two testes in man (Fig. 5.12) are composed predominantly of masses of *seminiferous tubules*, 0·12–0·3 mm in diameter, which ultimately drain into the storage site, the *epididymis*, an elongated cylindrical structure on the surface of the testis made up of the *ductuli efferentes*, which ultimately converge to a single *epidydymal duct*, emerging into the *vas deferens*. Transport of sperm through the epididymis results from peristaltic contractions of smooth muscle cells in the tubular walls, and by ciliary action of the cells lining the lumen.

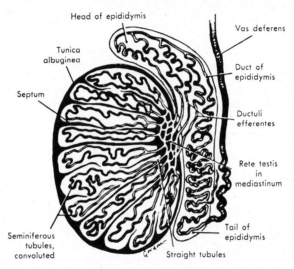

Fig. 5.12. Diagram showing the parts of the testis and epididymis. (Ham, "Histology", 6th Ed., Lippincott and Co.)

Spermatogenesis

Spermatozoa are derived from the primitive germ cells, or spermatogonia, constituting a part of the cellular lining of the seminiferous tubules. Associated with the spermatogonia are the *Sertoli cells*, whose ramifications extend from the basement membrane of the tubule up to the lumen; they presumably provide structural stability to an epithelium many of whose cells, the spermatogonia, are undergoing transformation to spermatocytes, spermatids and spermatozoa. The spaces between the tubules contain the *interstitial cells of Leydig*, responsible for the secretion of the male sex hormones. The process of spermatogenesis takes place in a cyclical fashion but the phases of activity

vary from one region to another. Since the process involves the formation of several histologically distinguishable cell types, the grouping of
cells in any region varies considerably. In general, the youngest
generation (spermatogonium) is closest to the basement membrane of
the tubule, whilst the most mature type, the spermatozöon, is close to
the lumen. The various stages in development give rise to cellular as-
sociations, and these are of a fixed type in man, some six arrangements
being described, e.g. one or two generations of spermatids are associated with spermatocytes and spermatogonia at the same step of
their respective development.

Stages. So far as the stages of development are concerned, it is sufficient to
appreciate that the spermatogonia lining the tubular walls undergo mitotic division
giving rise to more highly differentiated spermatogonia which eventually, after
meiotic division, become spermatids; the least differentiated and most primitive
spermatogonium is the dark staining *A-variety*; it divides mitotically to give the
Light-A variety from which, by further mitotic division, *Type-B* spermatogonia are
produced which then give rise to the resting spermatocyte. Clearly the continued
conversion of the most primitive *Dark-A* spermatogonia into more differentiated
types would deplete the stock of primitive cells, but this is prevented by the formation
of both *Dark-A* and *Light-A* daughter cells from the division of the *Dark-A* spermatogonium. The stages in development from primary spermatocyte to spermatid
involve, as we have seen, two meiotic divisions, during the first of which the number
of chromosomes is halved.

Spermiogenesis. The two meiotic divisions undergone by a primary spermatocyte give rise to four spermatids containing the haploid
number of chromosomes. The development of the spermatid to a
spermatozöon consists mainly of the modification of one pole to form
the *acrosome*—the apparatus that permits junction between spermatozöon
and ovum to take place and the subsequent transfer of the spermatozöon's nucleus to the ovum—and at the opposite pole the *tail*, whilst
the nucleus becomes highly dense and acquires the characteristic shape
shown in Fig. 5.13. Details of the morphological steps leading to the
definitive structure need not be entered into here; suffice it to say that
the centrioles—DNA-containing bodies in association with the nucleus
which, in somatic cells, as we have seen, organize the mitotic spindle
and asters—are responsible for the formation of the connecting piece
and flagellum, the distal centriole being responsible for the former and
the proximal for the latter. The flagellum has the characteristic
structure described earlier, consisting of the $9 + 2$ arrangement of
filaments, with the difference that the outer ring is made up of two
concentric rings of nine filaments each; and it is considered that the
outer dense filaments are the contractile elements that permit the
flagellar movement. The mitochondria surrounding the axial filament

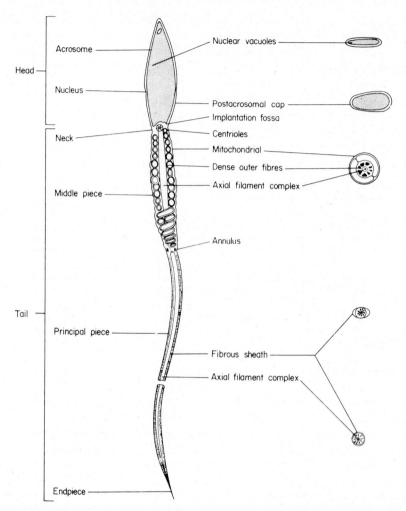

Fig. 5.13. The detailed structure of the mature spermatozöon. (Odell and Moyer, "Physiology of Reproduction", Mosby Co., St. Louis.)

in the middle piece are strategically placed to produce the metabolic energy involved in the flagellar movement.

The morphological changes taking place are described as *spermiogenesis*, and take place while the spermatid is engulfed in Sertoli cell cytoplasm.

Duration. The duration of the cycle of spermatogenesis, from the time when a stem cell spermatogonium is committed to cell division to the time when the spermatozöon is released from the Sertoli cell and lies free in the lumen, is some 74 ± 5 days.

Epididymis ✓

The sperm, after completion of development, are advanced into the efferent ductules of the testis and enter the epididymis where they are stored; the walls of this structure are lined by a secretory epithelium whose secretions provide the necessary metabolites for survival; it must be emphasized, however, that movement is passive, the flagellae being inactive.

Vas Deferens ✓

As indicated in Fig. 5.11, the vas deferens leads into the urethra during its course through the prostate gland; prior to this it dilates to form an enlargement, the *ampulla*, at the distal end of which it forms a large blind glandular evagination—the *seminal vesicle*. In the form of a *short* and *long ejaculatory duct*, it passes through the body of the *prostate* to enter the posterior wall of the urethra at the *colliculus seminalis*.

Seminal Vesicles. These two glands secrete a fluid that becomes integrated with the sperm mass during ejaculation; the secreted fluid has a characteristic chemical composition with high K^+ and low Na^+; citrate is the main anion whilst the sugar fructose, a substrate that the spermatozoa may utilize in metabolism, is present in high amounts.

Prostate

This is a lobular gland surrounding the proximal urethra (Fig. 5.11) and the ejaculatory ducts; it is about the size of a horse chestnut, being a conglomerate of some 30–50 small compound tubulo-alveolar glands giving origin to some 16–32 excretory ducts opening independently into the urethra around the colliculus seminalis. It produces a slightly acid secretion (pH 6·5) and provides the odour of semen; as with the seminal vesicular fluid, the main anion is citrate, but the main cation is sodium; a characteristic feature is the high concentration of zinc.

Bulbourethral and Urethral Glands

These glands, emptying into the posterior portion of the urethra, secrete large amounts of mucoproteins, and during the process of ejaculation the expulsion of their secretions antecedes that of the spermatozoa. Numerous smaller glands are widely dispersed along the length of the urethra.

Ripening of Sperm

The epididymis is something more than a storage tube, since it is well established that a certain period of ripening within the epididymis is necessary for fertility, so that young sperm immediately on entering are usually infertile; similarly, sperm that are too old are ineffective, and this explains why copulations after long intervals of abstention may be infertile.

The Seminiferous Tubule Fluid

Modern techniques of micropuncture have been successfully applied to obtaining fluid from the convoluted tubules and from their confluence in the rete testis. On the basis of such experiments, by Setchell and Waites, it has been concluded that the fluid, as primarily secreted in the convoluted tubules, has a high concentration of K^+ (112 mEq.) and low Na^+ (38 mEq.). On reaching the rete the fluid loses much of its K^+ and gains Na^+ and Cl^- so that the concentrations are now 14, 143 and 140 respectively, i.e. much closer to the values for extra-cellular fluid in other parts of the body. It is suggested that the semini-ferous tubules secrete a primarily K^+-rich fluid, which is diluted by a relatively Na^+-rich fluid secreted by the rete testis. This dilution is thought to occur by an ebb-and-flow process. That dilution occurs is suggested by the much lower spermatocrit (1 per cent) in the rete fluid than in the tubule fluid (14 per cent).

Coitus

The transfer of spermatozoa to the female reproductive tract is through the act of coitus, namely the introduction of the penis into the vagina with subsequent ejaculation of the spermatozoa and their accompanying glandular secretions, which together are given the name of *semen*. The rigidity required for penetration of the penis is provided by its engorgement by blood resulting from vasodilatation in response to impulses in the nervi erigentes, i.e. sacral autonomic parasympathetic fibres. The blood enters large collagenous sacs, the *corpora cavernosa*. These constitute a vast sponge-like system of irregular vascular spaces intercalated between the afferent arteries and efferent veins; in the relaxed state they appear only as thin clefts, but in erection they are large cavities filled with blood under pressure. Erection is associated with dilatation of the arteries, the veins playing a passive role, and these tend to become compressed as a result of the arterial expansion, thereby permitting the large increase in tissue volume. Because of this valve-like compression of the venous exits, the return of the penis into the flaccid condition, after the orgasm, occurs only slowly.

Ejaculation. Ejaculation, i.e. the transport of spermatozoa and secretions to the urethra and their ejection from the latter, is brought about primarily by muscular contraction, notably of the smooth muscle surrounding the epididymis and tubules, and by the spasmodic contraction of the bulbocavernosus muscle of the urogenital diaphragm. Reflux into the bladder is prevented by contraction of the sphincter at the base of the urethra, a process that prevents urine from entering the urethra at the same time.

The various components of the semen are ejected in order: first a small amount of pre-ejaculatory fluid is produced by the urethral and bulbourethral glands; next secretions from the prostate and seminal vesicles follow in order, then sperm from the ampulla of the ductus deferens and finally the main bulk of the spermatozoa from the tail of the epididymis.

Motility of Spermatozoa. During or after ejaculation the spermatozoa acquire a motility that had been inhibited while stored in the epididymis and ampulla. The exact mechanism for this acquisition of motility is not understood, but dilution *per se* in the seminal fluid is a significant factor, quite apart from its specific composition; thus shortage of fluid results in non-motile spermatozoa. Other factors are the ionic composition, pH and O_2-tension of the medium.

Migration of Spermatozoa to Oviduct

Speed of Movement

The semen, deposited in the vagina or, in some species such as the sow and rat, directly into the uterus, consists of a suspension of spermatozoa in the secretions of the accessory organs; of about 500 million or more that are deposited, only some 100 will be found in the oviducts at the time of fertilization. The passage from the vagina to the oviduct involves a lengthy journey, but this is completed remarkably rapidly; for example in the rat the journey of about 5 cm is accomplished in one minute, and in the human, sperm have been found in the oviduct some 30 minutes after coitus.

Uterine Contractions

The migration results from the sperm's own motility by flagellar action, amounting to some 28μ/sec in the mucus secretions of the uterus, but a predominant role is probably played in the uterine contractions which might suck semen into it and so accelerate movement. Thus, at the time of oestrus in many animals the oviductal and uterine muscles are active whilst, experimentally, transport can be increased by oestrogen in the non-oestrus rabbit. Again, fertility in animals may be increased by oxytocin injections which cause uterine contractions.

Prostaglandins. The presence of prostaglandins in the seminal fluid, moreover, lends further support to the importance of muscular contractions. It has been computed that the amount of prostaglandin E absorbed by the vagina from the semen after copulation would be sufficient to give a blood concentration that would cause uterine contractions. If the uterine end of the Fallopian tube contracted in preference to the fimbrial end, this might allow the spermatozöon longer in the tube in which to fertilize the ovum; at any rate male infertility has been associated with a low prostaglandin content of semen.

Uterine Secretions. The uterine secretions clearly have an important part to play; if they are too viscid they obstruct movement, whilst their chemical composition is important for nutrition of the sperm during its passage to the oviduct and to maintain it viable until fertilization occurs, which will not occur until the ovum arrives. In those species that ovulate in response to copulation, this period is of definite length, namely some 10 hr in the rabbit, but in the spontaneously ovulating animal without a fixed oestrus period of receiveness to the male, the spermatozöon may have to wait a much longer period, or it may meet an ovum as soon as it arrives. This timing is important, due to the limited periods during which both ovum and spermatozöon are capable of fertilization.

Capacitation. First, the spermatozöon, after leaving the male reproductive tract, must spend a further period of maturation, or *capacitation* as it is now called; only then can it penetrate the zona pellucida. Thus, if we take freshly ejaculated sperm and introduce it into oviducts of rabbits containing freshly ovulated ova, penetration of the zona does not occur, and the semen must be kept in the female genital tract for some 2–3 hr before this happens. Residence in the genital tract itself is not necessary, since capacitation will occur if the sperm are kept in the aqueous humour of the eye, but the fact that this occurs more rapidly during oestrus than in dioestrus suggests that the oviductal and follicular fluids are important. If capable spermatozoa are returned to seminal plasma they become "decapacitated" due to the presence of a high molecular weight protein in the fluid.

Loss of Capacity. Having developed its capability to fertilize, the spermatozöon retains this for only a limited period, being some 28–48 hr in man, 144 hr in the horse and 135 *days* in the bat; this period is shorter than the period during which the spermatozoa retain their motility, so that some other factor is lacking.

Disposal of Sperm

The spermatozoa remaining after coitus are largely disposed of within the female reproductive tract, either intracellularly by phagocytosis, e.g. by polymorphonuclear leucocytes, or extracellularly through enzymatic activity in the vaginal cavity. Leucocytic invasion of the uterus and endocervical cavity follows the appearance of the sperm and is similar to that occurring in response to any foreign body. The ciliary action of the epithelium of the oviducts may be important in removing nonfertilizing sperm.

Migration of the Ovum

In most species the time elapsing between ovulation and the arrival of the ovum in the uterine lumen is 3–4 days, although in the bat it requires several weeks and is much more rapid in the dog and cat, requiring only one day. The first stage, namely transport from the ovary through the ostium to the ampulla, requires only 2–5 minutes. Once there, contractions of the wall cause movement towards the uterus, but it remains at the distal end of the ampulla at the junction with the isthmus for some time, due to a sphincter-like obstruction. It is during this stay, which lasts about 3 days in primates, that fertilization and the early stages of cleavage take place. In most species the sperm are awaiting the ovum. The final stage, through the isthmic portion of the oviduct to the uterine cavity, is relatively short.

Limited Viability

As with the sperm, the viability of the ovum lasts only for a limited period. In the rabbit the period is remarkably short; thus freshly shed ova, obtained from a donor rabbit by injecting it with gonadotropins (Vol. 4), were transplanted into the oviduct of a recipient rabbit mated with a male rabbit 12 hr previously; through the first four hours after ovulation the ova were fertilized, but if 9 hours delay occurred before transplanting them, practically no ova were fertilized. In the human, the duration is given as 6–24 hr, and in the monkey 23 hr.

Oviductal Contractions

Contractions of the muscular wall of the oviduct certainly occur and this may be demonstrated by the spontaneous contraction taking place in isolated oviducts. The contractions are of the segmenting type rather than peristaltic, so that when a coloured oil is introduced into the oviduct it is caused to move, but not preferentially in either direction;

it results in spreading rather than the unidirectional progression that would be required to drive the ovum to the uterus. It must be appreciated that two mutually antagonistic processes are required of the oviduct, namely to facilitate progress of the sperm towards the infundibular end and transport of the ovum away from this to the tubero-uterine junction. A peristaltic wave would favour the one but oppose the other process, and it may be that the gradual spread achieved by segmentation is the appropriate compromise.

Resistance in Isthmus

It was observed that the coloured oil did not pass through the last 2 cm above the tubero-uterine junction, in spite of the segmenting movements, so that there appeared to be a functional block to further movement. This was emphasized by tying off the infundibular end, i.e. the end nearest to the ovary; in this case the secretions of the duct accumulated and caused it to balloon out in spite of the fact that the uterine end was not physically obstructed. Thus there is a definite resistance to free passage through the isthmus of the oviduct, a resistance that may be overcome experimentally by placing a tube in the last few centimetres of the duct leading into the uterus, thereby maintaining the junction patent.

Ciliary Movement

So far as progress of the ovum is concerned, the segmenting movements will contribute, but the ciliary action of the cells on the surface of the duct is probably more significant since, with a large body like the ovum, we may expect no definite preponderance of motion in one or other direction to result from segmentation. The ciliary action presumably helps to overcome the backward movement that would be induced by the flow of secretion, which apparently empties at the infundibular, rather than the uterine, end.

Prostaglandin Action

The possible involvement of prostaglandins in the uterine contractions that would favour migration of the spermatozoa has already been indicated. It is known that PGE_1 and PGE_2 cause contraction of the uterine end of the human Fallopian tube *in vitro*, but relax the distal three-quarters; these actions may well result in retention of the ovum, thereby increasing the chances of fertilization following coitus. As to the final "push" that must transfer the ovum into the uterus, little can be said.

Implantation and Development of the Ovum

Blastocyst

On its way along the Fallopian tube the fertilized ovum undergoes a series of cleavage divisions so that within the 3–4 days required to reach the uterus it has become a *morula*, a mulberry-shaped mass of blastomeres enclosed by the zona pellucida. Within the next few days, while free in the uterus, further cleavage leads to the stage called *blastocyst*; this mass of some 200 cells is differentiated into an outermost wall of *primary trophoblast*, within which is an eccentrically placed *inner cell mass* (Fig. 5.14). Certain formative cells within the inner cell mass will form the embryo, whilst all the remaining blastocystic cells will form what are called *extra-embryonic membranes*, i.e. structures concerned with the retention and nutrition of the embryo. The area of contact between the inner cell mass and the overlying trophoblast is the *embryonic pole* of the blastocyst.

Uterine Preparation

During this period the uterus, under the influence of progesterone secreted by the corpus luteum, has been undergoing preparative changes, and in experimental animals it can be shown that there has to be a fairly accurate synchrony between implantation and these changes. These are necessary since an egg will not survive if the development of the uterus is 24 hours ahead of it. Alternatively, oestrogens will hasten transport of the ovum so that it reaches the uterus prematurely and so fails to survive.

Envelopment of Blastocyst

The blastocyst attaches to the endometrium of the uterus and subsequently burrows in, as illustrated in Fig. 5.14. The zona pellucida now disappears and the polar trophoblast attaches to the endometrial surface and differentiates into an outer *syncytiotrophoblast* and an inner *cytotrophoblast*. As the blastocyst burrows deeper, the two trophoblastic layers spread to cover the abembryonic pole and thus completely envelop the blastocyst.

Development of Embryo and Cavities

The fluid within the blastocystic cavity is invaded by mesodermal cells derived from the inner surface of the cytotrophoblast, and at the same time a cavity, called the *primitive amniotic cavity*, forms between what will be the embryonic ectoderm and a layer of *amniogenic cells* derived from the polar trophoblast. The *primary yolk sac* is another cavity, delimited from the surrounding mesoderm by a layer of flattened

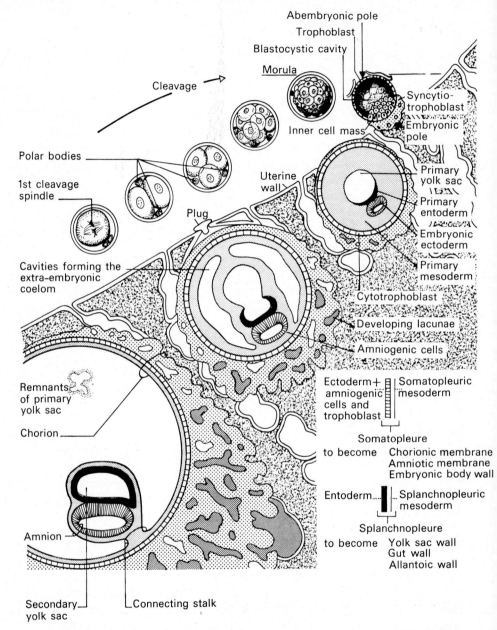

Fig. 5.14. Implantations and the initial stages of development of the embryo in the wall of the uterus. (Williams *et al.*, "Basic Embryology", Pitman, London).

cells (Heuser's membrane) and the *primary entoderm*, derived from the inner cell mass. The cells destined to form the embryo now constitute a two-layered disk consisting of the primary entoderm, forming the roof to the primary yolk sac, and the *embryonic ectoderm*. The primitive amniotic cavity is, as Fig. 5.14 shows, bounded by the ectoderm and the layer of amniogenic cells. While these events have been taking place the mesodermal tissue filling the cavity—the so-called *extra-embryonic mesoderm*—develops cavities which coalesce to form the *extra-embryonic coelom*. The stages leading to the development of the *secondary yolk sac, amnion* and *chorion* are easily envisaged in Fig. 5.14.

Further Embryonic Development. For details of further development of the embryo the reader must be referred to textbooks of embryology; it is sufficient to note that the embryo will develop and grow within the amniotic cavity, the secondary yolk sac becoming enclosed to form the alimentary tract. As the embryo develops, the coelomic cavity is encroached upon and by the end of the second month the amniotic cavity completely fills the chorionic vesicle, so that the amniotic membrane is in direct contact with the chorion; this relationship is maintained to the end of gestation.

Amniotic Fluid. During the first two months, the amnion closely enswathes the embryo and there is a large space between it and the chorion, the *extra-embryonic coelom*. Early in the third month the amniotic fluid increases rapidly in amount and the membranes fuse to obliterate the extra-embryonic coelom.

Nutrition of the Embryo

Lacunae

Nutrition of the embryo is through the development, in man and other animals, of an organ, the *placenta*, derived from the embryonic tissue, which permits a close association between the maternal and embryonic bloods. During implantation, the blastocyst erodes the uterine tissue to form a cavity in the decidua, and the trophoblast is probably responsible for engulfing nutrient material from the surrounding maternal tissue, the maternal blood coming into direct contact with the trophoblastic syncytium in the form of lacunae formed by the rupture of congested subepithelial capillaries into clefts in the syncytium. But soon this type of nutrition becomes inadequate and a blood-carried system develops.

Placenta

Within only 13 days after the beginning of implantation, a primitive vascular system develops in the embryo, chorion, yolk sac and

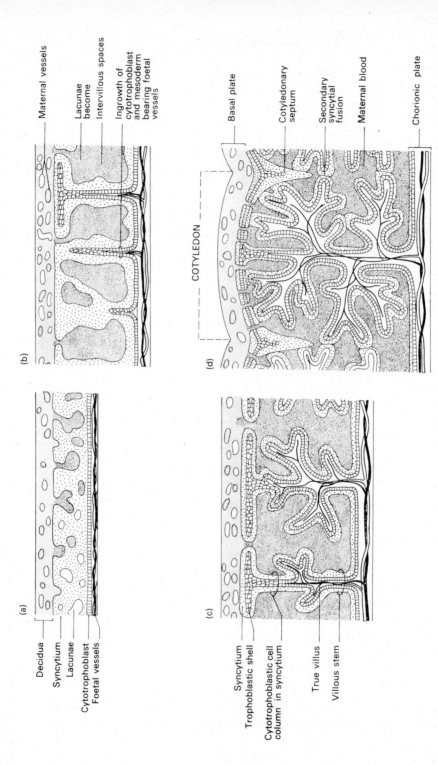

Fig. 5.15. Development of the placenta (note that in the upper figures development is shown from left to right as well as from above downwards). (Williams *et al.*, "Basic Embryology", Pitman, London.)

(a)

Decidua
Syncytium
Lacunae
Cytotrophoblast
Foetal vessels

(b)

Maternal vessels
Lacunae become
Intervillous spaces
Ingrowth of cytotrophoblast and mesoderm bearing foetal vessels

(c)

Syncytium
Trophoblastic shell
Cytotrophoblastic cell column in syncytium
True villus
Villous stem

(d)

Basal plate
Cotyledonary septum
Secondary syncytial fusion
Maternal blood
Chorionic plate
COTYLEDON

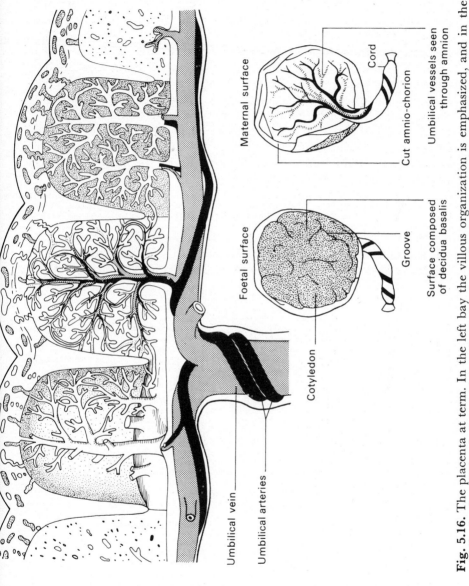

Fig. 5.16. The placenta at term. In the left bay the villous organization is emphasized, and in the middle the foetal circulation, with arteries in black. In the right bay the maternal blood percolating the intervillous spaces is emphasized. (Williams *et al.*, "Basic Embryology", Pitman, London.)

Maternal surface

Cord

Cut amnio-chorion

Umbilical vessels seen through amnion

Foetal surface

Groove

Surface composed of decidua basalis

Cotyledon

Umbilical vein

Umbilical arteries

connecting stalk. The vascularization of the chorion runs parallel with the development of villi which, as illustrated by Fig. 5.15, consist of projections of cytotrophoblastic cells along with the embryonic mesoderm bearing foetal blood-vessels; by the eighteenth day these villous projections contain blood islands and vessel rudiments, and by the 21st day these have united with each other and, by way of the connecting stalk, with the intraembryonic vessels to form a functional vascular system. The villi project into lacunae of the maternal blood. Development of this process leads to the mature placenta illustrated in Fig. 5.16. It must be emphasized that the foetal blood in the villus is always separated from the maternal blood by a layer of trophoblastic cells, and in this way a barrier between maternal and foetal circulations is maintained, a barrier that restrains the passage of many materials from one blood to the other.

Parturition and Puerperium

Figure 5.17 illustrates the situation of the foetus in the uterus at a late stage; it is enclosed in the amniotic sac which is fluid-filled so that the lungs of the new-born baby will be filled with this amniotic fluid.

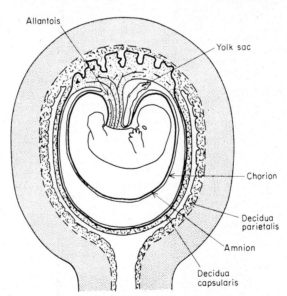

Fig. 5.17. Illustrating the foetus within the uterus. The foetus is surrounded by amniotic fluid enclosed in the amnion which lies in apposition to the chorion. The truly maternal layers are the decidua capsularis and decidua parietalis.

Chemical analysis of this fluid indicates that it is not a simple interstitial fluid formed as a filtrate from plasma but is a definite secretion, its characteristic electrolyte composition being the result of active processes taking place across the respiratory epithelium of the embryo.

Growth of Intra-Uterine Space

The maternal blood supply to the placenta is by way of the umbilical vessels. During the 270–280 days of human pregnancy the uterus grows so that the intra-uterine space increases from approximately zero to some 5–7 litres at term, about half of this volume being constituted by the foetus and the remainder by the amniotic fluid and placenta. Growth of the uterus is the result of an increase in the walls, in particular the muscle layers, which increase in weight from 70 g to 1000 g; this muscular development is the result of an increase in number of the fibres and a large increase in length.

Uterine Contractions

As pregnancy continues the weak rhythmic contractions of the uterine wall, occurring about every half-minute, tend to be replaced by more vigorous contractions until, at term, these become so vigorous as to be painful—labour pains, the pain being probably due to interference with the blood supply (*ischaemic pain*) and it is these contractions that ultimately lead to the expulsion of the infant, a process that may take anything from a few minutes to more than a day.

Changes in Cervix

Before this, the *parturitional stage*, is reached, several significant changes in the birth canal have taken place, notably a softening of the tissues of the cervix, whilst the mucus-secreting glands secrete copiously to keep the cervical canal filled with mucus. To allow passage of the foetus, the outer walls of the canal, formed of the bony pelvis, are able to relax by slackening of the ligaments, a process that, in animals like the rat, is assisted by actual absorption of bone at the symphysis pubis, i.e. the junction of the pubic bones in the mid-line on the ventral side of the pelvis.

Parturition

The final expulsion of the foetus occurs in stages; by the end of the first stage the cervix has become fully dilated as a result of the powerful uterine contractions; at some point during this process the foetal membranes, amnion and chorion, tear and the amniotic fluid escapes. During the second stage the foetus is expelled as a result of the uterine

contractions, which become ever more powerful, assisted by contraction of the abdominal muscles and diaphragm (bearing down).
During the third stage, after delivery of the foetus, the placenta and
foetal membranes are expelled as a result of further uterine contractions; in the human the umbilicus is tied off and cut to form the navel;
in animals this is achieved by biting; loss of blood is small by virtue
of constriction of the blood vessels.

Puerperium

The period immediately following parturition is called the *puerperium*,
and is accompanied by the initiation of lactation and the gradual
diminution in size of the uterus—involution—partly due to destruction
of the cells but mainly due to a reduction in their size. During this
period ovulation is usually suppressed but the situation varies with
species and individuals; in women lactation, when allowed to proceed,
tends to inhibit ovulation, and the onset of the menstrual cycle tends
to be delayed.

LACTATION

Structure of the Mammary Gland

The mammary glands produce the milk necessary to feed the infant
during its early development; they are considered to be modifications
of sweat glands (rather than of sebaceous glands). The human mammary
gland is composed of some 15–20 lobes, which are essentially independent glands with their own ducts opening separately at the surface
in the apical part, called the *nipple*. The individual lobe is built up of
numerous *lobules*, separated from each other by fine connective-
tissue strands—the *interlobular connective tissue*—which contrasts with the
coarser *interlobar* connective tissue. A section through a lobule shows it
to be made up of a system of tubules, and it is here, and in the alveoli
budding off from them, that the secretion of milk takes place, the
tubules emptying their secretions into small ductules which, by confluence, finally become the large ducts. Surrounding the nipple is the
areola, extending for 1–2 cm; it is pigmented, like the nipple, and
contains small modified mammary glands—*glands of Montgomery*—
whose ducts open through the skin of the areola. Sweat and sebaceous
glands are also present here.

Change during Pregnancy

The transitions from the non-pregnant to the pregnant, and then
to the lactating condition bring about striking changes in structure.

The tubules enlarge and give rise to *alveoli* by budding; and at the same time the large amounts of fat, held in the intralobular and inter-lobular connective tissue, decrease in amount so that the connective tissue layers are converted into septa in which the ducts are embedded. In general, the first phase of development during pregnancy consists

Inactive lobule   Active lobule

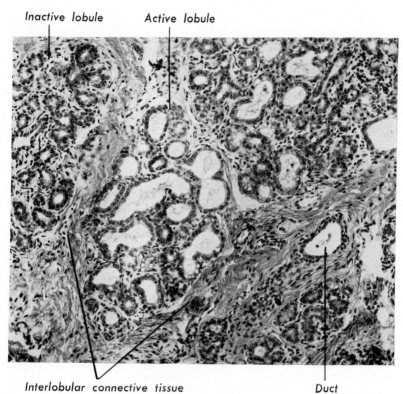

Interlobular connective tissue   Duct

Fig. 5.18. Section of mammary gland showing active and inactive glandular tissue. Fourth day post partum. Photomicrograph × 140. (Copenhaver, "Bailey's Textbook of Histology", 15th Ed., Williams and Wilkins, Baltimore.)

in cell proliferation to give the so-called alveolo-lobular condition; in women this takes place during the first five months; after this, the cells show signs of secretory activity, and the alveoli and small ducts become distended, increasing the size of the mamma. Figure 5.18 illustrates a section through a part of the gland in which both active and inactive lobules are present.

Secretory Tubule

The basic structure of the secretory tubule is a layer of *epithelial cells* lining the lumen. Beneath these are *basal cells*, resting on a basement membrane, whilst flattened *myoepithelial cells* are appressed to the inner aspect of the basement membrane. The epithelial cells have the

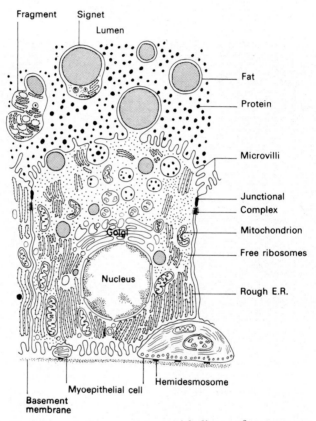

Fig. 5.19. Diagram of the secretory epithelium of mammary gland as interpreted from an electron micrograph. (Linzell and Peaker, *Physiol. Rev.*, 1971, **51**, 564.)

features characteristic of those lining cells capable of secreting fluid and specific substances (Fig. 5.19), with well marked Golgi apparatus and rough-surfaced endoplasmic reticulum. The apical surfaces of the cells have microvilli whilst the basal surfaces show infoldings, and the intercellular clefts exhibit the characteristic junctional complexes, including tight junctions, that are responsible for the low permeability of the epithelium to a variety of solutes when introduced into the duct. In the electron microscope the secretory cells appear to be of two main types, clear and dark, perhaps being responsible for different types of secretion.

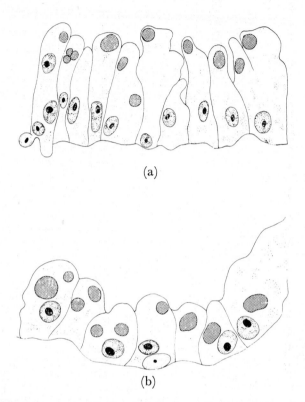

(a)

(b)

Fig. 5.20. Showing the epithelium of the lactating mammary gland in two conditions. In (a) the cells are tall and there are fat globules about to be ejected into the tubule. (b) represents an intermediate stage of secretion, with the cells much flatter. (After Richardson, *Brit. Med. Bull.* 1947, **5**, 123.)

Changes with Secretion. It is important to appreciate that the appearance of the epithelial cells can change radically according as the lobule, of which it forms a part, is in a condition of full secretion or has just been emptied and is beginning a new phase of elaboration of milk. Thus, when the alveoli and ductules are full, the cells are apparently stretched often to a very thin layer, but after emptying, when the lobule shrinks, the epithelium is often folded, with the cells so elongated that their apical cytoplasm projects into the lumen (Fig. 5.20).

Storage of Milk

The secretion of the epithelial cells—milk—is retained in the ducts until ejection is evoked, and then the alveoli and ducts are contracted by the action of the myoepithelial cells. Thus the mammary gland is different from other exocrine glands whose secretions are liberated more or less at the time of elaboration; milk secretion in the lactating animal is continuous, the product being stored until required.

Changes with Growth

The change in the mammary gland from the adult non-pregnant to the pregnant and lactating condition is the most striking, but after birth and up to adulthood there are continuous changes in the same general direction, namely the proliferation of the duct system and the ultimate formation of alveoli. It must be emphasized that there are many species-variations in the degree of development before pregnancy, and arguments from a single species can lead to misleading statements, e.g. that the alveolus, which arises as a budding from the duct system, is a feature peculiar to pregnancy; in fact, in animals with a prolonged luteal phase of the oestrus cycle (the pseudopregnant condition) not only can alveoli form but secretion of milk sufficient to nourish puppies can occur in the non-pregnant bitch. In general, before puberty is reached the changes consist of growth, keeping pace with the growth of the whole animal, with ramification of the duct system but no development of alveoli. With puberty and the onset of the oestrus cycle, more dramatic changes occur; the most prominent is the increase in size of the gland accompanied by the laying down of fat in the interlobular connective tissue and subcutaneously.

Oestrus

In lower mammals there are characteristic changes with each oestrus cycle, e.g. budding in the duct system, but this regresses after oestrus, so that on balance there is little development. In primates, including the human female, there are cyclical proliferative changes in the glandular tissue; thus in the human, a few days following cessation of menstrual flow there is a proliferation of duct tissue and this reaches its climax in the pre-menstruum; this is followed by a regressive phase. There is little doubt that these changes are related to the secretion of ovarian hormones (Vol. 4). Experimentally, when a condition of pseudopregnancy is induced in animals by sterile copulation or cervical stimulation (Vol. 4), mammary development characteristic of early pregnancy takes place but is followed by regression when the luteal phase subsides.

Chemical Composition of Milk

Protein and Carbohydrate

Milk is of necessity a complete food containing all the essentials for energy maintenance and growth. The mammary gland is not a

mere depot, accumulating the normal body constituents in a transferable form, but its cells are able to synthesize specific materials
peculiar to the milk from precursors in the blood plasma. Thus a new
protein, *caseinogen*, with a characteristic amino acid pattern is present;
as with fibrinogen, it is acted on by a proteolytic enzyme to form a
less soluble material, *casein*, the basis of cheese. Other proteins are
lactalbumin and *lactoglobulin*. The characteristic carbohydrate is *lactose*,

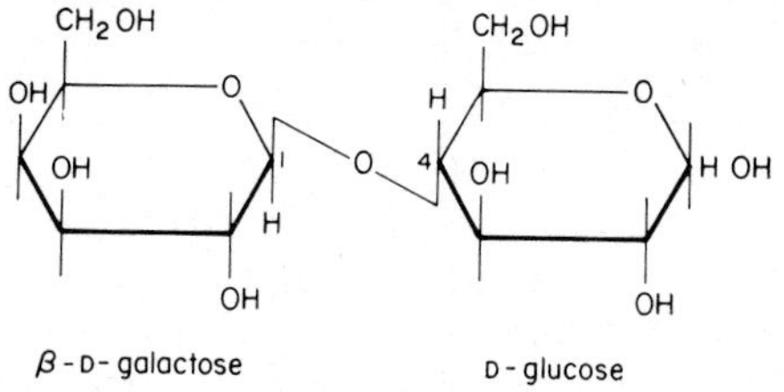

Fig. 5.21. The structural formula of lactose.

a disaccharide containing a glucose and galactose residue (Fig. 5.21);
the synthesis of galactose is peculiar to the gland, and its production
is used as a measure of lactation in experimental studies.

Species Differences

In Table II, concentrations of the more prominent constituents of
milk of several species are shown; there are some obvious species
differences, notably the very high fat and protein contents of reindeer
milk, the high concentration of lactose in human milk and its much
lower protein content, and so on.

TABLE II

Chemical composition of several species of milk
(After Kon and Cowie, "Milk: The Mammary Gland and its Secretions",
Academic Press.)

Species	Fat (g/100g)	Protein (g/100g)	Lactose	Na	K	Ca	Mg	Cl	P	Solids (g/100g)
					(mM/kg H_2O)					
Man	4·5	1·1	218	8·9	15	9·8	3·8	11	5·4	12·9
Cow	4·5	3·7	145	25	44·5	35	4·8	36·5	38	13·7
Reindeer	22·5	10·3	77							
Goat	4·5	3·3	142	10	50	40·5	9·6	48	46	13·2

Calcium and Phosphate

The high levels of calcium and phosphorus compared with those in blood are important from the point of view of bone growth; the presence of some 10 mmoles/litre of citric acid (170 mg/100 ml) ensures that a great deal of this ion is "sequestered" i.e. held in non-ionic form, and in this way a significant fraction is held in solution and not precipitated by the phosphates present; nevertheless a great deal is held in colloidal form as calcium salts of caseinogen, citric acid and phosphoric acid, so that only 35 per cent is present in the ionic form.

Lactose and Na^+

Milk is isotonic with the blood and this equality is maintained through the low concentrations of Na^+ and Cl^- which compensate for the high concentration of lactose, which in human milk contributes some 190 millimoles per litre. In general, as we should expect, there is an inverse relation between lactose concentration and sodium concentration (Fig. 5.22a), and lactose concentration and chloride concentration (Fig. 5.22b), whilst there is a direct relation between potassium and lactose concentrations which, of course, reflects an inverse relation between K^+ and Na^+ (Fig. 5.22d).

Active Transport. Quite clearly, the maintenance of a low concentration of Na^+ in the milk by comparison with that in the blood indicates a requirement for active transport of this ion at some stage. If, however, we envisage the secretion of milk as a primary formation of a lactose-filled vesicle within the cytoplasm of the secretory cell, with salts and water diffusing passively into it from the interstitial fluid, the active transport may well be exerted at the cell boundaries, controlling the cytoplasmic concentrations of Na^+ and K^+, as with so many other cells.

Fat

The fat of milk consists of droplets some 0·5 to 8 μ in diameter which are easily recognizable within the cytoplasm of the epithelial cells. The fat is mainly neutral fat, i.e. esterified with glycerol, and the fatty acids are both saturated, as with palmitic and stearic, and unsaturated, as with oleic acid; the proportion of unsaturated to saturated determines the fluidity at a given temperature. Linoleic acid has two double-bonds; it is described as an essential fatty acid since it cannot be synthesized in the animal body and is nevertheless required for synthetic purposes, as in the synthesis of prostanoic acid (p. 165). In human milk the percentages of saturated, monoethenoid and diethenoid fatty acids are: 48, 41 and 8 per cent respectively. So far as chain-length of the fatty acids is concerned, the 16- and 18-C-atom molecules constitute some 80 per cent of the total whilst the 10–14 C-atom acids make up the rest except for traces of shorter acids ranging from 4–8 C-atoms.

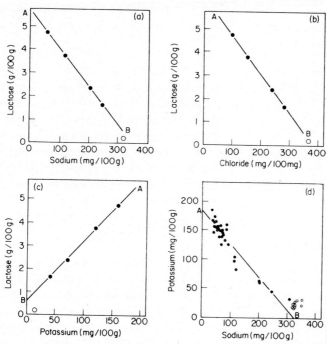

Fig. 5.22. Showing: (a) Inverse relation between lactose and sodium concentration in cow's milk; (b) Inverse relation between lactose and the chloride concentration in cow's milk; (c) Direct relation between lactose and potassium concentration in cow's milk; (d) Inverse relation between potassium and sodium concentration in cow's milk. ●: milk composition; ○: plasma (Barry and Rowland, *Biochem. J.*, 1953, **54**, 575.)

Iron

Of some interest is iron, large quantities of which are needed for multiplication of red blood cells and for providing the Fe-containing enzymes of oxidative metabolism. It is commonly stated that milk is deficient in iron when these requirements are taken into account, and certainly in some species a "suckling anaemia" will develop if the young are confined to maternal milk. The situation varies with the species, bovine milk having only 30 μg/100 ml, human 100, pig 180, and the dog 900 μg/100 ml. It is likely that, in some species, the stores in the liver and spleen, built up *in utero*, are drawn on during the suckling period, but if this occurs to any great extent it seems inadequate to meet the large demands of the growing infant, so that some deficiency of iron usually develops. It is interesting that some animals, such as the ox, man and cat, have a higher haemoglobin concentration in their blood when born than in adult life, so that we may regard the initial haemoconcentration as a store to be diluted during growth.

Amino Acids, etc.

So far as other constituents of the milk are concerned (such as amino acids, vitamins, trace elements), it is sufficient to say that, if the mother has been maintained during pregnancy on an adequate diet, these will be present in the milk in adequate quantities; deficiencies may well be reflected in the milk, although where calcium is concerned a deficiency of this in the mother's diet will not necessarily lead to a deficient milk, the maternal bones being sacrificed as a source.

The Secretion of Fat

Cellular Droplets

The most striking feature in the epithelial cell during secretion of milk is the formation of fat droplets, 1–8 μ in diameter, which migrate to the apex and may occupy practically the whole of the internal contents of the cell. Ultimately the droplets appear in the lumen, and Bargmann and Knoop suggested, on the basis of their histological studies, that they were actually pinched off by the plasma membrane, as illustrated schematically in Fig. 5.23.

Evidence strongly favouring this mode of formation is the appearance of fat droplets with a portion of cytoplasm surrounding them to give a signet-ring appearance as in Fig. 5.24. Sometimes the cytoplasm contains mitochondria, and in fact it has been argued that the other constituents of milk find their way out of the cell through such sacrifice of cytoplasm, giving rise to a truly apocrine (Vol. 1) type of secretion, but this is unlikely.

Membrane. If the fat droplet is, indeed, formed by pinching off the plasma membrane, we should expect that a membrane, similar in composition to the plasma membrane, might be separated from the droplets. By application of modern techniques of separating plasma membranes from mammary gland cells and the outer envelopes of the fat particles of milk it has been shown that this is probably true, the lipid envelope of the milk globule being made up of phospholipids and cholesterol similar to those of the plasma membrane of the cell. In the electron microscope, however, the isolated envelope of the milk globule tended to form plates by contrast with the tendency to form vesicles on the part of the plasma membrane, so that some change probably does take place when the milk globule is formed. It has been calculated that when the fat droplet comes close to the cell membrane, such strong attractive forces come into play that the plasma membrane

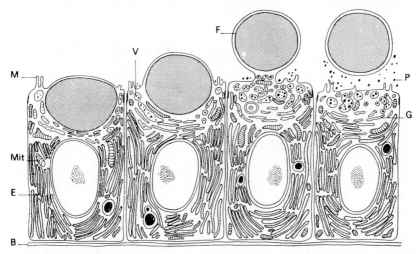

Fig. 5.23. Schematic representation of the secretion of fat droplets and protein granules. The fat droplet, F, is formed by pinching off a cytoplasmic oil droplet enclosed by a plasma membrane. The protein granules, P, are enclosed in vacuoles, V, which empty their contents into the extracellular space by exocytosis. M: microvillus; Mit: mitochondria; E: rough surfaced endoplasmic reticulum; G: Golgi apparatus; B: basement membrane. (Bargmann and Knoop, *Z. Zellf.*, 1959, **49**, 344.)

is able to pinch off the droplet spontaneously. In doing this, of course, the cell is sacrificing some of its own membrane, and it may be, as Patton and Fowks have emphasized, that the concurrent secretion of fluid and protein by exocytosis tends to restore the lost membrane.

Site of Synthesis

The actual site of synthesis of the fat droplets has been identified by the use of radioactive precursors. Mice were injected with ^{3}H-oleic acid, and the appearance of radioactivity in the gland was studied autoradiographically; within a minute practically all the label was identified in the rough-surfaced endoplasmic reticulum and in the lipid droplets, both intracellular and extracellular (Fig. 5.25). No activity was found over the granules in the Golgi system, which are the site of protein accumulation, so that lipid secretion does not depend on the Golgi apparatus, in marked contrast to the situation in liver cells where the lipid is accompanied by protein synthesis to form

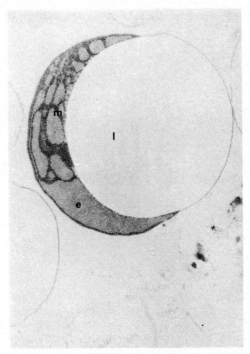

Fig. 5.24. Fat globules in goat's milk; one (l) has a crescent of cytoplasm (signet) that contains two mitochondria (m) and swollen endoplasmic reticulum (e) Scale 1 μ. (Courtesy of F. B. P. Wooding *in* Linzell and Peaker, *Physiol. Rev.*, 1971, **51**, 564.)

lipoproteins, which are accumulated in the Golgi system to form characteristic secretory granules.

Transport and Uptake of Fat

As we have seen, after a fat meal, the thoracic lymph contains large numbers of chylomicrons which pass into the blood stream. These fatty particles, some 300 to 6000 Å in diameter, appear in the electron microscope, after osmium fixation, as spherical bodies with a pale core

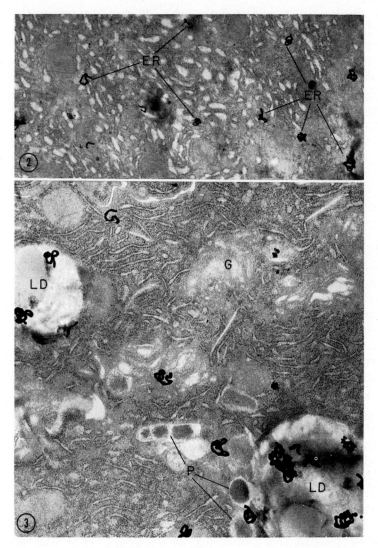

Fig. 5.25. Upper figure. 1 min after injection of oleic acid-^{3}H, the silver grains are seen over rough endoplasmic reticulum (ER) and some mitochondria (× 1600). Lower figure. 10–60 mins later the grains are seen to be concentrated over intracellular and intraluminal lipid droplets (LD). The granules (P) in the Golgi (G) vesicles are not labelled (× 25,000). (Stein and Stein, *J. Cell Biol.*, 1967, **34**, 251.)

and electron-dense surface layer, the latter being presumably the phospholipid-protein surface coating that tends to stabilize the particles. The chylomicrons may be regarded as a transport-form of absorbed long-chain fatty acids, and the mechanism of their subsequent uptake into the fat depots of the body, or site of metabolism, such as the liver, is of some general interest, and of particular interest so far as the mammary gland is concerned since there is no doubt that the long-chain fatty acids of the diet, appearing in the chyle and blood as neutral fat chylomicrons, appear in the milk as neutral triglyceride.*

Uptake from Blood. The uptake from blood is rapid, the half-life being of the order of 10–30 min, and by no means all is taken up by the liver, since the adipose tissue, heart muscle and lactating mammary gland all take up appreciable amounts. Escape from the vascular system in the liver is practicable through the large gaps in the sinusoid walls, but direct uptake into the extracellular spaces of adipose tissue and subsequent uptake into fat cells present problems, since the capillaries of adipose tissue do not exhibit fenestrations or gaps that would permit passage of such large particles.

The ability to take up fat varies from one tissue to another, and, in a given tissue, depends on the nutritional or other functional state of the animal. Thus uptake by mammary tissue occurs only during lactation, whilst uptake by adipose tissue occurs only when the animal is in positive energy balance. The factor in the tissue that determines whether it can take up blood triglyceride seems to be the presence of the triglyceride-splitting enzyme, phospholipid lipase.†

Cellular Hydrolysis

Biochemical studies of perfused tissue, be it a lactating mammary gland or adipose tissue of the abdomen, indicate that the triglyceride fat, perfused in the form of chylomicrons, is largely hydrolysed. Thus when the chylomicrons were doubly labelled, with ^{3}H in the glycerol and ^{14}C in the fatty acid portion, the fact of hydrolysis was established, since the incorporated fatty acids were largely combined with non-labelled glycerol, the hydrolysing tissue making use of its own, non-radioactive, glycerol for resynthesis to neutral fat. It has therefore

---

* With fatty acids of C_4 to C_{14} the precursors in milk are acetate; palmitate (C_{16}) is partly derived from acetate and partly from plasma triglyceride, i.e. chylomicrons. Oleate (C_{18}) and stearate (C_{18}) are almost entirely derived from plasma triglycerides.

† This enzyme has been described as "clearing factor" because it is released from tissues into the blood and catalyses the breakdown of chylomicrons, thereby reducing the milky appearance. Heparin, the anti-clotting factor contained by mast cells, when injected into the blood causes release of clearing factor or lipoprotein lipase. We may note that lipoprotein lipase is not the same enzyme as that catalysing the hydrolysis of fat in adipose cells.

been suggested that the transport out of the capillary involves hydrolysis of the triglyceride within the endothelial cells, the liberated fatty acids being emptied into the extracellular space of the fatty tissue and taken up by the fat cells to be reconverted to neutral fat.

Variations in Lipase Activity. Evidence for the importance of enzymatic splitting of fat is provided by analysis of the lipoprotein

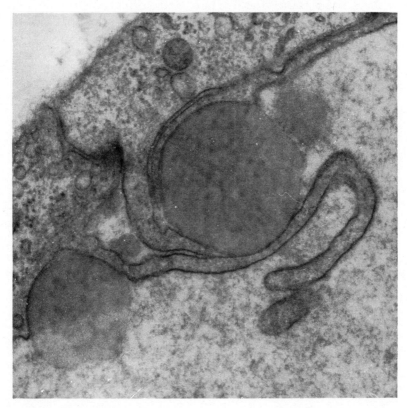

Fig. 5.26. Example of chylomicron sticking (left) and trapping (right) by cytoplasmic processes of endothelial cells. Both particles are very closely apposed to the cell membrane. From the mammary gland of the rat 18 mins after intravenous injection of chyle (unstained × 107,000). (Schoefl and French, *Proc. Roy. Soc. B.*, 1968, **169**, 153.)

lipase activity of tissues under conditions where fat absorption into the tissue from the blood is enhanced or inhibited. Thus the triglyceride uptake and lipoprotein lipase activity in adipose tissue are both decreased by fasting and diabetes, and increased by refeeding and insulin administration. In a similar way, with mammary tissue, both the uptake of chylomicrons and the phospholipase activity depend critically on whether the animal is lactating or not, and, if it is lactating, whether it is suckling. These changes are reflected, experimentally, in the uptake of chylomicrons from the blood perfused through the mammary gland blood-circulation. In the lactating and suckling condition some 8 per cent of the fatty acid content of the fat passing into the tissue is released as free fatty acids in the venous blood, compared with 1·5 per cent in non-suckling animals; these fatty acids presumably resulted from hydrolysis within the tissue. When the glands

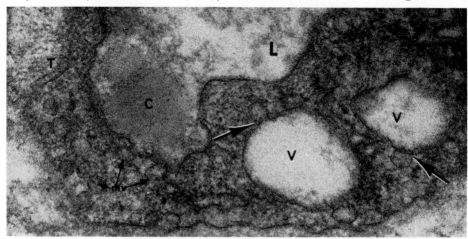

Fig. 5.27. Detail of a capillary endothelium in a parametrial fat pad perfused 5 mins with chylomicrons. A chylomicron (C) partially enveloped by an endothelial cell shows peripheral dispersion at the sites of microvascular invagination (MV). Note the junctions (arrows) between microvesicles and vacuoles (V). Both microvesicles and vacuoles contain flocculent material similar in electron opacity to that in the chylomicron. A tubular profile (T) 300 Å in diameter is evident in the cytoplasm (× 89,000).
(Blanchette-Mackie and Scow, *J. Cell Biol.*, 1971, **51**, 1.)

were analysed it was found that, in the suckling animals, 10 per cent of the perfused fat was retained compared with only 2 per cent in the non-suckling animals. In intact animals, moreover, the lipase activity of the mammary gland increases sharply at parturition and remains high so long as the mother suckles, whilst a period of non-suckling (as short as 9 hours) reduces the enzyme activity to about zero.

Engulfment of Chylomicrons. Electron microscopical studies of adipose tissue previously perfused with chylomicrons support the concept of hydrolysis within the capillary endothelium. Absorption of chylomicrons appeared to involve engulfment within the endothelial cell (Fig. 5.26), the large chylomicron becoming closely apposed to the cell membrane (Fig. 5.26). The actual process of engulfment probably takes place gradually, the chylomicron being eroded by the nipping off of pieces into microvesicles which subsequently empty into large vacuoles within the cytoplasm (Fig. 5.27). Sites of hydrolysis could be identified by incubating at 37°C tissue previously perfused with blood containing chylomicrons, and subsequently treating with lead salts, which formed electron-dense soaps with the liberated fatty acids. Granular and laminated precipitates were formed within the capillary endothelial cells and in the subendothelial space between endothelium and pericytes. Precipitates were found in microvesicles and the large vacuoles into which they apparently emptied.

Proteins and Lactose

Secretory Granule Formation

It will be recalled that Palade, in his classical study of the mode of synthesis and subsequent ejection of enzyme granules by the pancreatic acinar cell (Vol. 1), showed that the granule was synthesized on the endoplasmic reticulum. The secreted material was subsequently trans-ferred to membrane-bound vacuoles in the Golgi complex where they eventually matured, by a process of concentration, into secretory granules. Finally the membrane of the granule fused with the cell membrane, and the contents were emptied into the lumen. A precisely similar course of events has been described by Wellings and Philp for the elaboration of secretory granules in the mammary tubule, or alveolus, of the mouse. Granular material could be seen to collect in large vesicles of the Golgi complex, and these became mature droplets some 400–6000 Å in size similar in appearance to others seen in the lumen of the ductule. By the aid of autoradiography, after giving the lactating animal an injection of tritium-labelled leucine—an amino acid in high concentration in the milk-protein—they showed that the leucine first appeared in the endoplasmic reticulum, later in the Golgi apparatus and finally in the lumen.

Replacement of Membrane. Here, then, is a possible mechanism for restoring the cell membrane lost during elimination of the fat drop-lets, the Golgi droplet fusing with the plasma membrane as it empties its contents outside the cell in the characteristic process of exocytosis (Vol. 1).

Basic Mechanism of Secretion

In general, then, the secretion of milk may be divided into two main processes, namely (1) the pinching off of fat droplets, and (2) the emptying of Golgi-type vesicles through the apex of the epithelial cell.

Key Position of Lactose

The autoradiographic studies indicated that the Golgi vesicles contained protein, and it could well be that they also contained the remaining constituents of milk. Thus the vesicles could be the site of synthesis of lactose, the enzymes for this having been presumably synthesized on the endoplasmic reticulum along with the other proteins, and carried to the Golgi vesicles. Studies on the permeability of the apical cell membrane of the epithelium have shown that this is impermeable to lactose, so that its escape in large quantities from the

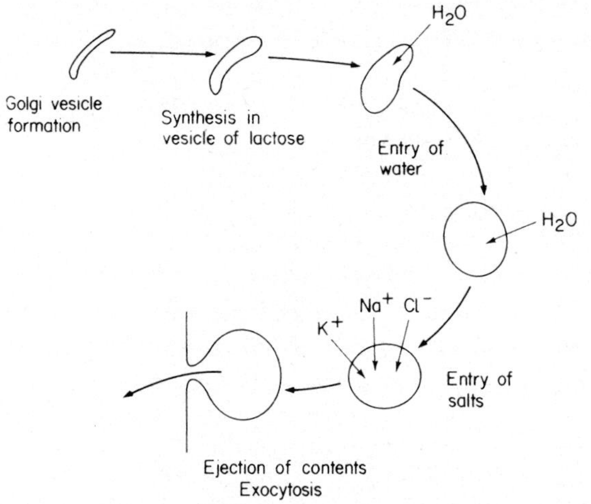

Fig. 5.28. Illustrates the development of the lactose-containing vesicles or granules, by synthesis of lactose within a Golgi vesicle. The osmotic pressure created by the synthesized lactose causes osmotic swelling associated with inward movement of cytoplasmic ions.

cell must be by way of some such exocytotic mechanism. The key position of lactose synthesis in the secretion of milk is indicated by several experimental studies. Thus, we may inhibit synthesis of lactose by depriving the perfused udder of glucose, and satisfying its other metabolic needs with acetate, fructose or mannose. In this case secretion of milk ceases, and is only resumed when glucose is provided. We may postulate, then, that the Golgi vesicle is the site of accumulation of the constituents of milk, a process that depends critically on the synthesis of lactose. Such a synthesis within a closed vesicle made up of a membrane impermeable to lactose, would provoke osmotic swelling leading to the entry of water and cytoplasmic solutes such as Na^+, Cl^-, K^+ etc. (Fig. 5.28).

Synthesis of Lactose

Lactose Synthetase

The final step in the synthesis of lactose is the reaction:

UDP-Galactose + Glucose → Lactose + UDP

(Fig. 5.29) a reaction catalysed by an enzyme-complex called *lactose synthetase*, which has been resolved into two separate proteins A and B. Protein B is *α-lactalbumin*, a constituent of milk, and its presence in this fluid in quite high concentrations (5 mg/ml in guinea pig milk)

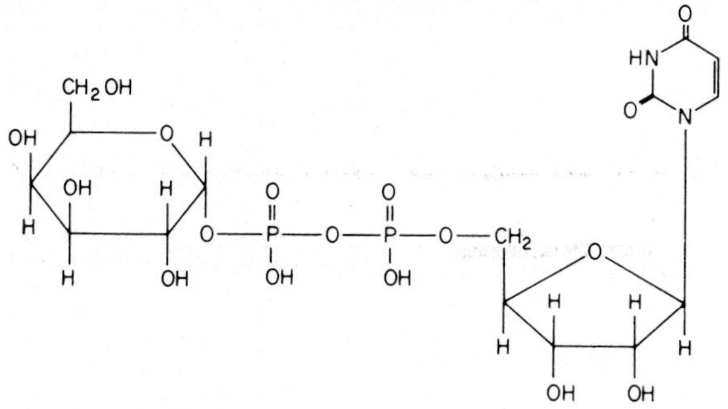

Fig. 5.29. The structural formula of UDP-galactose.

represents an unusual situation in which the enzyme required for synthesis of a component is lost in the secretion itself, a seeming extravagance which may, however, be of significance in the control of the secretion of milk.

Galactosyl Transferase. Protein A is an enzyme, *galactosyl trans-ferase*, which is not peculiar to the mammary cell being found in many cells where it is employed in the synthesis of N-acetyl lactosamine, a step in the formation of glycoproteins:

UDP-Galactose + N-acetyl-D-glucosamine ⟶ N-acetyl lactosamine
(NAL) + UDP

In the mammary cell its substrate-specificity is altered by the presence of α-lactalbumin so that it acquires an affinity for glucose and thereby acts as a galactosyl transferase for this molecule, producing lactose, i.e. *it becomes a lactose synthetase*. The efficacy of the enzyme in cata-lysing this reaction of lactose synthesis depends on the concentration of α-lactalbumin, the greater the concentration the greater the activity, whilst the activity of the same enzyme in the other reaction, namely the synthesis of N-acetyl lactosamine is reduced, as illustrated in Fig. 5.30, where it is seen that lactose–synthetase activity (curve B) increases with α-lactalbumin concentration whilst NAL–synthetase activity decreases (curve A).

Synthesis of α-Lactalbumin. Thus the synthesis of lactose depends vitally on the production of α-lactalbumin, and we may postulate that the A-enzyme is attached permanently to the Golgi membranes, whilst the B-enzyme—α-lactalbumin—is synthesized during milk secretion on the endoplasmic reticulum, whence it is carried to the Golgi vesicles to direct the catalysis of the UDP-Galactose + glucose

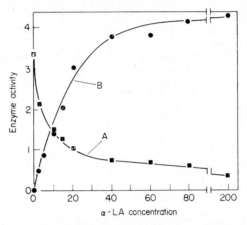

Fig. 5.30. The effect of the concentration of α lactalbumin (α-LA) on the NAL synthetase activity (curve A) and on the lactose synthetase activity (curve B) of A protein. Ordinate: enzyme activity, abscissa: concentration of α-LA in μg/100 μl. (Brew *et al.*, *Proc. Nat. Acad. Sci.*, 1968, **59**, 491.)

reaction by increasing the affinity of the A-enzyme for glucose. Inhibition of secretion could thus be brought about primarily by inhibition of synthesis of α-lactalbumin, which would bring lactose synthesis to an end as soon as the α-lactalbumin already in the cell had been eliminated in the milk.

Control by Specificity

As Brew remarked, this is a remarkable example of the control of an enzymatic reaction by grafting a new specificity on to an enzyme that spends most of its time carrying out a different reaction. That it is apparently unique may well be because the mammary gland has a metabolically unique feature, namely that of synthesizing lactose only during pregnancy and immediately after; thus, in the absence of pregnancy, the gland would never synthesize lactose throughout its life, but its NAL–synthetase activity, important for glycoprotein synthesis, would continue.

Electrochemical Aspects of Secretion

If the primary event in filling the Golgi vesicles with fluid and the non-fatty constituents of milk consists in the synthesis of lactose within these vesicles, then the control over the cytoplasmic composition of the secreting cell is of special interest, since it is conceivable that the vesicle fills by passive diffusion of solutes from cytoplasm, by virtue of the raised osmolality within the vesicle created by the lactose, as indicated in Fig. 5.28.

Ionic Relations

Linzell and Peaker have recently made an elaborate study of the ionic relations between milk, epithelial cytoplasm and extracellular fluid for the mouse and some other species. These were estimated by analysis of the gland and milk separately, the relative proportions of extracellular space and cells being estimated from the sucrose-space, whilst correction for the amount of milk remaining in the gland could be made on the basis of estimations of lactose, labelled with ^{14}C. The results of their analyses are shown schematically in Fig. 5.31, where the potential difference between the cytoplasm and the fluids is also shown. Thus if the extracellular fluid is used as the zero reference point, the intracellular potential is -41 mV whilst the potential across the whole cell is $+3$ mV.

Active Transport of Na^+. The interesting feature, shown by the middle block, is that the cytoplasm is in approximate electrochemical equilibrium with milk so far as Na^+ and K^+ are concerned, the negative potential of about -40 mV being sufficient to balance the concentration gradients. By contrast, these ions are not in equilibrium with the extracellular fluid, so that we must invoke active transport of Na^+ out of the cell linked with inward movement of K^+ presumably through the activity of a $Na^+–K^+$-activated ATPase, which seems to be localized to the basal and lateral parts of the plasma membrane. The chloride-ion is not at equilibrium on either side of the cell, so that active processes must be invoked to account for the concentration differences.

Golgi Vesicle. Figure 5.31 represents the situation regarding the cytoplasm and milk, but we may presume that an essentially similar situation would exist in relation to the Golgi vesicle within the cell before it had emptied its contents unless, of course, other changes in the secreted fluid took place after emptying and while the secretion was in the mammary ducts. If no further changes took place—and Linzell and Peaker's studies on the very low permeability of the ducts make such changes very improbable—then it would appear that the droplet could be formed by passive diffusion of Na^+ and K^+ into a

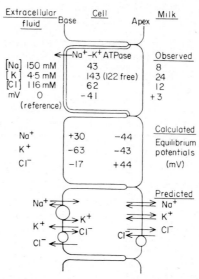

Fig. 5.31. Distribution of ions in mammary tissue of guinea pig. Top: measured concentrations in extracellular fluid and milk and calculated intracellular concentrations from an analysis of whole tissue and extracellular and milk spaces and measured membrane potentials. Middle: equilibrium potentials for each ion across apical and basal membranes calculated from Nernst equation. Bottom: scheme that could account for observed distribution of ions and membrane potentials. Active transport mechanisms probably exist for Na^+, K^+ and possibly for Cl^- on basal membrane, but possibly for Cl^- only on apical membrane. (Linzell and Peaker, *Physiol. Rev.*, 1971, **51**, 564.)

vesicle maintained with a zero or $+3$ mV internal potential. The passage of Cl^- into the vesicle, however, might require active transport, but until the involvement of other anions, including citrate and bicarbonate, is understood it is impossible to be more specific.

Changes in Tubule

As indicated earlier, the mammary gland stores its secretion within its tubular system, so that it is important to determine whether changes in composition take place during storage. One way of studying this would be to milk the animal very frequently, comparing the composition of the freshly secreted milk with that obtained after leaving a long period between milking; such experiments have given equivocal results, however, and a better approach is through a direct study of the permeability of the mammary ducts.

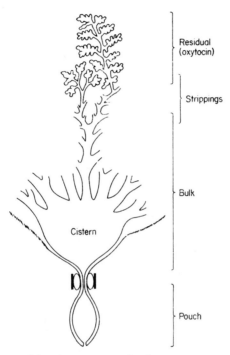

Residual (oxytocin)

Strippings

Bulk

Cistern

Pouch

Fig. 5.32. Diagram of the arrangement in the goat mammary gland and the location of fractions of milk removed in succession during a milking. Residual milk can only be removed after the injection of oxytocin. (Linzell and Peaker, *J. Physiol.*, 1971, **216,** 701.)

Permeability of Ducts. Thus in the goat, a pouch of teat may be prepared separated from the main cistern as in Fig. 5.32. When ^{14}C-lactose, Na$^+$, Cl$^-$, K$^+$, and Rb$^+$ were injected into this pouch through the teat-canal there was no loss into the blood, indicating a very low permeability of the epithelium lining the terminal duct. This does not prove, of course, that the smaller intramammary ducts share the same impermeability, although the structure of their epithelium is very similar. To determine the permeability of the smaller ducts the passage of the isotopes from blood into different portions of the secreted milk was measured. Thus, as illustrated in Fig. 5.32, the bulk of the milk already secreted is in the udder cistern, whilst the *"strippings"*, namely the final sample removed mechanically, come from small ducts, and the *residual milk*, obtained with the aid of oxytocin (Vol. 4), is derived from the smallest tubules and alveoli. Tritiated water passed rapidly into all fractions, as we should expect in view of the high permeability of animal cells to water; however ^{22}Na was excluded from the teat plus pouch, and the amount penetrating the bulk and strippings was small compared with that penetrating the residual milk, which had been derived from alveoli and ductules lined with secreting epithelium, and thus came into relation with cells that were permeable to the ion. Hence, in the smallest ducts, exchanges of material between blood and milk are by no means excluded, so that the composition of freshly secreted milk may be modified during its stay in the mammary gland.

Osmotic Work. The fact that the composition of milk is so different from that of the blood plasma means that, if such exchanges occurred rapidly, large amounts of osmotic work, involving large energy expenditure, would be required for maintaining the composition of milk, i.e. to prevent the lactose from escaping into the blood and Na^+ and K^+ penetrating into the milk.

Colostrum

This is the name given to the mammary gland secretion formed before the process of milk withdrawal has begun. It is thus present in the gland at parturition and represents the first food of the newborn infant. In addition, it occurs in some species during certain phases of the reproductive cycle, during weaning and in the newborn—the so-called witch's milk, this last being doubtless secreted by the immature mammary gland in response to the circulating maternal hormones. Cytologically the colostrum is recognized by the presence of colostral corpuscles—the corpuscles of Donne—which may well be macrophages that have ingested varying quantities of fat.

Immune Bodies

There are significant differences in chemical composition between colostrum and mature milk, the protein concentration being higher and the fat-content lower, but perhaps the most interesting feature is the circumstance that, in the colostrum of some species, notably the horse, pig and cow, there are large concentrations of immune bodies which, in these species, must be absorbed from the infant's intestine if it is to have the passive immunity to disease that is acquired by the infants of many other species, including man, by absorption from the mother across the placenta. Thus the ability to develop an active immunity to foreign bodies, such as bacteria and viruses, is not present in the very young, and is only acquired later; this is probably important physiologically since it means that the foetus, *in utero*, does not develop immune reactions to its mother's proteins.

Acquired Immunity. It is well known that many diseases, such as mumps, measles, diphtheria, etc., do not attack the very young, and this is because they have a passive immunity acquired *in utero* from the mother; certain species are an exception and must acquire this immunity from the colostrum. Thus, to cite an example, sows with some resistance to the virus of swine influenza possess, in their blood, protective immune bodies to this disease; the blood-serum of newborn piglets is free from these but they appear within 30 minutes of suckling. In a similar way ewes may be actively immunized against lamb dysentery by injection of killed bacteria (*Clostridium welchii* type B), and it is found that the lambs suckling from the ewe acquire this immunity passively. A very interesting feature of the colostrum of those species that must transmit immune bodies to the infant is the high degree of concentration of these bodies in the mammary secretion, compared with that in the blood.

Intestinal Absorption. Study of the intestinal absorption of colostrum of infant calves or piglets showed that absorption of these large molecules was similar to that of fat, in that they were incorporated into vesicles which appeared in the cytoplasm of the epithelial cells. With the aid of fluorescence-microscopy absorption of protein could be identified, and if animals were more than 18 days old they failed to exhibit the inclusions in the cytoplasm shown by the younger animals, showing that this capacity to absorb large molecules is a temporary phenomenon in the newborn.

Placenta. Finally we may note that the requirement for immune bodies in the colostrum is related to the structure of the placenta. Thus in man, where antibody transmission occurs typically before birth, the placenta is of the *haemochorial* type, uterine tissue being no part of the placenta which is made up of trophoblast, mesenchyme and endothelium. The horse and pig, typically transmitting after birth, have an *epitheliochorial* placenta, built up of uterine endothelium and epithelium as well as foetal structures, and we may presume that these extra barriers prevent transmission from maternal to foetal blood.

BIBLIOGRAPHY

The references given below are intended primarily as guides permitting the interested student to pursue any of the subjects in greater depth; they also constitute authority for many of the statements. To some extent consultation of some of the large academically orientated texts will be of assistance, and to avoid repetition these may be mentioned now:

As further reading to Chapters 1 and 2:

Davson, H. *A Textbook of General Physiology.* Churchill, London.

As further reading to Chapters 3, 4 and 5·

Davson, H. and Eggleton, G. (Eds.) *Principles of Human Physiology.* Churchill, London.
Keele, C. A. and Neil, F. *Samson Wright's Applied Physiology.* O.U.P., London.
Mountcastle, V. B. (Ed.) *Medical Physiology.* Mosby, St. Louis.
Ruch, T. C. and Patton, H. D. (Eds.) *Physiology and Biophysics.* Saunders, Philadelphia.

Chapter 1

Ahlquist, R. P. (1948). A study of adrenotropic receptors. *Amer. J. Physiol.*, **153,** 586–600.
Ahlquist, R. P. (1962). The adrenotropic receptor. *Arch. int. Pharmacodynam.*, **139,** 38–41.
Barondes, S. H. (Ed.) (1969). *Cellular Dynamics of the Neuron.* Academic Press, New York and London.
Blaschko, H. (1973). Catecholamine biosyntheses. *Brit. med. Bull.*, **29,** 105–109.
Bunge, R. P. (1968). Glial cells and the central myelin sheath. *Physiol. Rev.*, **48,** 197–251.
Burke, W. and Ginsborg, B. L. (1956). The electrical properties of the slow muscle fibre membrane. *J. Physiol.*, **132,** 586–598.
Ceccarelli, B., Hurlbut, W. P. and Mauro, A. (1972). Depletion of vesicles from frog neuromuscular junctions by prolonged tetanic stimulation. *J. Cell Biol.*, **54,** 30–38.
Coombs, J. S., Curtis, D. R. and Eccles, J. C. (1957). *J. Physiol.*, **139,** 198–231.
Cragg, B. G. (1970). What is the signal for chromatolysis. *Biol. Rev.*, **23,** 1–21.
Dahlström, A. (1969). Synthesis, transport and life-span of amine storage granules in sympathetic adrenergic neurons. *Symp. Int. Soc. Cell Biol.*, **8,** 153–174.
Davis, R. and Koelle, G. B. (1967). Electron microscopic localization of acetyl-cholinesterase and non-specific cholinesterase at the neuromuscular junction by the gold thiocholine and gold thiolacetic acid methods. *J. Cell Biol.*, **34,** 157–171.

Dodge, F. A. and Frankenhaeuser, B. (1958). Sodium currents in the myelinated nerve fibre of *Xenopus laevis* with the voltage clamp technique. *J. Physiol.*, **148**, 188–200.

Droz, B. and Koenig, H. L. (1969). The turnover of proteins in axons and nerve endings. *Symp. Int. Soc. Cell Biol.*, **8**, 35–50.

Dudel, J. and Kuffler, S. W. (1961). Presynaptic inhibition at the crayfish neuro-muscular junction. *J. Physiol.*, **155**, 543–562.

Eccles, J. C. (1952). The electrophysiological properties of the motoneurone. *Cold Spr. Harb. Symp. quant. Biol.*, **17**, 175–183.

Eccles, J. C. (1957). *The Physiology of Nerve Cells*. Johns Hopkins Univ. Press, Baltimore, and O.U.P.

Eccles, J. C. (1964). *The Physiology of Synapses*. Springer, Berlin.

Eccles, J. C., Katz, B. and Kuffler, S. W. (1941). Nature of the "end-plate potential" in curarized muscle. *J. Neurophysiol.*, **4**, 362–387.

Edelfrawi, M. E., Edelfrawi, A. T., Gilmour, L. P. and O'Brien, R. D. (1971). Multiple affinities for binding of cholinergic ligands to a particulate fraction of *Torpedo* electroplax. *Mol. Pharmacol.*, **7**, 420–428.

Euler, U. S. von (1948). Identification of the sympathomimetic ergone in adrenergic nerves of cattle (Sympathin N) with laevo-noradrenaline. *Acta physiol. scand.*, **16**, 63–74.

Falck, B., Hillarp, N.-Å., Thieme, G. and Torp, A. (1962). Fluorescence of catecholamines and related compounds condensed with formaldehyde. *J. Histochem. Cytochem.*, **10**, 348–354.

Fatt, P. and Katz, B. (1951). An analysis of the end-plate potential recorded with an intracellular electrode. *J. Physiol.*, **115**, 320–370.

Fatt, P. and Katz, B. (1952). Spontaneous subthreshold activity at motor nerve endings. *J. Physiol.*, **117**, 109–128.

Geffen, L. B. and Livett, B. G. (1971). Synaptic vesicles in sympathetic neurons. *Physiol. Rev.*, **51**, 98–157.

Guth, L. (1968). "Trophic" influences of nerve on muscle. *Physiol. Rev.*, **48**, 645–687.

Hodgkin, A. L. (1937). Evidence for electrical transmission in nerve. I and II. *J. Physiol.*, **90**, 183–210; 211–232.

Hodgkin, A. L. (1938). The subthreshold potentials in a crustacean nerve fibre. *Proc. Roy. Soc.*, *B.*, **126**, 87–121.

Hodgkin, A. L. and Huxley, A. F. (1945). Resting and action potentials in single nerve fibres. *J. Physiol.*, **104**, 176–195.

Hodgkin, A. L. and Huxley, A. F. (1952). Currents carried by sodium and potassium ions through the membrane of the giant axon of *Loligo*. *J. Physiol.*, **116**, 449–472.

Hodgkin, A. L. and Huxley, A. F. (1952). The components of membrane conductance in the giant axon of *Loligo*. *J. Physiol.*, **116**, 473–496.

Hodgkin, A. L. and Huxley, A. F. (1952). The dual effect of membrane potential on sodium conductance in the giant axon of *Loligo*. *J. Physiol.*, **116**, 497–506.

Hodgkin, A. L. and Huxley, A. F. (1952). Quantitative description of membrane current and its application to conduction and excitation in nerve. *J. Physiol.*, **117**, 500–544.

Hodgkin, A. L. and Katz, B. (1949). The effect of sodium ions on the electrical activity of the giant axon of the squid. *J. Physiol.*, **108**, 37–77.

Hösli, L. and Tebēcis, A. K. (1970). Actions of amino acids and convulsants on bulbar reticular neurone. *Exp. Brain Res.*, **11**, 111–127.

Hubbard, J. I., Llinas, R. and Quastel, D. M. J. (1969). *Electrophysiological Analysis of Synaptic Transmission.* Arnold, London.

Hunelus, F. C. and Davison, P. F. (1970). Fibrillar proteins from squid axons. I. Neurofilament protein. II. Microtubule protein. *J. Mol. Biol.*, **52**, 415–428; 429–439.

Jenkinson, D. H. (1973). Classification and properties of peripheral adrenergic receptors. *Brit. Med. Bull.*, **29**, 142–147.

Katz, B. (1939). *Electric Excitation in Nerve.* O.U.P.

Katz, B. (1969). *Nerve, Muscle and Synapse.* McGraw Hill.

Katz, B. and Miledi, R. (1968). The role of calcium in neuromuscular facilitation. *J. Physiol.*, **195**, 481–492.

Krnjevic, K. and Miledi, R. (1958). Acetylcholine in mammalian neuromuscular transmission. *Nature, Lond.*, **182**, 805–806.

Krnjevic, K. and Mitchell, J. F. (1961). The release of acetylcholine in the isolated rat diaphragm. *J. Physiol.*, **155**, 246–262.

Kuffler, S. W. (1942). Electrical potential changes at an isolated nerve-muscle junction. *J. Neurophysiol.*, **5**, 18–26.

Levi-Montalcini, R. and Angeletti, P. U. (1968). Nerve growth factor. *Physiol. Rev.*, **48**, 534–569.

Livett, B. G. (1973). Histochemical visualization of peripheral and central adrenergic neurones. *Brit. Med. Bull.*, **29**, 93–99.

Lloyd, D. P. C. (1943). Reflex action in relation to pattern and peripheral source of afferent stimulation. *J. Neurophysiol.*, **6**, 111–119.

Lubinska, L. (1961). Sedentary and migratory states of Schwann cells. *Exp. Cell Res.*, *Suppl.*, **8**, 74–90.

Lubinska, L. and Nimierko, S. (1971). Velocity and intensity of bidirectional migration of acetylcholinesterase in transected nerves. *Biol. Rev.*, **27**, 329–342.

Matthews, M. R. and Raisman, G. (1969). The ultrastructure and somatic efferent synapses of small granule-containing cells in the superior cervical ganglion. *J. Anat.*, **105**, 255–282.

McLennan, H. (1963). *Synaptic Transmission.* Saunders, Philadelphia.

Miledi, R., Molinoff, P. and Potter, L. T. (1971). Isolation of cholinergic receptor protein of *Torpedo* electric tissue. *Nature, Lond.*, **229**, 554–557.

O'Brien, R. D., Eldefrawi, M. E. and Eldefrawi, A. T. (1972). Isolation of acetyl-choline receptors. *Am. Rev. Pharmacol.*, **12**, 19–34.

O'Brien, R. D., Gilmour, L. P. and Eldefrawi, M. E. (1970). A muscarine-binding material in electroplax and its relation to the acetylcholine receptor. II. *Proc. Nat. Acad. Sci. Wash.*, **65**, 438–445.

Ochs, S. (1972). Rate of fast axoplasmic transport in mammalian nerve fibres. *J. Physiol.*, **227**, 627–645.

Owman, C. and Sjöstrand, N. O. (1965). Short adrenergic neurones and catechol-amine-containing cells in vas deferens and accessory male genital glands of different mammals. *Z. Zellforsch.*, **66**, 300–320.

Robertson, J. D. (1956). The ultrastructure of a reptilian myoneural junction. *J. biophys. biochem. Cytol.*, **2**, 381–394.

Schmitt, F. O. (1969). Fibrous proteins and neuronal dynamics. *Symp. Int. Soc. Cell Biol.*, **8**, 95–111.

Shanthaveerappa, T. R. and Bourne, G. H. (1962). The "perineurial epithelium", a metabolically active, continuous protoplasmic cell barrier surrounding peripheral nerve fasciculi. *J. Anat.*, **96**, 527–537.

Sherrington, C. S. (1906, 1947). *The Integrative Action of the Nervous System*. Constable, London; C.U.P.

Smith, R. S. and Koles, Z. J. (1970) Myelinated nerve fibers: computed effect of myelin thickness on conduction velocity. *Amer. J. Physiol.*, **219**, 1255–1258.

Thesleff, S. (1955). The mode of neuromuscular block caused by acetylcholine, nicotine, hexamethonium and succinylcholine. *Acta physiol. scand.*, **34**, 218-231.

Weiss, P. A. (1969). Neuronal dynamics and neuroplasmic "axonal" flow. *Symp. Int. Soc. Cell Biol.*, **8**, 3–34.

Zelená, J., Lubinska, L. and Gutmann, E. (1968). Accumulation of organelles at the ends of interrupted axons. *Z. Zellforsch.*, **91**, 200–219.

Chapter 2

Ambache, N. (1957). Properties of irin, a physiological constituent of rabbit's iris. *J. Physiol.*, **135**, 114–132.

Andersson, B., Larsson, S. and Persson, N. (1960). Some characteristics of the hypothalamic "drinking centre" as shown by the use of permanent electrodes. *Acta physiol. scand.*, **50**, 140–152.

Ahn, C. S. and Rosenberg, I. N. (1967). Proteolytic activity of the rat thyroid gland; studies using thyroid slices and subcellular fractions. *Endocrinol.*, **81**, 1319–1330.

Bakke, J. L. and Laurence, N. (1964). Influence of propylthiouracil and thyroxine on synthesis and secretion of TSH in the hypothyroid rat. *Acta Endocr.*, **46**, 111–123.

Bennett, H. S. and Kilham, L. (1940). The blood vessels of the adrenal gland of the adult cat. *Anat. Rec.*, **77**, 447–471.

Berson, S. A., Yalow, R. S., Glick, S. M. & Roth, J. (1964). Immunoassay of protein and peptide hormones. *Metabolism*, **13**, No. 10, Pt. 2, 171–189.

Birnbaumer, L. and Rodbell, M. (1969). Adenyl cyclase in fat cells. *J. biol. Chem.*, **244**, 3477–3483.

Celis, M. E., Taleisnik, S. and Walter, R. (1971). Release of pituitary melanocyte-stimulating hormone by the oxytocin fragment, H–Cys–Tyr–Ile–Gln–ASN–OH. *Biophys. Biochem. Res. Comm.*, **45**, 564–569.

Clegg, P. C. and Clegg, A. G. (1969). *Hormones, Cells and Organisms*. Heinemann, London.

Coupland, R. E. (1965). Electron microscopic observations in the structure of the rat adrenal medulla. I. Ultrastructure and organization of chromaffine cells in the normal adrenal medulla. II. Normal innervation. *J. Anat., London*, **99**, 231–254; 255–272.

Coupland, R. E. (1968). Corticosterone and methylation of noradrenaline by extra-adrenal chromaffin tissue. *J. Endocrin.*, **41**, 487–490.

Coupland, R. E., Pyper, A. S. and Hopwood, D. (1964). A method for differentiating between noradrenaline- and adrenaline-storing cells in the light and electron microscope. *Nature*, **201**, 1241–1242.

Cowie, A. T. and Tindal, J. S. (1971). *The Physiology of Lactation*. Arnold, London.

Dean, P. M. and Matthews, E. K. (1970). Glucose-induced electrical activity in pancreatic acinar islet cells. *J. Physiol.*, **210**, 255–264.

Douglas, W. W. (1968). Stimulus-secretion coupling: the concept and clues from chromaffin and other cells. *Brit. J. Pharmacol.*, **34**, 451–474.

Elliott, T. R. (1904). On the action of adrenalin. *J. Physiol.*, **31**, 20–21P.

Euler, K. von (1935). Uber die spezifische Blutdrucksenkende Substanz des menschlichen Prostata- und Samenblasensekretes. *Klin. Wochschr.*, **14,** 1182–1183.

Fawcett, D. W., Long, J. A. and Jones, A. L. (1969). The ultrastructure of endocrine glands. *Rec. Progr. Horm. Res.*, **25,** 315–368.

Fieser, L. F. and Fieser, M. (1959). *Steroids.* Reinhold, New York.

Gala, R. R. and Westphal, U. (1966). Further studies on the corticosteroid-binding globulin in the rat: proposed endocrine control. *Endocrinology.*, **79,** 67–76.

Garren, L. D., Ney, R. L. and Davis, W. W. (1965). Studies on the role of protein synthesis in the regulation of corticosterone production by adrenocorticotropic hormone in vivo. *Proc. Nat. Acad. Sci. Wash.*, **53,** 1443–1450.

Gill, G. N. and Garren, L. D. (1970). A cyclic 3′,5′-adenosine monophosphate dependent protein kinase from the adrenal cortex: comparison with a cyclic AMP binding protein. *Biochem. Biophys. Res. Comm.*, **39,** 335–345.

Goodman, I. and Hiatt, R. B. (1972). Coherin: a new peptide of the bovine neurohypophysis with activity on gastrointestinal motility. *Science,* **178,** 419–421.

Grahame-Smith, D. G., Butcher, R. W., Ney, R. L. and Sutherland, E. N. (1967). Adenosine 3′,5′-monophosphate as the intracellular mediator of the action of adrenocorticotropic hormone on the adrenal cortex. *J. biol. Chem.*, **242,** 5535–5541.

Greengard, P., Kuo, J. F. and Miyamoto, E. (1971). Studies on the mechanism of action of cyclic AMP in nervous and other tissues. In *Adv. Enzyme Regulation.* Vol. 9 (Ed. G. Weber), pp. 113–125. Pergamon, New York.

Harris, G. W. (1955). *Neural Control of the Pituitary Gland.* Arnold, London.

Harrison, R. G. and Hoey, M. J. (1960). *The Adrenal Circulation.* Blackwell Scientific Publ., Oxford, 1960.

Hayward, J. W. and Jennings, D. P. (1973). Activity of magnocellular neuroendocrine cells in the hypothalamus of unanaesthetized monkeys. II. *J. Physiol.*, **232,** 545–572.

Hedqvist, P. (1971). Prostaglandin E compounds and sympathetic neuromuscular transmission. *Ann. N.Y. Acad. Sci.*, **180,** 410–415.

Horton, E. W. (1969). Hypotheses in physiological roles of prostaglandins. *Physiol. Rev.*, **49,** 122–161.

Horton, E. W. (1972). *Prostaglandins.* Heinemann, London, 1972.

Joanus, S. D., Rosenstein, M. J. and Rubin, R. P. (1970). On the mode of action of ACTH on the isolated perfused adrenal gland. *J. Physiol.*, **209,** 539–556.

Kahn, R. H. and Lands, W. E. M. (Eds.) (1973). *Prostaglandins and Cyclic AMP.* Academic Press, New York and London.

Karlson, P. and Sekeris, C. E. (1962). Zum Tyrosinstoffwechsel der Insekten. IX. *Biochim. biophys. Acta*, **63,** 489–495.

Klyne, W. (1957). *The Chemistry of the Steroids.* Methuen, London.

Le Quesne, L. P. (1967). The response of the adrenal cortex to surgical stress. In *The Human Adrenal Cortex.* Ciba Study Group No. 27. Churchill, 1967.

Libet, B. (1968). Long latent periods and further analysis of slow synaptic responses in sympathetic ganglia. *J. Neurophysiol.*, **30,** 494–514.

Lipmann, F. (1971). Effects of cyclic AMP, its mechanism of action, and comments on the energetics of its 3′-phosphate bond. In *Adv. Enzyme Regulations.* Vol. 9 (Ed. G. Weber). Pergamon, New York.

Litwack, G. and Sanger, S. (1972). Subcellular actions of glucocorticoids. In *Biochemical Actions of Hormones. Vol. II* (Ed. G. Litwack). Acad. Press, 1972.

Mannetti, G. V., Shlatz, L. and Reilly, K. (1972). Hormone-membrane interactions (pp. 207–239). In *Insulin Action* (Ed. I. B. Fritz). Academic Press, New York and London.

Matsuo, H., Baba, Y., Nair, R. M. G., Anmura, A. and Schally, A. V. (1971). Structure of porcine LH- and FSH-releasing hormone. I. The proposed amino acid sequence. *Biophys. Biochem. Res. Comm.*, **43**, 1334–1339.

Matthews, E. K. and Saffran, M. (1973). Ionic dependence of adrenal steroido-genesis and ACTH-induced changes in the membrane potential of adrenocortical cells. *J. Physiol.*, **234**, 43–64.

Matthews, M. R. and Raisman, G. (1969). The ultrastructure and somatic efferent synapses of small granule-containing cells in the superior cervical ganglion. *J. Anat. London*, **105**, 255–282.

Mayerson, B. J. (1964). Central nervous monoamines and hormone induced estrus behaviour in the spayed rat. *Acta physiol. scand.*, **63**, Suppl. 241.

McCann, S. M. and Porter, J. C. (1969). Hypothalamic pituitary stimulating and inhibitory hormones. *Physiol. Rev.*, **49**, 240–284.

Mess, B., Zanisi, M. and Tima, L. (1970). Site of production of releasing and inhibiting factors. In *The Hypothalamus* (Ed. L. Martini, M. Molla and F. Fraschini), pp. 259–276. Academic Press, New York and London.

Midgley, A. R. (1966). Radioimmunoassay: a method for human chorionic gonadotropin and human luteinizing hormone. *Endocrinology*, **79**, 10–18.

Milligan, J. V. and Kraicer, J. (1970). Adenohypophysial transmembrane potentials: polarity reversal by elevated internal potassium concentration. *Science*, **167**, 182–184.

Monod, J., Changeux, J. P. and Jacob, F. (1963). Allosteric proteins and cellular control systems. *J. mol. Biol.*, **6**, 306–329.

Motta, M., Piva, F. and Martini, L. (1970). The hypothalamus as the center of feedback mechanisms. In *The Hypothalamus* (Ed. L. Martini, M. Motta and F. Fraschini), pp. 463–484. Academic Press, New York and London.

Nair, R. M. G., Kasten, A. J. and Schally, A. V. (1971). Isolation and structure of hypothalamic MSH release-inhibiting hormone. *Biophys. Biochem. Res. Comm.*, **43**, 1376–1381.

Palay, S. L. (1970). The fine structure of secretory neurons in the preoptic nucleus of the goldfish. *Anat. Rec.*, **138**, 417–443.

Pastan, I., Roth, J. and Macchia, V. (1966). Binding of hormone to tissue: the first step in polypeptide hormone action. *Proc. Na⁺ Acad. Sci. Wash.*, **56**, 1802–1809.

Pena, A., Dvorkin, B. and White, A. (1966). Effects of a single injection of cortisol on amino acid-incorporating activities of rat liver and thymic preparations in vitro. *J. Biol. Chem.*, **241**, 2144–2150.

Pitt-Rivers, R. and Cavalieri, R. R. (1964). Thyroid hormone biosynthesis. In *The Thyroid Gland*. Vol. 1 (Eds. R. Pitt-Rivers and W. R. Trotter), pp. 87–112. Butterworth, London.

Pohorecky, L. A. and Wurtman, R. J. (1971). Adrenocortical control of epinephrine synthesis. *Pharmacol. Rev.*, **23**, 1–35.

Poisner, A. M. and Trifana, J. M. (1967). The role of ATP and ATPase in the release of catecholamines from the adrenal medulla. *J. Pharmacol.*, **3**, 561–571.

Popa, G. T. and Fielding, U. (1930). A portal circulation from the pituitary to the hypothalamic region. *J. Anat. Lond.*, **65**, 88–91.

Porter, J. C. *et al.* (1970). A procedure for the cannulation of a pituitary stalk portal vessel and perfusion of the pars distalis in the rat. *Endocrinology*, **87**, 187–201.

Rall, T. W. and Sutherland, E. W. (1961). The regulatory role of adenosine— 3',5'-phosphate. *C.S.H. Symp.*, **26**, 347–354.

Ramwell, P. W. and Shaw, J. E. (1970). Biological significance of the prostaglandins. *Rec. Progr. Horm. Res.*, **26**, 139–187.

Riggs, T. R. (1970). Hormones and transport across cell membranes. In *Biochemical Actions of Hormones* (Ed. G. Litwack), Ch. 5. Academic Press, New York and London.

Robertis, E. de, DeLores Arnaiz, G. R. and Albenci, M. (1967). Subcellular distribution of adenyl cyclase and cyclic phosphodiesterase in rat brain cortex. *J. biol. Chem.*, **242**, 3487–3498.

Robison, G. A., Butcher, R. W. and Sutherland, E. W. (1971). *Cyclic AMP*. Academic Press, New York and London.

Sachs, H. *et al.* (1969). Biosynthesis and release of vasopressin and neurophysin. *Recent Progr. Hormone Res.*, **25**, 447–491.

Sandberg, A. and Slaunwhite, R. W. (1963). Transcortin: a corticosteroid-binding protein of plasma. V. *J. clin. Invest.*, **42**, 51–54.

Sanger, F. (1960). Chemistry of insulin. *Brit. Med. Bull.*, **16**, 183–188.

Schayer, R. W. (1967). A unified theory of glucocorticoid action. II. *Persp. Biol. Med.*, **10**, 409–418.

Schimmer, B. P., Ueda, K. and Sato, G. H. (1968). Site of action of adrenocorticotropic hormone (ACTH) in adrenal cell cultures. *Biophys. Biochem. Res. Comm*, **32**, 806–810.

Shoppee, C. W. (1958). *Chemistry of the Steroids*. Methuen, London.

Spaziani, E. and Gutman, A. (1965). Distribution volumes of sugars in rat uterus, ileum and skeletal muscle as affected by estradiol. *Endocrinology*. **76**, 470–478.

Spaziani, E. and Suddich, R. P. (1967). Hexose transport and blood flow rate in the uterus: effects of estradiol, puromycin and actinomycin, D. *Endocrinology*. **81**, 205–214.

Takabatake, Y. and Sachs, H. (1964). Vasopressin biosynthesis. III. *Endocrinology*. **75**, 934–942.

Tata, J. R. (1964). Distribution and metabolism of thyroid hormones. In *The Thyroid Gland*. Vol. I (Eds. R. Pitt-Rivers and W. R. Trotter), pp. 163–186. Butterworth, London.

Tata, J. R. (1970). Regulation of protein synthesis by growth and developmental hormones. In *Biochemical Actions of Hormones* (Ed. G. Litwack), Ch. 3. Academic Press, New York and London.

Turkington, R. W. (1972). Molecular biological aspects of prolactin. In *Lactogenic Hormones*. Ciba Symp., pp. 111–127. Churchill-Livingston.

Verney, E. B. (1947). The antidiuretic hormone and the factors which determine its release. *Proc. Roy. Soc., B.*, **135**, 25–105.

Westphal, U. (1970). Binding of hormones to serum proteins. In *Biochemical Actions of Hormones* (Ed. G. Litwack), Ch. 6. Academic Press, New York and London.

Wilber, J. F. and Porter, J. C. (1970). Thyrotropin and growth hormone releasing activity in hypophyseal portal blood. *Endocrinology*, **87**, 807–811.

Wilson, B., Raghapathy, E., Tonoue, T. and Tong, W. (1968). TSH-like actions of dibutyryl-cAMP on isolated bovine thyroid cells. *Endocrinology*, **83**, 877–848.

Wissig, S. L. (1964). Morphology and cytology. In *The Thyroid Gland*. Vol. 1 (Eds. R. Pitt-Rivers and W. R. Trotter), pp. 32–70. Butterworth, London.

Wurtman, R. J. and Axelrod, J. (1966). Control of enzymatic synthesis of adrenaline in the adrenal medulla by adrenal cortical steroids. *J. biol. Chem.*, **241**, 2301–2305.

Wurtman, R. J., Axelrod, J. and Kelly, D. E. (1968). *The Pineal*. Academic Press, New York.

Zambrano, D. and Robertis, E. de (1966). The secretory cycle of supraoptic neurons in the rat. *Z. Zellforsch.*, **73**, 414–431.

Chapter 3

Adrian, R. H., Chandler, W. K. and Hodgkin, A. L. (1969). The kinetics of mechanical activation in frog muscle. *J. Physiol.*, **204**, 207–230.

Adrian, R. H., Constantin, L. L. and Peachey, L. D. (1969). Radial spread of contraction in frog muscle fibres. *J. Physiol.*, **204**, 231–257.

Beeler, G. W. and Reuter, H. (1970). The relation between membrane potential, membrane currents and activation of contraction in ventricular myocardial fibres. *J. Physiol.*, **207**, 211–229.

Bendall, J. R. (1969). *Muscles, Molecules and Movement*. Heinemann, London.

Bennett, M. R. (1972). *Autonomic Neuromuscular Transmission*. C.U.P.

Bennett, M. R. (1973). An electrophysiological analysis of the storage and release of noradrenaline at sympathetic nerve terminals. *J. Physiol.*, **229**, 515–531.

Bennett, M. R., Burnstock, G. and Holman, M. E. (1966). Transmission from perivascular inhibitory fibres to the smooth muscle of the guinea pig taenia coli. *J. Physiol.*, **182**, 527–540.

Benz, L., Eckstein, B., Matthews, E. K. and Williams, J. A. (1972). Control of pancreatic amylase release *in vitro*: effects of ions, cyclic AMP, and colchicine. *Brit. J. Pharmacol.*, **46**, 66–77.

Bolton, T. R. (1973). Effects of electrogenic sodium pumping on the membrane potential of longitudinal smooth muscle from terminal ileum of guinea pig. *J. Physiol.*, **228**, 693–712.

Bozler, E. (1948). Conduction automacity and tonus of visceral muscles. *Experientia*, **4**, 213–218.

Brading, A., Bülbring, E. and Tomita, T. (1969). The effect of sodium and calcium on the action potential of the smooth muscle of the guinea-pig taenia coli. *J. Physiol.*, **200**, 637–654.

Breeman, C. von *et al.* (1972). Excitation-contraction coupling in rabbit aorta studied by the lanthanum method of measuring cellular calcium influx. *Circulation Res.*, **30**, 44–54.

Bülbring, E. (Ed.). (1970). *Smooth Muscle*. Arnold, London.

Bülbring, E. and Tomita, T. (1970). Effects of Ca removal on the smooth muscle of the guinea-pig taenia coli. *J. Physiol.*, **210**, 217–232.

Carlson, F. D., Hardy, D. and Wilkie, D. R. (1967). The relation between heat produced and phosphorylcreatine split during isometric contraction of frog's muscle. *J. Physiol.*, **189**, 209–235.

Case, R. M. and Clausen, T. (1971). Calcium ions and release of enzymes from rat pancreas in response to gastrointestinal hormones. *Acta endocr. Copenhagen Suppl.* **155**, 203.

Casteels, R. (1970). The relation between the membrane potential and the ion distribution in smooth muscle cells. In *Smooth Muscle* (Ed. E. Bülbring *et al.*). Arnold, 1970, pp. 70–99.

Close, R. (1967). Properties of motor units in fast and slow skeletal muscles. *J. Physiol.*, **193**, 45–55.

Constantin, L. L., Franzini-Armstrong, C. and Podolsky, R. J. (1965). Localization of calcium-accumulating structures in striated muscle fibres. *Science*, **147**, 158–160.

Devine, C. E. and Somlyo, A. P. (1971). Thick filaments in vascular smooth muscle. *J. Cell Biol.*, **49**, 636–649.

Dewey, M. M. (1969). The structure and function of the intercalated disc in vertebrate cardiac muscle. *Comparative Physiology of the Heart; Current Trends. Experientia Suppl.*, **15**, 10–28.

Dewey, M. M. and Barr, L. (1964). A study of the structure and distribution of the nexus. *J. Cell Biol.*, **23**, 553–585.

Douglas, W. W. (1968). Stimulus-secretion coupling: the concept and clues from chromaffin and other cells. *Br. J. Pharmacol.*, **34**, 451–474.

Douglas, W. W. (1974). Involvement of calcium in exocytosis and the exocytosis-vesiculation sequence. *Biochem. Soc. Symp.*, **39**, 1–28.

Douglas, W. W., Kanno, T. and Sampson, S. R. (1967). Effects of acetylcholine and other medullary secretogogues and antagonists on the membrane potential of adrenal chromaffin cells. *J. Physiol.*, **188**, 107–120.

Douglas, W. W. and Nagasawa, J. (1971). Membrane vesiculation at sites of exocytosis in the neurohypophysis and adrenal medulla: a device for membrane conservation. *J. Physiol.*, **218**, 94–95P.

Douglas, W. W. and Poisner, A. M. (1962). Importance of calcium for acetylcholine-evoked salivary secretion. *Nature, Lond.*, **196**, 379–380.

Douglas, W. W. and Rubin, R. P. (1963). The mechanism of catecholamine release from the adrenal medulla and the role of calcium in stimulus-secretion coupling. *J. Physiol.*, **167**, 288–310.

Dreizen, P., Gershman, L. C., Trotta, P. P. and Stracher, A. (1967). Myosin. Subunits and their interactions. *J. Gen. Physiol.*, **50**, No. 6, Pt. 2, 85–118.

Ebashi, S. and Ebashi, F. (1964). A new protein component participating in the superprecipitation of myosin B. *J. Biochem., Tokyo*, **55**, 604–613.

Ebashi, S., Ohtsuki, I. and Mihashi, K. (1972). Regulatory proteins of muscle with special reference to troponin. *Cold Spr. Harb. Symp. quant. Biol.*, **37**, 215–223.

Endo, M., Tanaka, M. and Ogawa, Y. (1970). Calcium induced release of calcium from the sarcoplasmic reticulum of skinned skeletal muscle fibres. *Nature*, **228**, 34–36.

Euler, U. S. von and Lishajko, F. (1968). Inhibitory action of adrenergic blocking agents on reuptake and net uptake of noradrenaline in nerve granules. *Acta physiol. scand.*, **74**, 501–506.

Fawcett, D. W. and McNutt, N. S. (1969). The ultrastructure of the cat myocardium. *J. Cell Biol.*, **42**, 1–45.

Ford, L. E. and Podolsky, R. J. (1970). Regenerative calcium release within muscle cells. *Science*, **167**, 58–59.

Ford, L. E. and Podolsky, R. J. (1972). Calcium uptake and force development by skinned muscle fibres in ECTA buffered solutions. *J. Physiol.*, **223**, 1–19.

Gasser, H. S. and Hill, A. V. (1924). Dynamics of muscular contraction. *Proc. Roy. Soc., B*, **96**, 398–437.

Gillis, J. M. (1969). The site of action of calcium in producing contraction in striated muscle. *J. Physiol.*, **200**, 849–864.

Gordon, A. M., Huxley, A. F. and Julian, F. J. (1966). Tension development in highly stretched vertebrate muscle fibres. *J. Physiol.*, **184**, 143–169.

Gray, E. G. and Willis, R. A. (1970). On synaptic vesicles, complex vesicles and dense projections. *Brain Res.*, **24**, 149–168.

Haselgrove, J. C. (1972). X-ray evidence for a conformational change in the actin-containing filaments of vertebrate striated muscle. *Cold Spr. Harb. Symp. quant. Biol.*, **37**, 341–352.

Hecht, H. H. (1965). Comparative physiological and morphological aspects of pacemaker tissues. *Ann. N.Y. Acad. Sci.*, **127**, 49–83.

Hill, A. V. (1938). The heat of shortening and the dynamic constants of muscle. *Proc. Roy. Soc., B*, **126**, 136–195.

Hodgkin, A. L. and Horowicz, P. (1960). Potassium contractures in single muscle fibres. *J. Physiol.*, **153**, 386–403.

Hoffman, B. F. and Suckling, E. E. (1953). Cardiac cellular potentials: effect of vagal stimulation and acetylcholine. *Amer. J. Physiol.*, **173**, 312–320.

Hokin, L. E. (1966). Effects of calcium omission on acetylcholine-stimulated amylase secretion and phospholipid synthesis in pigeon pancreas slices. *Biochim. biophys. acta*, **115**, 219–221.

Hutter, O. F. and Trautwein, W. (1956). Vagal and sympathetic effects on the pacemaker fibres in the sinus venosus of the heart. *J. gen. Physiol.*, **39**, 715–733.

Huxley, A. F. (1957). Muscle structure and theories of contraction. *Progr. Biophys.*, **7**, 255–318.

Huxley, A. F. (1959). Ionic movements during nerve activity. *Ann. N.Y. Acad. Sci.*, **81**, 221–246.

Huxley, A. F. and Taylor, R. E. (1958). Local activation of striated muscle fibres. *J. Physiol.*, **144**, 426–441.

Huxley, H. E. (1972). Structural changes in the actin- and myosin-containing filaments during contraction. *Cold Spr. Harb. Symp. quant. Biol.*, **37**, 361–376.

Katz, A. M. (1970). Contractile proteins of the heart. *Physiol. Rev.*, **50**, 63–158.

Kendrick-Jones, J., Lehman, W. and Szent-Györgyi, A. G. (1970). Regulation in molluscan muscles. *J. mol. Biol.*, **54**, 313–326.

Lacy, P. E., Howell, S. L., Young, D. A. and Fink, C. J. (1968). New hypothesis of insulin secretion. *Nature, Lond.*, **219**, 1177–1179.

Lane, B. P. and Rhodin, J. A. G. (1964). Cellular interrelationships and electrical activity in two types of smooth muscle. *J. Ultrastr. Res.*, **10**, 470–488.

Legato, M. J. and Langer, G. A. (1969). The subcellular localization of calcium ion in mammalian myocardium. *J. Cell Biol.*, **41**, 401–423.

Lehman, W., Kendrick-Jones, J. and Szent-Györgyi, A. G. (1972). Myosin-linked regulatory systems: comparative studies. *Cold Spr. Harb. Symp. quant. Biol.*, **37**, 319–330.

Lowey, S., Slayter, H. S., Weeds, A. G. and Baker, H. (1969). Substructure of the myosin molecule. I. Subfragments of myosin by enzymic degradation. *J. mol. Biol.*, **42**, 1–29.

Lowy, J. and Small, J. V. (1970). The organization of myosin and actin in vertebrate smooth muscle. *Nature*, **227**, 46–51.

Matthews, E. K. and Petersen, O. H. (1973). Pancreatic acinar cells: ionic dependence of the membrane potential and acetylcholine-induced depolarization. *J. Physiol.*, **231**, 283–295.

Matthews, E. K., Petersen, O. H. and Williams, J. A. (1973). Pancreatic acinar cells: acetylcholine-induced membrane depolarization, calcium efflux and amylase release. *J. Physiol.*, **234**, 689–701.

Moore, P. B., Huxley, H. E. and De Rosier, D. J. (1970). Three-dimensional recon-
struction of F-actin, thin filaments and decorated thin filaments. *J. mol. Biol.*,
50, 279–295.

Morad, M. and Orkand, R. K. (1971). Excitation-contraction coupling in frog
ventricle: evidence from voltage clamp studies. *J. Physiol.*, **219,** 167–189.

Nachmias, V. T., Huxley, H. E. and Kessler, D. (1970). Electron microscope
observations on actomyosin and actin preparations from *Physarum polycephalum.*
J. mol. Biol., **50,** 83–90.

Nagasawa, J., Douglas, W. W. and Schulz, R. A. (1970). Ultrastructural evidence
of secretion by exocytosis and of "synaptic vesicle" formation in posterior
pituitary glands. *Nature*, **227,** 407–409.

Natori, R. (1954). The property and contraction process of isolated myofibrils.
Jikeikai Med. J., **1,** 119–126.

Niedergerke, R. (1955). Local muscular shortening by intracellularly applied calcium.
J. Physiol., **128,** 12–13P.

Perry, S. V., Cole, H. A., Head, J. F. and Wilson, F. J. (1972). Localization and
mode of action of the inhibitory protein component of the troponin complex.
Cold Spr. Harb. Symp. quant. Biol., **37,** 251–262.

Podolsky, R. J. (1962). The structural changes in isolated myofibrils during calcium-
activated contraction. *J. gen. Physiol.*, **45,** 613–614A.

Poisner, A. M. and Bernstein, J. (1971). A possible role of microtubules in catecholamine release from the adrenal medulla: effect of colchicine, Vinca alkaloids
and deuterium oxide. *J. Pharmacol.*, **177,** 102–108.

Ramsey, R. W. (1944). Muscle physics. In *Medical Physics* (Ed. Glaser). Year Book
Publishers, Chicago.

Rice, R. V. *et al.* (1970). The organization of contractile filaments in a mammalian
smooth muscle. *J. Cell Biol.*, **47,** 183–196.

Rice, R. V. and Brady, A. C. (1972). Biochemical and ultrastructural studies on
vertebrate smooth muscle. *Cold. Spr. Harb. Symp. quant. Biol.*, **37,** 429–438.

Ritchie, J. M. (1954). The duration of the plateau of full activity in frog muscle.
J. Physiol., **124,** 605–612.

Rome, E. (1972). Structural studies by X-ray diffraction of striated muscle
permeated with certain ions and proteins. *Cold Spr. Harb. Symp. quant. Biol.*, **37,**
331–339.

Rubin, R. P. (1970). The role of calcium in the release of neurotransmitter substances and hormones. *Pharmacol. Rev.*, **22,** 389–428.

Rüegg, J. C. (1971). Smooth muscle tone. *Physiol. Rev.*, **51,** 201–248.

Slayter, H. S. and Lowey, S. (1967). Substructure of the myosin molecule as visualized
by electron microscopy. *Proc. Nat. Acad. Sci. Wash.*, **58,** 1611–1618.

Spudich, J. A. (1972). Effects of cytochalasin B on actin filaments. *Cold. Spr. Harb.
Symp. quant. Biol.*, **37,** 585–593.

Spudich, J. A., Huxley, H. E. and Finch, J. T. (1972). Regulation of skeletal muscle
contraction. II. *J. mol. Biol.*, **72,** 619–632.

Staley, N. A. and Benson, E. S. (1968). The ultrastructure of frog ventricular cardiac
muscle and its relationship to mechanisms of excitation-contraction coupling.
J. Cell Biol., **38,** 99–114.

Winegrad, S. (1961). The possible role of calcium in excitation-contraction coupling
of heart muscle. *Circulation*, **24,** 523–529.

Winegrad, S. (1965). Autoradiographic studies of intracellular calcium in frog
muscle. *J. gen. Physiol.*, **48,** 455–479.

Winegrad, S. (1971). Studies of cardiac muscle with a high permeability to calcium produced by treatment with ethylenediaminetetracetic acid. *J. gen. Physiol.*, **58**, 71–93.

Wood, E. H., Heppner, R. L. and Weidmann, S. (1969). Inotropic effects of electric currents. *Circulation Res.*, **24**, 409–445.

Yoshimura, H. and Imai, Y. (1967). Studies on the secretory potential of acinal cells of dog's submaxillary gland and the ionic dependency of it. *Jap. J. Physiol.*, **17**, 280–293.

Chapter 4

Ada, G. L. and Byrt, P. (1969). Specific inactivation of antigen-reactive cells with ^{125}I-labelled antigen. *Nature*, **222**, 1291–1292.

Adelstein, R. S. and Conti, M. A. (1972). The characterization of contractile proteins from platelets and fibroblasts. *Cold Spr. Harb. Symp. quant. Biol.*, **37**, 599–605.

Allison, V. F., Lancaster, M. G. and Crosthwaite, J. L. (1963). Studies on the pathogenesis of acute inflammation. *Amer. J. Path.*, **43**, 775–795.

Aoki, T. *et al.* (1969). Antigenic structure of cell surfaces. *J. exp. Med.*, **130**, 979–1001.

Ascheim, E. and Zweifach, B. W. (1962). Quantitative studies of protein and water shifts during inflammation. *Amer. J. Physiol.*, **202**, 554–558.

Ashford, T. P. and Freeman, D. G. (1967). The role of the endothelium in the initial phases of thrombosis. *Amer. J. Path.*, **50**, 257–273.

Bangham, A. D. (1964). The adhesiveness of leukocytes with special reference to zeta potential. *Ann. N.Y. Acad. Sci.*, **116**, 945–949.

Behnke, O. (1968). Electron microscopical observations on the surface coating of human blood platelets. *J. Ultrastr. Res.*, **24**, 51–69.

Behnke, O. and Zelander, T. (1967). Filamentous substructure of microtubules of the marginal bundle of mammalian blood platelets. *J. Ultrastr. Res.*, **19**, 147–165.

Bettex-Galland, M. and Lüscher, E. F. (1959). Extraction of an actomyosin-like protein from human thrombocytes. *Nature*, **184**, 276–277.

Bettex-Galland, M. and Lüscher, E. F. (1965). Thrombosthenin, the contractile protein from blood platelets. *Adv. Prot. Chem.*, **20**, 1–35.

Bokisch, V. A., Müller-Eberhard, H. J. and Cochrane, C. G. (1969). Isolation of a fragment (C3a) of the third component of human complement containing anaphylotoxin and chemotactic activity. *J. exp. Med.*, **129**, 1109–1130.

Booyse, F. M. and Rafelson, M. E. (1969). A contractile protein model for platelet aggregation. *Blood*, **33**, 100–103.

Booyse, F. M. and Rafelson, M. E. (1972). Mechanism and control of platelet-platelet interaction. *Microvasc. Res.*, **4**, 207–213.

Born, G. V. R. and Cross, M. J. (1964). Effects of inorganic ions and of plasma proteins on the aggregation of blood platelets by adenosine diphosphate. *J. Physiol.*, **170**, 397–414.

Bowden, D. H. and Adamsen, I. Y. R. (1972). The pulmonary interstitial cell as immediate precursor of the alveolar macrophage. *Amer. J. Path.*, **68**, 521–528.

Boyden, S. V., North, R. J. and Faulkner, S. M. (1965). Complement and the activity of phagocytes. In *Complement*. Ciba Symp. pp. 190–213.

Cohen, E. P. and Parks, J. J. (1964). Antibody production by nonimmune spleen cells incubated with RNA from immunized mice. *Science*, **144**, 1012–1013.

Crawford, N. (1971). The presence of contractile proteins in platelet microparticles isolated from human and animal platelet-free plasma. *Brit. J. Haemat.*, **21,** 53–69.

Dumonde, D. C. *et al.* (1969). "Lymphokines": non-antibody mediators of cellular immunity generated by lymphocyte activation. *Nature,* **224,** 38–42, 43–44.

Dutton, R. W. and Mishell, R. I. (1967). Cell populations and cell proliferation in the *in vitro* response of normal mouse spleen to heterologous erythrocytes. *J. exp. Med.,* **126,** 443–454.

Erslev, A. J. (1971). Feedback circuits in the control of stem cell differentiation. *Amer. J. Pathol.,* **65,** 629–639.

Fagraeus, A. (1948). Antibody production in relation to the development of plasma cells. *Acta Med. Scand.,* **130** (Suppl. 204).

Fawcett, D. W. (1955). An experimental study of mast cell degranulation and regeneration. *Anat. Rec.,* **121,** 29–51.

Fisher, J. W. *et al.* (1971). Chemical agents which stimulate erythropoietin production. In *Kidney Hormones* (Ed. J. W. Fisher). Academic Press, New York.

Goldstein, A. L., Asanuma, Y. and White, A. (1970). The thymus as an endocrine gland: properties of thymosin, a new thymus hormone. *Rec. Progr. Hormone Res.,* **26,** 505–532.

Goldstein, G. and Mackay, I. R. (1969). *The Human Thymus.* Heinemann, London.

Gottlieb, A. A., Glisin, V. R. and Doty, P. (1967). Studies on macrophage RNA involved in antibody production. *Proc. Nat. Acad. Sci. Wash.,* **57,** 1849–1856.

Gowans, J. L. and Knight, E. J. (1963). The route of re-circulation of lymphocytes in the rat. *Proc. Roy. Soc. B.,* **159,** 257–282.

Graham, P. and Schild, H. O. (1967). Histamine formation in the tuberculin reaction of the rat. *Immunology,* **12,** 725–726.

Grant, L. (1965). The sticking and emigration of white cells in inflammation. In Zweifach, B. W., Grant, L. and McClaskey, R. T. *The Inflammatory Response.* Ch. 5. Academic Press, New York and London.

Hakomori, S. and Strycharz, G. D. (1968). Investigations on cellular blood-group substances. I. *Biochem.,* **7,** 1279–1286.

Harris, H. (1960). Mobilization of defensive cells in inflammatory tissue. *Bact. Rev.,* **24,** 3–15.

Harris, T. N., Hummeler, K. and Harris, S. (1966). Electron microscopic observations on antibody producing lymph node cells. *J. exp. Med.,* **123,** 161–172.

Henson, P. M. (1971). Interaction of cells with immune complexes: adherence, release of constituents, and tissue injury. *J. exp. Med.,* **134,** 114–135S.

Henson, P. M. and Cochrane, C. G. (1970). Cellular mediators of immunological tissue injury. *J. Retic. Soc.,* **8,** 124–138.

Hill, W. C. and Nissen, B. (1971). The antigen receptor in delayed-type hypersensitivity. II. *J. Immunol.,* **106,** 421–426.

Hovig, T. (1963). Release of a platelet-aggregating substance (ADP) from rabbit blood platelets induced by saline "extract" of tendons. *Thromb. Diath. Haem.,* **9,** 264–278.

Humphrey, J. H. (1967). Cell mediated immunity. General perspectives. *Brit. med. Bull.,* **23,** 93–97.

Hurley, J. V. (1964). Substances promoting leukocyte emigration. *Ann. N.Y. Acad. Sci.,* **116,** 918–935.

Jacherts, D. (1971). The flow of information during primary antibody synthesis. In *The Role of Lymphocytes and Macrophages in the Immunological Response* (Ed. D. C. Dumonde). Springer, Berlin.

Jerne, N. K. and Nordin, A. A. (1963). Plaque formation in agar by single antibody-producing cells. *Science*, **140,** 405.

Kabat, E. A. (1956). *Blood Group Substances*. Academic Press. New York and London.

Kahlson, G. and Rosengren, E. (1968). New approaches to the physiology of histamine. *Physiol. Rev.*, **48,** 155–196.

Kahlson, G. and Rosengren, E. (1971). *Biogenesis and Physiology of Histamine*. Arnold, London.

Kitchin, A. G., Megirian, R. and Laffin, R. J. (1970). The effect of serum fractions on *in vitro* colloidal gold phagocytosis. *J. Retic. Soc.*, **8,** 55–65.

Kjaerheim, A. and Hovig, T. (1962). The ultrastructure of haemostatic blood platelet plugs in rabbit mesenterium. *Thromb. Diath. Haemorr.*, **7,** 1–15.

Lee, C. Y. (1972). Chemistry and pharmacology of polypeptide toxins in snake venoms. *Anni. Rev. Pharmacol.*, **12,** 265–286.

Levine, P. and Stetson, R. E. (1934). An unusual case of intragroup agglutination. *J. Amer. Med. Ass.*, **113,** 126–127.

Lewis, G. P. (1964). Plasma kinins and other vasoactive compounds in acute inflammation. *Ann. N.Y. Acad. Sci.*, **116,** 847–854.

Lewis, T. (1927). *The Blood Vessels of the Human Skin and their Responses*. Shaw and Son, London.

Lorand, L. (1965). Physiological roles of fibrinogen and fibrin. *Fed. Proc.*, **24,** 784–793.

Macfarlane, R. G. (1965). Hemostatic mechanisms in tissue injury. In *The Inflammatory Response* (Ed. Zweifach, B. W., Grant, L. and McClaskey, R. T.), pp. 465–494. Academic Press, New York and London.

Majno, G. and Palade, G. E. (1961). The effect of histamine and serotonin on vascular permeability: an electron microscopic study. *J. biophys. biochem. Cytol.*, **11,** 571–605.

Mandel, T. and Byrt, P. (1971). The uptake of antigens and non-antigenic markers by mouse spleen and peritoneal cells. In *The Role of the Lymphocyte and Macrophage in the Immune Response*. (Ed. D. C. Dumonde), pp. 38–42. Springer, Berlin.

Mandel, T., Byrt, P. and Ada, G. L. (1969). A morphological examination of antigen reactive cells from mouse spleen and peritoneal cavity. *Exp. Cell Res.*, **58,** 179–182.

Marchesi, V. T. and Gowans, J. L. (1963). The migration of lymphocytes through the endothelium of venules in lymph nodes. *Proc. Roy. Soc. B.*, **159,** 283–290.

McKay, D. G. (1972). Participation of components of the blood coagulation system in the inflammatory response. *Amer. J. Path.*, **67,** 181–203.

Mehrishi, J. N. (1972). Molecular aspects of the mammalian cell surface. *Progr. Biophys.*, **25,** 3–70.

Meldrum, B. S. (1965). The actions of snake venoms on nerve and muscle. The pharmacology of phospholipase A and of polypeptide toxins. *Pharmacol. Rev.*, **17,** 393–445.

Mishell, R. I. and Dutton, R. W. (1967). Immunization of dissociated spleen cell cultures from normal mice. *J. exp. Med.*, **126,** 423–442.

Morley, A., Rickard, K. A., Howard, D. and Stohlman, F. (1971). Studies on the regulation of granulopoiesis. IV. *Blood*, **37,** 14–22.

Mosier, D. E. (1967). A requirement for two cell types for antibody formation in vitro. *Science*, **158,** 1573–1575.

Mourant, A. E. (1946). A new human blood group antigen of frequent occurrence. *Nature*, **158**, 237–238.

Mudd, S., McCutcheon, M. and Lucke, B. (1934). Phagocytosis. *Physiol. Rev.*, **14**, 210–275.

Müller-Eberhard, H. J. (1969). Complement. *Annu. Rev. Biochem.*, **38**, 389–414.

Müller-Eberhard, H. J. (1972). The molecular basis of the biological activities of complement. Harvey Lectures, 66, 75–104.

Mustard, J. F. and Packham, M. A. (1970). Factors influencing platelet function: adhesion, release and aggregation. *Pharmacol. Rev.*, **22**, 97–187.

Narahashi *et al.* (1972). Effects of scorpion venom on squid axon membranes. *Amer. J. Physiol.*, **222**, 850–857.

North, R. J. (1969). Cellular kinetics associated with the development of acquired cellular resistance. *J. exp. Med.*, **130**, 299–314.

Nossal, G. J. V. *et al.* (1968). Cell to cell interaction in the immune response. III. *J. exp. Med.*, **128**, 839–853.

Petris, S. de, Karlsbad, G. and Pernis, B. (1963). Localization of antibodies in plasma cells by electron microscopy. *J. exp. Med.*, **117**, 849–862.

Pisano, J. J. (1968). Vasoactive peptides in venoms. *Fed. Proc.*, **27**, 58–62.

Ponder, E. *Haemolysis and Related Phenomena*. Grune and Stratton, New York.

Prada, M. da *et al.* (1967). Subcellular localization of 5-hydroxytryptamine and histamine in blood platelets. *Nature*, **216**, 1315–1317.

Putnam, F. W., Titani, K., Wikler, M. and Shinoda, T. (1967). Structure and evolution of kappa and lambda light chains. *Cold Spr. Harb. Symp. quant. Biol.*, **32**, 9–28.

Race, R. R. and Sanger, R. (1968). *Blood Groups in Man*. 5th Ed. Blackwell, Oxford.

Ratnoff, O. D. and Lepow, I. H. (1963). Complement as a mediator of inflammation. *J. exp. Med.*, **118**, 681–697.

Roser, B. (1970). The origins, kinetics and fate of macrophage populations. *J. Retic. Soc.*, **8**, 139–161.

Sander, G. E. and Huggins, C. G. (1972). Vasoactive peptides. *Annu. Rev. Pharmacol.*, **12**, 227–264.

Schild, H. O. and Willoughby, D. A. (1967). Possible pharmacological mediation of delayed hypersensitivity. *Brit. med. Bull.*, **23**, 46–51.

Silva, W. D. da and Lepow, I. H. (1967). Complement as mediator of inflammation. *J. exp. Med.*, **125**, 921–946.

Silverman, M. S. (1970). The macrophage in cellular and humoral immunity. *J. Retic. Soc.*, **8**, 105–123.

Stohlman, F. (1971). Erythropoietin and erythroid kinetics. In *Kidney Hormones* (Ed. J. W. Fisher), pp. 331–341. Academic Press, New York and London.

Thomas, L. (1964). Possible role of leucocyte granules in the Schwartzman and Arthus reactions. *Proc. Soc. exp. Biol., N.Y.*, **115**, 235–240.

Tidball, M. E. and Scherer, R. W. (1972). Relationship of calcium and magnesium to platelet histamine release. *Amer. J. Physiol.*, **222**, 1303–1308.

Unanue, E. R. and Cerrottini, J. C. (1969). Persistence of antigen on the surface of macrophages. *Nature*, **222**, 1193–1195.

Van Oss, C. J. and Stinson, M. W. (1970). Immunoglobulins as specific opsonins. I. *J. Retic. Soc.*, **8**, 397–406.

Ward, P. A. (1968). Complement factors involved in chemotaxis of human eosinophils and a new chemotactic factor for neutrophils from C'5. *I. Immunol.*, **101**, 818–819.

Warren, B. A. (1971). The platelet pseudopodium and its involvement in aggregation and adhesion to vessel walls. *Brit. J. exp. Path.*, **52**, 378–382.

Weiss, L. (1972). *The Cells and Tissues of the Immune System.* Prentice Hall, New Jersey.

Weissman, I. L. (1967). Thymus cell migration. *J. exp. Med.*, **126**, 291–304.

Weissmann, G., Spilberg, I. and Krakauer, K. (1969). Arthritis induced in rabbits by lysates of granulocyte lysosomes. *Arthr. Rheum.*, **12**, 103–116.

Weissmann, G., Zurier, R. B. and Hoffstein, S. (1972). Leukocytic proteases and the immunologic release of lysosomal enzymes. *Amer. J. Path.*, **68**, 539–559.

Weissmann, G., Zurier, R. B., Spieler, P. J. and Goldstein, I. M. (1971). Mechanisms of lysosomal enzyme release from leukocytes exposed to immune complexes and other particles. *J. exp. Med.*, **134**, 149–165.

White, J. G. and Krivit, W. (1966). The ultrastructural localization and release of platelet lipids. *Blood*, **27**, 167–186.

Wiener, A. S. and Peters, H. R. (1940). Hemolytic reactions following transfusions of blood of the homologous group, with three cases in which the same agglutinogen was responsible. *Ann. int. Med.*, **13**, 2306–2322.

Wolstencroft, R. A. *et al.* (1971). Lymphocyte mitogenetic factor in cell-induced immunity. In *The Role of Lymphocytes and Macrophages in the Immunological Response* (Ed. D. C. Dumonde), pp. 28–37. Springer, Berlin.

Wood, W. B. (1951/52) Studies on the cellular immunology of acute bacterial infections. *Harvey Lectures*, **47**, 72–98.

Wright, A. E. and Douglas, S. R. (1903). An experimental investigation of the role of the blood fluids in connection with phagocytosis. *Proc. Roy. Soc.*, **72**, 357–370.

Wright, A. E. and Douglas, S. R. (1904). Further observations in connection with phagocytosis. *Proc. Roy. Soc.*, **73**, 128–142.

Yoffey, J. M. (1973). Stem cell role of the lymphocyte-transitional cell (LT) compartment. In *Haemopoietic Stem Cells.* Ciba Symp. Elesevier, Amsterdam.

Young, I. and Friedman, H. (1967). The morphologic demonstration of antibody formation in follicles of lymphoid tissue. In *Germinal Centre in Immune Responses* (Ed. C. Cottier *et al.*), p. 102. Springer, New York.

Zucker-Franklin, D. (1969). Microfibrils of blood platelets: their relationship to microtubules and the contractile protein. *J. clin. Invest.*, **48**, 165–175.

Zweifach, B. W. (1963). Peripheral vascular factors in the genesis of stasis and thrombosis. *Fed. Proc.*, **22**, 1351–1355.

Chapter 5

Adams, C. E. and Chang, M. C. (1962). The effect of delayed mating on fertilization in the rabbit. *J. exp. Zool.*, **151**, 155–158.

Adams, C. E. and Chang, M. C. (1962). Capacitation of rabbit spermatozoa in the fallopian tube and in the uterus. *J. exp. Zool.*, **151**, 159–165.

Adamson, T. M., Boyd, R. D. H., Platt, H. S. and Strang, L. B. (1969). Composition of alveolar liquid in the foetal lamb. *J. Physiol.*, **204**, 159–168.

Annison, E. F., Linzell, J. L., Fazakerley, S. and Nichols, B. W. (1967). The oxidation and utilization of palmitate, stearate, oleate . . . etc. *Biochem. J.*, **102**, 637–647.

Balfour, W. E. and Comline, R. S. (1962). Acceleration of the absorption of unchanged globulin in the new-born calf by factors in colostrum. *J. Physiol.*, **160**, 234–257.

Bargmann, W. and Knoop, A. (1959). Uber die Morphologie der Milchsekretion. *Z. Zellforsch.*, **49**, 344–388.

Barry, J. M. and Rowland, S. J. (1953). Variations in the ionic and lactose concentration in milk. *Biochem. J.*, **54**, 575–578.

Black, D. L. and Asdell, S. A. (1958). Transport through the rabbit oviduct. *Amer. J. Physiol.*, **192**, 63–68.

Blanchette-Mackie, E. J. and Scow, R. O. (1971). Sites of lipoprotein lipase activity in adipose tissue perfused with chylomicrons. *J. Cell Biol.*, **51**, 1–25.

Brew, K., Vanaman, T. C. and Hill, R. L. (1968). The role of α-lactalbumin and the A protein in lactose synthetase: a unique mechanism for the control of a biological reaction. *Proc. Nat. Acad. Sci. Wash.*, **59**, 491–492.

Colwin, A. L. and Colwin, L. H. (1961a). Fine structure of the spermatozoon of *Hydroides hexagonus* (Annelida) with special reference to the acrosomal region. *J. biophys. biochem. Cytol.*, **10**, 211–230.

Colwin, A. L. and Colwin, L. H. (1961b). Changes in the spermatozoon during fertilization in *Hydroides hexagonus* (Annelida). I. Passage of the acrosomal region through the vitelline membrane. II. Incorporation with the egg. *J. biophys. biochem. Cytol.*, **10**, 231–254; 255–274.

Colwin, L. H. and Colwin, A. L. (1963). Role of the gamete membranes in fertilization in *Saccoglossus Kowvalevskii* (Enteropneusta). I and II. *J. Cell Biol.*, **19**, 477–500; 501–518.

Cowie, A. T. and Tindal, J. S. (1971). *The Physiology of Lactation*. Arnold, London.

Dickmann, Z., Chewe, T. H., Bonney, W. A. and Noyes, R. W. (1965). The human egg in the pronuclear stage. *Anat. Rec.*, **152**, 293–302.

Hamilton, W. J., Boyd, J. D. and Mossman, H. W. (1959). *Human Embryology*. 2nd Ed. Heffer, Cambridge.

Hamosh, M., Clary, T. R., Chernick, S. S. and Scow, R. O. (1970). Lipoprotein lipase activity of adipose and mammary tissue and plasma triglyceride in pregnant and lactating rats. *Biochim. biophys. acta*, **210**, 473–482.

Hardwick, D. C., Linzell, J. L. and Price, S. M. (1961). The effect of glucose and acetate on milk secretion by the perfused goat udder. *Biochem. J.*, **80**, 37–45.

Horton, E. W. (1969). Hypotheses on physiological roles of prostaglandins. *Physiol. Rev.*, **49**, 122–161.

Jones, B. M. and Kemp, R. B. (1969). Self-isolation of the foetal trophoblast. *Nature*, **221**, 829–831.

Keenan, T. W. *et al.* (1970). Biochemical and morphological comparison of plasma membrane and milk fat globule membrane from bovine mammary gland. *J. Cell Biol.*, **44**, 80–93.

Kon, S. K. and Cowie, A. T. (1961). *Milk: The Mammary Gland and its Secretions*. Academic Press, New York.

Linzell, J. L. (1955). Some observations on the contractile tissue of the mammary glands. *J. Physiol.*, **130**, 257–267.

Linzell, J. C. and Peaker, M. (1971). Mechanism of milk secretion. *Physiol. Rev.*, **51**, 564–597.

Linzell, J. L. and Peaker, M. (1971). Intracellular concentrations of sodium, potassium and chloride in the lactating mammary gland and their relation to the secretory mechanism. *J. Physiol.*, **216**, 683–700.

Linzell, J. L. and Peaker, M. (1971). The permeability of mammary ducts. *J. Physiol.*, **216**, 701–716.

Mendelson, C. R. and Scow, R. O. (1972). Uptake of chylomicron-triglyceride by perfused mammary tissue of lactating rats. *Amer. J. Physiol.*, **223**, 1418–1423.

Odell, W. D. and Moyer, D. La R. (1971). *Physiology of Reproduction*. Mosby, St. Louis.

Richardson, K. C. (1947). Some structural features of the mammary gland. *Brit. Med. Bull.*, **5,** 123–129.

Richardson, K. C. (1949). Contractile tissues in the mammary gland, with special reference to myoepithelium in the goat. *Proc. Roy. Soc. B.*, **136,** 30–45.

Runnström, J. and Kriszat, G. (1952). The cortical propagation of the activation impulse in the sea urchin egg. *Exp. Cell Res.*, **3,** 419–426.

Schoefl, G. I. and French, J. E. (1968). Vascular permeability to particulate fat: morphological observations on vessels of lactating mammary gland and of lung. *Proc. Roy. Soc. B.*, **169,** 153–165.

Schwartz, N. B. (1969). A model for the regulation of ovulation in the rat. *Rec. Progr. Hormone Res.*, **25,** 1–55.

Schwartz, N. B. (1970). Control of rhythmic secretion of gonadotropins. In *The Hypothalamus* (Ed. Martini, L., Motta, M. and Fraschini, F.), pp. 515–528. Academic Press, New York and London.

Setchell, B. P., Voglmayr, J. G. and Waites, G. M. H. (1969). A blood-testis barrier restricting passage from blood into rete testis fluid but not into lymph. *J. Physiol.*, **200,** 73–85.

Soderwall, A. L. and Blandau, R. J. (1941). The duration of the fertilizing capacity of spermatozoa in the female genital tract of the rat. *J. exp. Zool.*, **88,** 55–64.

Stein, O. and Stein, Y. (1967). Lipid synthesis, intracellular transport, and secretion. II. *J. Cell Biol.*, **34,** 251–263.

Toker, C. (1967). Observations on the ultrastructure of a mammary ductule. *J. Ultrastr. Res.*, **21,** 9–25.

Wellings, S. R. and Philp, J. R. (1964). The function of the Golgi apparatus in lactating cells of the BALB/c Crgl mouse. *Z. Zellforsch.*, **61,** 871–882.

Williams, P. L. and Wendell-Smith, C. P. (1969). *Basic Human Embryology*. Pitman, London.

Zamboni, L. and Mastroianni, L. (1966). Electron microscopic studies on rabbit ova. *J. Ultrastr. Res.*, **14,** 95–117.

SUBJECT INDEX

A

Absolute refractory period, 15–16
Accommodation, nerve, 24, 25–26
Acetylcholine,
  adrenal medulla, 175
  amount released per impulse, 37–38
  autonomic ganglia, 106–107
  autonomic postganglionic fibres, 107
  botulinum toxin, 61–62
  cardiac action, 247
  CNS transmitter substance, 84–85
  curarine, blockage by, 40
  denervation hypersensitivity, 54–55
  eserine potentiation, 39
  glandular secretion release, 279, 282, 283–284
  hemicholinium, effect on, 45–46
  homeostasis of stores, 47
  multiple neurotization, 61
  muscarine, 38, 107
  nicotinic actions, 38, 107
  ouabain inhibition of release, 49
  Renshaw synapse, 86
  smooth muscle, 258–259, 263, 268
  stores, release from, 46–47
  structure of, 38
  synthesis, 45–47, 55–59
  transmitter substance, 35–36
  trophic substance, 60–61
  vesicle appearance, 67
  Wedensky inhibition, lack in, 45
Acetylcholinesterase, 38–39, 264, 269
Acetylthiocholine, 38–39, 45–50
Acid phosphatase, secretory apparatus, 170
Acrosome, 387–388, 399–400
  filament, 386
ACTH, 133
  adrenal cortex activation, 179
  adrenal medulla, interaction, 182–183
  binding to cell surface, 153

ACTH—*continued*
  cyclic AMP activation, 151
  cycloheximide, inhibition, 156
  erythropoiesis, 309
  half life, 169–170
  lipolytic effect, 159–160
  puromycin inhibition, 156
Actin, 221–222, 225–228, 277
  microfilaments, 285–280
Actinomycin D,
  FSH action, inhibition, 156
  messenger RNA, inhibition, 155
  neuronal chromatolysis, 60
  PNMT synthesis, 183
  prolactin inhibition, 156–157
  sodium transport, inhibition, 161–163
Action potential, 10–13
  cardiac muscle, 239–240, 249–250
  depolarization of membrane, 16–26
  diphasic, 10–14
  direction of spread, 11
  end plate potential, 40
  foot of, 30–31
  hormonal release, pancreas, 129–130
  inward sodium current, 20
  local current spread, 28–30
  mechanism of, 11–34
  monophasic, 11–12
  muscle, 36–37, 40–41, 43, 200
  outward potassium current, 14, 20–22
  propagation of, 26–34
  sequence of change, 12–13
  sodium movements, 14
  sodium permeability, inactivation of, 22–23
  velocity of transmission, 11
  voltage clamp, 18–23
Active state, muscle, 201, 204
Actomyosin, 222–223, 225–228, 277
  thrombosthenin, 325
Adenohypophysis, 132–133
Adenosine-3′, 5′-phosphate, 150–160